CAMBRIDGE STUDIES
IN ENGLISH LEGAL HISTORY

Edited by
D.E.C. YALE
Fellow of Christ's College and
Reader in English Legal History at the University of Cambridge

LAW AND POLITICS IN JACOBEAN ENGLAND:

THE TRACTS OF LORD CHANCELLOR ELLESMERE

LOUIS A. KNAFLA

Associate Professor of History
University of Calgary

CAMBRIDGE UNIVERSITY PRESS

Cambridge
London · New York · Melbourne

Published by the Syndics of the Cambridge University Press
The Pitt Building, Trumpington Street, Cambridge CB2 1RP
Bentley House, 200 Euston Road, London NW1 2DB
32 East 57th Street, New York, NY 10022, USA
296 Beaconsfield Parade, Middle Park, Melbourne 3206, Australia

First published 1977

Photoset and printed in Malta
by Interprint (Malta) Ltd

Library of Congress Cataloguing in Publication Data

Knafla, Louis A 1935–
Law and politics in Jacobean England

(Cambridge studies in English legal history)

'Ellesmere's tracts' (p.   ): A coppie of
a wrytten discourse by the Lord Chaunccllor Else-
more concerning the royall prerogatiue. ca. 1604. –
The speech of the Lord Chancellor of England, in the
Eschequer Chamber, touching the post-nati. [etc.]

Includes indexes

1. Egerton, Thomas, Baron Ellesmere and Viscount
Brackley, 1540?–1617. 2. Law – Great Britain –
Addresses, essays, lectures.   3. Great Britain –
History – James I, 1603–1625 – Sources.   I. Egerton,
Thomas, Baron Ellesmere and Viscount Brackley, 1540?–
1617. II. Title. III. Series
KD621. E35 K55   340'.0942   76-4757
ISBN 0 521 21191 3

CONTENTS

PREFACE

The consolidation of the state under the aegis of monarchy was one of the salient features of the English, as well as the Continental experience in the sixteenth century. In England the cultivation of royal power presaged that of Parliament and the common law. Such growth was due largely to the respect for authority that was instilled in society by the Tudor monarchs and the governing class. Confidence in the Crown and its policies had become a trait of the English political personality in the sixteenth century; a trait that endured until the waning years of Queen Elizabeth and the coming of the Stuarts.

There is little doubt, however, that by the turn of the century English society was witnessing a growth of tension in the relations between the members of the governing class, and between society and the State. Divisive social and economic problems, religious controversy, corruption in the governing process, conflicts in the courts, and confusion in the law were factors which contributed to this growth of tension. The institutions of society and the State were approaching a crossroads where either their reform or collapse would become inevitable. Thus crucial questions of State that involved the prerogatives of the Crown, the powers of Parliament, the responsibilities of the courts of law, and the rights and obligations of the citizen remained unresolved, and became the subject of increasing public discussion. They also began to appear in the prose and poetry, and the political and religious writings of the age.

Numerous memoranda, pamphlets, tracts, and treatises have provided us with sources for the study of the crisis in the governing class, and in the relations between society and the State in the early seventeenth century. There are, however, few sources whose authority has been established that provide us with the copious thought of those individuals who actually managed the affairs of government. Much of the existing literature was composed by courtiers or writers who were patronised to present that which their sponsors wished to have believed. Administrators – apart from those with antiquarian interests – were habitually too occupied in carving out careers in the labyrinth of government to address themselves directly to the crucial questions. As with public officials in all ages, their time was too absorbed in dealing with the matters that came to hand. Those men who did reflect on the crucial questions of State would be wary of disclosing their frank reflections on the printed page and thereby incurring either the opprobrium of the king or the nefarious attacks of political factions. The published, and particularly the unpublished, writings of Chancellor Ellesmere are a case in point. They represent in their broadest significance a group of documents expressive of the growth of that tension within the governing class, and within the institutions of government and the law.

Ellesmere was both an assiduous administrator and a minister of the first rank who was deeply concerned with the hotly contested questions of the times. He disclosed his opinions openly in his private writings, publishing only the least controversial. All of his tracts except the *Post-Nati* were composed in a semi-formal manner. His analysis was usually cogent and pithy; the style concise and abrupt. His perspective was generally moderate for a period of sharp political, constitutional, and legal conflict. At these times Ellesmere combined the perspicacity of the administrator with the meditation of the jurist. But there were occasions when his opinions were either radical or reactionary, and these instances reflected the influence of the conflicts of the age on one of the most seasoned statesmen of Jacobean England.

If a thread exists which provides a recurring theme to Ellesmere's tracts, it can be found explicably in the law. The Chancellor was from the beginning a lawyer. And whether he was discussing the forms of action at common law, or Parliament and the prerogatives of the Crown, his ideas stemmed from a legal framework which dominated more of the thought of the period than historians have generally acknowledged. The chancellor's close association with judges and legal writers such as Sir Edmund Anderson, John Popham, Sir Francis Bacon, Sir Edward Coke, Sir John Davies, and William Lambarde give his writings a specific importance in the literature of the law. His tracts, in reflecting a reading of Continental politics and jurisprudence, are also important sources for European constitutional and legal thought. Their most immediate significance, however, stems from Ellesmere's long experience in government and the courts of law, an experience which covered more than thirty-five years of public office. In this respect his tracts are part of the political, constitutional, administrative, and legal history of the era.

Ellesmere's tracts have not been readily available since the mid-seventeenth century. At his death in March of 1616–17, contemporaries such as Sir Francis Bacon commented upon 'the precious jewels' which the famed Lord Chancellor had left in the care of his chaplain and later successor, John Williams. The jewels referred to were Ellesmere's manuscript tracts. Contemporaries at Williams' death in 1650 had noted the disappearance of the tracts, and their loss was attributed to the dispersal of archives during the Civil Wars. An extensive search has resulted in the discovery of the original, or early copies of seven of his tracts on the royal prerogative, Parliament, government, and the law in manuscript collections at numerous libraries in North America and Great Britain. These tracts form the basis of this book.

The work has been organised around the tracts to facilitate an examination of Ellesmere's ideas within the context of his life and career. After an introductory biographical sketch, Part One comprises an analysis of Ellesemere's thought on a series of political and legal problems in the reign of James. Part Two contains a critical edition of Ellesmere's tracts on those subjects in the order in which they were composed. Together, these two parts have been designed not only to make, with the appropriate background, an interpretation of the subject, but also to present as much of the record as possible.

Ellesmere as a man has often been misunderstood, both by contemporaries and modern writers. Since the issues in which he became involved were public issues, contemporaries often forced him into the various categories of their thoughts. Thus he was accepted by 'royalists' and 'puritans', both of whom found nourishment in his career. But, while he was a common lawyer, his greatest enemies were at times common lawyers. Dilemmas such as this will never be resolved definitively. They will, however, become understandable when writers cease to base their work on those 'select' sources which have bred a genre of historical literature for the period that is often as inaccurate as it is biased. Only by examining the wide range of notes, letters, memos, tracts, and treatises, within the context of an essentially large body of personal and public records, will writers come to a knowledgeable understanding of the history of men, and their ideas and institutions, in the early seventeenth century. My purpose here is simply to resurrect some of the thought and work of Ellesemere as a lawyer, judge, and statesman, to raise some of the questions which contemporaries asked about law and politics, and to indicate some of the material from which I hope the answers will come.

A number of research libraries throughout North America and the United Kingdom have made this study possible. The libraries and their staffs in North America whom I wish to thank for their assistance in making the sources available are as follows: the Univesity of California libraries at Berkeley and Los Angeles, the Folger Shakespeare Library, Washington, D.C., the Harvard Law and University libraries, Cambridge, Massachusetts, the Henry E. Huntington Library, San Marino, California, the Newberry Library of Chicago, the New York Public Library, the Stanford Law School Library, Stanford, California, the University of Toronto libraries, Ontario, and the Yale Law School and University libraries, New Haven, Connecticut.

In the United Kingdom the principal centres for sources used in London were the British Museum, the Duchy of Cornwall Record Office, the Historical Manuscripts Commission, the House of Lords Records Office, the Inner Temple Library, the Institute of Historical Research, the Lambeth Palace Library, Lincoln's Inn Library, the Univesity of London Library, the Public Records Office, and the Warburg Institute. Outside London, I had recourse to several of the college libraries at Oxford and Cambridge, particularly at Corpus Christi and Exeter colleges, Oxford, the Bodleian Library, Oxford, the Cambridge University Library, the John Rylands Library, Manchester, the National Library of Wales, Aberystwyth, Trinity College Library, Dublin, and the University College of North Wales, Bangor. Equally important were the county record offices where I had the pleasure of doing research: namely, those of Cheshire, Flintshire, Oxfordshire, Northamptonshire, Shropshire, and Warwickshire, and of the City of Chester. Finally, I want to give special acknowledgement to those havens for scholars where most of my writing was done – to the staffs of the libraries of the Institute of Historical Research, the Henry E. Huntington Library, and the University of Calgary.

Research and writing demand good criticism, and regardless of the results of this work I have been fortunate to receive the generous critical advice and suggestions of a number of scholars. For the

subject area of politics and society these include Elizabeth Read
Foster, Lamar Hill, Joel Hurstfield, James Larkin, Sir John Neale,
Brian O'Farrell, G. Dyfnalt Owen, Marc Schwarz, Roy Schreiber,
A. J. Slavin, Lawrence Stone, and Penry Williams. On matters
concerning law and administration, I want to thank Lewis Abbott,
J. P. Anglin, Thomas G. Barnes, Marjorie Blatcher, William Huse
Dunham, J. A. C. Grant, Charles Gray, W. J. Jones, S. F. C. Milsom,
Walter C. Richardson, A. W. B. Simpson, and Samuel E. Thorne. For
intellectual, cultural, and religious topics I wish to acknowledge the
help of Leland Carlson, Mark H. Curtis, French Fogle, Fritz Levy,
James McConica, Michael MacDonald, Anthony G. Petti, Paul S.
Seaver, and John Steadman. Finally, I would like to thank specially
those individuals who read the work from beginning to end in one
form or another, and whose painstaking criticism contributed to the
final shape of the study: John Baker, James Cockburn, Geoffrey
Elton, and David Yale. Any errors, confusion, or misunderstanding
that remain are solely of my own doing.

   A number of institutions and agencies provided me with both
financial support and encouragement in the pursuit of this study.
These include from the beginning the Regents of the University of
California, the Trustees of the Henry E. Huntington Library, the
University of Calgary, and the Canada Council. Grants from the latter
two organizations made possible the six transatlantic journeys which
this study ultimately required. I also wish to thank Mr David Yale,
the Editor of the English Legal History Series, and the staff of the
Cambridge University Press for their assistance and patience with the
manuscript. With respect to the demands which this project has made
on my family, I can say freely that their willingness to accept Ellesmere
as an adopted 'lord' to guide the time-tables of their lives has made,
from beginning to end, the eventual appearance of this work possible.

Highgate
Easter, 1975   L.A.K.

ABBREVIATIONS

Add. MS	Manuscript in the Additional collection, British Museum.
APC	*Acts of the Privy Council of England*, ed. R. A. Dasent *et al.* (1907–25), vols. XXXII–XXXV.
AJLH	*The American Journal of Legal History.*
Alnwick MS	Manuscript of the Duke of Northumberland, Alnwick Castle, Northumberland.
AmPhS	*Proceedings of the American Philosophical Society.*
Archeion	*Archeion; or, a Discourse upon the High Courts of Justice in England by William Lambarde*, ed. Charles McIlwain and Paul Ward (Cambridge Mass. 1957).
Bacon, *Elements*	Sir Francis Bacon, *The Elements of the Common Laws of England* (1630). *STC* 1134.
Bacon, *Letters*	*The letters and life of Francis Bacon including all his occasional works*, ed. James Spedding *et al.* (1857–74), vols. I–VII.
Bacon, *Works*	*The works of Francis Bacon: literary and professional works*, ed. James Spedding *et al.* (1861), vols. I–II.
Barlow MS	Manuscript in the Barlow coll., Bodleian Library, Oxford.
Barr. MS	Barrington manuscript, Inner Temple Library, London.
BIHR	*Bulletin of the Institute of Historical Research.*
B.M.	The British Museum, London.
B.M. RB	Rare book at the B.M. with marginal notes.
Bodl.	The Bodleian Library, Oxford.
Bowyer Diary	*Parliamentary diary of Robert Bowyer*, ed. D. H. Willson (Minneapolis, Minn. 1931).
'Brief Chanc.'	'A Breviate or direccion for the Kings Learned councell collected by the Lord Chauncellor Ellesmere, mense Septembris 1615'. Folger MS V.b. 90.

Buccleuch MS	*The Manuscripts of His Grace the Duke of Buccleuch and Queensbury*, H.M.C. (1926). Vols. I–III.
Bulstrode, *Reports*	*The Reports of Edward Bulstrode* (2nd ed. 1688).
C	Chancery document, Public Record Office, London.
C.33	Chancery decree and order entry books, Public Record Office, London.
Camden	Camden Society Publications. Old, New, and Third Series.
Cary, *Reports*	George Cary, *Reports or Causes in Chancery* (2nd ed. 1665).
Chetham Soc.	Chetham Society. *Remains Historical and Literary connected with the Palatine Counties of Lancaster and Chester*. Old, New, and Third Series.
Choyce Cases	*Choyce Cases in Chancery* (1652).
CJ	*The Journals of the House of Commons* (n.d.), I (1547–1628).
Cleo. MS	Cleopatra manuscript in the Cottonian coll., British Museum.
CLJ	*The Cambridge Law Journal.*
Cockburn, *Assizes*	J. S. Cockburn, *A history of English assizes 1558–1714* (Cambridge 1972).
Co. Lit.	Coke, Sir Edward. *The First Part of the Institutes of the Laws of England* (1794 ed.). Two vols.
Co. Rep.	*Les Reports* [Part One] (1600), through Part Eleven – *La unz^{me} part* (1615).
Coke MS Rep. A	Autograph manuscript reports of Edward Coke, 1579–88. British Museum, Harleian MS 6687.
Coke MS Rep. C	Autograph manuscript reports of Edward Coke, 1591–1606. British Museum, Harleian MS 6686.
Coke MS Rep. E	Autograph manuscript reports of Edward Coke, 1608–11. Cambridge University Library MS Ii. v. 2/12.
Collect. Jurid.	*Collectanea Juridica*, ed. Francis Hargrave (1791–2), Vols. I–II.
Const. Docs.	*Constitutional documents of the reign of James I*, ed J. R. Tanner (Cambridge 1930).
Cotton MS	Manuscript in the Cottonian coll., British Museum.

Cowell, *Interpreter*	Dr John Cowell, *The Interpreter* (Cambridge 1607), *STC*5900.
CP	Court of Common Pleas.
Cranfield MS	*Calendar of the manuscripts of Major General Lord Sackville: Cranfield papers*, H.M.C. (1940–66), vols. I–II.
C.R.O.	The Cheshire Record Office, Chester.
Croke, *Reports*	*Reports of Cases in Kings Bench and Common Bench* (1669), parts I–III.
Crompton, *L'Authoritie*	Richard Crompton, *L'Authoritie et Iurisdiction des Courts de la Maiestie de la Roygne* (1594). *STC.* 6050.
CSPD.	*The Calendar of State Papers, Domestic. Elizabeth, James I.*
C.U.L.	The Cambridge University Library, Cambridge.
CymRS	Cymmrodorion Record Series, *Transactions.*
Davies, *Primer Report*	Sir John Davies, *Le Primer Report del Cases & Matters en Ley* (Dublin 1615), *STC* 6361.
D.C.O.	The Duchy of Cornwall Office, Buckingham Palace Gate, London.
Debates 1610	*Parliamentary debates in 1610*, ed. S. R. Gardiner (1861).
Discourse	*A Discourse upon the Exposicion & Understandinge of Statutes With Sir Thomas Egerton's Additions*, ed. Samuel E. Thorne (San Marino Calif. 1942).
DNB	*The dictionary of national biography.*
Dyer, *Novel Cases*	James Dyer, *Cy Ensuont Ascuns Novel Cases* (1585). *STC* 7388.
E	Exchequer document, Public Record Office.
E. 101	Various Court of Exchequer accounts, fines, and amercements, Public Record Office.
EcHR	*The Economic History Review.*
'Eg. on Coke'	'The Lord Chancellor Egertons Observacions vpon ye Lord Cookes Reportes'. British Museum, Hargrave MS 254.
Eg. Papers	*The Egerton Papers*, ed. J. P. Collier (1840). Camden Soc. vol. XII.
EHR	*English Historical Review.*
Ellesm. MS	Bridgewater and Ellesmere manuscript coll., Huntington Library.
F–H MS	Finch–Hatton manuscript, Northamptonshire Record Office.
Finch, *Law*	Henry Finch, *Law, or a Discovrse Thereof*

	(2nd ed. 1627). *STC* 10871.
Fitzherbert, *Brevium*	Anthony Fitzherbert, *La Nouvella Natura Brevium* (3rd ed. 1553, col. 1560).
F.L.O.	Flintshire Record Office, Hawarden, Clwyd.
Folger	The Folger Shakespeare Library, Washington D.C.
Gardiner, *Hist.*	Samuel Rawson Gardiner, *History of England from the accession of James I to the outbreak of the Civil War 1603–1642* (rev. ed. 1881–85), vols. I–IV.
Godbold, *Reports*	*Reports of Certain Cases*, rev. John Godbold and ed. W. Hughes (1652).
'Govt. 1615'	Ellesmere, Baron. 'Thinges to be considered of before a parlement to be called'. Huntington Library, Ellesmere MS 2610.
Hake, *Epieikeia*	Edward Hake, *Epieikeia, a dialogue on equity in three parts* ed. D. E. C. Yale (1953).
Hale MS	Manuscript in the Hale coll., Lincoln's Inn Library.
Harg. MS	Hargrave manuscript, British Museum.
Harl. Misc.	*The Harleian Miscellany* (1808–13).
Harl. MS	Harleian manuscript, British Museum.
Harv. Law	The Harvard Law Library, Langdell Hall, Cambridge, Mass.
Hastings MS	*Report on the manuscripts of the late Reginald Rawdon Hastings*, H.M.C. (1928–47), vols. I–IV.
Hasts. MS	Hastings manuscript, Huntington Library.
Hawarde, *Reportes*	*Les Reportes del Cases in Camera Stellata 1593 to 1609*, ed. W. P. Baildon (1894).
HLQ	*Huntington Library Quarterly.*
H.M.C.	Historical Manuscripts Commission, London. Reports and Papers.
Hobart, *Reports*	*The Reports of That Learned Sir Henry Hobart Knight* (1641).
Holdsworth, *HEL*	Holdsworth, Sir William. *A history of English law*, vols. I (7th ed. 1956), II (4th ed. 1946), III (5th ed. 1942), IV–V (3rd ed. 1945), VI–VII (7th ed. 1956).
Holkham MS	Manuscript of the Earl of Leicester, Holkham Hall, Norfolk.
Hunt.	Henry E. Huntington Library and Art Gallery, San Marino, Calif.
Hunt. RB	Rare book with marginal notes in the Huntington Library.
Ind.	Manuscript index, Public Record Office.

Inst.	Coke, Sir Edward. The Second Part of the Institutes; The Third Part of the Institutes; The Fourt Part of the Institutes (1797 ed.).
I.T.	The Inner Temple Library, London.
'Iudicature'	Ellesmere, Baron. 'Memorialles for Iudicature. Pro Bono Publico.' Huntington Library, Ellesmere MS 2623.
James, *Works*	*The political works of James I*, ed. Charles Howard McIlwain (Cambridge Mass. 1918).
JBS	*The Journal of British Studies.*
Jones, *Chancery*	W. J. Jones, *The Elizabethan Court of Chancery* (Oxford 1967).
J.R.L.	The John Rylands Library, Manchester.
KB 27	Plea rolls, Court of King's Bench, civil side, Public Record Office.
Lans. MS	Lansdowne manuscript, British Museum.
L.I.	The Lincoln's Inn Library, London.
Littleton, *Tenures*	Thomas Littleton, *Les Tenures* (32nd Law French ed. 1581).
LJ	*Journal of the House of Lords beginning Anno Vicesimo Elizabethae Reginae* (n.d.), vol. II.
LQR	*The Law Quarterly Review.*
Moir, *Parl. 1614*	Thomas Moir, *The Addled Parliament of 1614* (Oxford 1958).
Moore, *Cases*	*Cases Collect et Report per Sir Francis Moore* (1663).
N.L.W.	The National Library of Wales, Aberystwyth.
Nott's Chanc. Cases	*Lord Nottingham's Chancery Cases*, ed. D. E. C. Yale (1957, 1961). Selden Society vols. 73 (I) and 79 (II).
N.R.O.	The Northamptonshire Record Office, Delapré Abbey, Northampton.
'Parl. 1604–10'	Ellesmere, Baron. 'Speciall observacions touching all the sessions of the last parlement anno 7 Regis.' Huntington Library, Ellesmere MS 2599.
Parl. 1610	*Proceedings in Parliament 1610*, ed. Elizabeth Read Foster (New Haven, Conn. 1966). 2 vols.
P & P	*Past and Present.*
P.C.C.	Prerogative Court of Canterbury, wills, Public Record Office.
Petyt MS	Petyt manuscript, Inner Temple Library.
Plowden, *Commentaries*	Edmund Plowden, *Les Commentaries ou Reportes* (2nd ed. 1578). *STC* 20041.

Post-Nati	Ellesmere, Baron. *The Speech of the Lord Chancellor of England, in the Eschequer Chamber, touching the Post-Nati* (1609).
Practice Chanc.	*The Practice of the High Court of Chancery Unfolded* (2nd ed. 1692).
'Prerog.'	'A Coppie of a wrytten discourse by the Lord Chauncellor Elsemore concerning the Royall Prerogatiue'. Harvard Law Library MS 4006.
Prestwich, *Cranfield*	Menna Prestwich, *Cranfield: politics and profits under the early Stuarts* (Oxford 1966).
P.R.O.	The Public Record Office, London.
'Prohibitians'	'Some Notes, and Remembrances, concerning Prohibitians, for Staying of suites in the Ecclesiasticall Courts, and in the Courts of the Admiraltie' (1611), Barlow MS9.
Rawl. MS	Rawlinson manuscript, Bodleian Library, Oxford.
Rep. Chanc.	*Reports of Cases Taken and Adjudged in the Court of Chancery* (3rd ed. 1736).
Rolle, *Reports*	*Le Reports de divers Cases, Banke le Roy* (1675).
Rot. Parl.	*Rotuli Parliamentorum* (1767), vols. I–II.
Royal MS	Manuscript in the Royal coll, British Museum.
Sackv. MS	Sackville manuscript, H.M.C., London.
Salisbury MS	*Calendar of the Manuscripts of the Most Hon. Marquess of Salisbury*, H.M.C. (1895–1970), parts VI–XXI.
SC	Court of Star Chamber, complaints and proceedings, Public Record Office.
Sloane MS	Manuscript in the Sloane collection, British Museum.
SP	Documents in the State Papers, Public Record Office.
SPD 14, 15	State Papers Domestic: Elizabeth, James I and Addenda.
S.R.O.	Shropshire Record Office, Shrewsbury, Salop.
STC	*A Short-Title Catalogue of Books Printed in England, Scotland, & Ireland and of English Books Printed Abroad 1475–1640*, ed. A. W. Pollard and C. R. Redgrave (1926).
State Trials	*Cobbett's Complete Collection of State Trials*, ed. W. Cobbett and T. B. Howell (1809), vols. I–II.
Stat. Realm	*The Statutes of the Realm* (1810–19), vols. I–VI.
Staunford, *Prerogative*	Sir William Staunford, *An Exposicion of the Kinges Prerogative* (1567). *STC* 23213.

Stowe MS	Stowe manuscript, British Museum.
Tanner MS	Tanner manuscript, Bodleian Library, Oxford.
Tourneur MS Rep.	Manuscript report of Timothy Tourneur, British Museum Add. MS 35, 957.
TRHS	*Transactions of the Royal Historical Society.*
U.C.N.W.	University College of North Wales Library, Bangor, Wales.
V.C.H.	Victoria County History.
West, *Symboleog.*	William West, *The Second Part of Symboleo-graphy* (5th ed. 1601).
Yale Law	The Yale Law Library, New Haven, Conn.
Y.U.L.	The Yale University Library.
Yelv. MS	Yelverton manuscript, British Museum.
Yelverton, *Reports*	*The Reports of Sir Henry Yelverton* (1735 ed.)

NOTES ON STYLE

The year has been referenced for beginning at both January 1 for modern convenience and March 24 for the identification of contemporary documents. All dates within these are cited as 1603/4.

When a law report is cited, the first time it is cited in the same manner as a contemporary work; the standard short form is used for later references to the same report.

References from the *Short-Title Catalogue* have been included where there are several contemporary editions of a work, or more than one printing in the same year.

Where a source exists in print as well as in manuscript, the printed version is cited if the matter concerned is reproduced accurately from the manuscript.

The place of publication for printed works is London unless otherwise noted.

All quotations in the text of Part One (Law and Politics) have been completely modernised in spelling, capitalisation, and punctuation. The titles of manuscripts and printed works, however, have been published in the original.

Editorial conventions followed in Part Two are listed on page 196.

TABLE OF STATUTES

TABLE OF CASES

(Abbreviations: Ad – Admiralty, As – Assize, Ch – Chancery,
CP – Common Pleas, Ex – Exchequer, Ex Ch – Exchequer
Chamber, GD – Gaol Delivery, HL – House of Lords, KB –
King's Bench, KC – King's Council, Pa – Parliament, PC – Privy
Council, Re – Requests, SC – Star Chamber, SI – Serjeants Inn,
Sp Co – Special Commission, Wa – Wards.)

INTRODUCTION

The life and career of Sir Thomas Egerton, Lord Ellesmere, bears vivid testimony to the axiom that the shape and texture of Britain's landscape has had a major influence on its people. Egerton's world was the northern borderland of England and Wales, an area which comprised Cheshire, Denbighshire, Flintshire, and northern Shropshire. Known as the northern lowland region of the Welsh marches,[1] this area of Britain had been in the backwater of Britain's historical development from the mid-fourteenth century to the advent of Tudor rule. But it witnessed in the sixteenth century a significant revival. The intensification of dairy farming, together with the mining of coal and iron ore, broadened the region's wealth and increased its exports. This invigorated economic foundation spurred the growth of the port of Chester and the market towns of Oswestry, Whitchurch, and Shrewsbury. A new Anglo-Celtic gentry class, acquiring the lands of the decimated feudal nobility, developed in both town and country to provide the basis of a new ruling elite. Grammar schools were founded, contributing to an increase in literacy, the development of the arts, and a religious reformation.[2] Thus in the sixteenth century the people of this region had economic, social, cultural, and religious experiences which began to bring them into the mainstream of English life on the Midland plain that stretched below them.

[1] Dorothy Sylvester, *The rural landscape of the Welsh borderland* (1969), 35–8. The region was bordered on the north by the Dee estuary and the Wirral peninsula, on the west by the Welsh massif, on the south by the upland promontory of southern Shropshire, and on the east by the south-west flank of the Pennines. Sylvester's book is an outstanding examination of the features of the area. To assess the historical relationships, see the essay of D. E. C. Eversely in *An introduction to English historical demography* (1966), 14–43.

[2] The best general account is that of Penry Williams, 'The Welsh borderland under Queen Elizabeth', *Welsh Historical Review* I (1960), 19–36. See also A. H. Dodd, *The Industrial Revolution in North Wales* (Cardiff, 2nd ed. 1951), 5–18, 55–61, 169–91, 300–7; and *The agrarian history of England and Wales, 1500–1640*, ed. Joan Thirsk (Cambridge 1967), 124–47, 265–73, 360–81, 587–616. Some of these themes are assessed for Cheshire by J. S. Morill, *Cheshire 1630–1660* (Oxford 1974), 14–24; and for northern Wales by G. Dyfnalt Owen, *Elizabethan Wales* (Cardiff 1964), 12–38, 58–103, 123–9, 149–58, 169–84.

The future Lord Chancellor was raised in the Dee valley, a stretch of rich greensward which forms the western half of this lowland region. The Dee valley is separated from the more sparsely settled Wever valley to the east by a wooded central ridge which bisects the region from north to south. From this central ridge, which runs from Frodsham down to Nesscliffe, one can overlook the 'valley of the goddess', a prosperous land lying between the central ridge and the Welsh massif amidst the serpentine winding of the Dee. Stretching for more than forty miles from the Irish Sea to Llangollen, the valley is dominated by the ancient city of Chester, which rests at the foot of the Dee. Access to the English Midlands is through the Midland Gap, a belt of morainic country that spreads between the southern reaches of the central ridge and the Pennines.[1]

Throughout the centuries the economy of the Dee valley had been largely pastoral and the agrarian landscape open field. The land was moderately populated, the demographic structure consisting of either closely settled nucleated villages or multi-parish townships. The people represented a mixture of Celtic (Welsh) and Anglian (English) blood and customs, the Welsh adopting the social structure of Anglian society, and the English absorbing the family tribal characteristics of their Celtic neighbours. This blending marked these people with a bold and egregious spirit. With their total dedication to the family, its servants and relations, this group placed their emphasis on the local power and influence of a group of interrelated people rather than on money. Thus any kind of business or profession was acceptable as long as it had its uses. This attitude led not only to an acquisitive participation in a variety of economic ventures, but also to a wide range of cultural pursuits.[2]

The home of these activities, the Dee valley also comprised the borderland of two English and Welsh counties; and the homogeneity of its communities made administrative distinctions merely nominal. The absence of great lords and effective institutions of government had left by the sixteenth century a distinct influence on political and

---

[1] Sylvester, *Welsh borderland*, 257–75, 293–313, 463–70. Some detailed sketches near contemp. are those of John Speed, *Histoire of Great Britaine* [1611] (3rd ed. 1632), 61–70; and Daniel Defoe, *A tour thro' the whole island of Great Britain* [1724–7], ed. G. D. H. Cole (1927), I, 464–71.

[2] The most perceptive reconstruction of this society is that of Owen, *Elizabethan Wales*. See also the comments of David Mathew, *The Celtic peoples and Renaissance Europe* (1933), 76–92, 230–61.

social development.[1] The conflicting authority of bodies such as the Council in the Marches of Wales, the County palatine of Chester and its courts of Great Sessions and Exchequer, the Western Assize Circuit, and the four county administrations enabled the communities to ignore established authorities and develop autonomously.[2] Allegiance was owed to prominent families whose manor house, chapel, market, lake, and park dominated the immediate surroundings. Only the ruins of the occasional castle served as a reminder of the habit of ducal and provincial authority which had existed in the not too distant past.

The lower section of the valley, which culminated in the environs of Chester, was called the Dee Vale Royal. On this gentle lowland drift prosperity unfolded rapidly in the middle decades of the sixteenth century, contributing to a large increase in population and to the foundation of satellite villages. With prominent royal estates in the area, the sons of gentry families became attracted to the universities and the inns of court of south-east England in search of further education and advancement. Educated at the centre of English life, those individuals who were successful returned to the Vale Royal to use their newly won prestige and influence to marshal the family and its connections in the quest for land and power. Spilling over into other parts of the lowland area, they first concocted ancient pedigrees to add a measure of distinction to an inconspicuous past. Securing both royal and local offices, they then utilised their influence and credit to make attractive marriages and to gather land. Capitalising their sources of agrarian production, several families emerged in the later decades of the sixteenth century to play the role of the marcher lords of much earlier times.[3]

[1] Local riots became endemic throughout the first two-thirds of the sixteenth century. Examples for Egerton's relations can be found in A. H. Dodd, *A history of Wrexham* (1957), 34–51; and S. C. 5/A.23/22.

[2] For example, when a Chester royal steward was asked if he owed his obligations to the sheriff or to the exch. court, he replied that he would not speak until instructed by the Earl of Leicester: C.R.O. Cholmondeley MS E. 112. Some of the admin. problems are still reflected in the records: --P.R.O. *Lists and Indices*, 40 (1963 ed.), iii–vi. The influence of these problems on one of the typical local communities has been assessed by W. B. Stephens and Norah Fuidge, 'Tudor and Stuart Congleton', in *History of Congleton*, ed. W. B. Stephens (Manchester 1970), 48–71.

[3] Dorothy Sylvester, 'The manor and the Cheshire landscape', *Trans. of the Lancs. and Cheshire Antiq. Soc.* 70 (1960), 1–15. The general background is in J. Beck, *Tudor Cheshire* (Chester 1969). The families are listed and discussed by William Camden, *Britannia* [1586], ed. Edmund Gibson (rev. ed. 1695), 554–63.

Thomas Egerton was such a man: born in the eastern section of the lowland region – the Wever river valley – of a newly squired family, the Egertons of Ridley.[1] The family seat was established at Ridley in 1514 by Sir Ralph Egerton, the second son of Sir Ralph Egerton of Oulton who had been rewarded for his heroism in the French wars of Henry VIII. The second son made his own family seat at Ridley, near that of his father and older brother. His son and heir, Richard Egerton, fathered an illegitimate boy, Thomas, in 1541 as a result of a teenage affair with Alice Sparke, a servant girl from the neighbouring village of Bickerton.[2] Shortly afterwards, Richard married Mary Grosvenor of Eaton Hall, the daughter of the old and prominent Grosvenor family which had remained a prominent force in the Vale Royal for several centuries. While the evidence is not explicit, it appears that Mary Grosvenor became responsible for providing for Thomas, and she sent her husband's illicit offspring to the home of a neighbouring Welsh family only a few miles from Eaton Hall, the Ravenscrofts of Bretton.[3] The Ravenscrofts were a newly risen Welsh gentry family who in the past decades had intermarried into the well-established Grosvenor and Stanley families. Together, the Grosvenors and Ravenscrofts, but particularly the Ravenscrofts, assumed responsibility for the bastard son. The strong ties between foster parents and their children that characterised the region[4] would prove in this instance to be enduring ones.

Although Thomas Egerton's early education cannot be identified, it is quite possible that he attended one of the early grammar schools founded in Denbighshire in the 1540s. Certainly his thoroughly disciplined life reflected the rigour of a grammar school education in

---

[1] E. W. Ives, 'Patronage at the Court of Henry VIII: the case of Sir Ralph Egerton of Ridley', *Bull. of the John Rylands Lib.*, 56 (1973–74), 346–8.

[2] There is no record of his birth. The approximate date is Oct. 1541 to Jan. 1541/2. The author has derived this from notes of his daughter Mary and his grandchildren in family tables and calendars at the Hunt. Lib. – Ellesm. MSS 995, 997, 998; and *A brief Treatise containing many proper Tables and easie rules*, ed. Richard Grafton (1599), Hunt. RB 61189–90. Contemp. oral opinion was rehearsed in *The Gentleman's Magazine*, 84 (1914), pt. 1, p. 225. Sir Ralph Egerton had so many illegitimate daughters that he could not remember their names: P.C.C. Porch 33.

[3] Ellesm. MS. 415; George Ormerod, *The history of the County Palatine and City of Chester* (2nd ed. 1882), II, 833–6: and Robert Glover's 'Visitation of Cheshire' [1580], Chetham Soc. 97 (1876), 97. The background is sketchy: J. H. Hanshall, *The history of the County Palatine of Cheshire* (Chester 1823), 805–6. Contemp. opinion was noted by Dr Godfrey Goodman, *The court of King James the First* [Chas. I], ed. Edmund Gibson (rev. ed. 1839), 273.

[4] For example, SPD 12/107/4–14.

the northern Welsh Marches.[1] Raised by the Ravenscroft family, he matriculated to Brasenose College, Oxford, in 1556. Brasenose had become a university centre for students from north-west England in the first half of the sixteenth century, and at the date of Egerton's matriculation eighteen of the twenty-one College fellows originated from the western border counties.[2] Egerton spent three years at Brasenose. Entering the mainstream of English intellectual life, he adopted a great reverence for the college and the university that he retained throughout his later career. Afterwards he sent his sons and those of his estate agents to Brasenose,[3] bearing personal testimony to the importance of a university education as a prerequisite for success in the renaissance state. Moreover, he aided other individual scholars with financial assistance, provided the College with many gifts, exercised an influence in the appointment of its officials, and intervened to resolve internal disputes.[4] But Egerton's future participation in the life of Brasenose was not in itself an isolated phenomenon. He also became a permanent figure in the university community, where he assisted in the affairs of other colleges and in the relations of the university to the town, eventually becoming Chancellor of Oxford University in 1610.[5]

Egerton's university education served as a means to a larger end. He did not graduate from Brasenose College. Instead, after spending three years at Oxford he went to law school – the inns of chancery and of court in London. Furnivall's and Lincoln's Inn had several students

[1] A. H. Williams, 'The origins of the old endowed grammar schools of Denbighshire', *Denbighshire Historical Society Transactions* 2 (1953), 26–7; and Owen, *Elizabethan Wales*, 198–208. The background of such schools and their curriculum has been cogently and fully assessed by Joan Simon, *Education and society in Tudor England* (Cambridge 1966), 197–268, 299–332.

[2] Compiled from the *Brasenose College register 1509–1909*, Oxford Hist. Soc. 50 (1909), I, 18–28. The subject is discussed by the Rev. David Mathew, 'Wales and England in the early seventeenth century', *CymRS* (1955), 36–45.

[3] *Brasenose register*, I, Index. Many of his later seventeenth- and eighteenth-century family descendants also matriculated at Brasenose.

[4] His work and influence can be seen, for example, from the letters of Richard Dalton and Richard Kylbens in Ellesm. MSS 51, 423, 430, 1927; and the accounts given in G. H. Wakeling, 'History of the College 1603–1660', *Brasenose quatercentenary monographs* 2 (Oxford 1909), pt. 1, no. 11, pp. 8–11. His gifts are noted in A. J. Butler, 'The College plate', *Brasenose register* III, 16–20. For his attempts to settle disputes see H. E. Salter, *Oxford City properties*, Oxford Hist. Soc. 83 (1926), 358–62.

[5] Ellesm. MSS 424–6, 1926, 1928, 1942, 1959, 1962, being personal and official univ. corresp. His election of 2 Nov. 1610 in *CSPD James*, IX, 135.

from the Cheshire–Shropshire area.[1] Since neither the Ravenscrofts
nor the Grosvenors had any family member in the law profession, it
is possible that they used their connections with the Bishop of Chester
and the Earl of Derby to have their foster son at college preferred to
an inn of chancery. The union of England and Wales in 1536 made the
Anglo-Welsh families realise that they had to gain expertise in the
English land law and make useful connections in the English law
profession.[2] The development of extra-curricular forms of education
at the universities in the sixteenth century had enabled students to
matriculate there for the purpose of receiving instruction suitable
for political and legal careers rather than participating in the statutory
curriculum, which was devoted largely to studies for the Church.[3]
Thus, although there is no evidence of the course of study which
Egerton undertook at Brasenose, his own papers indicate that he
studied classics, logic, history, and civil law,[4] subjects crucial to the
development of a legal mind in any age.

In the autumn of 1560 Egerton entered Furnivall's Inn, an inn of
chancery which introduced students to common law studies before
going on to an inn of court.[5] Furnivall's was administered by
Lincoln's Inn, one of the four inns of court in London, and in the
autumn of the following year Egerton matriculated to the senior institution.[6] His early common-law studies were not restricted to the
classroom. Raised in the rather lawless borderland country, where the
love of sport and conflict was strong, he seems to have spent his
summers outdoors. Thus in the summer of 1562 we find him cited in
a Star Chamber deposition for riding through an estate in the Dee
valley sword in hand with several compatriots, who allegedly de-
molished an enclosure.[7] The charge implies that Egerton and the
others had sought to frighten the complainant into settling a land
dispute out of court. This was justice 'northern style' by 'the well-
tempered sword.'[8]

[1] Wilfrid Prest, *The Inns of Court under Elizabeth I and the early Stuarts 1590–1640* (1972), 32–8.

[2] I would like to thank Dr G. Dyfnalt Owen for his suggestions on this topic.

[3] Mark H. Curtis, *Oxford and Cambridge in transition, 1558–1642* (Oxford 1959), 107–48.

[4] His studies at Brasenose College and Lincoln's Inn are discussed in Chap. I.

[5] *Early records of Furnivalls Inn*, ed. D. S. Bland (Newcastle 1957), f. 93.

[6] *The Records of the Honourable Society of Lincoln's Inn*, Vol. I – admissions (1896), 67.

[7] S. C. 5/B.2/9 (S.C. Trin. 1562).

[8] Roger North on circuit, quoted in J. S. Cockburn, *A history of English assizes 1558–1714* (Cambridge 1972), 40. Lawlessness in Egerton's area is described by Dodd, *Wrexham*, 34–51.

But northern-style justice was becoming irrelevant in this crucial period in the history of English common law studies as agrarian, industrial, and commercial change were affecting English life pervasively. The Courts of King's Bench and Chancery were being confronted with endless lists of suitors, and new developments in the forms of action and the pattern of litigation had also increased the complexity of the law. Moreover, the growth in jurisdiction of conciliar and provincial courts to handle the increasing problems of enforcement contributed to the proliferation of law suits and the uncertainty of the law itself.[1] Thus the new aristocracy came to demand, more than ever before, expert legal counsel to assist in dealing with the manifold problems which confronted them. And so did the Tudor State. The demand for lawyers had become nearly insatiable.[2]

The inns of court, moreover, were no longer concerned solely with legal studies. They were also becoming fashionable centres for intellectual, social, and cultural activities which had come to express the ideals of humanistic study.[3] The humanists of early Tudor England had addressed themselves to the deficiencies of the curriculum at the inns, and they demanded that these institutions adopt the love and respect for pure learning which was being nurtured at the universities. Prominent Tudor publicists such as John Rastell and Sir Thomas Elyot recommended a humanistic education at the universities as a prerequisite for legal studies at the inns.[4] Seeking a transformation of the ruling elite, they proclaimed that the power of learning was so great that its graduates could – in Elyot's words – 'become men of so excellent wisdom that throughout all the world should be found in no common weal more noble counsellors, our laws not only comprehending most excellent reasons but also being

[1] S. F. C. Milsom, *Historical foundations of the common law* (1969), 59–73, and Chaps. VIII–IX, XI–XII *passim*; and Sir Charles Ogilvie, *The king's government and the common law 1471–1641* (Oxford 1958), 79–86, 118–29.

[2] Louis A. Knafla, 'The matriculation revolution and education at the Inns of Court in Renaissance England', in *Tudor men and institutions*, ed. A. J. Slavin (Baton Rouge La. 1972), 234–41; and J. H. Baker, 'A history of the Order of the Serjeants at Law' (Univ. Coll. Fac. of Law, London; Ph.D. diss. 1968), 266–97.

[3] Knafla, 'Matriculation revolution', 245–8; and the approach of Wilfrid Prest, 'Legal education of the gentry at the Inns of Court, 1560–1640', *P&P*, 38 (1967), 20–39.

[4] A theme of Pearl Hogrefe, *The Sir Thomas More circle* (Urbana Ill. 1959); Leland Miles, *John Colet and the Platonic tradition* (La Salle Pa. 1961); and Mark Curtis, 'Education and Apprenticeship', *Shakespeare and his own time*, ed. Allardyce Nicoll (Cambridge 1964).

gathered and composed of the pure meal and flour sifted out of the best laws of all other countries'. [1]

Lincoln's Inn had begun to form an influential community of interest in mid-sixteenth-century England. Its graduates included John and William Rastell, and Richard Tottel, the most important legal printers of the age. [2] These men, exercising a monopoly of printing legal publications, had a considerable influence on common law studies. Moreover, they were also editors devoted to the promotion of humanistic ideals through the study of *bonae literae*. Having connections with intellectual circles and the royal court, they had a considerable influence on the students at Lincoln's Inn. Thus Thomas Egerton not only pursued common law studies at the Inn, but he also developed more fully his general interests in law, philosophy, and history which he had begun in tutorials at Brasenose College. [3] Altogether Egerton spent eight years at Lincoln's Inn and a few more as an attorney out of chambers. These years, bestowing upon him the knowledge and skill of the legal profession, formed the decisive period in his intellectual development.

The beginning of Egerton's law career proper dates from his call to the Bar in 1572. He seems to have made a lucrative career before the courts, conducting legal affairs firstly for the Grosvenor and Ravenscroft families and their relations, [4] and secondly for the Bishop of Chester and the Earls of Derby and Leicester — two of the most prominent men in the northern Marches. [5] Egerton established his legal practice before the Council in the Marches of Wales, the Western Circuit of the Assize courts, the Chancery, and the Court of King's

---

[1] Sir Thomas Elyot, *The Boke Named the Governour* [1531], ed. Foster Watson (1907), 64. See also John Rastell, *Of Gentylnes and Nobylyte* [1525] ed. A. C. Partridge and F. P. Watson (1950), Epilogue.

[2] A. W. Reed, *Early Tudor drama* (1926), 1–27, 104–17; H. J. Byrom, 'Richard Tottel — his life and work', *The Library*, new. ser. 8 (1927), 220–2; Howard Graham, 'The Rastells and the printed English law book of the Renaissance', *Law Lib. J.* 47 (1954), 7–18; and L. W. Abbott, *Law reporting in England 1485–1585* (1973), 9–81, for a discussion of the early printers within the ms. tradition to 1558.

[3] These subjects are discussed at length in Chap. I.

[4] For example, he was the executor or overseer of the wills of Richard and Anthony Grosvenor by 1575: *Wills and inventories* Chetham Soc. 51 (1860), 153; and P.C.C. Daughtry 20. Examples of family case work are C.2/B.8/21; C.2/E.4/42, 61–2; C.3/60/11; C.3/248/42; C.3/268/9, 22, 30; P.R.O. Requests 2/165/152; and Harl. MS 2007.

[5] His briefs of early cases are in Ellesm. MS 482, especially at ff. 90–147. For the Derby–Leicester–Egerton relationship see Cotton MS Vespasian C. VIII, f. 30r; for Egerton and Leicester, Goodman, *Court of James*, 271–5, 280–3; for Egerton and Derby, *Eg. Papers*, 96, 131. Later cases are in Ellesm. MSS 5647–5713, 5810–92.

Bench. As a lawyer he placed a high premium on original research. He made the effort to go back to the sources, and to frame a historical outline of the major factors. He would then construct a logically un-impeachable case, and present it in a grave, yet dynamic manner. His brief for the Dean and Chapter of Chester against the Crown is a useful example.[1] The Dean and Chapter sought a writ of entry for manors originally granted them by the Crown, but their entrance had been barred because of the defects of certain statutes which were alleged to confirm the letters patent from the Queen. Since that time the monarch sought to bestow the lands to royal favourites. Egerton wrote an elaborate essay on how an analytical reconstruction of the words, phrases, and sections of the statutes, within the context of their intentions, made irrelevant the defects of the acts and confirmed the right of the Dean's entrance. Briefs such as these brought to him the success which resulted in his appointment to serve as legal counsel for the Crown in 1581.

Success as a lawyer also brought the acquisition of wealth, and Egerton relied extensively for advice and assistance on those families who stood behind him in his law career. His earliest purchases of land in the 1560s were made, and placed in secret trust for him by George and Ralph Ravenscroft, who also served as his trustees.[2] Later, their successors William and Thomas Ravenscroft would perform similar roles. Egerton's first two estate agents, John Allen and Thomas Whitby, had worked for the Ravenscroft family.[3] And in 1576 he married Elizabeth Ravenscroft, the youngest daughter of the family who had taken him into their home. When Egerton set up his own household, he chose Henry Johns and John Panton (both of whom had worked for the Ravenscrofts) as his servants.[4] Afterwards, Panton's son became the first person whom Egerton as a bencher of

---

[1] Ellesm. MS 482, ff. 34–52. Egerton's own agents became the holders of the fee farm. Some of the local background which surfaced is sketched by Michael B. Pulman, 'An interjection of the royal prerogative into the legal and ecclesiastical affairs of Cheshire in the fifteen seventies', *Albion* (1974), 226–36. See as well the *Bracebridge Case*, the briefs in Ellesm. MS 482, ff. 124–9; documents in C.2/B.b.8/21; and the reports in Plowden, *Commentaries*, 416–24, for background.

[2] Some of the lands held in trust were noted in Thomas Wilbraham's will: C. R. O. Tollemache MS DTW Q. Misc. 2/2 (1612). See also Ellesm. MS 560.

[3] Documents in the C.R.O. Cholm. MSS, and the Ellesm. MSS.

[4] The Ravenscrofts of Bretton, their relations and lands, have been recorded for the period from the Ellesm. MSS, and the N. L. W. Glynne, Plas Gwyn, and Plymouth MSS. For Panton and Johns, see Ellesm. MSS 636–7, 658–62; and N. L. W. Gen. MSS 9086–9101 (Panton papers).

Lincoln's Inn would have 'specially admitted' to an inn of court. The two elder Ravenscroft daughters who were raised with Egerton, Maude and Alice, married into the Hope of Greenhope and Massey of Aldeford families, and the Hopes and Masseys provided Egerton with agricultural advice and managed some of his lands.[1] A third Ravenscroft daughter, Katherine, married Robert Davies of Gwysaney who, together with the Ravenscrofts themselves, would oversee Egerton's Denbighshire estates.[2] The Grosvenor family was also influential in his affairs.

The Grosvenors, from as early as 1570, had written Egerton into their wills as the recipient of gifts of money, as the Earl of Derby did in 1572.[3] The Grosvenors had intermarried often in the fifteenth and sixteenth centuries with the Ravenscrofts, the Pulestons of Emrall, and the Wilbrahams of Woodhay.[4] Roger Puleston and Richard Wilbraham served as two of Egerton's early stewards, as their sons did later. They also made him large loans.[5] Other men who provided him with services by the 1580s included Thomas Dymocke, and Ellis and Richard Younge, who had served the Grosvenor and Puleston families; Richard and Roger Brereton of Tatton and Worsley, who were major figures with the Derby family; and Thomas and William Mostyn of Talacre, whose family had intermarried often with the Ravenscrofts.[6] Local families who also participated in the development of Egerton's interests included the Mainwarings of Drayton, Salop, who had worked for the Derby family and were related to the Masseys and Breretons; and the Duttons of Dutton, a family who had served the Earls of Derby and Leicester, and loaned Egerton funds for

[1] Refs. to the Hopes and Masseys have been located only in the Ellesm. MSS.

[2] Robert Davies – U.C.N.W. Davies of Gwysaney MSS.

[3] Thomas Grosvenor, P.C.C. Lyon 20 (will proved in 1601); Anthony Grosvenor, C.142/180/21, and P.R.O. Wards 7/19/127 (1577); Elizabeth Grosvenor, P.C.C. Woodhall 51 (1601); and William Grosvenor, P.C.C. Woodhall 53 (1601). The will of Edward, Earl of Derby, P.C.C. Daper 38 (1572); and of Henry, Earl of Derby, P.C.C. Dixy 66 (21 Sept. 1593).

[4] Corresp. in Ellesm. MSS 132, 227; and N.L.W. Add. MS 251/D. The Pulestons of Emrall, their relations and lands, have been noted from N.L.W. Puleston MSS; the Wilbrahams of Woodhay from C.R.O. MSS DDX/28, 210; and the Grosvenors of Eaton from Chester Town Hall, Grosvenor MSS, and C.R.O. Cholm. MSS H. 127–55.

[5] Ellesm. MSS 1176–7.

[6] Letters, for example, in Ellesm. MSS 8, 10, 15A, 54; Harl. MS 1926, ff. 53v–108r; U.C.N.W. Mostyn MSS 101–2; N.L.W. Wynn of Gwydir MSS 1458–60; and C.R.O. Cholm. MSS H. 121–70, B.70–84, C.468–85, 958. For the Mostyns, U.C.N.W. Mostyn MSS, and N.L.W. Thorne MSS; and for the Breretons, Ellesm. MSS, Hasts. MSS, and C.R.O. Cholm. MSS.

further land purchases in the late 1570s and early 1580s.[1]

These family relations brought Egerton a very crucial knowledge of the land market, financial aid, advice, and trusted service. They also brought him into the lucrative orbit of the royal commission. For example, in the years 1571–3 Egerton and a number of the near and distant relations who assisted, and worked for him, were appointed to royal commissions whose functions ranged from holding inquisitions *post mortem* on convicted felons and attainted nobles, to searching for 'concealed and encroached lands' and 'secret enclosures'.[2] These commissions awarded for Cheshire, Denbighshire, and Flintshire carried broad powers, and they often led to the confiscation of land. Such confiscation would be followed by a sale, and the commissioners would often figure prominently in that transaction. Thus, when Egerton's friends and agents dominated a commission to investigate defaulters on debt to the Crown in 1572, a manor seized in lieu of non-payment was then granted to Egerton when he volunteered the payment of the debt.[3] Practices such as these had been used in the past by prominent families such as the Stanleys and the Grosvenors. This kind of opportunity would become even more readily available to Egerton with his rise into the legal service of the Queen.

Egerton's other business interests in this period were in mining, industry, and commerce. The northern Welsh borderlands were relatively rich in coal and iron-ore deposits, and new techniques in mining together with increased demand made the exploitation of these natural resources very profitable in the mid-sixteenth century.[4] The central ridge was the area rich in iron ore, and the area at the foot of the Welsh massif contained large deposits of coal and lead. The Grosvenors of Eaton had secured a number of coal and lead mines by royal grant in 1551, and they acquired the large coalfield near Ewlowe in 1571 through a complicated transfer after the death of a cousin,

[1] The Mainwaring papers are in the Bedfordshire Rec. Off. Countess of Cowper MSS, vol. 30, and the J.R.L. Mainwaring MSS; Dutton papers are in C.R.O. MSS EDC 2/7 and DVE C. III–V. Later, John Dutton married the first daughter of Egerton's eldest son, Thomas. Relevant corresp. is in Ellesm. MSS 18, 54, 65, 132, 146, 158, 237, 654, 753; and Hasts. MS 1265. The Dutton loans are in the U.C.N.W. Mostyn MSS, 'Dutton bonds' uncat.

[2] U.C.N.W. Mostyn MSS 648–72; E.123/10/265; and E.178/496–503, 1422, 1884, 2858, 3430. The potential for such searches in the early 1570s, and the later protests, are explored by C. J. Kitching, 'The quest for concealed lands in the reign of Elizabeth I', *TRHS*, 5th ser. 24 (1974), 63–78.

[3] E.178/495. See also the papers in Ellesm. MSS 1254–76, 1331–85.

[4] Dodd, *Indust. Revo. No. Wales*, 16–8, 169–91.

John Booth.[1] Their claim, however, was contested. Besides employing Thomas Egerton for their legal defence, George Ravenscroft and John Whitby – who were working for both Thomas Grosvenor and Egerton – entered the mine with a group of men and carried off '300 wain loads of coal'.[2] The business was obviously too attractive to wait for further delays.

Later, Egerton himself became more directly involved in the coal and iron-ore business. He secured a grant from the Queen for leasing the Lordship of Bromfield and Yale which included the right to mine iron ore with a royalty reserved to the Crown.[3] He also assisted financially in aiding his estate agents Robert Davies of Gwynsaney and Roger Mostyn to purchase coalfields and woodland in northern Flintshire.[4] Prior to this purchase, Mostyn and his neighbours had been cited in an Exchequer deposition for tearing down William Ratcliffe's water mill for the smelting of iron ore.[5] Although the circumstances surrounding this industrial sabotage are unknown, it is at least apparent that there was considerable competition in mining and industry, and that Egerton and his coterie were involved.

In commercial matters Egerton began his law career working not only for his relatives and patrons, but also for the Company of Merchant Adventurers. He defended their interests in a law suit in 1573, and became a deputy-governor of the Company by 1575.[6] Publicly, he defended their interests in letters to Burghley and the Privy Council in the years 1578–81.[7] After his appointment to the Solicitorship in 1581 he continued to support them and became a member of the Board. Later, he participated in the interests of the East India Company when it was chartered in 1601.[8] However, in commercial ventures as well as mining and industry, Egerton did not become too deeply committed. No one area of business or professional life was allowed to dominate his career with the single-minded intensity which he gave to legal practice and the law.

---

[1] N.L.W. Gen. MS 8.062/E; and *Denbs. Hist. Soc. Trans.* 7 (Denbigh 1958), 41–2.

[2] E.123/5/343 (17 May 1577).

[3] Lans. MS 78, ff. 85–7; N.L.W. Gen. MS 18.062/E; and P.R.O. Ind. 9800/558.

[4] F.L.O. Mostyn MSS uncat. (box for 1590s). See as well the U.C.N.W. Gwysaney MSS 218–47.

[5] The deposition for the exch. ct. in E.133/6/926 (Trin. 1590).

[6] *APC Eliz. 1571–5*, p. 160; and *1575–7*, pp. 43–4.

[7] *CSP Foreign, 1578–9* (1903), 382–3; *1581–2* (1907), 146–9; *1582* (1909), 418; **and** Ellesm. MS 2373.

[8] *CSP Colonial Ser. East India, China and Japan*, *1513–1616* (1862), 238.

Egerton's advent to public office occurred in June, 1581, when he was promoted to the post of Solicitor-General.[1] According to oral tradition, the Queen and her ministers had decided that he would not plead against the Crown again. Egerton's rise to public office came, however, only after a re-examination of his religious position. He had retained the Catholic faith of his stepmother throughout his early life. At Lincoln's Inn he was suspended in May 1569 for observing the Catholic rites and ceremonies just when he was going to be called to the Bar. But he was restored by the governors of the Inn.[2] He was suspended again in June 1570 for observing the Catholic faith, and an order was set down that if he was certified as reconciled by the Bishop of London he could be called to the Bar at the next moot. Not until eight months later did he make the decision to give up his observance of the Catholic faith, and once certified by the Bishop, he was called to the Bar in the spring of 1572.[3]

While Egerton gave up his practice of the Old Faith he did not at first embrace the Anglican Church. We find in the Diocese of London returns of 1577 for the 'peculiar' jurisdiction of the inns the citation of Thomas Egerton for not attending divine service. At this time Egerton was at the height of a very promising legal career, and once again he had to make a crucial decision. The decision appears to have been made quickly, and he is listed at the bottom of the inquiry as having been fully reconciled.[4] His career would now move rapidly, both at Lincoln's Inn and in the law profession. As official positions became vacant in the legal service of the Crown, Egerton would be among the leading contenders; and in some instances he would become the unchallenged candidate.

Egerton's stature at Lincoln's Inn developed fully after his final reconciliation with the Established Church in 1577. In the following year he was given new chambers in the Inn and appointed steward for the Lent Reading. And in 1579 he was called to the Bench, becoming one of the governors of the Inn.[5] He gave his first Reading to the students on the interpretation of letters patent in 1581.[6] As a bencher, Egerton seems to have given advice and financial aid, made

---

[1] Ellesm. MS 498; C.66/120/9v (28 June 1581).
[2] *The records of the Honourable Society of Lincoln's Inn – the black books* (1897), I, 371.
[3] *Ibid.* 372, 381, 458.
[4] *Catholic Record Society Miscellanea* 12 (1921), 101.
[5] These, and other refs. to his activities at Lincoln's Inn, 1577–9, are in the *Black books*, I, 404–15.
[6] *Ibid.* 423. Notes of the Reading are in C.U.L. Dd. 11. 87, ff. 152r–9v.

loans, and assisted in the raising of additional funds for the construction of new buildings.[1] He presented his second Reading to
Furnivall's Inn on leases in 1585, and was elected to the prestigious
post of treasurer in 1587.[2] Later, he gave a third Reading on
tenures.[3] Egerton's efforts on behalf of the Inn did not go unrewar-
ded. In the following decade he received more privileges of making
'special admissions' than any other bencher with the exception of
Chancellor Puckering.[4] He also ushered in a new generation of law
students from the ·northern Welsh Marches. Egerton had a total of
twenty-three different men who had assisted him at various times
in his household, and in his agrarian and industrial ventures down to
1594. Of these men, twenty would send at least one of their sons to
Lincoln's Inn by the end of the Elizabethan period,[5] thereby contributing to that new pattern of patronage which was re-ordering the
structure of English society.

Egerton was advanced to public office at a propitious time in the
history of the Tudor State. He, together with his predecessor John
Popham, seem to have marked the emergence of the Solicitor- and
Attorney-Generalship to a substantial place in the administration
of English government and the law.[6] Egerton's work as Solicitor-
General became very quickly a full-time occupation. An examination
of his personal papers reveals that his knowledge of land and commerce was relied on extensively by the Queen and her Privy Council.
For example, he drafted letters patent for grants of Crown land,
offices, local fairs and markets, and monopolies. He also participated
in the direct administration of the Queen's lands. In this capacity he
rewrote legal instruments defining boundaries, tenures, and conditions, and presented new or additional questions to be asked of her
tenants.[7] Work such as this was supplemented with his prosecution
of suits before the central courts for the maintenance of royal rights,
the discovery of concealed titles, and debts owed to the Crown.[8]

---

[1] *Black books*, I, 429, 432, 440, 460–1.
[2] *Ibid.* II, 6, 9–10. Notes of the lecture are in Lans. MS 1119, ff. 43–60.
[3] Notes in Lans. MS 1121, ff. 20–38; and on 'The Rehearsall' in Harl. MS 5265, ff. 136r–
7v.
[4] *Black books*, II, 39 etc. He also angered many of his colleagues with his 'hard speeches'
and demands: for example, at pp. 50, 58, 71.
[5] Lincoln's Inn, *Admissions*, I, 74–91.
[6] The view is my own. For the context, see the comments of Baker, 'History of Serjeants',
398–404; and W. J. Jones, *Politics and the Bench* (1971), 29, 40–2.
[7] Ellesm. MSS 1254–76, 1331–85.
[8] Ellesm. MS 482, *passim*.

Combining Egerton's personal records with those of the 'Acts of the Privy Council', it is readily apparent that his work as Solicitor-General included not only the care of royal rights and land, but also the resolution of disputes between central and local officials, borough governments and their inhabitants, lay and ecclesiastical bodies, and the examination and prosecution of criminal offences against the State.[1] However, Egerton's public reputation was based on his prosecution of cases of treason and conspiracy in the 1580s and early 1590s, and it was this role as a public prosecutor that gave him a public reputation which would make possible future elevation to even higher offices of state.

The role that Egerton played in the great treason trials of 1585–92 came at a time when outstanding lawyers were being given major responsibilities as legal counsel for the Crown. Egerton was known as an indefatigable researcher, a man who covered every aspect of the case himself from research in the original records to the examination and counsel of witnesses, the preparation of the briefs, and the conduct of the trial. He was also a dynamic figure who impressed in the court room. A significant change occurred in royal policy around 1579 with the appointment of Edmund Anderson as Queen's Serjeant and John Popham as Solicitor-General. Both men were known not only as intelligent and hard-working, but also as unusually tough in their legal attitudes and severe in application. Thus when Gilbert Gerrard – a rather weak and mediocre figure – was kicked upstairs as Master of the Rolls in the summer of 1581, Popham was appointed to the Attorney-Generalship and Egerton to the Solicitorship.

Egerton joined Anderson and Popham in the autumn term of 1581, and in the first two cases they handled Egerton remained in the background.[2] The initial case was the trial of Vaux, Tresham, Catesby, and others for treason, where Egerton observed the attack of Anderson and Popham which brought the defendants' conviction. The second case was the prosecution of Edmund Campion and others for high treason. Again, Egerton was largely an observer as Anderson

---

[1] Particularly the *APC Eliz.* 1581–2 to 1590–1, *passim*. This kind of work continued uninterrupted with his appointment to the Attorney-Generalship in 1592: *APC Eliz. 1592, 1592–3*. These activities account for the great mass of copy petitions, grants, charters, and letters patent in the Ellesm. MSS coll. at the Hunt. Lib. that date from the 1580s.

[2] *APC Eliz. 1581–2*, pp. 248–68. Egerton's notes on the proceedings in Ellesm. MS 2663 have been edited by Anthony G. Petti, *Recusant documents from the Ellesmere manuscripts*, Cath. Rec. Soc. 59 (1968), 5–9. I wish to thank Professor Tony Petti for discussing these and other docs. with me.

launched one of the first genuinely vicious prosecutions of his career in a style with which he would become justifiably symbolised, and then used torture to secure a forced confession.[1] The following spring Anderson was raised to the Chief Justiceship of the Court of Common Pleas, Popham and Egerton becoming the two prosecuting officers of the Crown. These two lawyers would prepare and lead the prosecution of some of the most famous treason cases in England's history.

The threat posed by the Scottish Catholic Queen and a Spanish invasion were two of the major problems which confronted England in the years 1585–9, and the spectre of a rebellion for the overthrow of the Elizabethan settlement by a Catholic Queen supported by a Spanish army necessitated a severe and unbending Crown policy towards potential traitors.[2] The major criminal trials were those of Henry Percy, Earl of Northumberland, Anthony Babington and his fellow conspirators, Mary Queen of Scots, Philip Howard, Earl of Arundel, and Lord John Perrot. In addition, dozens of other individuals were implicated in several webs of intrigue and conspiracy. Egerton and Popham would participate in every one of these cases with a number of other legal counsellors, but the bulk of the work was in the hands of those two officials who prepared most of the briefs and took turns with each defendant who faced the court. Catholicism was definitely no longer a sticking point for Thomas Egerton as he became a dedicated professional supporter and champion of the Established Church.

The general pattern of the two prosecutors appears to have been established in the trial of the Earl of Northumberland in 1585. Here, although each man took his turn in the trial, Popham was more noteworthy for laying down the particulars of the evidence, and Egerton in confronting the defendant personally to draw out his guilt.[3] In the trial of the Babington group for conspiracy in the following year we can read from the record examples of Egerton's devastating courtroom manner. When one of the alleged conspirators, Tilney, stated that the priest Ballard did not come to him disguised to speak of a treason, the Solicitor replied:

---

[1] *State Trials*, I, 1050–83 (Nov. 1581). Anderson's daughter Katherine later married an Egerton relative – Sir George Booth of Dunham Massey, as did three of her own children.

[2] R. B. Wernham, *Before the Armada* (1966), Chap. VII. Egerton's general exams are noted in *CSPD 1581–90*, p. 339 (July 1586).

[3] *State Trials* I, 1120–2 (June 1585).

'Tilney, you say true; he came not disguised, but I will tell you how he came; being a popish priest, he came in a grey cloak laid on with gold lace, in velvet hose, a cut satin doublet, a fair hat of the meanest fashion, the band being set with silver buttons; a man and a boy after him, and his name, captain Fortescue.'[1]

The trial resulted in fourteen executions.

Egerton's work was quite conspicuous in the causes against the Babington group and Mary Queen of Scots. In the Babington trial he examined the famous ciphers and attested to their authenticity, interrogated the group of men one by one to reveal their confusion, and, with Popham, prepared the indictments.[2] The Solicitor undertook similar work in Mary's cause, which began in October, 1586, with the examination of the evidence and the interrogation of witnesses.[3] According to Lord Treasurer Burghley, the Solicitor was 'best acquainted with the matters wherewith the Scottish Queen, her secretaries, and those traitors that were executed and others were touched concerning the practices for the destruction of her majesty'.[4] In the public trial of the Scottish Queen Egerton had the difficult task of proving her complicity in the plot against Elizabeth, and afterwards he drafted with Popham and Burghley's amendments the petition for her execution.[5] Mary's beheading was followed by the gathering of the Spanish Armada, and its defeat brought another series of cases for the conviction of prominent individuals who may have given it support. The two most famous were Howard and Perrot.

Philip Howard, Earl of Arundel, had been in the Tower since 1585, and in 1589 the Crown placed him on trial for treason before the House of Lords. The articles charged were many, ranging from complicity in the Armada and raising up a potential Catholic Queen, to praying for the cause before, during, and after its defeat. The trial was conducted before the Lords by Popham and Egerton. Popham

---

[1] *Ibid.* I, 1150. The trials are recorded at pp. 1127–62.

[2] SPD 12/193/1–2. 46, 54 (15–20 Sept. 1586). Egerton's notes are pr. from Ellesm. MS 1197 in Petti, *Recusant docs.* 23–4. The proceedings are in *State Trials*, 1127–40 (Sept. 1586).

[3] Witnesses interrogated and racked are noted in *APC Eliz. 1568–70*, pp. 271–2. Notes and materials are in *CSP Scotland*, IX, 44, 61–2, 77–8; and Cotton MS Caligula C. IX, ff. 469–72, 632–8. The indictments and petition for the execution with Egerton's notes are in Ellesm. MS 1191, pr. in Petti, *Recusant docs.* 23–31.

[4] Ellesm. MS 1846. See also the Yelv. MS in Add. MS 48.031.

[5] *State Trials* I, 1141–1228 (Oct. 1586 to Feb. 1586/7). Other important accounts are in the Cotton MS Caligula C. IX; and Yelv. MS 31. Egerton's brief is I.T. Barrington MS 29, ff. 609–19.

prosecuted most of the articles, but Egerton concluded the case with evidence which he had collected from the forced confessions of prisoners who were alleged to have overheard the Earl's prayers through the prison walls in the course of several years. [1] Egerton's method was to take thirteen pieces of evidence, enlarge and conceptualise every one of them, and then conclude each point with a sworn statement and the repeated declaration – 'proved'. Capitalising on a dramatic situation, he tangled the men who sat arraigned before him in a web of evidence which brought their conviction and the death sentence. [2] The Earl, although sentenced to death, was allowed to live under sentence in solitary confinement until he died from privation in 1595.

The Solicitor's approach was similar in the prosecution of John Perrot, Lord Lieutenant of Ireland, for high treason in April 1592, before a special commission in the Court of King's Bench. The charge was complicity in the invasion plans of 1588–9. In this cause Popham and Egerton had been collecting evidence for the past two years, and Egerton's marginalia appeared throughout the examinations which led to the pressing of an indictment. [3] In the arraignment the Solicitor once again made the final plea, and this time the trial ended in a shouting match with exclamations of 'You did me wrong' (Perrot) and 'I never did you wrong' (Egerton), reverberating around the hall. [4] Between the conclusion of the trial and the day on which a verdict was to be rendered, the Earl of Essex and others sought to intervene on Perrot's behalf, but the Attorney and Solicitor-General convinced Burghley that the accused must go the way of all traitors if convicted. [5] Perrot, a broken man, committed suicide before the death sentence was carried out.

The larger problem of treason in these years stemmed from the problem of recusancy, and the legal staff of the Crown bore the responsibility for the discovery, apprehension, and prosecution of recusants by parliamentary statute. Egerton's early work was dele-

---

[1] Egerton's copy of the articles in Ellesm. MS 1196 has been ed. by Petti, *Recusant docs.* 32–3. See as well a different copy with additional notes by Egerton in B.M. Egerton MS 2074, ff. 64–87, and Ellesm. MSS 5794–5809.

[2] *State Trials* I, 1249–64 (April 1589). Most of the materials bearing on this trial were coll. and pr. fully in *Unpublished documents relating to the English martyrs*, ed. John Hungerford Pollen, Cath. Rec. Soc. 21 (1919), I, 170–289.

[3] Alnwick MS 6, ff. 50v–8v, 87–97, 143–9, 159–69, 204–97; and SPD 12/241/10B–15v. See also Ellesm. MSS 6224–9.

[4] *State Trials* I, 1329 (April–May 1592).

[5] SPD 12/238/82, 155.

gated to commissions which were composed largely of his relatives and estate agents, most of whom had, or were acquiring, legal experience. A group of them were engaged on such commissions for the western border counties and the north in the period 1583–90. [1] One of the commissions examined the Solicitor's remaining Catholic relative, Mary Egerton (née Grosvenor) his stepmother. She was listed with the recommendation of 'leniency'. [2] Egerton protected her carefully to the end of her natural life.

A change in Egerton's attitude towards recusancy occurred following the defeat of the Armada, and his papers provide suitable evidence of the change. The recusants to be ignored were the 'simple' people who had been 'misled in these actions'. [3] The ones to be examined were those capable of committing treason. The essential problem, as he stated in a letter to the Privy Council, was 'to discern those that carry traitorous and malicious minds against her majesty and the state, from those whose simplicity is misled by ignorant and blind zeal'. [4] As soon as the Perrot trial was over, the Solicitor and Attorney-General were ordered to launch a major investigation of recusants. With Popham's elevation to the King's Bench, Egerton became the Attorney-General and was joined by Edward Coke who succeeded him in the Solicitorship.

The policy of the Crown against recusants had been clear since the early 1580s, and it was enacted by Parliament in the spring of 1593 with 'An Act against Popish Recusants'. [5] The result of this statute was that the Solicitor and Attorney-General conducted a new series of examinations, which led to another group of trials. The legal officers also invented some new techniques for the discovery of traitorous recusants. Deploring the inability to gain sufficient testimony, Coke and Egerton placed a new emphasis on investigating servants and wives, and Egerton himself drew up proposals for the interrogation of 'wives'. [6] The result of this policy was a new scourge of the

[1] SPD 12/183/35, 12/230/57, 12/232/45, 12/257/66, 12/243/1. Also the items edited in Petti, Recusant docs. 29–30, 33–6. The men most active were Ralph Egerton, Richard Harding, Roger Puleston, Roger and Thomas Wilbraham, and Richard Younge.

[2] SPD 12/164/183 (22 Oct. 1585). Despite her fines, when she died in 1597 she still left considerable gifts to Egerton, his children and grandchildren, and more than £2,200 in land. She always used her maiden name, Grosvenor.

[3] His draft articles are in SPD 12/212/70 (20 July 1588). Some of his early exams. of recusants are in SPD 12/232/45, 84.

[4] SPD 12/212/70, 147. See also SPD 12/191/15.

[5] 'An Acte against Popishe Recusants', 35 Eliz. c. 2, Stat. Realm IV, 843–6.

[6] Mentioned in an exam. of Miles Gerrard on 10 Jan. 1592/3: Harl. MS 6995, f. 167.

country, and Egerton found himself at York in December of 1593, waiting for his shipment of 'one trunk, a casket, two bags, and two boxes of writings'. [1]

Egerton's presentation of bills of information against fifty-five recusant couples in February 1593/4, was the first group submission of the Crown's legal counsel to meet the problem of recusancy which was now deemed to be so serious. [2] A number of Crown prosecutions were launched in the courts against these and other individuals, particularly persons suspected as 'spies'. The Attorney-General recommended that once such recusants were 'proved' dangerous and committed for trial they be kept in strict security. If they should fail to co-operate with the Crown they were to receive 'such torture upon the wall as is usual for the better understanding of the truth of matters against her majesty and the state'. [3]

The Attorney was also concerned with the Crown's image before the law. When a recusant was convicted as a traitorous spy he advocated nothing short of an immediate public execution following the delivery of the judgment. Thus, when the chief physician to the Queen, Dr Roderigo Lopez, was implicated in February of 1593/4 for a plot on her life, Egerton conducted an engaging court-room prosecution against the doctor in the Court of King's Bench, describing him as 'a perjured and murdering villain and Jewish doctor, worse than Judas himself'. [4] He was convicted. The Queen, however, did not want the sentence of execution carried out; and neither did her Treasurer, Lord Burghley. But when Lopez became ill in the Tower of London, the Attorney wrote a worried letter to the Privy Council: 'If this should be deferred, and Lopez die before execution, great dishonour and scandal might ensue'. [5] After more than two months of further delays the Attorney, who was now taking up his new office as Master of the Rolls, finally had his wish. Dr Lopez, unlike Arundel and Perrot, did not die before his execution. He was escorted from

---

[1] Harl. MS 6996, f. 50, and Ellesm. MS 2834. Notes from other places are in Harl. MS 6996, f. 19, and Lans. MS 74, f. 202.

[2] E.159/406/71–99 (Hill. 1593/4). Egerton's later exams. are in Ellesm. MSS 2101–58. Coke's are in E.159/407/231–2. See also 11 Co. Rep. ff. 56v–62v.

[3] SPD 12/230/57, 112 (11 June 1590), and later 12/243/93 (23 Dec. 1592). Some of his interrogatories for spies are in CSPD, 1591–4, pp. 425–36. For the authority to resort to the rack in such instances he had noted his own copy of Elizabeth's procl. A Declaration of the favourable dealing of her Maiesties Commissioners . . . (1583), Hunt. RB 89493, sig. Aa. iii, and the last folio un-numbered.

[4] The indictments are in SPD 12/247/102, the case at ff. 213–26.

[5] SPD 12/268/26 (14 Mar. 1593/4).

the Tower to Westminster on the morning of June 7 with two other
Portuguese prisoners, and brought to the King's Bench where they
were 'laid on hurdles, and conveyed by the sheriffs of London over
the bridge, up to Leadenhall, and so to Tyburn and there hanged, cut
down alive, held down by the strength of men, dismembered, bowel-
led, headed, and quartered, their quarters set on the gates of the
city.' [1]

Besides dealing with recusants, another area of legal activity that
engaged the labour of Egerton from 1592–4 was the prosecution of
Separatists. John Whitgift, Archbishop of Canterbury, had led the
onslaught against Puritan preaching and writing from the time of his
appointment in 1593. [2] The Separatists were the most threatening
members of the Puritan movement, and the Attorney-General found
them frustrating. Again, as with the recusants, he had estate agents
with legal training participate in many of the commissions of investigation. [3] His first major trial of Separatists was that of Henry
Barrow and associates in the spring of 1593. Prior to this he had
secured a copy of Barrow's *Plaine Refutation* and his 'Fragment directed to the Parliament', and studied both works closely. He filled the
margins of his copies with notes and underlined statements which
in his mind appeared to be treasonous: statements such as, 'Her
Majesty's government the yoke of Antichrist'. [4] Before the trial he
held a series of conferences with Barrow and John Greenwood, and
he came away from them thoroughly exasperated. As he wrote to
Puckering after a session with Barrow: 'I have spent this whole after-
noon at a fruitless, idle conference, and am but now returned both
weary and weak.' [5]

A second group of Separatists comprised John Penry, Robert
Bowle, and others, who were examined and tried for their role in
financing, publishing, and distributing Separatist literature. Again,
the Attorney held conferences with them, and emerged bewildered
when they proclaimed loyalty to the Queen and the State after publishing works which declared that the institutions of parish, cathedral,

---

[1] John Stow, *Annales, or, a Generall Chronicle of England* [1592] (1930), 768–9. The K.B. prison referred to was the Marshalsea in Southwark.

[2] Patrick Collinson, *The Elizabethan Puritan movement* (1967), 243–72.

[3] For ex. Gabriel Goodman and Richard Younge in Ellesm. MSS 2101–21, pr. by Leland Carlson in *The writings of John Greenwood and Henry Barrow, 1591–1593* (1970), 319–72. For these and other critical docs. I want to thank Dr Carlson for his advice and suggestions.

[4] Leland Carlson, *The writings of Henry Barrow 1587–1590* (1962), 122–3.

[5] Carlson, *Greenwood and Barrow 1591–93*, 284–6.

and the ecclesiastical hierarchy were 'antichristian'.[1] In the end
the Attorney had no sympathy and advocated their execution. His
position was well set out in a memorandum on 'Reasons against
Publicke Disputation with Barow'.[2] He stated that all the arguments
that men could ever make on the general questions of religious
doctrine and Church government had been put forward in the reigns
of Henry VIII, Edward VI, Mary, and in the early years of Elizabeth.
The discussion of these general questions had been completed, and
final, irrevocable decisions had been made for the peace and prosperity
of the kingdom. Thus that which is denied to Catholics must also now
be denied to Separatists, and both must submit or 'suffer the fate of
heretics of all ages'.[3]

Egerton's reputation grew significantly in the law courts and
councils of Elizabethan England, and its growth on the national
level was accompanied with increased recognition in his county. His
patronage of justices of the peace in the northern Marches became
significant in the 1580s as his relatives and agents entered the ranks
of the commissions of the peace.[4] He was also asked to aid in the
promotion of trade and industry in the city of Chester and its
environs, and he responded dutifully.[5] As a result he attained the
patronage of numerous city offices of an administrative, economic,
and legal nature, and one of his agents kept notes on cases heard
before the Chester Common Hall of Pleas.[6] His influence in the city
and the county then spread to the county palatine, where he received
the appointment of Deputy Baron of the Exchequer Court, and a
position in the Council in the Marches of Wales.[7]

A successful career as Solicitor and Attorney-General for the
Crown also brought considerable influence in other parts of the
country as Egerton's legal services were now being sought by noble
men and women, bishops and cathedral chapters, boroughs and

---

[1] Ellesm. MS 2097, ed. Carlson, *ibid.* 221–2. For the exams. see pp. 292–3, and the
transcripts of Ellesm. 2093–6 at pp. 308–15.

[2] Harl. MS 6848, f. 212. Egerton is in my opinion the author of this memo.

[3] *Ibid.* See as well SPD 12/199/2, and 12/257/66.

[4] Lans. MS 35, ff. 135r–40v.

[5] Lans. MS 40, f. 46r–v; and the proposals in Chester Town Hall MS M/L/1/53, and
A/F/7/24/36–9. The area and its problems are noted in George Lerry, 'The industries of
Denbighshire from Tudor times', *Denbs. Hist. Soc. Trans.* 7 (Denbigh 1958), 41–2.

[6] Chester Town Hall MS M/L/1/35–48, 112; the Randle Holme Collection, *passim* (Harl.
MSS 1995–2190); and the lists in Ormerod, *Chester*, 1, 65–89, 214–22. The notes of Robert
Whitby are in Harl. MS 2004, ff. 153–236.

[7] P.R.O. Ind. 17314–5.

universities. From the lay aristocracy he received life annuities from Henry Stanley, Earl of Derby, Robert Dudley, Earl of Leicester, Edward Seymour, Earl of Hertford, William, later Lord Paget, Philip Howard, Earl of Arundel, and Elizabeth Fitzgerald, Countess of Lincoln.[1] All but Arundel were devout Protestants. Other annuities came from the Bishops of Chester, Bath and Wells, Coventry and Lichfield, and the University of Cambridge.[2] He received fees for becoming steward of the Queen's lands in Denbighshire and Flintshire, Westminster, and Winchester; and also from being recorder of the boroughs of Cambridge, Lichfield, and Lincoln. [3]

Egerton's ever-widening range of aristocractic contacts and emoluments increased the potential for the acquisition of land. The last major portion of his eventual land holdings in the Welsh borderlands was acquired in the years 1584–90 when he was in the midst of crucial prosecutions for the Crown. These lands came to him in a number of ways: by royal grant in return for his services, by the death of his relations, and by purchase. In most instances the choices originated from his trusted relatives and estate agents. In Cheshire he acquired the manor of Dodleston at the death of Anthony Grosvenor in 1584.[4] Since Dodleston was less than two miles from the Eaton and Bretton Halls – the ancestral homes of the Grosvenor and Ravenscroft families – he made it his personal household down to the very end of his career. He then acquired several large Cheshire manors in the next five years: Cholmeston, Edge, Newhall, and Oldcastle.[5] His chief manors in Denbighshire and Flintshire were acquired in the same period, and most of them were in the Flintshire areas that bordered his Cheshire estates. In Flintshire this included the manors of Coleshill, Kirchinan, Over, and Northope, together with a number of individual parcels.[6] In Denbighshire he purchased the manor of Hem Hewlington and leases to the lordships of Holt, and

---

[1] Ellesm. MSS 503–4; 503; 502; 500; 499, 510; and 7; respectively.

[2] Ellesm. MSS 505; 502, 508; 516; and 507; respectively.

[3] P.R.O. Ind. 6800/479v; Ellesm. MSS 518; 516; 506; 534; *Annals of Cambridge*, ed. Charles Henry Cooper (Cambridge 1893), II, 556; Ellesm. MSS 502; and 501; respectively.

[4] Harl. MS 2002, f. 398; and Ellesm. MSS 732, 766A. When the advowson expired Egerton purchased it as well, and appointed Roger Ravenscroft rector when the post became vacant: C.R.O. EDP 106/1/1.

[5] Ellesm. MSS 732, 766A; C.66/1333/28–9, and C.66/1369/1–2; S.R.O. Bradford MS 6/62; and C.R.O. MS DVE/M/VII/13–4.

[6] Summarised in Ellesm. MS 509. The acquisition of Coleshill is in Ellesm. MSS 753, 1767, 1779–82; Kirchinan, in Ellesm. MSS 1833–6, 1591; and Northope, Ellesm. MSS 1814–25. See as well Ellesm. MSS 560A, 658–60, and N.L.W. Gen. MS 1231/D.

Bromfield and Yale, which included fees from the twenty-one manors that belonged to the latter lordship.[1]

Later, in the 1590s, Egerton augmented his land holdings in Cheshire, Denbighshire, and Flintshire, and expanded his estates into southern Cheshire and Warwickshire, the area which comprised the Midland Gap and the western end of the Midlands. In Cheshire he acquired twelve small holdings near his larger estates together with the manors of Beichton and Brewer's Haugh. He also purchased some land and buildings in the city of Chester, including the dissolved abbey of White Friars.[2] In Denbighshire he bought the substantial manor of Gresford and several small parcels in this county and Flintshire.[3] Most of Egerton's acquisitions in south-east Cheshire and Warwickshire came from his new family ties with the prominent gentry families of Venables of Kinderton and Leigh of Newnham Regis, respectively. The daughter of Sir Thomas Venables was married to Egerton's eldest son, Thomas; and Francis, the son and heir of Sir Thomas Leigh, married Egerton's daughter Mary.[4] This also brought Egerton into a lasting friendship with the wealthy landed and commercial gentleman, Sir Thomas Leigh of Stoneleigh. With these marriage connections came the substantial manors of Dunchurch, Kington, Maxstoke, and Talton with several nearby parcels.[5]

Fees, offices, and land increased Egerton's credit and sources of revenue, and they also provided potential for the future patronage and political influence that would be so important to his later career. Spreading out from his base in Cheshire, Denbighshire, and Flintshire, his prestige and influence began to be felt in the neighbouring counties of Lancashire, Shropshire, and Warwickshire. For example, royal commissions for the Crown's common law affairs in these counties

[1] C.66/1433/21; P.R.O. Ind. 9800/558; Lans. MS 78, ff. 85–7; C.66/1328/16–9; Ellesm. MSS 509, 1766, 6160; and S. C. 2/226/44–5. An initial but limited study of his family and lands from the 1580s to his death in 1617 is in Louis A. Knafla, 'New Model Lawyer' (Ph.D. diss. Univ. of Calif. Los Angeles 1965), Chap. V.

[2] Ellesm. MSS·766A, 887; and C.66/1408/1.

[3] Ellesm. MSS 509, 1822–3, 1848–51B, 1858; N.R.O. Ellesm. MSS X.469/40, X.893/1. Some of the corresp. is in Ellesm. MSS 8–10, 24–7, 417.

[4] S.R.O. Venables MS 484; and C.R.O. MS DVE/M/5. They established relationships with the Grosvenors (Ellesm. MSS 638–9), the Breretons, Hopes, and Mainwarings (C.R.O. Vernon MSS).

[5] C.66/1363/11–2; 66/1431/11–2; 66/1462/33–4; 66/1464/9–10, 22; Ellesm. MSS 413, 629, 636–7; P.R.O. Duchy of Lanc. MS 30/11/125–32; P.R.O. Wards 7/20/193; and The history of the county of Warwick, ed. L. F. Salzman, V.C.H. (1947), IV, 139–40; VI, 81.

flowed to relatives and estate agents like Ralph Egerton, William Ravenscroft, Thomas Wilbraham, and Richard Young.[1] There were also commissions for the collection of Crown debts and parliamentary taxes, which went to working relatives such as Roger Brereton, Thomas Hanmer, Thomas Leigh, William Mainwaring, Roger Puleston, and George Ravenscroft; and in most cases these men formed a considerable majority of the commission. They also assured themselves of not being over-taxed. [2]

Other avenues of profit were secured from the Crown by gaining the appointment of relatives and agents for literally every kind of royal commission issued: commissions to investigate Crown leases, castles, concealed lands, the lands of fugitives, and inquisitions *post mortem*.[3] In commissions such as these – especially in the 1590s – one begins to note the names of relatives and estate agents new and old, of older trusted colleagues and their sons fresh out of Lincoln's Inn.[4] Many of these men also entered the ranks of the various county officialdoms as justices of the peace, and the commissions for the peace from the time of the Armada onwards became littered with the retinue of the Solicitor and Attorney-General.[5] Eventually, the most successful became members of Parliament for the local boroughs and counties. Thus in the last two decades of Elizabeth's reign the Brereton, Hanmer, Holcroft, Massey, Mostyn, Panton, Puleston, Ravenscroft, Salesbury, Thelwall, and Whitby families, in addition to that of his own, had come to control the borough and county seats of Denbigh, Flint, and Chester, in addition to boroughs in Lancashire and Shropshire. [6]

---

[1] A. H. Dodd, *Studies in Stuart Wales* (Cardiff 1952), 49–75; and Penry Williams, *The Council in the Marches of Wales under Elizabeth I* (Cardiff 1958), for lawyers in his patronage: pp. 201–4, 263–6, 300–4.

[2] E.123/10/41, 178/1887, 178/3419; and E.123/10/257.

[3] As C.54/1222 (1585), and 54/1335 (1589); E.178/1153, 1422, 1913, 3400, 3404–8, 3417–9; and P.R.O. B/204B/131–3.

[4] Ralph and William Brereton, Robert Davies, Richard and Thomas Grosvenor, Thomas Hanmer, John Hope, Edward Hughes, George and Henry Mainwaring, William Marbury, John, Roger, and Thomas Mostyn, Edward and Roger Puleston, George, Thomas, and Ralph Ravenscroft, John Thelwall, and Ellis and Richard Younge.

[5] The list, for ex. in Harl. MS 1926, ff. 76–119.

[6] MPs who owed their seats at least in part to his influence from 1584 to 1603 were as follows, organised by county: Cheshire – Thomas Egerton jun., John Done, Thomas Holcroft, Thomas Lawton, and Edward Whitby; Denbighshire – John Panton, Roger Puleston, Simon Thelwall, and Robert Wroth; Flintshire – John Cope, Thomas Mostyn, Thomas Hanmer, William Massey, Roger Puleston, Robert and William Ravenscroft; Shropshire – John Egerton, George Lawley, William Leighton, Roger Owen, and John Poole.

Such offices were also useful for the exploitation of the surrounding countryside by these extended family groups. For example, in the era of the Irish wars from 1588–1600, Richard Brereton, Roger Puleston, and Roger Wilbraham were given the royal authority to supply and pay the troops being gathered with arms and victuals, and provided for their transportation.[1] This aspect of their work was linked closely to their mining and commercial interests. Besides being involved in the coal and iron industry, Roger Wilbraham secured a large royal grant to develop the brine houses, and the salt and lead boilers in Nantwich.[2] Perhaps the formation of these various enterprises was related to Egerton's promises to assist the growth of employment opportunities in the Chester area.

Egerton used his offices and influence not only to promote the welfare of his relatives and estate agents, but also to protect their interests. And they needed protection. The more turbulent aspects of life in the Welsh marches which have been revealed fully for the later medieval era had not been tamed significantly by the mid-sixteenth century. In the first half of the century Egerton's relatives had been the object of constant law suits for a wide variety of crimes, ranging from the involvement of the Breretons and Venables in cases of adultery, and the citation of the Breretons and Pulestons for local riots, to the use of fraud by the Pulestons, Grosvenors, and Ravenscrofts in the attempt to acquire rights to land and local offices.[3] By the 1580s these families were acquiring through Egerton offices and influence which, together with their intermarriages, promoted a sense of camaraderie to protect themselves from events of their own instigation. However, the range of their nefarious affairs could still benefit from the assistance of the Crown Solicitor. Egerton, as a private lawyer in the 1570s, was placed in the role of fighting his relatives' interests against the prosecutions of the Crown. Thus, in defending Richard Brereton against a royal suit in the King's Bench, he had written to his brother-in-law that he was at last making a successful defence: 'I now begin to learn to play the Solicitor

[1] *Salisbury MSS*, XIV, 148–9. See also N.L.W. Chirk Castle MS F/9873; Harl. MS 1926, ff. 62r–72v; and E.101/532/4–6.

[2] P.R.O. Ind. 6800/185, 250.

[3] C.R.O. MSS EDA 12/2/4, 14; S. C. 5/A.44/35; and E. 123/1/205, C.R.O. MSS EDC 2/8/27, 53, respectively. Other family law suits were recorded in *Exchequer proceedings concerning Wales*, ed. T. I. J. Jones (Cardiff 1955), 197; *A catalogue of Star Chamber proceedings relating to Wales*, ed. Ifan ab Owen Edwards (Cardiff 1929), 53, 171.

prettily.'[1] The Solicitor was John Popham. Later, as Solicitor himself, Egerton would use Popham's assistance in defending a suit against his son's father-in-law, Thomas Venables, to deprive him of lands which he had recovered after being pardoned by an attaint of felony.[2] Egerton's loyalty to his relatives was seldom questioned during the course of his career.

But what of the families whom he opposed? From them there was considerable enmity, particularly from families who in the competition for land, influence, and power were forced to abandon the Welsh borderlands. These families included the Bostocks of Wem, who sold and moved to Berkshire and Oxfordshire; and the Egertons of Caldecote, one of the two prominent Egerton families in the later middle ages who lost their local influence to the bastard son and, faced with additional problems, moved to Staffordshire.[3] Later, when Egerton was being suggested for the office of Chamberlain of Chester, Peter Warburton, a lawyer who had a legal career free of faction, wrote to his patron, Sir Robert Cecil: that while Egerton was a very able man, he would exercise the office 'for his own person and profit'.[4] The repercussions of the exercise of such an influence was revealed vividly in a letter from the schoolmaster of Shocklache. Protesting a move to oust him, he wrote to his patron, Sir Richard Egerton of Ridley of that group of the Attorney's men who 'conspire to overthrow our school, government, and authority, and your patronage. . . I may be bold to stir a little in their dunghill, which they have heaped up, full of subordination, bribery, lineage, railing, scurrilous and reproachful speeches, untrue reports, slanders, boastings, defiances, and all impiety.'[5] The protest was of little avail.

Egerton's promotions after the close of the major treason trials which followed the national crises of the 1580s came rapidly and without opposition. In the midst of the Arundel and Perrot trials Lord

---

[1] Letter repr. by Lord John Campbell, *The lives of the Lord Chancellors and Keepers of the Great Seal of England* (1856), II, 177–8. The context is in Ellesm. MSS 8, 15A.

[2] 'Venables Case' (K.B. Mich. 1585), in John Leonard, *Reports and cases of law* (1658 ed.), II, 122–7; III, 185–92, and Ellesm. MS 6084.

[3] For the Bostocks see Arthur E. Preston, *The church and parish of St Nicholas, Abingdon*, in Oxford Hist. Soc. 99 (1935), 458–66; for the Egertons of Caldecote, Add. MS 34.815, ff. 317–20. Thomas Egerton had also supported long-time antagonists of the Egertons of Ridley, esp. the Breretons: Ives, 'Sir Ralph Egerton', 349–50, 366–9; and later the assassins of Sir John Egerton of Oulton: Ellesm. MSS 199–222.

[4] *CSPD, 1591–94*, p. 438.

[5] Hasts. MS 1534, f. 1.

Keeper Hatton had died, and Egerton and Puckering were the chief candidates for the position. The decision, however, was postponed until after the trials were concluded, and the office was given to Puckering on 27 April 1592.[1] That Egerton was considered as having an almost equal chance at the position speaks highly of the esteem in which he was held in London and Westminster. Although certainly he was more talented than Puckering, he was no royal favourite, which Puckering certainly was, and Egerton still lacked the courtly connections which were still essential for high office. However, within ten days of Puckering's appointment, Christopher Wray, the Chief Justice of the King's Bench, died, and Popham was the natural choice for the Chief Justiceship. Egerton was selected immediately to replace Popham as Attorney-General, and the warrants for the promotion of both men went out in the same week.[2]

That following winter of 1592 witnessed the burial of Gilbert Gerrard, Master of the Rolls, and Egerton was rumoured as his successor. The appointment, however, was delayed by more than a year. Although no evidence has come to hand to document an explanation of this unusual delay, there is a reasonable conjecture. A year previously Egerton had been one of the two leading candidates for the presidency of the Chancery, and the history of the office of Master of the Rolls – Gerrard's mastership was a case in point – had not been a conspicuous one. It appears that Egeron wanted nothing less than the presidency of a court and, as Puckering was three years younger, the immediate possibilities of succeeding him must not have looked very good. On the other hand, the two other Chief Justices, while still very vigorous men who would live well into their seventies, had just turned sixty. Perhaps Egerton had let it be known that he was not yet interested in the Mastership of the Rolls.

In the meantime, other offices and honours came to the new Attorney-General in the course of the following fourteen months while the office of the Master of the Rolls lay open. Puckering's chancellorship was becoming not only undistinguished but also tinged with corruption. Egerton received the prestigious post of the Chamberlain of Chester at the death of Henry, Earl of Derby, in February 1593/4, against the claims of Henry's eldest son Ferdinando, and was

[1] The Queen's difficulty in coming to a decision was noted by Lord Burghley: *CSPD*, *1591–94*, p. 222. See his letter to Sir Thomas Heneage in SPD 12/242/25.

[2] C. 66/1385/17–8; and Ellesm. MS 511 (28 May 1592).

knighted.[1] Egerton now had most of the major offices in the western borderlands: the Chamberlain of Chester, membership in the Council in the Marches of Wales, Lord Lieutenant of Denbighshire and Flintshire, Receiver-General of Crown rents in the northern marches, and lessee of the largest royal estates in the area. He also had a considerable personal ownership of property and industrial wealth in the area, and his coterie of related agents predominated in the countryside as justices of the peace, members of Parliament, and royal commissioners, standing as permanent fixtures in the administration of local, provincial, and central government in the region. Finally, Egerton was appointed to the Mastership of the Rolls in the spring of 1594.[2] It appeared that he had placed his cards on Puckering's succumbing to his growing obesity, and he was proved right. In two years' time Puckering too would be buried, and Egerton as Lord Keeper of England would move to the presidency of the Chancery.

Puckering died on 30 April 1596, and Egerton's notice of appointment was announced three days later, the official ceremony occurring on May 6.[3] The new Lord Keeper retained the Mastership of the Rolls, became president of the Court of Star Chamber and Speaker of the House of Lords, and was sworn to the Privy Council. According to moderate observers at the royal court, he came to his offices 'with a general applause both of court, city, and country, for the reputation he hath of integrity, law, knowledge and courage ... yea, against the desire and endeavour, as it is thought, of the omnipotent couple'.[4] His swift appointment – made by Elizabeth without hesitation – must have reflected the esteem in which she held him.[5] The swearing in of the new Lord Keeper was made a significant event of state. The notebook of Simeon Powle, the Clerk of the Crown, contains the fullest des-

[1] C. 66/1413/11 (2 March 1593/4); Ellesm. MS 513; and with an addition of lands C. 66/1423/15–6 (9 July 1594). Egerton's role in the office and his impact on the court is discussed by W. J. Jones, 'The Exchequer of Chester in the last years of Elizabeth', in *Tudor institutions*, 129–35, 149–54, 163–7.

[2] C. 66/1409/17 (10 April 1594). There were some technical problems in the passing of the seal: Harl. MS 7042, f. 79r.

[3] C. 54/1530/14 (6 May 1596). For the rapid call, without competition, see the comments cited in Thomas Birch, *Memoirs of the Reign of Queen Elizabeth* (1754 ed.), I, 478–9.

[4] See Anthony Bacon's letter pr. by Birch, *Memoirs*, I, 491. This matter is also mentioned by William Camden, *Annales rerum Anglicarum* (1625), II, 128; and Edward Grimstone in Ellesm. MS 2682. The 'omnipotent couple' were William and Robert Cecil.

[5] I wish to acknowledge Sir John Neale for discussing with me Egerton's appointment and speeches.

cription of that occasion. Near the end of the ceremony Elizabeth was
said to declare that 'I began with a lord keeper (and he was a wise man
I tell you), and I will end with a lord keeper'; and Burghley, the now
ancient Lord Treasurer, replied that she would bury four or five
more. Elizabeth, after a brief conversation with Egerton, then said in
departing from the hall that 'none of Lord Treasurer's men will come
in to fetch him away as long as I am here.'[1] This was a prophetic remark on the political machinations of the Cecil family which would
eventually embroil Egerton himself.

Egerton's life and career had proceeded successfully from his first
marriage and reconciliation with the Church in the 1570s to his appointments of 1596. But the next four years witnessed a series of
personal tragedies which would lead to the opening of new directions
in both his personal life and public career. First, Egerton's wife Elizabeth had died in the year of the Armada, 1588, leaving him with two
sons, Thomas and John, and a daughter, Mary. The sons were sent
to Brasenose College, Oxford, and Lincoln's Inn, and the daughter
went into the home of his sister Dorothy Brereton of Tatton and
Worsley.[2] Remaining a widower for several years, he then married
Lady Elizabeth Wolley, a wealthy widow of the ancient gentry family
of More of Loseley who had earlier buried her first husband, Sir
John Polstead of Abury, and more recently her second, Sir John
Wolley – who was Latin Secretary and Privy Councillor – in February 1595/6. Egerton married Lady Wolley shortly after his promotion to the Lord Keepership, and they appear to have been a
compatible couple.[3] Since Lady Wolley was a leading member of
the Queen's household, she provided Egerton with his first personal
entry into the royal court.

This temporary revival of his personal affairs was cut short in the
eight months of 1599 when Egerton witnessed the death of his second
wife, his stepmother, Mary, and his eldest son, Thomas.[4] The deaths
of these loved ones were followed immediately by the Essex affair.
The Earl of Essex had employed, befriended, and benefited Egerton's
two sons prior to his dismal failures in Ireland at tremendous expense
to the Crown. When Essex was reprimanded by the Queen in autumn

---

[1] Tanner MS 168, f. 92. The whole occasion is described at ff. 88v–92v.

[2] Ellesm. MSS 8, 10, 15, 15A.

[3] C. 142/349/74. The marriage, without the permission of the Queen, was later pardoned
by the Church: Ellesm. MS 517 (7 Oct. 1597).

[4] *The Topographer* (1789), I, 126–7.

of 1599, the Lord Keeper was required to maintain him in the custody of his home for ten months. Afterwards, when Egerton and others went to Essex House to save the Earl from a further act that would bring his illustrious, if ill-fated, career to a cruel conclusion, they were imprisoned by his guards as Essex assembled arms to take the City of London.[1] When the Earl came to trial for his treason the Lord Keeper had little mercy, recommending that the Earl be stripped of everything he had and be left for the hangman's silken noose.[2]

Egerton recovered from these events only to be besieged by scheming women who were looking for an attractive match. Included among these was the Countess Dowager of Russell, a very rich, strong, and domineering woman who had made legal history by lecturing the Lords of the realm for more than half an hour in the Court of Star Chamber.[3] The Countess wanted Egerton for either herself or her daughter. Her letters were mixed with praise and abuse. In one letter she called him 'an arrogant hypocrite', and then warned him to take her offers more seriously, 'lest it be suspected that your lord loved so much, as that they will fear your lord hath none left for another'.[4] Egerton replied to such letters with unconcern,[5] and it appears that what he had in mind was another woman with even a greater degree of ancestry, land, and influence.

Most of the important turning points in Egerton's personal life were based on decisions that affected significantly his lands and social status. A dowry from Lady Wolley had brought his first lands outside of the Welsh marches and its approaches. Several important manors and other parcels came into his hands from the county of Surrey, and he struck a close friendship with Lady Wolley's brother, Sir George More of Loseley, who became responsible for the supervision of Egerton's Surrey estates.[6] Meanwhile, the will of his stepmother, Mary, brought him additional Cheshire lands, and the death of his stepsister Dorothy's husband William Brereton (without heirs) pro-

---

[1] Add. MS 38.139, f. 184, and 39.830, ff. 27–30; B. M. Egerton MS 2877, f. 79v; B. M. Sloane MS 1775, ff. 54r–5v; and Stowe MS 151, ff. 2v–4v, and 275, f. 15. Essex was at York House from 1 Oct. 1599 to 5 July 1600. The rebellion occurred on 8 Feb. 1600/1.

[2] H.M.C. *The Manuscripts of Lord De L'Isle and Dudley* (1936), II, 398–449, 467; Harl. MSS 677, f. 33, 1323, f. 23, 6854, f. 24. He was executed on Feb. 8.

[3] Hawarde, *Reportes*, 271–81.

[4] Ellesm. MSS 46, f. 1, and 47, f. 1, respectively.

[5] Ellesm. MSS 48, 47A–B.

[6] C. 142/249/74; and Ellesm. MSS 158, 225.

vided him with a number of lands in Lancashire.[1] These acquisitions
extended his holdings northwards into Lancashire as well as south-
wards into the Midland Gap, provided an initial base in south-east
England, and augmented his revenues significantly at relatively no
cost to himself. His marriage to Alice, Countess of Derby, achieved
a similar but even more important result.

Alice was a daughter of Sir John Spencer of Althorp, Northamptonshire, an ancient and wealthy Midlands family. Her marriage to Ferdinando Stanley, Earl of Derby, was accompanied with a very significant dowry from the Spencer lands.[2] The Earl of Derby had extensive
estates in the Midlands, and Ferdinando's early death without heirs
in the year after his accession to the Earldom left Alice, Countess
of Derby, with the largest portion of his lands, the remaining holdings in Lancashire going to Ferdinando's younger brother, William.[3]
Meanwhile, the Countess of Derby had entered the Queen's household and became one of the most prominent women at Elizabeth's
court. She was also, possessed with Spencer and Derby lands, one of
the wealthiest.

Egerton had been close to the Derby family from the very beginning of his career, and he was obviously known to young Alice.[4] But
Alice was titled, wealthy, and a beautiful, cultured woman. She was
perhaps too high in stature for Egerton in 1596 when he married
Lady Wolley. Alice enjoyed her single status as Countess at the royal
court after her husband's death in 1594, and came to know Egerton
much better after his appointment to the Chancery and the Privy
Council, and his marriage to Lady Wolley.[5] By 1600 Egerton was in
a different position. He was now prominent in the Council and the
royal court, and held one of the highest offices of state. He was also
wealthy with land, patronage, and prestige in his own right. With

---

[1] C. 142/159/73; Ellesm. MSS 732, 766G; and N.R.O. Ellesm. MS X. 721–3, 909–12.
Egerton had been a witness to the original grant of lands worth more than £1,500 from Geoffrey
Brereton of Tatton to his son Richard and wife Dorothy: Ellesm. MS 555. Later litigation is in
P.R.O. Requests 2/163/45, etc. Dorothy was the eldest daughter of Mary Grosvenor and Sir
Richard Egerton of Ridley. Her husband settled lands on Thomas Egerton after the death of
their only child. Some of their warm corresp. is still extant: Ellesm. MSS 8, 10, 15, 15A.

[2] *A history of the county of Middlesex*, ed. Susan Reynolds, V.C.H. (1962), III, 239–40, 253–7;
and Add. MS 29.438, f. 10.

[3] *Salisbury MSS*, IV, 515. Documents for his estates are in Ellesm. MS 784. For later disputes: C. 24/390, 403–4, 89/9/10, 89/10/33, 54.

[4] *The Stanley papers*, ed. F. R. Raines, Chetham Soc. 31 (1853), 19, 43, 65; and Ellesm.
MSS 11, 14.

[5] *Stanley papers*, 106–7.

Lady Wolley's death he had become one of England's most prized widowers who held, at the age of fifty-eight, an even more promising career. Alice, meanwhile, was still widowed with two unwedded daughters. Having entered a noble's family, she must have yet aspired to the making of an ennobled dynasty. Therefore, in 1600 an Egerton–Derby marriage became possible, and in October it occurred secretly without the Queen's consent.[1]

In a complicated series of transactions Egerton married Alice Derby, and his son and heir, John, was betrothed to Alice's eldest daughter, Frances.[2] A decree in Chancery confirmed the descent of the major portion of the Derby eastern Midlands estates to Alice by the hand of her prospective husband,[3] and these lands would come into the hands of the Egerton–Derby heirs, John and Frances. However, a substantial portion of the estates were to be retained by Alice should Egerton die before her. The result of this web of transactions is that Egerton, in 1600–1, became one of the major landowners in the Midlands. Embracing a triangle of holdings in the three counties of Hertfordshire, Buckinghamshire, and Northamptonshire, Egerton acquired some of their most prosperous estates: Ashridge, Brackley, Gaddesden, and Harefield.[4] He was now one of the richest gentlemen in Britain, and in 1602 he and Alice welcomed Queen Elizabeth on her last royal progress in one of the most lavish entertainments of the era, the three-day event costing more than £2,000.[5] The career of the illegitimate son of lesser Cheshire gentry had reached the top.

Egerton's friends and relatives would continue to rise with their patron. Two new men became the centre of the coterie which Egerton formed in the Midlands: Sir Arthur Mainwaring of Ightfield, Salop, a cousin of Lady Wolley who had handled her affairs, and Thomas

---

[1] Ellesm. MSS 213–4.

[2] Ellesm. MSS 224, 706–7; and P.C.C. Weldon 22, Meade 9.

[3] Ellesm. MSS 775, 778, 784; and E. Williams, *Early Holborn and the legal quarter of London* (1927), I, 690–1, 725. Later, Egerton sat in judgment on Alice's claim for part of the Isle of Man: Ellesm. MS 152, ff. 1–2.

[4] N. R. O. Ellesm. MSS X. 460/8, 471/8, 1729/1, 8; J. H. Todd, *A history of Ashridge* (1878), 64–5; *History of the county of Buckinghamshire*, ed. William Page, V.C.H. (1925), III, 333, 360, 380, 407–9, 463–4; and *A history of the county of Hertfordshire*, ed. William Page, V.C.H. (1907), II, 203–14, 446–52.

[5] John Nichols, *The progresses and public processions of Queen Elizabeth* (1823), III, 581–6. Beware of J. P. Collier's forged documents – Ellesm. MSS 123–6 – which were pr. in the *Eg. Papers*. Alice became very prominent at the court of James: *Jacobean J.* 69, 127–8, 181, 208.

Chamberlain, a steward of Lady Derby's estates. These men, to-gether with some members of the Grosvenor, Marbury, and Panton families who had assisted Egerton in the west, now came to admini-ster his estates in the east.[1] Egerton himself gained a host of new offices that stemmed from his Midlands conquest: High Steward of Cambridge, Kingston, New Sarum, Oxford, and St Alban's; and Lord Lieutenant of Buckinghamshire.[2] Moreover, the pattern whereby local royal commissions, JPs, and MPs were drawn from his retinue of relatives and estate agents that had been created in the northern Welsh marches in the late sixteenth century would now be repeated in the eastern Midlands in the early years of the seventeenth century.[3] And the more promising men would ride on his coat tails into the halls of central government, acquiring offices in the Chancery and other departments of state. [4]

The last years of Elizabeth's reign witnessed Egerton's increasing participation in the political, administrative, and economic affairs of her government. As Speaker of the Lords he became prominent in the Parliaments of 1597 and 1601.[5] In diplomatic matters he took part in the negotiations with the Dutch that resulted in a treaty, and was involved in discussions with the French.[6] Administratively, he attempted to bring about the reform of procedures in the Chancery and its inner departments,[7] and his efforts at administrative and legal reform brought him face to face with problems of efficiency and finance. Thus by the end of Elizabeth's reign Egerton began to object to the wanton spending of the royal court, the existence of fraud in the farming of customs duties, and corruption in the use of monoplies,

[1] Ellesm. MSS 146, 176–82, 233, 766A, 767. Also, the wills of Elizabeth and Arthur Mainwaring: P.C.C. Lyon 19, Sainberbe 49.

[2] Ellesm. MS 51A, and Cooper, *Annals Cambridge*, 556–64, 599–600; Ellesm. MS 519; Ellesm. MS 523; *Survey of the antiquities of the City of Oxford*, ed. Andrew Clark (Oxford 1899), 37, and *Oxford council acts*, ed. H. E. Salter (Oxford 1928), 140; *CSPD Eliz.* IX, 432; and Ellesm. MS 52; respectively.

[3] A list of all his agents as of the summer of 1603 is in his household accounts for June and July: Ellesm. MSS 288–91.

[4] Some exs. are in Ellesm. MSS 30–1, 48, 138, 155; Hasts. MSS 2522–3, 15.602; Add. MS 5756; E. 351/1482, 1621–38, 2609–11, 2630–43; P.R.O. A.O. 1/1358–60; and P.R.O. Ind. 17289–90.

[5] Heywood Townshend, *Historical Collections* (1680), 79–82, 130, 150–1, 176–8, 335–6; and Sir John Neale, *Elizabeth I and her Parliaments 1584–1601* (New York 1958), 366–7, 371–9, 387, 425–7.

[6] Camden, *Annales*, II, 610; Thomas Rymer, *Foedera*, XVI (Hague 1741), 343, 783; and H.M.C. *De L'Isle and Dudley*, III, pp. lxvii–lxviii.

[7] W. J. Jones, *The Elizabethan Court of Chancery* (Oxford 1967), 61–92; and Ellesm. MSS 2820, 2916. The topics are discussed at length in Chap. VII.

measures which were severely eroding the economic foundations of the monarchy.[1] Comparing the management of Crown affairs with that of his own, perhaps he became sceptical of the ability of the Queen and her favourites to manage the affairs of state successfully in a world he had come to know all too fully.

The death of Queen Elizabeth on 24 March 1603, brought at last the Scottish king, James VI, to the English throne. Egerton and Cecil were the two men who remained with Elizabeth down to her dying words, and these two men also rode at the front of the procession that brought James to London for his coronation.[2] Egerton had never been part of the Cecil faction. In the Privy Council of Elizabeth he had regarded himself as a counter-weight, a moderate who was attempting to steer a middle course in a nefarious political world. Thus the accession of James brought no earldoms or dukedoms, but it did bring him a title of nobility, and the manor, church, park, and lake of Ellesmere which commanded the southern tip of the central ridge in the borderlands that bore the name of his new rank, Baron Ellesmere.[3]

Sworn into office to continue the presidency of the Chancery with the most prestigious title of Lord Chancellor on 24 July 1603,[4] Ellesmere had some of the essential characteristics for success. Industrious, tough, frugal, bright, ingenious, and independent, he displayed the ability to build and to survive. He used his skill and industry to become an outstanding lawyer, his ingenuity and cunning to make useful marriages, connections, and contracts, and his independence to remain his own man.[5] Knowledgeable in the character of men, he used them too where it would count, securing their

---

[1] For example, his S.C. speeches for 1596–1602 printed in the *Salisbury MSS*, X, 182–85, 208; and notes from *The journal of Sir Roger Wilbraham*, ed. Harold Spencer Scott, Camden Misc. 10 (1902), 12–3, 19, 30–2, 44, 50. These subjects are discussed in Chaps. III–IV.

[2] John Nichols, *The progresses ... of King James the First* (1828), I, 324–6 (15 March 1603/4).

[3] *Collins' Peerage of England* (1812), III, 179; *Gentleman's Mag.* 63 (1793), pt. I, p. 42; Defoe, *Tour*, II, 474; and Ellesm. MSS 766C-F. The society and economy of the Ellesmere area is similar to that of Myddle: see David Hay, *An English rural community: Myddle under the Tudors and Stuarts* (Leicester 1974). Egerton received other grants of lands in the north Salop area, including the large estate of Whitchurch, and made purchases of his own: Ellesm. MSS 732, 766F.

[4] *Wilbraham's J.* 60–1; Rymer, *Foedera*, XVI, 495; and *CSPD Eliz.* VIII, 29.

[5] One of his critics credited him with these abilities: Add. MS 35.957, f. 81v. These general characteristics of success for the period have been set down and elucidated by H. J. Habbakuk and Mary Finch in *The wealth of five Northamptonshire families 1540–1640*, ed. Mary E. Finch (Oxford 1956), xi–xvi, 165–70; and Lawrence Stone, *The crisis of the aristocracy 1558–1641* (Oxford 1965), esp. Chaps. II, IV–VIII, XI; and his *Family and fortune* (Oxford 1973), Chaps. I, VI–VII.

long-term support by giving in return his loyalty and assistance. He was also to acquire wealth where it could be best obtained, to conserve it, and to put it to good advantage. Although no complete analysis of his wealth has been made, tentative calculations would place his income at £10,000–12,000 per year at the accession of James.[1]

The new Lord Chancellor was not, with most of his colleagues, born in the reign of Elizabeth. In fact, like most of the privy councillors at the accession of James, he had been educated in the middle decades of the sixteenth century. Egerton, however, represented the figure of a revived lord of the marches. Like William Salesbury of Lleweni,[2] he was born in rather humble circumstances and had to rely on both skill and force to move to the top. Thus he was at the same time brutal and creative, interested in any way of making money by land, commerce, or industry, devoted to family, relations, and friends, and loyal to local interests. But he was also much more than a Salesbury of Lleweni. Like Henry Stanley, the fourth Earl of Derby (his early patron),[3] he had ambitions beyond his county and the region of the northern Welsh marches.

Ellesmere had sought the highest legal offices of state and spared no effort to gain them. He was not, however, solely a legal or political man. Like the Earl of Derby, he considered himself a knowledgeable man – a patron and promoter of the new religion, the new philosophy, and the new learning. But, despite these slightly 'modern' characteristics, Ellesmere would remain in essence a country gentleman. Although he went to London with the aspiration of power, influence, and nobility, he left the world not only with his successes, but also with the major part of his rural borderland values unimpaired. It was, in fact, the resiliency of his character that makes the study of his mind necessary for an understanding of the man, his work, and his writings.

[1] For his official income from offices see Alnwick MS 11; C. 66/1452/24–5; Harl. MS 5756, ff. 16–48; and the contemp. assessment by Edward Montagu in *Buccleuch MS*, H.M.C. (1926), III, 182. Calculations of some official revenues have been made by Dr Jones, *Chancery*, 88–91; and an estimate for chancellors generally by G. E. Aylmer, *The King's servants* (1961), 209–11.

[2] Glanmor Williams, 'The achievement of William Salesbury', *Denb. Hist. Soc. Trans.* 14 (Denbigh 1965), 75–96.

[3] *DNB*, s.v. Henry Stanley, Earl of Derby. Considerable unpub. material exists for Henry Stanley which has yet to be examined or evaluated in the N.R.O. Fitzwilliam and Ellesmere MSS colls.

PART ONE

LAW AND POLITICS

THE MAKING OF A LEGAL MIND

The journey into the mind of an Elizabethan lawyer is at best a hazardous affair, but it is also a journey that must be attempted if we are to acquire that knowledge of how the law was learned, interpreted, and applied in an era of decisive legal change.[1] Since knowledge of the law also became an avenue for entering the practical world of government and politics, the mind of the Elizabethan lawyer becomes even more important than has been realised for an understanding of the history of the seventeenth century, and especially the watershed of Jacobean times. The availability of the early notes and textbooks of Thomas Egerton from his residence at Lincoln's Inn in the 1560s and 1570s provide us with an important group of sources for examining the development of a legal mind in the sixteenth century that is crucial for our understanding of the early seventeenth.[2] Moreover, when combined with his later papers and personal correspondence from the 1580s and 1590s, these sources make possible an examination of not only a legal mind, but also the religious, social, and cultural values that underlie Egerton's role in the political and legal problems of the age.

Egerton's legal career was based not only on his studies at Lincoln's Inn, but also on the learning which he had acquired at grammar school and university. Although there is no direct evidence of his studies prior to admission to Brasenose College, his notes and writings at Lincoln's Inn contain sufficient material related to his collegiate studies to investigate his intellectual development beginning with his years at Oxford in the late 1550s. The evidence indicates that he studied the classics, history, and civil law, and was influenced

---

[1] The only attempts to do this for England, with varying results, have been the studies of J. W. Gough, *Fundamental law in English constitutional history* (Oxford 1955); and J. G. A. Pocock, *The ancient constitution and the feudal law* (Cambridge 1957). For the Continent, considerable work of this nature has been done. A biog. ex. is that of Donald R. Kelley, 'Guillaume Budé and the first historical school of law', *Amer. Hist. Rev.* 72 (1967), 807–34.

[2] The sources are cited in Louis A. Knafla, 'The law studies of an Elizabethan student', *HLQ* 32 (1969), 221–40.

by the methodological revolution of logic and rhetoric that came to affect university life so dramatically in the course of the sixteenth century. Taking the subject of classics, it appears that although Egerton never revealed any scholarly interest in Greek studies, he did make a habit of citing those Greek and Roman writers 'fashionable' to the sixteenth century Englishman, especially Aristotle, Cicero, Plato, and Seneca.[1] However, the only works with which he became conversant were Aristotle's *Politics* and *Ethics*, works which he pillaged for philosophical concepts and legal maxims that he used consistently in the legal opinions that flowed from his pen down to the end of his career.[2]

The works of the civilians were much more prominent in Egerton's studies. Often he cited precedents from Justinian's *Corpus Juris Civilis* and chiefly the *Digest*.[3] Later he would use such works to make occasional analogies between the rules of common and civil law.[4] Egerton was also interested in civilians as practising lawyers. Thus when he collected notes on the problem of morality and corruption in the English law profession he cited not only the maxims of civilians, but also those of the great ancients such as Cicero and Demosthenes.[5] Egerton's interest in the civilians was not restricted, however, to the old civil law. He appears to have been interested particularly in the new methodology that led to the legal renaissance of Continental Europe in the sixteenth century,[6] a methodology which stemmed in a more popular guise from the work of Peter Ramus at the University of Paris that was being introduced to Oxford and Cambridge in the third quarter of the sixteenth century.

The Ramistic programme of logic and rhetoric became popular with English undergraduates, and Egerton's interest appears to have occurred precisely at the time of its English inception. The new logic

[1] His ms. notes in his copies of Fitzherbert, *Natura Brevium*, Hunt. RB 59688, on the title page; Littleton, *Tenures*, Hunt. RB 62234, f. 11r; and in Ellesm. MS 482, f. 97r.

[2] Ellesm. MS 485, f. 2v; his notes in Fitzherbert, the title page; and his Littleton, rear fly leaf. Later comments are in Ellesm. MS 496, Chaps. V, VII; and the *Post-Nati*, 105.

[3] Notes in Ellesm. MSS 465, 475, 481, 482 loose leaf 1 and f. 190v, MS 485, and later MSS 453, 2610.

[4] The series of analogies, for ex. in the *Post-Nati*, 37, 43, 49–50, 58, 61–2, 107.

[5] Notes in Ellesm. MSS 482 f. 72v; 485 f. 3r; in his copy of Fitzherbert, title page recto-verso; and later in Ellesm. MS 2610, ff. 1r, 11r.

[6] The penetrating studies of Julian H. Franklin, *Jean Bodin and the sixteenth-century revolution in the methodology of law and history* (New York 1963); and Donald R. Kelley, 'The rise of legal history in the Renaissance', *Hist. and Theory* 9 (1970), 174–94; and his studies in *Foundations of modern historical scholarship* (New York 1970), Chaps. II–III.

and rhetoric was taught by some of the more radical instructors in the new tutorial system that was being developed as a teaching device at Oxford and Cambridge from mid-century. In bypassing the established curriculum, these instructors were introducing new subjects of study into the university community which would appeal to the education of a genteel laity that was matriculating to the colleges in increasing numbers for general knowledge and the professions rather than for the service of the Church. Thus the second half of the sixteenth century would witness in England not only the advent of the new logic and rhetoric, but also of the academic study of subjects such as history, literature, languages, and the new sciences.[1] And Thomas Egerton would later contribute encouragement and financial aid to assist their development.[2]

The variety of Ramism that was introduced into England was its most practical and virile strain. It was based on the premise that each man was a microcosm of the world, possessing within himself an ontological bond which wedded both the material and spiritual elements of nature. Hence the only true form of learning was 'natural' learning, based on man's native speech and language. Within this context the Ramistic science of logic was the discovery of knowledge and the system of rhetoric, its expression. Technically, the new logic that was developed in England consisted of the critical study of the sources, the use of a device called 'invention' (*inventio*) to discover all possible facts and points of view, the use of dichotomies to organise facts and create propositions, and the examination of propositions and arguments through the appropriation of words and phrases. The purpose of the new logic was to enable the student who mastered it to go out and discover, and re-order anew that body of knowledge which comprised the profession to which he would dedicate his life.[3]

[1] The thesis of Mark H. Curtis, *Oxford and Cambridge in transition* (Oxford 1959), 107–48. See also *supra*, pp. 6–8.

[2] As one of his patronees wrote: you 'so tendereth and fostereth the professions of true wisdom, that [you are] worthily named the reviver and restorer of wisdom: yes I have heard it sundry times blayed, that England never had the like zealous patron of scholars' – William Vaughan, *The Golden-Grove* (1600), sig M4v. Other scholars whom he patronised included Anthony and Francis Bacon, Jacques Bellot, Edward Brerewood, Richard Brett, Charles Butler, John Case, Giovanni Florio, Albericus Gentilis, George Goodwin, Richard Hakluyt, John Hall, Arthur Hopton, Thomas Hyggons, Thomas Lodge, George Paul, Robert Peterson, John Rosinus, John Shaw, and Tobias Shaw. His patronage of literary figures such as Samuel Daniel and John Davies of Hereford is the focus of Virgil B. Heltzel, 'Sir Thomas Egerton as patron', *HLQ* 11 (1948), esp. 115–24.

[3] Louis A. Knafla, 'Ramism and the English Renaissance', in *Science, technology, and culture*, ed. L. A. Knafla, M. Staum, T. Travers (Calgary 1976), 26–50.

Egerton acquired these skills of Ramism in tutorials at Brasenose
College and during his years at Furnivall's and Lincoln's Inn. His
patronage of Ramists such as Charles Butler, George Case, and
George and John Downame demonstrated his interest in the new
logic and rhetoric.[1] In fact, Case taught the new methodology to
Egerton's sons Thomas and John at his own home in Oxford, and
dedicated some of his major works to father and sons.[2]

Egerton also acquired at Brasenose an interest in historical
studies. The study of English antiquities was perhaps a natural subject for a college in which many students and Fellows came from a
provincial area that had long sought to maintain its ancient privileges
and traditions against the centralising tendencies of the Tudor State.
The evidence of later letters suggests that Egerton studied with
Ferdinando Pulton, an historical and legal scholar who was a college
Fellow at that time.[3] He also met Sampson Erdeswicke, the antiquarian and historian who had completed his B.A. degree at Christ's
College, Cambridge, and had been admitted to Brasenose as a gentleman commoner.[4] Egerton maintained these early associations. He
followed in Pulton's footsteps to Lincoln's Inn and became one of
the first patrons of his published works.[5] In fact, Egerton's interest in
ancient sources and customs of the past was to be developed further
at the inns of court.

The education which Egerton received at Lincoln's Inn can be
documented from the printed legal works which he noted copiously,
together with a number of miscellaneous notes and papers that have
come down to us in his hand. The major texts which he acquired for
his personal law library consisted of nine basic works: Fitzherbert's
abridgement of older common law cases, Phaer's collection of legal
instruments for conveyancing, Rastell's collection of precedents for

[1] Butler – the *Rhetoricae Libri Duo* (1598 and 1600 eds). Downame – the dedicated copies
of his treatises and sermons: Hunt RB 60224 (1603), 60836 (1607), and 60217 (1611). Case –
his Latin poem on 'Justice', Ellesm. MS 34/B/30 (*c.* 1600) and his *Lapis Philosophicus*
(Oxford 1599).

[2] Case's dedications to John Egerton were his *Ancilla Philosophiae* (Oxford 1599), Hunt.
RB 98528; and the *Speculum Moralium* (Oxford 1585), Hunt. RB 98524.

[3] *Brasenose College register 1509–1909*, Oxford, Hist. Soc. 50 (1909), 1, 18; and Ellesm.
MSS 1963–4.

[4] *Brasenose reg.* 1, 19; and Reginald Jeffrey, 'History of the College, 1547–1603', *Brasenose
quartercentenary monographs* 2 (Oxford 1909), pt. 1, no. 10, p. 6.

[5] Pulton's *An Abstract of al the penall Statutes which be generall, in force and use* (3rd ed.
1577), Hunt. RB 61076.

pleading, two editions of the statutes, the texts of Littleton and Perkins on the land law, and Staunford's collections for the study of criminal law.[1] These works were annotated fully and bear the symbols of Egerton's study on almost every page. He also abridged and indexed separately those texts which he used most extensively,[2] and compiled a voluminous commonplace book in which he attempted to digest the legal knowledge which he had acquired under alphabetical headings.[3] Egerton's early law books are a remarkable source of an analysis of his legal studies, and they reveal the manner in which he acquired a knowledge of the common law.

Training in logic and rhetoric was instrumental to Egerton's common law studies, and the Ramistic influences were pervasive. For example, Egerton's use of 'invention' to locate arguments and contradictions can be found in the margins throughout his law books. The devices which he used to explain the subject of his inquiry appear to have been copied from those which were contained in the printed marginal headnotes of John Perkins' popular study of English land law, one of the first printed law books which revealed the influence of Ramist methodology.[4] The devices used most frequently were words and phrases like *'quere'* and *'nota le diversitie'*. The *quere* notation was used to question either the applicability of a case to a particular incident, an interpretation of a statute, or the decision of a judge. Thus the use of phrases in law French such as *'Quere si ceo extend al terres deins le cytye de Chester'*, and *'quere of atteynder by this statute'*, appeared copiously among the marginal notations in his law books.[5] The *diversitie* notation was used to signify the contradictions or ambiguities in a work. This notation

---

[1] Knafla, 'Law studies', 223–4.

[2] For ex. the surviving ms. indices of his Littleton (Ellesm. MS 1160), Plowden (Ellesm. MS 1165), and the *Digest* (Ellesm. MS 34/A/5).

[3] Ellesm. MS 496, a small, fat paper vol. of 396 folios. There are more than five hundred topics listed in the table of contents, but less than one-fourth were pursued in the text, which was eventually crammed full. It was begun by 1570 and up-dated through approx. 1585.

[4] John Perkins, *Incipit per Utilis Tractatus* (4th ed. 1545), Hunt. RB 62897, and ff. 3v–5r, 21v–5v. This was a popular text on the land law – learned, subtle, and witty – which has not received any adequate study by modern scholars.

[5] Ms. notes in his copies of Dyer, *Novel Cases*, Hunt. RB 59138, ff. 5r, 7r–v, 13v, 19r, 24r, 26r, 32v, 33r, 35r–v, 39v, 40v, for ex; Littleton, *Tenures*, ff. 106r, 117v, 119v, 123r, 144r, 166v, for ex; and William Rastell's *A Collection of Entrees* (1566), Hunt. RB 69108, ff. 632r–43v. Also exs. from Ellesm. MS 482, ff. 249r–50v, 253r, 277r, 288r.

was usually followed by comments like '*nota la difference le forme de bref*', and '*diversitye convenant en fait, and covenant en leye*'.[1] He also used it extensively in revising his own briefs to cases as a practising lawyer in the 1570s,[2] critiquing his arguments before presenting them to the court.

The intentions of men – whether they were those of legislators or of parties before a court – were often regarded as a key element of the law. Thus Egerton often noted places in his briefs of cases where the question of intent became a legal issue.[3] When deceit was involved he made very bold emendations in the text. Particularly in cases involving the assignment, delivery, or payment of leases, and the acquisitions of grants on false pretences which, if upheld, would cause the grantor to be deceived (for example, '*deceyt, graunt le roy voyde or Roy est deceyve*').[4] This concern with deceit was allied to a moral concern of what constituted good and bad law. In this regard we find additional terms such as '*objeccion*' and '*contra*' in the marginal notes to his texts.

Egerton's use of the terms '*objeccion*' and '*contra*' was primarily to criticise faulty pleading, doubtful legal processes, and questionable interpretations of statutes. It was also often used after a *quere* notation. Thus we find comments like '*protestation contrary al substance del plee*', and '*contra formam statute*'.[5] Sometimes he would challenge a particular decision of the Bench. For example, in one instance he noted: '*Vide quod le verdit conclude sur speciall matter en ley, conter le ley.*'[6] Devices such as these were merely part of the rather elaborate methodological apparatus which Egerton brought to bear on his legal studies. In order to understand how they progressed, one must examine the legal topics in which he became particularly interested.

---

[1] Egerton's notes in *The Abridgment of the Boke of Assises* (1555), Hunt. RB 60686, ff. 6r, 86r, 88r–v, 111v; Dyer, *Novel Cases*, for ex. ff. 248r, 257r, 258r, 270v, 286r, 287r, 288v; Fitzherbert, *Natura Brevium*, for ex. ff. 131r, 143r, 193v, 194r; Littleton, *Tenures*, for ex. ff. 30r, 44v, 49r, 58v, 66r, 74v, 80v; Plowden, *Commentaries*, Hunt. RB 62961, for ex. ff. 351r, 366r, 374r, 376r, 380r–v, 394r; and Staunford, *Prerogative*, Hunt. RB 69540, for ex. ff. 40v, 41r, 58r, 65r.

[2] Ellesm. MS 482, ff. 106r, 125r, 158v, 162v–3r, 171r, 190r, 198r–v, 226r–v, 231r, 246v, 250v, 252r, 319v.

[3] Ellesm. MS 482, ff. 56v, 57r, 62v–3r, 72v, 106v, 125v, 144r, 146r, 188r–9v, 228r–9v, 247r, 258r, 289v.

[4] Notes in Dyer, *Novel Cases*, ff. 168v, 241v, 268r, 339v; in Fitzherbert, *Natura Brevium*, ff. 97v, 98v, 99v, 116r; and in Ellesm. MS 482, *passim*.

[5] Ms. notes in his Dyer, ff. 317v and 312r, respectively. See as well comments in Ellesm. MS 482, ff. 81r, 87r–8v, 90r, 124v–9r, 250r, 269v–77r, 288r.

[6] Ellesm. MS 482, f. 124v, 'Mr. Bracebridge his Case'.

These included the subjects of land and criminal law, and the interpretation of statutes.

Egerton's study of the land law was based primarily on the Year Books, the statutes, and a few major texts. The chief works which he utilised were Thomas Littleton's *Tenures*, Anthony Fitzherbert's *Nouvelle Natura Brevium*, and John Perkins' *Incipit Tractatus*.[1] It appears that he used Fitzherbert for his source book and Littleton for a commentary, and the two were annotated as if they were in fact companion volumes. Perkins' essay was not annotated for its subject matter, but he incorporated many references into his copy of Littleton. The *Tenures* became not only his major text, but also his guide to the sources. Thus he added to the general discussion and arguments in his Littleton references from the cases in Fitzherbert, and the cases in his Fitzherbert were annotated from his collection of Year Books and the statutes.[2] He then tried to keep his collection of sources up to date by adding references from recent cases at court to his copy of Fitzherbert.[3]

Egerton's study of the criminal law was undertaken in a similar manner. His major textbook for this subject was William Staunford's *Prerogative* supplemented with an edition of the statutes, a collection of cases on liveries and maintainers for justices of the peace, and a *Boke of Assises*.[4] In this instance his Staunford served much the same purpose for criminal law as his Littleton served for matters concerning land. The Staunford, like his Littleton, had chapter numbers placed at the top of every page. Subheadings were inserted, the arguments in the text were bracketed, all supplementary material was referenced in the margins, and a full methodological apparatus was used for the assessment of the text. Afterwards he added relevant points of law from the imposing commonplace book he was compiling from cases which he had observed before the courts.[5] Egerton's use of his law books reflects a critical, hard-working examination of

---

[1] His autograph copies of Littleton's *Tenures* (25th Law French ed. 1557), Hunt. RB 62234; Fitzherbert's *Natura Brevium* (3rd Law Fr. ed. 1553 col. 1560), Hunt. RB 59688; and Perkins' *Incipit per Utilis Tractatus* (4th Latin ed. 1545), Hunt. RB 62897.

[2] The Year Book cases in his commonplace book, Ellesm. MS 496; and his copies of the *Magna Carta cum aliis antiquis Statutis* (10th ed. 1556), Hunt. RB 59487; and William Rastell's *A Collection of All the Statutes* (4th ed. 1565), Hunt. RB 59501.

[3] Contemp. cases which Egerton added to his Fitzherbert in the 1570s and 1580s were at ff. 28r, 61r, 85r, 145v, 152r, for ex.

[4] His copies of Staunford's *Prerogative* (1567), Hunt. RB 69540; *A Collection ... concerning Liveries* (1571), Hunt. RB 99044; and the *Boke of Assises* (1555), Hunt. RB 60686.

[5] Egerton's copy of Staunford's *Prerogative*, and his commonplace book – Ellesm. MS 496.

the common law. But perhaps the most important single document of his legal studies at the inns of court was his roughly hewn and precocious tract on the interpretation of statutes, which was composed around 1565.[1]

One of the earliest treatises on statute law to be written in the English language, this tract reveals a major area of Egerton's interest in the law, and illuminates the background of some of the controversies in which he later became embroiled. His initial interest in statutes was derived from the need to cope with the impact of the Reformation Parliament on the land law. Thus his focus was not on the land law itself, but in explaining a method for the interpretation of statutes that would facilitate an examination of those statutes both old and new which were relevant to any particular kind of tenure. In this regard Egerton began his tract with some observations on the role of statutes in the English common law, and addressed himself to some of the greater legal and constitutional problems which had arisen in the course of the sixteenth century. His opening discussion defined the positive law as statutes and proclamations, holding that Parliament not only declared custom but also made the law. Its sovereignty was full and unimpeachable, its authority 'absolute and bindeth all manners of persons, because that all men are privy and parties thereto'.[2] Since Parliament was the only institution that could abolish old laws and make new ones, statutes were regarded as the highest form of law in England. This kind of reasoning caused Egerton to take the very logical step of breaking with legal tradition and most contemporary writers by making statutes the first, primary, and most important source of law in the commonwealth.[3]

---

[1] The *Discourse*. While Professor Thorne lacked definitive evidence to ascribe the tract to Egerton, such authorship has been assumed by T. F. T. Plucknett, 'Ellesmere on Statutes', *LRQ* 60 (1944), 242–9. See as well the comments of Max Radin, 'Early statutory interpretation in England', *Illinois Law Rev.* 38 (1943), 16–40. The evidence that demonstrates Egerton's authorship will be contained in the present author's unpublished article on statute law and its interp. in the sixteenth century.

[2] *Discourse*, 108; and reinforced at pp. 103, 113, 169–70. Early notes supporting his later stand can be found in his copies of Dyer, *Novel Cases*, f. 129v; Plowden, *Commentaries*, f. 79v; Rastell, *Coll. Statutes* (1565 ed.), ff. 34r, 552r, 576v; *ibid.* (1572 ed.), Hunt. RB 59499, fly leaf 4r, f. 560v; and Staunford, *Plees Coron*, f. 162v.

[3] *Discourse*, 103–13; and later in Folger MS V.a. 378, f. 6v. The new legal tradition developed by Christopher Saint-German, *A Treatise Concerning the Division between the Spiritualtie and Temporaltie* (n.d.), 228; Sir Thomas Smith, *De Republica Anglorum*, ed. L. Alston (Cambridge Mass. 1906), Chaps. I–III; James Whitelocke, in *Select statutes and other constitutional documents*, ed. G. W. Prothero (2nd ed. Oxford 1898), 351–2; Henry Finch, *Nomotechnia* (1613), s.v. 'Cestascavoir'; and Sir Edward Coke, 4 *Inst.* 36.

The major body of the tract was arranged into three sections: the organisation of statutes, the exposition of rules for interpreting them, and the means to construe and apply words and sentences. Perhaps his most important contribution was the general discussion of rules for understanding statutes.[1] Here Egerton presented various methods, and concluded with three major rules: discovering the mischief that was complained of in the petition that led to the framing of the bill, analysing the preamble or debates to discern the intentions of Parliament, and assessing from the Year Books and Law Reports how the act was applied in the courts after its passage. By discussing the criteria for properly understanding statutes, Egerton had placed on paper some observations which were obviously current at the inns of court, observations which would be examined more fully by Edmund Plowden in his *Commentaries* (1572), and set down as legal rules in *Heydon's Case* (1584).[2]

The organisation of statutes and the use of words were two other subjects equally relevant to the problems confronting law students in the early Elizabethan period. Egerton's dissection of statutes in terms of their preamble, body, and proviso revealed an ability to discuss the composition of statutes with clarity.[3] The preamble contained the cause, purpose, and intent of the statute; the body comprised the subject and the remedy; and the proviso defined the scope of actions which fell under its purview. Whether all statutes were formed this way was a crucial problem that Egerton never faced. In discussing the body of the statute he was confronted with questions as to how specific words and sentences should be regarded in restricting or enlarging their meaning. This brought him to an analysis of the equity of statutes, of the limitations of statutes, and of interpreting them in the affirmative or the negative. With its precise use of grammar, his discussion reflected an incisive mind.[4]

The inquiry and research which Egerton made into statutes and statute law reflected one instance of how lawyers in the last third of the sixteenth century had exhibited a keen interest in this subject. Egerton himself analysed and annotated profusely the statutes he

---

[1] *Discourse*, 117–22, 140–61.
[2] Plowden, *Commentaries*, ff. 10r, 82r, 205r–v, 366v, 464r–v, 467r–v; and *Heydon's Case*, 3 *Co. Rep.* 7v (K.B. 1584).
[3] *Discourse*, 114–7, 172–3.
[4] *Ibid.* 123–40, 161–72. Similar interps. were expounded by Plowden in his *Commentaries*, ff. 82r–v, 109, 363r–7r, 465r–7r. Egerton noted these afterwards in his own copy of Plowden – Hunt. RB 62961.

studied in contemporary editions, abridged them into his commonplace book, and noted important ones in the flyleaves of his various
legal texts.[1] When he became an officer of state he collected and
noted statutes pertaining to the legal rights of the Crown.[2] Later in
his career as Chancellor he would play a significant role in promoting
and encouraging the proper editing and publication of the statutes of
the realm.[3]

Egerton's abiding interest in statutes and the sources of the law
stemmed from his historical curiosity that was begun at Brasenose
College with Erdeswicke and Pulton, nurtured at Lincoln's Inn, and
brought to fruition after being called to the Bar in 1572. Pulton
had moved from Brasenose to Lincoln's Inn a year before Egerton,
and his interest in the study of penal statutes – when viewed in the
light of his later correspondence – indicates that he may have worked
with Egerton on the preparation of the *Discourse*.[4] Two other scholars
of history with whom Egerton developed lifetime friendships at
Lincoln's Inn were William Lambarde, who became the famous
Kentish antiquarian and legal historian, and Francis Thynne, the
later antiquarian, author, and Lancaster Herald. Lambarde, who
pioneered the study of ancient legal customs in England and possessed
a keen legal and historical mind, shared some of Egerton's early legal
practice, exchanged historical works as gifts, sent autographed copies
of his own books,[5] and was later promoted by the new Lord Keeper
to important offices in Chancery Lane and the Tower.[6] Thynne, one
of the most industrious heralds and antiquarians of the period, dedi-

---

[1] His copy of *Magna Carta cum Statutis*, Ellesm. MS 496, and his notes in the *Boke of
Assises*, rear fly leaf, and Rastell's *Coll. Statutes* (1572 ed.), third fly leaf from the rear.

[2] Ellesm. MSS 482, 2611.

[3] A full discussion of Egerton's notes and writings on statutes and their interp. is in
Thorne, *Discourse*, Introduction; and in Knafla, 'New model lawyer', Chap. III.

[4] Their corresp. in Ellesm. MSS 1963–4, 2979; Egerton's copy of Pulton's *An Abstract of
al the penall Statutes*; and Pulton's major works – *A Kalendar, or Table, comprehending the
effect of all the Statutes* (1606); and *A Collection of sundrie Statutes* (1618).

[5] Some of their joint law business and corresp. is Ellesm. MSS 39, 2649, 2649B.
Lambarde's ms. dedications to Egerton were two copies of his *Eirenarcha: OR of The Office of
Justice of the Peace* (1581), Hunt. RB 17273, title page; *ibid.* (1588 ed.), Hunt. RB 62135,
letter pinned to the title page; and a ms. copy of Gervasius of Tilberic, 'de necessaris
Scaccarii observantiis Dialogue', the letter of presentation pr. in *HLQ* 11 (1948), 202–3.
A useful study of Lambarde has been done by Retha Warnicke, *William Lambarde* (1973).

[6] Joseph Haward, *Miscellanea Genealogica et Heraldica*, ser. 1 (1876), II, 100–2; and
Paul Ward, 'William Lambarde's collections on Chancery', *Harvard Lib. Bull.* 7 (1953),
572–5. Lambarde also placed his wife and children in trust to Egerton at his death: P. C. C.
Woodhall 63.

cated four of his most important manuscript treatises to Egerton. [1] In one particular letter he spoke nostalgically of 'those younger years when Lincoln's Inn society did link us all in one chain of amity'. [2]

It was also in those years at Lincoln's Inn in the 1560s and 1570s that Egerton became more deeply acquainted with ancient customs and laws, and with the studies of the legal humanists of the Continent. He acquired manuscript collections of the laws of Canute, the customs of the Normans, and the oldest registers of writs. [3] He collected at the same time the later commentaries of Bracton and Britton. [4] Egerton's growing historical interests were not restricted, however, to his native country. He acquired works on the laws of Moses, the Roman Republic, and the Roman Church. [5] In fact, it was due perhaps to his interest in the civil law that he became acquainted with the work of the legal humanists that was changing the course of legal studies on the Continent so dramatically in the sixteenth century.

Beginning in the late 1570s, Egerton began to cite in the loose-leaf pages and margins of his law books, and occasionally in his manuscript briefs of cases, the writings of prominent European jurists such as Jacobus Acontius, Joachim Hopper, Lambert Daneau, and, later, Jean Bodin. [6] Thus the Dutch jurist Hopper, whom Egerton came to regard as 'one of the gravest and best learned lawyers of our

[1] Thynne's manuscript volumes with letters of presentation were the 'Parte of the first part of the Comentaries of Britayne' (26 Aug. 1587), Ellesm. MS 1137; 'The names and Arms of the Chauncellors' (13 June 1597), Ellesm. MS 26/A/6; 'Animadversions uppon the Annoticions on Corrections of Some imperfections of impressions of Chaucer's workes' (16 Dec. 1599), Ellesm. MS 34/B/11; and 'Emblems and Epigrams' (n.d.), Ellesm. MS 34/B/12.

[2] Ellesm. MS 34/B/12, unnumbered f. 3r. One should also mention Egerton's later relation Sir Francis Leigh, a patron of antiquarians who was a friend of William Camden and John Selden.

[3] Canute's 'laws' are trans. in Ellesm. MS 1124, from a copy of William Lambarde's; and Ellesm. MS 1164. He also had a history of England from ancient times which he noted: Ellesm. MS 1128 (34/B/26).

[4] *Henrici de Bracton de Legibus & Consuetudinibus Angliae Libri* (1569), Hunt. RB 97059; and *Britton* (n.d.), Hunt. RB 60508.

[5] Egerton acquired the laws of Moses from John Shaw, who taught his eldest son, Thomas, at Brasenose – Folger MS V.a. 6; and an edition of the laws of the Hebrews – Ellesm. MS 1182A. His ancient history texts were John Rosinus, *Romanarum Antiquitatum* (Lyons 1585), Hunt, RB 49603; and Henry Savile, *The Ende of Nero and beginning of Galba* (1591), Hunt. RB 69625. The coll. of canon law was Ellesm. MS 34/A/5.

[6] Acontius: notes in Fitzherbert, *Natura Brevium*, front and rear fly leaves; Hopper: *Post-Nati*, 85–6; Daneau: Notes in his Fitzherbert, title page, f. 1, and rear fly leaf; and Bodin: Ellesm. MS 465, f. IV, and 'Brief Chanc'. f. 1r.

age', was cited often for his concept of the historicity of the law: its limitation to time and place, and the necessity for continual evaluation, analysis, and reframing to meet the needs of the present.[1] In Egerton's own words, 'All human laws are but *leges temporis*, and the wisdom of judges was only valid for their time'.[2] It was from these and similar sources that he developed a judicial and historical approach to the law that would provide the basis for his work as jurist and statesman in the early seventeenth century. He also acquired a means to preserve it: a travelling bookcase to hold pocketbook copies of works on philosophy, theology, poetry, law, and history, which would accompany him on his long trips between London and the northern Welsh marches.[3]

Egerton's interest in historical change was also affected by the developments in the law which occurred in the early stages of his legal career – the renaissance of the common law which was to have such a great impact on the substance of the law and the judicial system.[4] The problems which legal change posed to a student and a lawyer were reflected poignantly in Egerton's law books. At the time of being called to the Bar, he acquired a copy of one of the earliest printed reports of recent cases, Plowden's *Commentaries*. He annotated the arguments throughout, and then appears to have entered items from his Plowden profusely into his Fitzherbert and his collections of statutes, with further cross-references to his Littleton.[5] Later, after Egerton became Solicitor-General, Dyer's important collection of recent common law cases was published. Egerton's copy of Dyer reveals the manner in which he refurbished his working library of legal texts.[6] On the one hand, he now entered references from his Dyer into his Fitzherbert–Littleton apparatus. On the other hand, he indexed his Dyer according to legal topics and the forms of action, placed references to these at the tops of the pages, and then entered into Dyer at the appropriate places those still pertinent items of the

---

[1] *Post-Nati*, 85.

[2] Ellesm. MS 2755, f. 1, and again in the *Post-Nati*, 47.

[3] At the Hunt. Lib. It was similar to three others which the author has seen elsewhere from the same period: Francis Bacon's at the Toledo Museum of Art, Ohio; the 'Brotherton' case at the Brotherton Lib. Leeds Univ.; and Julius Caesar's at the B.M. Most of the books were pr. and bound at the Planton Press, Leyden, 1557–1620. I wish to thank Mr Carey Bliss of the Hunt. Lib. for his assistance in making these known to me.

[4] Louis A. Knafla, 'Humanism and the Common Law Renaissance', *Humanities Rev.* 4 (1976).

[5] *Supra*, nn. 4–5, pp. 44, 1–2 pp. 46.

[6] His copy of Dyer, *Novel Cases*, Hunt. RB 59138.

old learning which were contained in his Littleton. By the time he became Attorney-General, his Dyer (a collection of new cases) had replaced his Littleton (a study of the old law) as his major common law text. [1]

This change in Egerton's legal studies was also exhibited in his study of statutes. Thus, when he gave his first Reading on statutes in 1581, he chose a relatively new act on the making and interpretation of letters patent. [2] Rather than lecture on an old statute, as was the normal custom just prior to this period, Egerton was among that new generation of Readers to turn to an examination of new statutes in the lecture cycle at the inns of court. [3] When he later presented his Double Reading as Attorney-General, he selected one of the most controversial statutes of the Reformation Parliament concerning land – the statute of leases. [4] The subject matter of these Readings reflected not only his legal interests, but also those of the law which he litigated so profusely both as a practising lawyer and as legal counsel to the Queen in the 1570s and 1580s.

The ideas and attitudes of a common lawyer which comprise the totality of his mind stretch far beyond the arena of the law. They comprise in microcosm one particular sum of the society in which he lives. Thus the manner in which Egerton as Lord Chancellor utilised the learning, power, and influence that he had acquired in the reign of Elizabeth was determined in part by the ideas and attitudes which developed in the course of his long life and career. It is to this end that an analysis of his religion, of his social and cultural values, and of his political and legal attitudes is necessary before we can come to a meaningful understanding of his major writings in the reign of James.

Egerton's religious background was nourished, as we have seen, by the Catholic Faith. Retaining his religious orthodoxy, he probably studied some Catholic theology at Brasenose in the last years of Queen Mary, 1556–8. Perhaps these studies went hand in hand with his

[1] He also had to acquire another working copy of Littleton's *Tenures* (32nd Law Fr. ed. 1581), Hunt. RB 62239. In a sense Coke may have been exceptional in maintaining the topics and order of the land law discussion found in Littleton for his *Co. Lit.*

[2] The stat. of 18 Eliz. on 'Letters Patent', notes on the Reading in C. U. L., Camb. MS Dd. 11.87, ff. 152r–9v.

[3] Louis A. Knafla, 'The matriculation revolution and education at the Inns of Court in Renaissance England', *Tudor men and institutions*, ed. A. J. Slavin (Baton Rouge La. 1972), 251–5.

[4] The stat. of 32 Henry VIII on 'Leases', notes on the Reading in Lans. MS 1119, ff. 43–60.

readings on Roman civil and canon law.[1] They were certainly acknowledged by his frequent citation of Church Fathers together with classical authors in the notes of his earliest law books, which can be ascribed to the early and mid 1560s.[2] We have seen in the previous chapter that he maintained the Old Faith at least to 1569, and perhaps to 1577. How he maintained it can be explained by his Catholic stepmother, his patronage by families with Catholic elements, and his close friendships with Pulton and Thynne – both of whom resided with Egerton at Lincoln's Inn and remained loyal to the Old Faith.[3] These factors also explain some of the difficulty he might have experienced in relinquishing it.

The evidence for his religious change can also be documented. As a practising lawyer in the 1570s he obtained the works of John Calvin and Thomas Cranmer,[4] and afterwards he cited religious references almost exclusively from the Old Testament and the early Church Fathers. Ecclesiastical institutions had always been at the centre of secular government in the Welsh borderlands.[5] Thus, once Egerton was convinced that he had 'erred' in matters of religion, he must have regarded the other old believers as stubborn and possibly treasonous.[6] His vigorous prosecution of Catholic 'traitors' in the late 1580s, and the rapid promotions he achieved in the 1590s, must have made him an attractive figure to the newly Established Church.[7]

Egerton was courted zealously by both Anglican and Puritan writers in the 1590s, and some of them hailed him – like Philip Sidney earlier[8] – as a future leader of their religious aspirations in Britain

---

[1] *Supra*, pp. 13, 39–40.

[2] Ellesm. MS 482, ff. 247v, 269r, 287v; and notes in his first copies of Fitzherbert, *Natura Brevium*, title page, f. 1, and rear fly leaf; and of Littleton, *Tenures*, last two fly leaves.

[3] *Supra*, pp. 48–9, and Pulton and Thynne, s.v. *D.N.B.*

[4] His autograph copies of *Sermons of Maister John Calvin* trans. Arthur Golding (1580), Hunt. RB 98692; and of Cranmer's *Defensio Verae* (1557), Hunt. RB 60044. The citations are in Ellesm. MSS 129 f. 1v; 456; 465; 485 ff. 1v, 2v, 3v; 1872 f. 4v; and the *Post-Nati*, 84–5, 97–8, 105–7, 116–7.

[5] G. Dyfnalt Owen, *Elizabethan Wales* (Cardiff, 1964), 215–30.

[6] Also the Duttons: C.R.O. EDC 2/7.

[7] Chaderton became Bishop of Chester in 1577, and with the aid of Derby and Leicester had led the attack against Cheshire Catholics for their conversion. He also established lectureships throughout the northern Welsh marches – fourteen by 1584 – and founded the Puritan movement in the county: J. S. Morrill, *Cheshire 1630–1660* (Oxford 1974), 17–9. Later, as Bishop of Lincoln, he wrote to Egerton reminiscing about their 'merry' and 'pleasant' times when they were 'set down by your Lord's little table in your gallery at Dodleston': Ellesm. MS 75, f. 1v.

[8] James M. Osborn, *Young Philip Sidney 1572–1577* (New Haven Conn. 1972).

and for a Protestant Europe. At first the evidence indicates that he gave patronage to rabid anti-Catholics for tracts against the policies of Rome which were subversive to the Established Church.[1] These religious writers, united in their antipathy to Rome, tied their anti-papal feelings to the Protestant cause throughout Europe and supported England's war against Spain vigorously. The enemy was 'Roman' Catholicism as the servant of the Habsburg Empire, and thus the enemies in England were those Jesuits and seminary priests who, as the alleged spies of the tyrant Philip II, sought the overthrow of the English State. Their writings help explain Egerton's prosecution of recusants in the 1590s, and his verbal expressions of antipathy against them. As he penned on a bill of information, these are 'natural vipers, ready to eat out the belly of your mother'.[2] However, in matters strictly religious Egerton seems to have remained a relatively tolerant man. Purely religious concerns never came between close friendships such as those with Pulton and Thynne, both of whom retained their Catholicism while accepting the newly established order in Church and State. In reading the work of the famous Dutch author Jacobus Acontius, Egerton noted his idea of toleration that provided for freedom of religious practice as long as it was not designed to overthrow the established order.[3]

A second group of religious men to court Egerton in the 1590s consisted of noted Calvinist preachers and theologians who looked upon him as a supporter of the movement for Church reform. These men attacked the 'evils' which had remained in the Established Church: simony, pluralities, non-residency, and unlearned curates and preachers. They addressed Egerton in the dedications of their pamphlets and treatises to praise him for his support of these reforms.[4] John Norden, for example, when writing of how 'the most godly do even groan in their souls to consider the present state and

---

[1] These writers included Thomas Bell, Thomas Bilson, Edward Bulkeley, John Donne, John Downame, John Golburne, Edward Hutchins, Gerard de Malynes, Gabriel Powell, Ralph Ravens, Hugh Roberts, Matthew Sutcliffe, Cipriano de Valera, and Andrew Willet. The context has been set down by William S. Maltby, *The black legend in England* (Durham N.C. 1973).

[2] Folger MS X.d. 337, f. 14v (SC 14 Feb. 1600).

[3] Jacopo Acontio, *Stratagemata Satanae* (Basel 1564), quoted by Egerton in his copy of Fitzherbert, front and back fly leaves.

[4] Particularly Laurence Chaderton, John Downame, Roger Fenton, Christopher Goodman, John Norden, and John Shaw. Egerton's proposals are in Ellesm. MS 2029. The best summary of his position was that of John Shaw, 'The perill of pluralities, Non-residencie, and choppinge of Benefices', Ellesm. MS 34/B/34 (1598), 1–2.

condition of things', then exclaimed that 'now of a sudden every godly eye seemeth to be fixed on you ... that many things may be reformed'. Norden went on to couple Church reform to the reform of English society, and he preached the abolition of drunkenness, swearing, gaming, smoking, idleness, lust, and pride.[1] Pleas such as this must have struck a good response in Egerton, a man who believed in a simple style of living and who had condemned these sins himself.

Egerton's response to such demands was a rather positive one. Not only was he in favour of ecclesiastical reform, but he also patronised a learned, Calvinistic clergy in the church livings of the Welsh border-lands as well as the Midlands. He was the first lay Chancellor to have household chaplains, and Drs John Dove, John King, and John Williams, although not Puritans, were able Calvinist theologians and outstanding preachers.[2] And Williams would later, after Bacon, take his place as a chosen successor for the Woolsack.

A similar pattern can be seen in the men whom Egerton patronised to the ecclesiastical benefices which came to his gift: learned, zealous Anglicans and moderate Puritans.[3] Moreover, he expanded his patronage of benefices in· the course of his public career.[4] For example, he became partly responsible for a succession of notable preachers resident at Lincoln's Inn, including John Donne. The poet, preacher, and writer had previously been the Lord Keeper's private secretary, and later he became preacher of Lincoln's Inn, chaplain to James I, and Dean of St Paul's.[5] As one writer noted,

[1] Norden's dedicatory tract in ms. without formal title, headed 'inward spirits rejoice' (c. 1596/7), Ellesm. MS 33/A/35, ff. 1v and 2v, 7r respectively.

[2] The best general study of preaching in the period is that of Irvonwy Morgan, *The godly preachers of the Elizabethan Church* (1965). For Dove and King see Millar Maclure, *The Paul's Cross sermons, 1534–1642* (Toronto 1958), 3, 79–80, 98–101, 106, 130–5, 146–52, 161, 218–22; and George Hennessy, *Novum repertorium ecclesiasticum parochiale londinense* (1898), pt. 10, p. 90. For Williams, see Elizabeth Dew Roberts, *Mitre and sceptre* (1938). Williams alone received five benefices from Egerton: Lans. MS 985, ff. 80r–1v.

[3] Particularly men such as Roger Fenton, Joseph Hall, Henry Hoddesdon, Edward Hutchins, Francis Osborne, William Osborne, John Rawlinson, Francis Rollenson, and Matthew Sutcliffe. They also made dedications and presentations to Egerton.

[4] Tanner MS 179, Egerton's record of benefices to which he made presentations. For the eccles. patronage which he had at his disposal, and its context, see the useful survey of Rosemary O'Day, 'Ecclesiastical patronage of the Lord Keepers 1558–1642', *TRHS* 23 (1973), esp. 93–100.

[5] Irvonwy Morgan, *Prince Charles' Puritan chaplain* (1957), 109–11; and Sir William Bell, *Lincoln's Inn: its history and traditions* (1947), 68–73. Some of Donne's relevant corresp. is in Folger MSS L.b. 526–34, 538. In an ms. dedication pinned to a copy of *The Pseudo-Martyr* (1610), he said 'that those poor sparks of understanding or judgement which are in me, were derived and kindled from you, and owe themselves to you' – quoted in Sotheby & Co. *Catalogue of the remaining portion of the Bridgewater Library* (1951), 16.

Egerton's two feet were as 'fiery pillars' of the Church, even when he became 'burned' by his private secretary.[1]

The new Lord Keeper not only patronised a learned Calvinist clergy, but he also placed great emphasis on good preaching. Often he required preachers to enter into bonds to ensure giving sermons as a prerequisite for their installation.[2] According to one incumbent, Egerton appointed only 'masters of assemblies who can drive in the nail'.[3] However, such a reputation often led to misunderstanding. Several radical Puritans, from Andrew Willet of East Anglia to John Shaw of Yorkshire, who envisaged a restructured Church and a 'changed' people, sought Egerton's assistance and heralded him as 'a *chosen* leader'.[4] According to Willet, the Lord Keeper was 'the captain appointed by the lord to lead the soldiers into battle, and never had they better encouragement since you took over leadership of the field'.[5] Willet's excesses, however, were topped by those of Edward Topsell, who declared that ever since he had become 'a judge in England ... so many learned men have had free ingress into temples, that 40,000 at the least have been gained by their preaching to march after your lordship'.[6]

Egerton's religious beliefs had turned from Catholicism to Calvinism by the reign of James. His beliefs, however, were incorporated into a mind that held statesmanship pre-eminent. Thus in James's first speech to Parliament in 1604, Egerton noted the King's conception of the religious duties of his subjects as if it were also a warning to his councillors: the maintenance of the true ancient church, the authority of antiquity, and the obedience owed to the King as the father of the Church.[7] Part of Egerton's success in maintaining this 'holy pretence' of the King was due to his own belief in the 'Godly Prince': that strange millenarian concept of the Christian Emperor who would lead a holy crusade against Antichrist (the Pope), reform the Church with the guidance of the laity, and form with his

[1] Francis Rollenson, *Twelve Prophetical Legacies* (1612), sig. 3v.

[2] Tanner MS 179.

[3] Mr Barlow, 'The Rehearsall Sermon', Ellesm MS 34/B/42, f. 2r–v. Chaderton, Downame, Goodwin, King, Shaw, and Williams are discussed in the admirable study of Paul S. Seaver, *The Puritan lectureships* (Stanford, Calif. 1970).

[4] i.e., a predestined leader, with the assurance of salvation: 'R.B.' in Ellesm. MS 34/A/13, f. 2v (16 Jan. 1603/4).

[5] Andreas Willet, *Tetrastylon Papismi* (1599), sig. 4A.

[6] Edward Topsell, 'The Fowles of Heaven', Ellesm. MS 33/A/13, f. 2r.

[7] *The Kings Maiesties Speech* (1604), Hunt. RB 61876, Egerton's notes at sigs. 2v–3r, B4r–v.

councillors the 'Watch-men of Christ'.[1] The belief was nothing less than an acceptance of the tradition of John Foxe which Egerton had eventually embraced, a tradition that included both Anglicans and Nonconformists by the early seventeenth century.

That Egerton should become receptive to Calvinism is more easily comprehended when we inquire into his social and cultural values. From his appointment as Solicitor-General in 1581 down to his death in 1617, Egerton was a man who believed in the hard and thrifty life of the provincial countryside. From the woody dingle of Dodleston up to the forest and lake of Ellesmere, and down to the broad expanse of the lower Midlands, the 'country' was for Egerton the only place to live. For example, within a month of Egerton's admittance to the Privy Council, one of his agents wrote to Cecil apologising for Egerton's delay in not coming to London until the first day of the legal term.[2] Thereafter, a series of letters follows from Egerton to both Cecil and Essex on the virtues of country life versus that of the city and the court. He defined the country in these letters as woods, open fields, neat houses, clean air, a plain diet, fishing and exercise, and freedom of movement.[3] In fact, his list of rustic virtues was an appropriate tonic for the vices which the Calvinist writers whom he patronised had harangued in their works.

Even when Egerton was in attendance at the court of Elizabeth he never hesitated to beg the Queen's permission to return to Dodleston as soon as the law terms were no longer sitting. As he wrote eloquently in a letter to Essex, 'It seems to me that heaven is in the country, where there be no rubbish of Court nor State affairs to stop.'[4] He even appears to have preferred an Islington cottage or a small manor house at Pyrford, Surrey, to urban life in London. As he wrote in defence of going to Pyrford, 'this barren place yieldeth me spare diet, good air, and convenient exericse.'[5] However, even in the midst of a heavy schedule he would often leave York House and Westminster for the fields and heath of outer London. We have, for example, this

---

[1] This and other concepts have been derived from the provocative studies of William L. Lamont, *Godly rule* (1969), esp. Chaps. I–II; and William Haller, *Foxe's 'Book of Martyrs' and the elect nation* (New York 1963).

[2] *Salisbury MS*, V, 246–7, John Harper to Cecil (16 June 1596).

[3] *Ibid.* IX, 14, 22, 25, 119–20. It should be mentioned that the villages, and even towns, of the Welsh borderlands were far less populated, and more dependent on the agrarian landscape, than those in central, southern, or eastern England: Owen, *Elizabethan Wales*, 93–8.

[4] *Salisbury MS*, IX, 25 (13 Jan. 1598/9).

[5] *Ibid.* IX, 191, Egerton to Cecil (2 June 1599). For his Islington house, Henry B. Wheatley, *London past & present* (1891), II, 269.

youthful and picturesque letter to Cecil from a man in his late fifties, where he declares that 'yesterday I made a wilful escape; and broke from the physicians and from an unclean and unwholesome house. I am now seeking clean air on Hounslow Heath.'[1]

Egerton also loved the countryside for its spartan life. He expressed a deep dislike of rich foods, excessive drink, and tobacco, and he lectured his son John on his 'unnecessary pastimes'.[2] These feelings help to explain his abhorrence of doctors. Thus in a letter to Cecil, where he complained of feeling ill, he was in 'fear to fall into the physicians hands, which I account as a curse'.[3] Although Egerton otherwise was a very healthy man, he continually used the excuse of 'ailments' to escape the feverish, restless life of the royal court for the open landscape. In fact, according to one of the women who courted him, he had 'as sound of a body as any'. The only ailment he appeared to have was an occasional siege of the gout in one foot.[4] He never ceased, however, to be concerned with the health of his family and relatives in Cheshire, Denbighshire, Shropshire, Northamptonshire, and Hertfordshire. One particular series of letters contains vivid personal statements on the course of the plague and the movement of his friends and relatives in the countryside to avoid it.[5] He was also pleased to speak of his happiness for their being permanently resident in the Western borderlands or the Midlands rather than in London.

These simplistic, rustic tastes stemmed from that tradition of the pastoral life which had been embedded so deeply in the artisan and gentleman status groups of late medieval and early modern England. The word 'rural' had become symbolic of the landscape, the agrarian community, thrift, industry, and the pleasures of nature's environment. In the world of literature it had become embodied in the 'pastoral' tradition, a corpus of literary conventions based on the above features, and identifying rural life with a simple life, a simple life with a good life, and a good life with Christian virtue and salvation.[6] Whether it stemmed from the hands of Shakespeare, Sidney,

---

[1] *Salisbury MS*, X, 81 (26 March 1600).

[2] Further, that 'Repentence cannot cure you, but yet let it warn you': Ellesm. MS 195 (26 July 1608). For his comments on 'drink', see *Att-Gen v. Welby*, Hawarde, *Reportes*, 315–6 (SC 29 Nov. 1606). For tobacco, the *Post-Nati*, 84–5.

[3] *Salisbury MS*, X, 70, Egerton to Cecil (14 March 1599/1600).

[4] Ellesm. MS 46, f. 1r, from the Lady Russell (n.d.); and his letter to Cecil – 'I am prisoner under two cruel gaolers, podagra and melancholia. The one fetters my feet: the other oppresses my heart', *Salisbury MS*, XII, 583 (2 Jan. 1603/4).

[5] Ellesm. MSS 176–9, 181, 407, to his son John (29 July to 21 August 1603).

[6] I would like to thank Professors Michael MacDonald and Max Patrick for their discussions on this complex subject.

or Spenser, or from a west Midlands poet like Drayton,[1] it represented a stream of English life that had always been at the centre of
its existence.

The rustic, pastoral element in Egerton's character never left him.
It must have added a fascinating touch to the life of the institutions
of which he became part in Whitehall and Westminster. He was
renowned, for example, for his stories. One of them was the tale of a
friar stealing a dying man's lands by getting him to answer 'yea' to a
series of simple questions, interjecting questions about gifts of
land to the friar. The man's son, meanwhile, stood by witnessing the
disappearance of his inheritance. Finally, the son interrupted the
friar and asked the father if he should bash the friar over the head;
the father uttered 'yea', and the son then bashed the friar and re-
gained access to his inheritance.[2] He told a similar story at one of the
judges' dinners. After an evening of much drinking and laughter by
some of them, a stern prayer was given. According to the diarist,
Egerton replied: '"God save, defend me from the fair grace of God";
viz. when one hath broken his arm with a fall, that he broke not his
neck is called in Cheshire the fair grace of god.'[3]

The one social problem which Egerton never did resolve was the
life of the court, which made so many demands on his time. Whenever
he made the compromise, however, he made it gallantly. He objected
strongly, for example, to a public feast and progress upon his receipt
of the Barony of Ellesmere and the title of Lord Chancellor.[4] But
he made it anyway. He also complained bitterly of the costumes of
office, but when he had his robes designed he looked 'like a Chancellor
of France'.[5] Thrift and hard work were virtues on which Egerton
thrived. The agents who managed his estates spoke of his hatred of
large expenses and his preference for keeping a 'simple, humble
household'.[6] This life style caused one prominent renaissance lady
to complain that 'your lord keepeth not the table nor the part honourable and fit for ye place'.[7] Here again the dilemma became apparent.

---

[1] William Shakespeare's *Much Ado about Nothing*, Sir Philip Sidney's *Arcadia*, and Edmund
Spenser's *Shepherd's Calendar*. According to a letter of Samuel Daniel, Egerton knew and
cherished 'Master Spenser': Ellesm. MS 138.

[2] Hawarde, *Reportes*, 431.

[3] *Journal of Roger Wilbraham*, ed. Harold Spencer Scott, *Camden Misc.* 10 (1902), 19.

[4] Ellesm. MS 389 (recounted on 4 Sept. 1616).

[5] Thomas Fuller, *The History of the Worthies of England* (1840), I, 270–1.

[6] The testimony of Coleman and Hope given in Geoffrey Goodman, *The court of King
James the First* (1839), 280–3.

[7] Ellesm. MS 47, the Countess Dowager Russell to Egerton (c. 1600), f. 1r.

He had married Lady Wolley and the Countess of Derby for their
wealth and position at court, but he could never fully bring himself
actually to live at the royal court or in the fashionable renaissance
palaces which he inherited from his wives. Thus, although he admired
and was extremely proud of Alice Derby, often he could not tolerate
her and the elaborate household which she maintained. In fact, the
rate of her spending brought their relationship to one of strife and
conflict that carried on beyond his death.[1]

Egerton's industrious nature never seemed to know any limits. The
men who knew him very late in life, when he was well into his
seventies, marvelled at the pace he set in administering the matters of
state. Cranfield, Bacon, and Buckingham paid him such testimony.[2]
To the men at court, especially those who owed their daily purse to
the benevolence of the monarch, a 'country' Chancellor was the
embodiment of disaster, and they never ceased to attack him as a
hypochondriac unfit for service to the State.[3]

It is difficult to exaggerate the extent to which the social and cultural values which Egerton inherited from the northern borderlands
of the Welsh marches, moulded by the religious concerns of Calvinism, influenced the development of his attitudes towards politics and
the law. Personally, Egerton was a very out-going individual, whether
in a court room or out in the countryside. When he was admitted to
the Privy Council in 1596, he sought the friendship of all members,
including the Cecil and Essex factions.[4] But he never hesitated in
establishing an independent point of view, and in drawing upon his
personal followers in the borderlands to build eventually his own
base of support in the House of Commons, the departments of state,
and the lower echelons of government. He also never hesitated in
dropping a political ally should he discredit himself. As we have
seen, he would work for the Earl of Arundel and assist the Earl of
Essex until they made fatal, and irreconcilable, moves; when that

[1] Ellesm. MSS 213, 389; and comments in drafts of his will – Ellesm. MSS 224, 706–7,
722. For Alice's attempt to break his will after his demise, see Ellesm. MSS 213–4, 284,
726; and N. R. O. Ellesm. MS I, 149, 400–1.

[2] Recounted in Goodman, *Court of James*, 280–3. The early grammar schools of the
Welsh marches were well known for their rigour and discipline. This factor, together with
his illegitimate origins, must have contributed to the tremendous drive and ambition that
characterised his life and career.

[3] *Infra*, Chaps. III, VII.

[4] The Egerton to Cecil correspondence, *supra*; and Egerton to Lord Henry Howard,
Ellesm. MS 130 (13 April 1603).

occurred he presided over their executions.[1] In fact, Egerton's
astute judgment of individuals was considered by opponents to be one
of his most prized assets.[2]

Politically, Egerton was a moderate. On the one hand he was loyal
to the Queen and her Council, but on the other hand he never hesitated to speak for reform when he considered it intrinsically essential.
His moderate attitudes were due to the rich variety of his experiences
in matters of social and cultural life, religion, and government: the
interplay of court and country, Catholic and Protestant, and local and
central institutions. These experiences created a sense of dualism in
his political attitudes. Thus in writing on the subject of authority
he would cite first St Augustine of Hippo on God ordaining Kings and
authorising them to rule their subjects, and then St Cyprian of
Carthage on the necessity of obtaining the popular consent of the
citizens to govern the State.[3] Like Lambert Daneau, the eminent
French Calvinist jurist, he conceived of the State as a federation of
social groups linked together by a series of contracts which were
articulated from the smaller to the larger units.[4] The role of the
Crown was to provide these groups with a basic foundation of unity
and the effective means of leadership.

What gave stability to Egerton's political career was his tough-
mindedness. In his early years as Lord Keeper he had no hesitation in
drafting and changing the language and terms of royal grants which
had been secured by the favourites of the Crown.[5] For example,
Richard Orrell had been a scandalous official in several Elizabethan
departments of state. Possessing the support of the Queen, Orrell
was nonetheless cited and tried by Egerton for misdemeanours in the
Court of Star Chamber. Prior to judgment, Orrell petitioned the
Queen for clemency. The Lord Keeper, before passing the petition to
the Queen, wrote across its face: 'I never saw a more proud and
foolish petition than this.'[6] Orrell was not spared.

---

[1] *Supra*, pp. 17–18, 30–1.

[2] Ellesm. MS 46, Lady Russell to Egerton (c. 1600); and Add. MS 35.957, f. 81v, a
lawyer's critical assessment.

[3] For Augustine: Ellesm. MS 485, f. 1v; notes in Fitzherbert, *Natura Brevium*, Hunt. RB
59688, title page and rear fly leaf. For Cyprian: Ellesm. MS 485, f. 2v, 3v; and notes in
Littleton, *Tenures*, Hunt. RB 66634, second to last fly leaf.

[4] Lambert Daneau, *Ethica Christiana sive de rerum creatanum origine et usu* (Geneva 1576);
and Egerton's notes from it in his copy of Fitzherbert, title page verso.

[5] Ellesm. MSS 1410–24, 1445–81, 1500–13, 1552–75.

[6] Ellesm. MS 2926 (c. 1600). He had earlier defrauded the Queen of a descent from the Earl
of Derby: Ellesm. MS 919. Egerton's ability to exercise the control of the offices he acquired
was emphasised by several contemp. observers: Ellesm. MS 2958, f. 1, and Lans. MS 174, ff.
236–9.

The Lord Keeper, becoming Chancellor, maintained his control in the reign of James. He continued to take great liberty in re-writing drafts of grants to pass the great seal. He also did not hesitate to refuse the royal will when he thought it misguided. It appears that James admired the tenacity of his Chancellor. Several times early in the reign the King had his favourites communicate to Egerton a royal expression of support despite the fact that the Chancellor had refused to accept the precise terms of the grants desired by the King.[1] This kind of reputation enabled him to withstand the vicissitudes of political life in the early seventeenth century. It also made him a most desirable patron. Thus when Sir John Harington wrote to the Earl of Shrewsbury for aid in a suit at court, he requested that Shrewsbury obtain the views of Egerton, 'who may strike the greatest stroke therein.'[2] His career was full of striking strokes, and his attitude towards law and justice provides us with a suitable, and closing, exemplification of this aspect of his character.

Egerton was not only a tough-minded politician, but he was also a hard legal officer of the Crown. The ability which he displayed in pursuing matters to the end as Solicitor and Attorney-General became the hallmark of his work as Master of the Rolls and Lord Keeper. As Master of the Rolls he chastised the Masters of the Chancery often for not having causes properly entered and committing causes which should not be committed.[3] He was also forever telling the judges of assize and the justices of the peace to get on with their work in the country rather than to spend so much time making merry in London. The laws, he contended, were not being enforced in the country because 'many justices of the peace were basket justices, to gather hens and capons *colore officii*, but not to distribute justice to the relief of the subjects'.[4] He was equally hard on the lawyers who appeared before him as president of the Chancery or the Star Chamber.

[1] Letters of Sir Thomas Chaloner and Lord Erskine to Egerton, printed in the *Eg. Papers*, 363–4 (23 April 1603), and 400 (25 Feb. 1604/5), respectively; and Egerton's corresp. with Erskine – Ellesm. MSS 152, 156, 160. As Thomas, Viscount Fenton wrote: the King was 'not displeased that you are backward in subscribing or passing of things, ... and [has] many times gotten thanks from his majesty': *The Manuscripts of the Earl of Mar & Kellie*, H.M.C. 60 (1930), II, 74 (21 Feb. 1616/7).

[2] Sir John Harington to the Earl of Shrewsbury, in *Nugae Antiqua*, ed. Thomas Park (1804), I, 348, from Heralds' Coll. MS M, f. 285.

[3] Bacon, *Works*, II, 71.

[4] See as well his proposals in Ellesm. MS 2616, and his other speeches in the S.C. – esp. those reproduced in William Camden, *Tomus Alter* (1629), 249; *Wilbraham J.* 44; Simons D'Ewes, *The Journals of all the Parliaments ... Elizabeth* (1682), 618–9; H.M.C. *Hastings MS*, IV, 229; and Folger MS X.d. 337, ff. 12v–7r. Egerton thrived on hard litigation, and was known as 'a good hearer of causes' – Add. MS 35.957, f. 81v (the author's trans. from the Latin).

This rustic jurist did not have a very high opinion of the legal profession. For example, when handed a petition he disliked, he developed, according to Francis Bacon, the following style in dealing with it: '"What, you would have my hand to this now? Well so you shall. Nay you shall have both my hands to it." And so would, with both his hands, tear it in pieces.'[1] In one instance when he received a petition that was too verbose, he had the lawyer paraded around the courtroom with his head shoved through the petition up to his chin.[2] When Sir William Townshend had requested advice, or hints of progress on his case, Egerton replied in a draft letter: 'I can not marvel that you trouble yourself and me so often, with writing of the proceeding in the cause,' and concluded that 'I will neither burn nor conceal your letters, but let plain truth appear open faced without masking.'[3] On several occasions he took steps to have attorneys disbarred, and in one instance he referred to them openly in court as 'dangerous vermin' and 'caterpillars of the commonwealth'.[4] Direct and decisive actions such as these must have caused numerous authors to dedicate books to him in homage to his unbending standards on the Bench.[5]

In one famous *cause* before the Star Chamber at the turn of the century, Robert Pye, a barrister of the Inner Temple, was accused by Egerton of perjury, and told that he should have been a butcher like his father. When Pye was convicted, Egerton ordered that he be whipped, pilloried, have both ears cut off, fined 100 marks, and be condemned to 'perpetual punishment' (life imprisonment).[6] Not even former associates like Serjeant Heale, a prominent lawyer, were spared harsh treatment. Heale had been congratulated by Egerton for his outstanding depositions, and on one occasion had lent the Lord

---

[1] Bacon, *Works*, II, 176 (Apophthegm 13).

[2] Richard Mylward in 1596: Harv. Law MS 1035, ff. 71–7, abstracted in Cecil Monro, *Acta Cancellariae* (1847), 692–3.

[3] Ellesm. MS 173 (Oct. 1607).

[4] Hawarde, *Reportes*, 133, *Q's Att. ex parte Merrike v. Pie* (SC 5 May 1602). Other equally unyielding comments are given at pp. 42–3, 55–6, 80–2, 128; and later in his tract on 'Iudicature'.

[5] For ex. Thomas Churchyard in Hunt. RB 14616 (1596), Sir John Davies in Hunt. RB 60953–4 (1615); George Goodwin in Ellesm. MS 34/B/31 (1598); Edward Hutchins in Hunt. RB 21243 (1596); and Thomas Playfer in Ellesm. MS 36 (1596). See as well the comments of Samuel Daniel, *Memoirs*, ed. Samuel Egerton Brydges (1802), v–xi; Dr Godfrey Goodman, *Court of James*, 275–6; and Richard Robinson, 'A Briefe Collection', *Camden Misc.* 20 (1953), 12.

[6] The case cited above: Hawarde, *Reportes*, 133.

Keeper £400 (without perhaps having been reimbursed).[1] But Heale was then implicated in the Cobham plot against the Crown, and was also accused of fraud in the exercise of his office. Once he was tainted with these charges Egerton would no longer stand by him. When Heale was tried in the Star Chamber, a majority of the Court voted for acquittal, a few moved for conviction and a fine of £1,000, but Egerton voted for disbarment, imprisonment, and a fine of £2,000.[2] Although the decision was recorded as an acquittal by the reporters of the Court, the fine rolls indicate that Heale paid an amercement of £1,000.[3] Egerton was not to be bested completely, not even by a majority of the court.

Neither was Egerton forbearing in his attitude towards torture and capital punishment. We have seen, for example, how he never hesitated to resort to the rack as a legal officer of the Crown once he felt justified in its use. When Henry Barrow was racked, there was an objection, and Egerton produced a precedent: a proclamation of 1583 where he noted that the rack could be used if the accused 'will not tell the truth'. The purpose of the proclamation was to correct 'tortures unjustly reported to be done upon them for matters of religion'.[4] The use of the rack to obtain justice was a mild procedure for Egerton when compared with the alternative of justice being undone. The Lord Keeper was also concerned with appropriate remedies for punishment. Thus in a case for slander before the Star Chamber he had occasion to complain of the insufficient means of punishment for this offence, and brought a suggestion to the attention of his colleagues on the Bench: the practice of 'the Indians by drawing blood out of the tongue and ears, to be offered in sacrifice'.[5]

The 'country' Chancellor must indeed have been something to watch in the halls of Parliament, the Council chambers, and the courts at Westminster. Possessed with a strong base of regional power

---

[1] The congratulations were in *Beverley v. Pitt & others* (SC 21 Oct. 1957), Hawarde, *Reportes*, 83–4. The loan and alleged support for a grant of the office of M. R. are noted in Heale's letter to Egerton pr. in *Eg. Papers*, 315 (14 Nov. 1600).

[2] Hawarde, *Reportes*, 171–6. Heale's implication in the Cobham plot is suggested in the *Ashburnham Manuscripts*, H.M.C. 8th Rep. App. Pt. III (1881), 13–22. See also the original of the Wilbraham J. in Folger MS M.b. 22, f. 99.

[3] Hawarde, *Reportes*, 411. The Heale encounter was much more complex. The author wishes to thank Professor James Cockburn for his comments on the case, apropos his forthcoming article on Serjeant Heale.

[4] *A Declaration of the favourable dealing of her Maiesties commissioners* (1583), Hunt. RB 89493, sig. Aa. iii and f. 3, respectively.

[5] *Att-Gen. v. Pickering* (SC 14 May 1605), Hawarde, *Reportes*, 229.

and influence in the north-west borderlands and the Midlands, commanding the loyalty of a large coterie of relatives and agents in Parliament and the departments of state, and attracting the enthusiastic support of numerous academics, preachers, and literary writers, he was in a position to play a major role in the history of the early seventeenth century. According to one benefactor, Egerton had procured 'from the nurseries of learning and religion, fit workmen for the building of His temple, and He hath vouchsafed to make you one of those sacred Senators, which are the pillars of the kingdom'.[1] The country Chancellor, having acquired land, office, influence, and power, had come to believe this. He was blessed with an ability to grasp problems and get the job done; thus it is not surprising that he would leave an indelible mark on the reign of James I.

[1] John Shaw, 'The perill', Ellesm. MS 34/B/34, p. 1.

KINGSHIP AND THE PROBLEM OF SOVEREIGNTY

James Stuart's idea of Kingship – that it was indefeasible and held by hereditary divine right – posed a formidable problem to the administrators of Jacobean England, most of whom had been nurtured in the government of Queen Elizabeth. King James defined his prerogative to rule as absolute, and he believed that all institutions of government and law existed solely by his grace.[1] Even though he fully accepted the proposition of governing in partnership with the Privy Council, Parliament, and the courts of law, he spoke continually of his exalted role. This pontifical 'mystery of state' had roots deep in the ecclesiological substratum of medieval thought.[2] It had formed, moreover, an underlying assumption of political and constitutional thought down through the sixteenth century. But James's speeches on his idea of kingship brought the 'mystery' of state out into the public marketplace, and prompted the more self-seeking members of society to commend and advance it orally and in the press. This public exposition created a new literary tradition in the early years of his reign: the composition of satirical political poems and panegyric on the person and presence of the monarch.[3]

The speeches and writings of King James – and their influence on the spoken and written word – had small utility for the sober statesmen who staffed his government. Ellesmere, as Lord Chancellor, was an individual entrusted to recognise and to administer the powers of the Crown. In this respect Ellesmere's tract on the royal prerogative, together with his discourse on the history of kingship which was

[1] The best analysis of James's political ideas is still that of Charles Howard McIlwain in the introd. to his ed. of James, *Works*, pp. xv–lxxx.

[2] Ernest H. Kantorowicz, 'Mysteries of state: an absolutist concept and its late medieval origins', in his *Selected studies* (Princeton N.J. 1965), 381–98. The semi-divine regard for Tudor monarchs has been described succinctly in G. R. Elton's *The Tudor constitution* (Cambridge 1960), 12–20. For Jacobean times see the study of W. H. Greenleaf, *Order, empiricism and politics* (1964). An interesting analysis from a literary perspective is that of David G. Hale, *The body politic* (New York 1972).

[3] Ruth Nevo, *The dial of virtue* (Princeton N.J. 1963), 3–11, 20–1.

contained in the *Post-Nati*, comprise an interesting assessment of his conception and administration of the prerogative in early Stuart England.[1] The Chancellor was no philosopher. But in 1608 he had to rule on the status of the *post-nati* in Calvin's Case. Holding that Scotsmen born after the accession of the Scottish King to the English throne could inherit land in England, he believed that he had a major obligation to explain convincingly why allegiance was owed to the monarch as a natural man by all his subjects regardless of their place of birth.

The study of the royal prerogative in the sixteenth century had been based on the medieval concept of the king's two bodies. The monarch was regarded as possessing both a natural and a politic body. His politic body consisted of the incorporation of the monarch and his subjects, whereof he was the 'head' and his subjects the 'members'. His natural body was that part of him which mystically never died.[2] This concept of the King's two bodies in one person was widely held in England, and it was defined in the writings of prominent judges such as Edmund Plowden and Sir Edward Coke.[3] A few judges also reduced it to considerable examination. Sir Thomas Fleming, for example, equated the natural body (or capacity) of the sovereign with his absolute power, and the politic body with his ordinary power. Thus the monarch through his natural capacity ruled absolutely in a number of affairs (such as ecclesiastical and foreign policy), and through his political capacity governed in conjunction with the established institutions of State (as Parliament and the Privy Council).[4]

Chancellor Ellesmere believed in a concept of the King's single, natural body. Thus when the Chancellor delivered his opinion on the *Post-Nati* before the judges in the Exchequer Chamber in June 1608, he

---

[1] For the writings of historians on this general subject there are the very useful, and sometimes penetrating, studies of Francis D. Wormuth, *The royal prerogative, 1603–1649* (Ithaca N.Y. 1939); Margaret A. Judson, *The crisis of the constitution* (Rutgers N.J. 1949); and J. W. Gough, *Fundamental law in English constitutional history* (corr. ed. Oxford 1961).

[2] Ernest H. Kantorowicz, *The king's two bodies: a study in mediaeval political theology* (Cambridge 1957), 7–23.

[3] Plowden, *Commentaries*, ff. 212–3, 220, 238, 242, 261; and Coke in *Calvin's case*, 7 *Co. Rep.* 12r–v.

[4] Chief Baron Fleming in *The Case of Impositions* (1606), *State Trials*, II, 387–94. A lawyer's attempt to list the prerogs. in this manner, specifying what the King could and could not do, is in 'Prerogatives of the King', Harl. MS 1323, ff. 210–5 (*c.* 1613–15). A general discussion of the contemp. scene is Sir William Holdsworth's 'The prerogative in the sixteenth century', *Columbia Law Rev.* 21 (1921), 554–71; and Wormuth, *Royal Prerog.* 1–98.

assumed that all the rights and privileges of the English people had evolved from the natural bodies of their monarchs.[1] The Chancellor's assumption was in sharp contrast to that of the counsel for the plaintiff and the two chief justices who had preceded him, all of whom had discussed explicitly the concept of the two, quite different, capacities of the King.[2] While Ellesmere did not state his objection to their position in his public speech, he did so in his notes, where he penned a definition from Pliny's dictionary for those men who believed in the theory of the King's two bodies: 'Amphisbena – a serpent having a head at each end, both striving to be the master head.'[3] The Chancellor's interest in the contemporary debate, together with its practical ramifications, now caused him to take an additional step. His rough tract or memorandum on the royal prerogative that he composed in 1608–9 represents the attempt of an administrator to reconcile the concept of a single, natural body of state with the elements of government which he administered daily.

The growth of the Tudor State in the sixteenth century had created the paradox of a strong monarchy, a proliferation of national, regional, and local institutions and bureaucracies, and a broad range of parliamentary legislation. These developments had encouraged the newly enriched aristocracy, which now numbered the Chancellor among its members, to devote more of their work and interest to the governing process. Ellesmere brought a practical mind to this task. Hardened by meeting life's challenges successfully, converted to Calvinism, and educated in the new methodology, he did not hesitate to come to terms with complex and controversial subjects. Although his conclusions were practical rather than philosophical, he did manage to reconcile the problem of an undivided allegiance in the political and constitutional thought of the period.[4]

---

[1] *Post-Nati*, 73–5 and *passim*. He denied the double-body theory explicitly in his criticisms of the issues in this case – Ellesm. MS 1215, f. 2r. The author wishes to thank Professor William Dunham for discussing Ellesmere's concept of the prerog. and other ideas from the *Post-Nati*.

[2] Bacon, in *State Trials* II, 597–8; Coke in 7 *Co. Rep.* 12r–v and Fleming in Hawarde, *Reportes*, 361–3.

[3] Quoting Pliny's *Natura Historica* in Ellesm. MS 1215, f. 3v.

[4] The problem and numerous related ones were set out in the discussions on *Calvin's Case*, particularly the famous dialogue on 'Certein errors uppon the statute made 25 E. 3'; two of the fuller versions from among the many extant copies are B. M. Sloane MS 2716, ff. 1–37v, and Hale MS 80, ff. 150–71. Ellesmere's position was similar to the one which became ascribed to Serjeant Browne. The standard opinion that Ellesmere was merely a follower of the King's view is summarised by W. J. Jones, 'Ellesmere and Politics, 1603–17', in *Early Stuart studies*, ed. Howard S. Reinmuth (Minneapolis Minn. 1970), 30–3.

All prerogatives, according to Ellesmere, stemmed from one incontrovertible source: the natural body of the sovereign. They could be broken down, however, into two aspects. First, 'the absolute prerogative which is in Kings according to their private will and judgment'; and second, 'that absolute prerogative which according to the King's pleasure [is] revealed by his laws'.[1] Since all government had its roots in the sovereign's absolute prerogative, this prerogative must be composed of personal privileges that stemmed from the body of the monarch, and legal ones that stemmed from the laws of the State.

The King's personal privileges were based on his general power to rule in the manner of his predecessors. Such privileges were derived from the private will and judgment that the monarch possessed as a substitute of God on earth. The wisdom, power, and gifts which God gave to the monarch enabled him to become the father of his people and the head of their commonwealth. These particular attributes were part of the 'person' of the King. They were aspects which he could not delegate to other men.[2] Ellesmere's more extensive views on this first aspect of the King's prerogative were nourished by his earlier acquaintance with the historical studies of Continental legal humanists, and his ideas can be understood when they are placed within the context of those studies.[3]

The origins of an historical approach to the law can be found in the work of European jurists, which dates from the late fifteenth century. Scholars such as André Alciat, Ulrich Zasius, and Guillaume Budé first brought a humanistic knowledge of grammar and philology to the study of the civil law.[4] They used these two disciplines to purge the civil law manuscripts of their medieval corruptions, and then to study them within their original historical context. A second generation of legal humanists developed in the 1540s and 1550s to create from these reconstructed texts a new science of law. Influenced by the

---

[1] 'Prerog.' ff. 1–3v. This distinction may seem to be a 'fine' one by historians, but it is crucial for political philosophy. The author wishes to thank Professor Anthony Parel for helping to clarify these distinctions.

[2] This position was established decisively in his marginal notes, which criticised severely an anon. tract on the subject: Ellesm. MS 1215, ff. 1–3v.

[3] The most accessible studies of legal humanism are by Pierre Mesnard, *L'essor de la philosophie politique au XVIe siècle* (2nd ed. Paris 1951); Myron P. Gilmore, *Humanists and jurists* (Cambridge Mass. 1963); Julian H. Franklin, *Jean Bodin and the sixteenth-century revolution in the methodology of law and history* (New York 1963); and Donald R. Kelley, *Foundations of modern historical scholarship* (1970).

[4] For Alciat, *Dictionnaire de biographie française*, I, 1330–3; for Zasius, *Allgemeine deutsche Biographie*, XLIV, 708–15; and for Budé, *Nouvelle biographie generale*, VII, 718–26. Their roles and context have been assessed by Kelley, *Foundations*, Chap. II.

methodological revolution that was characterised by Ramism, jurists such as Hugues Doneau and François Duaren attempted to explain the history of the law, and to reconstruct a new legal system that would reflect more thoroughly the needs and demands of Continental states and societies in the sixteenth century.[1] Their successors – Jacques Cujas, François Baudouin, François Hotman, and Jean Bodin – produced the scholarly legal work which marked the historiographical revolution of sixteenth-century Europe.[2]

Although most English historians have ignored any serious consideration of the legal humanists of the Continent,[3] the Englishmen of the sixteenth century did not. Young Elizabethan scholars such as William Lambarde, Francis Thynne, Robert Bowyer, Robert Cotton, John Spelman, Henry Finch, and John Dodderidge, knowledgeable in the philological, legal, and historical studies of Continental jurists, began to apply that expertise to an examination of the origins and development of their own native laws and institutions.[4] Ellesmere read the work of several legal humanists and became part of this new tradition which came to influence English legal thought so decisively in the late sixteenth and seventeenth centuries.[5] Like his contemporary, Bodin, he criticised the wasteful occupation of past writers, and used a critical understanding of historical and legal evidence to discover the foundations of his State and the historical changes which had brought about its present constitution.[6]

[1] Neither of these individuals has received much attention from modern historians apart from Kelley's general comments. For Duaren, Nouv. biog. gen. XIV, 669–71; and for Doneau, Nieuw nederlandsch biografisch woordenboels, I, 729–33.

[2] A useful analysis of Cujas is that of Pierre Mesnard, 'La place de Cujas dans la querelle de l'humanisme juridique', Revue historique de droit français et étranger, 4th ser. 28 (1950), 521–37. For Baudouin, Biographie nationale de Belgique, I, 842–7; for Hotman, Nouv. biog. gen. XXV, 225–34; and for Bodin, Pierre Mesnard, 'Jean Bodin à Toulouse', Bibliothèque d'humanisme et renaissance 12 (1950), 31–59; Franklin, Bodin and method; and Kelley, Foundations, Chap. IV.

[3] J. G. A. Pocock, The ancient constitution and the feudal law (Cambridge 1957), Chaps. I–III; and to a lesser extent, F. Smith Fussner, The historical revolution 1580–1640 (1962), 26–32.

[4] Louis A. Knafla 'Humanism and the common law renaissance', Humanities Assoc. Rev. 28 (1977).

[5] Among the notes from his law school days are some on Guillaume Budé and Hugues Doneau: Ellesm. MS 482, loose leaf f. 1 and f. 146. The law books which he acquired at that time, esp. his Fitzherbert, Natura Brevium, Hunt. RB 59688, and his Littleton, Tenures, Hunt. RB 62234 and 62239, contain random notes on such matters.

[6] Bodin in Method for the easy comprehension of history, trans. Beatrice Reynolds (New York 1945), the 'Preface'; and Ellesmere in the Post-Nati, 60–2. Ellesmere cited Bodon on legal problems in his 'Brief Chanc.', and Ellesm. MS 465. He had purchased a copy of Hotman's De Furoribus Gallicis (1573), Hunt. RB 59775.

Ellesmere's views on the personal privileges of the monarch were derived generally from the historical studies of the *feudum* by the French scholars Charles Dumoulin, Cujas, and Hotman, and more specifically from the Scots Adam Blackwood and Thomas Craig.[1] His manuscript notations indicate that he dated the English constitution from the Norman Conquest, when King William I had introduced feudal tenures into England.[2] The Chancellor believed, for example, that the English common law developed from the customs which grew out of the adjudication of cases involving feudal tenures. Therefore, he resolved that the King – in creating feudal tenures and in appointing judges to sit in his place – was initially responsible for giving laws to his people.[3] He buttressed the argument by making a collection 'From Ye Register' of laws and customs which had evolved from the Norman period.[4] Ellesmere, in holding to this conception of the origins of the English constitution in the personal privileges of the monarch, expressed a view of sovereignty that differed from many of his contemporaries.

English common lawyers, civil lawyers, and politicians tended to place sovereignty either in the customs and the law, or in the theoretical office of the monarch. Many common lawyers placed sovereignty in the common law, and the law over the King. These men defined the common law as immemorial custom, and believed that custom originated in the old folk moots of the Anglo-Saxon era, and became the common law of the central courts in the centuries of Norman and

---

[1] Useful discussions of these Continental and Scottish studies are those of Donald R. Kelley, '*De origine feudorum*: the beginnings of an historical problem', *Speculum* 39 (1964), 213–6; and Pocock, *Ancient const.* 70–123. The influence of such studies on English historical thought has been analysed by F. J. Levy, *Tudor historical thought* (San Marino Calif. 1967), 33–78, 202–11, 237–51; and Fussner, *Hist. revo.* 299–311. Ellesmere took notes from Blackwood in the Law French abridgement of his treatise on statutes (Ellesm. MS 496, cap. 2), and made extracts from Blackwood's works (Ellesm. MS 2538). He praised him fully in the *Post-Nati*, 43–5.

[2] In Ellesmere's other copy of Littleton's *Tenures* (25th Law Fr. ed. 1557), Hunt. RB 62234, front fly leaf 3r; and in his notes for *Calvin's Case* dated 4 June 1608: Ellesm. MS 1872, f. 3r.

[3] This is resolved in both the 'Prerog.', ff. 2v–3v, and the *Post-Nati*, 105–8. He emphasised the feudal tenures as a foundation of the royal prerog. in speeches to the House of Lords: *Parl. 1610*, I, 42–3, 202. The radical extension of this view, that the laws and institutions of the Normans introduced authoritarianism and a despotic ruling class, is assessed by Christopher Hill, 'The Norman yoke', *Puritanism and revolution* (1958), 50–122, esp. 50–70.

[4] 'Of the Antiquity of the Register', Ellesm. MS 1164; the quotation in his endorsement. The ms. was prepared perhaps by William Lambarde: see the *Archeion*, 108–17.

Angevin rule.[1] However, a number of civilians and politicians conceived of a monarch who was totally absolute, dispensing a natural or
divine law to his subjects. Men such as these exalted the undivided
power and sovereignty of the King.[2] The two general interpretations
have been referred to frequently as the dominant conceptions of the
royal prerogative in the early seventeenth century. However, such an
examination of legal records and manuscript treatises suggests that a
moderate view may have been the more accepted one.

Authors such as William Camden and Sir John Dodderidge wrote
treatises on the royal prerogative which accommodated a strong
monarchy with a mixed government. According to this interpretation,
prerogatives were rights accompanied with obligations.[3] Thus, although the King had certain inalienable rights, he also had a number
of obligations which he could not negate. This interpretation led other
writers to list what the King could, and could not do.[4] The position
that Chancellor Ellesmere took was to stand for monarchy by divine
right, but also to assume within the institution of monarchy a separation of the legal and personal aspects. This separation enabled him
to believe on the one hand in divine right monarchy and, on the other
hand, in the existence of the law of the land as a law unto itself in the
name of the King.[5] The outlines of Ellesmere's process of thought can
be seen in his treatise on Calvin's Case: the case of the *Post-Nati.*

[1] For ex. common lawyers such as Sir Edward Coke, 3 *Co. Rep.* 'Preface' (1602); Sir John
Davies, *Le Primer Report des Cases & Matters en ley resolves & adjudged en les Courts del Roy en
Ireland* (Dublin 1615), sigs. *2r–v, *4r–5r; Bulstrode Whitelock, Stowe MS 333, Chaps.
XIV–XVI; and the author of 'Omne Jus', Hale MS 80, ff. 42–50. The concept of an im-
memorial common law has been studied by J. G. A. Pocock, *Ancient Const.* 30–69. William
Dunham Jun. has placed it in the context of the royal prerog. in 'Regal power and the rule of
law: a Tudor paradox', *J. of Brit. Studies* 3 (1964), 24–56.
[2] Prominent exs. of civil lawyers were Cowell's *Interpreter, s.v.* 'Prerogative'; and Charles
Merbury, *A Briefe Discourse of Royall Monarchie* (1581), 1–5, 38–52. Philosophical treatises
which provided an explanation of this point of view included 'De Jure Maiestatis', Ellesm.
MS 1166, and 'A Treatise of the Praerogatiue', Rawl. MS D. 369, ff. 1v–9v. For privy
councillors including Bacon and the Howards see generally David Harris Willson, *The privy
councillors in the House of Commons 1603–1629* (Minneapolis Minn. 1940); and G. P. V. Akrigg,
Jacobean pageant (Cambridge Mass. 1962).
[3] 'William Camden's "Discourse concerning the Prerogative of the Crown"', ed. F. S.
Fussner, *Proceeds. of the Amer. Phil. Soc.* 101 (1957), 204–15; and Dodderidge's 'A breefe
Proiect', Harl. MS 5220, ff. 3–21.
[4] For ex. Thomas Ashe, *Le Second Volume Del Promptuarie* (1614), 223–30; William
Lambarde's *Archeion*, 108–22, 131–48; and the anon. 'Prerogatives of the King', Harl.
MS 1323, ff. 210–5. A major source was Staunford's colls. in his *Prerogative.*
[5] Ellesmere's concept, however, was regarded as 'too high' by some members in the H. of
C.: *Parl. 1610*, II, 156–7.

The Chancellor took great care in his opinion on the *Post-Nati* to list examples of the laws which English kings had given to their people from the reign of Henry II to that of Henry VI.[1] Ellesmere had come to view society not as a corporation, but as groups of people with differing customs and laws. What gave these people unity was their allegiance to the person of the sovereign. The Chancellor explained, for example, that the people of Normandy, Aquitaine, and Ireland had diverse customs and laws which were given to them by different monarchs at different times, and that they had become subject to the same sovereign and capable of all the rights allowed to his denizens.[2] He also pointed out that within England the people of Wales, the County palatine of Chester, Kent, and the islands of Guernsey and Jersey had derived their customs and laws in the same manner, and had acquired similar rights.[3] It was within this context that Ellesmere in the *Post-Nati* defended the right of the Scot Robert Calvin to hold land in England as a subject of King James of Scotland; that the pronouncement of laws was a personal, God-given right of monarchs, and as kingship was a personal rather than a public office, that King James of Scotland was no more nor less a sovereign than King James of England.[4]

Ellesmere's views on the personal privileges of the King were similar to those of Bodin. Both believed that the royal prerogative was composed of rights belonging to the monarch as well as rights embodied in the laws of the State. Both considered the giving of new customs and laws as part of the personal privileges of the monarch. Where Ellesmere differed from Bodin was in his conception of sovereignty and the royal prerogative in the English experience. Sovereignty, for Bodin, represented the corporate power of the republic and was vested in the public office of the monarch. For Ellesmere, sovereignty represented the allegiance owed by communities who formed a society or commonwealth, and was vested in the private person of the monarch. In this respect the Chancellor did not imitate Bodin's concept of sovereignty like many other English

---

[1] *Post-Nati*, 31–46, 67–77. Numerous tracts on this subject were written in 1604 at the outset of the proposals for union. Some have been coll. in SP 14/7/40–1, 63–71, 80.

[2] *Post-Nati*, 18–23, 47–58, 64–76. He compiled a list of such customs and laws in his coll. of proceedings on the union: L. I. Maynard MS 83, the two loose leaves between ff. 6–7.

[3] *Post-Nati*, 79–81.

[4] *Ibid.* 4–7, 117–8.

writers who studied and made use of his ideas.[1] While Ellesmere envisaged the royal prerogative in part as privileges personal to the body of the King, he also made a significant provision for the delegation of the sovereign's legal privileges to those men who were entrusted to administer them.

The second aspect of the King's prerogative consisted of those legal privileges which were contained in the laws of the State. Ellesmere conceived of the law as an essential part, and expression of the absolute prerogatives of the monarch. He described the laws in effect as positive law: law that was made in written form by the King (proclamations), the King in Council (acts and letters), the King in Parliament (statutes), and the King's judges of the courts of law.[2] The monarch was personally involved in the making of all positive law except for the decisions of the judges. Ellesmere, believing that the monarch was personally involved in the making of all law, thus stated that the judges held their offices in place of the sovereign; that the judges were empowered by the King to execute his legal privileges in the courts of law.[3] This point of view determined his attitude towards judicial interpretation.

The role of judges and law officers was to adhere strictly to the positive law. For example, an officer who concealed offences against the positive law violated the trust reposed in him by the monarch for whom he acted. So too did a common law judge who administered more, or less, than the strict letter of the law. Ellesmere objected strongly to such actions, and reasoned that men who went beyond the letter of the law would 'rather desire to be kings than to rule the people

[1] Bodin's chief disciples in England were Charles Merbury (his *Briefe Discourse*); Sir John Hayward in *An Answer to the First Part of a Certaine Conference Concerning Succession* (1603); and Edward Forsett in a *Comparative Discourse of the Bodies Natural and Politique* (1606).

[2] Ellesmere discussed how unwritten law had devolved to written law in the *Post-Nati*, 31–58. For a different view see the address of the Speaker of the Commons on 7 July 1604 in *Parl. Hist.* 1046–50; and Coke in *The Case of Proclamations* (1611), *State Trials* II, 725–6. The general definition was discussed by Henry Finch, *Nomotechnia* (1613), *s.v.* '*Cestascavoir*'. The origins of the doctrine have been studied by S. B. Chrimes, *English constitutional ideas in the fifteenth century* (Cambridge 1936); 197–207; and John Dykstra Eusden, *Puritans, lawyers, and politics in early seventeenth-century England* (New Haven Conn. 1958), 114–26.

[3] 'Prerog.', ff. 1–2v. A number of precedents for procedures concerning offences against the legal privileges of the King were coll. for Ellesmere by George Carew: Ellesm, MS 446. The Chancellor had stated this concept earlier in the SC – Hawarde, *Reportes*, 100 (1598), 164 (1603).

under him, who will not administrate justice by law but by their own wills'.[1] The Chancellor's strong belief in a judiciary that would interpret the law strictly was illustrated by the manner in which he composed instructions for drafting proclamations and statutes.[2] Not even courts of equity were exempted from this responsibility. Hence his commitment to hasten the development of the Court of Chancery to a court whose adjudication was based on equitable principles drafted into rules of law.[3]

Ellesmere's interest in the role of judges and officers in administering the law grew out of his study of the controversy over the possession of the *merum imperium* (full power, or sovereignty) in Western Continental countries.[4] The question of who possessed full power, and the extent to which judges or magistrates held or exercised that power, was a crucial factor in the growth of the national State. The central position in Continental thought was that the King alone possessed the *merum imperium*, an interpretation that grew out of the work of Alciat and Dumoulin. The dissenting position on the Continent was based on the premise that the power was possessed by the judges themselves. There were, however, two schools of thought on the manner in which the judges held the *merum imperium*. According to Bodin and Charles Loyseau, the judges exercised the power of their public office as a public right, but Johannes Althusius and Hugo Grotius believed that judges held office by means of their private right.[5]

A number of English jurists were interested in the question of the *merum imperium*, and there were two conflicting interpretations. According to Dr John Cowell it was possessed by the King, and the duty of the office-holder was to sit and to act in his place.[6] Sir Henry

---

[1] 'Prerog.', ff. 4r–6v; the quote at f. 5r. He referred to Bodin's views on this subject in Ellesm. MS 465.

[2] For ex. his suggestions to Lord Keeper Puckering in a letter of 17 Jan. 1593/4: Harl. MS 6996, f. 58.

[3] This is a theme of his 'Brief Chanc.', and his work as Chanc. in the reign of James (*infra* Chap. VII).

[4] Ellesmere cited Bodin on the problem of the *merum imperium* in the preface to his 'Brief Chanc.' f. 1r. The controversy in France is discussed by William Church, *Constitutional thought in sixteenth-century France* (Cambridge Mass. 1941); and in Spain by Bernice Hamilton, *Political thought in sixteenth-century Spain* (Oxford 1963). For England see J. H. Salmon, *The French religious wars in English political thought* (Oxford 1959).

[5] The most lucid analysis of the various interps. is that of Myron Gilmore, *Argument from Roman law in political thought 1200–1600* (Cambridge Mass. 1941), 48–71, 93–126. See also Ralph Giesey, *The juristic basis of dynastic right to the French throne* (Philadelphia 1961), 30–7.

[6] Cowell, *Interpreter*, *s.v.* 'Office (*Officium*)'. The entry here, however, is confusing. See the extensive discussion *s.v.* 'Praerogative of the King'.

Finch, however, declared that sovereignty was vested in the holder of the office, and that the occupant had a public right to exercise the office as he deemed appropriate.[1] Ellesmere adopted an intermediate position on this issue.[2] He believed with Cowell and Bodin that the King alone possessed the *merum imperium*. But he also believed that the monarch had delegated the exercise of that right to his judges. Thus they were obliged to adhere strictly to the positive law. 'That judges be appointed who know the law, and that they be limited to govern according to the law, is a thing of necessity and of extraordinary care'.[3]

The legal privileges of the King placed important limitations on all office-holders, limitations that were designed to protect the people in their full enjoyment of the positive laws of the commonwealth. The purpose of monarchy was to guarantee through the royal prerogative the expression of the private prerogatives of the people, and to ensure that the institutions of law and government did not encroach upon them. Thus Ellesmere declared in the *Post-Nati* that there was no greater bond between the monarch and his people than the right of citizens to have recourse to their sovereign against the wrongs committed by other persons or institutions, whether committed in a private or a public capacity. Their recourse was the King's laws. The laws protected the rights of the people and preserved the unity of the commonwealth.[4]

The Chancellor also believed, however, that the legal privileges of the King were binding upon the monarch himself: that the sovereign was charged to observe the laws which he and his predecessors had created. In this respect the institutions of government – in which the monarch was the foremost member – had acquired obligations for which they, and he, had become responsible.[5] The Chancellor later emphasised this side of the King's absolute prerogatives when he became frustrated with James's policies in governing the

---

[1] Finch, *Law*, 162–4. He makes the qualification at the beginning that the man must be competent or the grant of the office is void.

[2] *Post-Nati*, 48–66, 72–105.

[3] He made these points in the 'Prerog.', ff. 1–2r, 5r–6v, and the quote at f. 9v. The quotation is a paraphrase of one of James's speeches which Ellesmere noted and bracketed in his own copy: *The Kings Majesties Speech* (1603), Hunt. RB 61876, sig. 4v.

[4] 'Prerog.', ff. 7r–8v.

[5] Ellesmere's position on this important limitation of the Crown was quite similar to that of George Buchanan: *De Jure Regni apud Scotos*, ed. Charles Flinn Arrowwood (Austin Texas 1949), Chap. 27. See as well John Ponet, *A Shorte Treatise of Politike power* (1556), sig. cvii verso. Later, Puritan writers would find refuge and recourse in 'the highways of God and King' – the courts of law: Eusden, *Puritans and lawyers*, 121–6.

State. In addressing the House of Lords in 1614 he turned around nicely the legal privileges of the monarch in declaring that 'the King hath no prerogative but that which is warranted by law and the law hath given him'.[1]

Ellesmere's idea of the personal and legal aspects of the royal prerogative provided a firm theoretical foundation for the unity of British society. Sovereignty was vested in the 'person' of the sovereign. 'The Crown is but an ensign of sovereignty'.[2] Ellesmere's most eloquent plea for his views on the royal prerogative grew out of his desire to maintain the unity of British society under the law, and he made it in speaking before the judges and councillors on behalf of Anglo-Scots Union:

This bond of allegiance whereof we dispute, is *Vinculum fidei*; it bindeth the soul and conscience of every subject, severally and respectively to be faithful and obedient to the King: And as a soul or conscience cannot be framed by policy; so faith and allegiance cannot be framed by policy, nor put into a politic body. An oath must be sworn by a natural body; homage and fealty must be done by a natural body, a politic body cannot do it.

Now then, since there is but one King, and sovereign to whom this faith and allegiance is due by all his subjects of England and Scotland, can any human policy divide this one King, and make him two Kings? . . . Nay shortly, can any man be a true subject to King James as King of England, and a traitor or rebel to King James as King of Scotland? Shall a foot breadth, or an inch breadth of ground make a difference of birth-right of subjects born under one King? . . .

As the King nor his heart cannot be divided, for he is one entire King over all his subjects, in which soever of his Kingdoms or dominions they were born, so he must not be served nor obeyed by halves; he must have entire and perfect obedience of his subjects . . . Divide a man's heart, and you lose both parts of it, and make no heart at all; so he that is not an entire subject but half faced, is no subject at all; and he that is born an entire and perfect subject, ought by reason and law to have all the freedoms, privileges, and benefits pertaining to his birth-right in all the King's dominions.[3]

---

[1] H.M.C. *Hastings MSS* IV, 263. A few years earlier he would have emphasised that for matters of 'state' the King could still in law bind his people: Hawarde, *Reportes*, 329 (SC Mich. 1607).

[2] *Post-Nati*, 73.

[3] *Ibid.* 101–3. He later summarised this view in a speech to the Lords: *Parl. 1610* I, 64.

LORDS AND COMMONS

The problem of James and his Parliaments has been one of the most frequently discussed topics in the history of his reign. The initial Parliament of the first Stuart has been seen by most historians as heralding the rise of the House of Commons to political maturity, the seizing of the legislative initiative from an inept King, and the auspicious beginnings of a 'struggle for sovereignty' which culminated in the Long Parliament and the Civil Wars of the 1640s.[1] This view has not always been fully subscribed to by historians of the period, and recently it has been challenged.[2] Nonetheless, regardless of the roles which scholars have attributed to the Parliament of 1604–10, its importance in the political history of the age cannot be denied.[3] Ellesmere's tract on this Parliament, composed shortly after its dissolution, is, when placed in the context of his other papers, an important document for the study of Crown and Parliament in the first decade of James's reign.

The first session of the Parliament of 1604 assembled in the spring. Requests by the King for a subsidy, a revision of the laws, and an Anglo-Scots union were placed aside in the House of Commons for a discussion of the grievances that had been smouldering in late Elizabethan England. These included royal interference with the

[1] This is the thesis that has been established by the studies of Wallace Notestein, 'The winning of the initiative by the House of Commons', *Proceeds of the Brit. Acad.* (1924), 3–51; David Harris Willson, *The privy councillors in the House of Commons 1604–1629* (Minneapolis Minn. 1940); and William M. Mitchell, *The rise of the revolutionary party in the English House of Commons, 1603–1629* (New York 1957). The quotation is the title of the book of George L. Mosse (East Lansing Mich. 1950).

[2] G. R. Elton, 'A high road to civil war?', *From the Renaissance to the Counter-Reformation*, ed. Charles H. Carter (New York 1965), 325–47; George Donaldson, *Scotland: James V to James VII* (Edinburgh 1965), 183–237; Charles H. Carter, *The secret diplomacy of the Hapsburgs, 1598–1625* (New York 1964), 109–19; and J. S. Roskill, 'Perspectives in English parliamentary history', *Historical studies of the English Parliament, 1399–1603*, ed. E. B. Fyrde and Edward Miller (Cambridge 1970), II, 296–323.

[3] Wallace Notestein, *The House of Commons 1604–1610* (New Haven Conn. 1971). See also the still useful commentary of Gardiner, *Hist.* I, 160–95, 285–99, 324–40, 348–54; II, 63–87, 105–11.

privileges of members of Parliament, corruption in wardship, purveyance, and monopolies, the dispensation of penal statutes, abuses in ecclesiastical courts, and festering social and economic problems. The refusal of King James and his chief minister, Robert Cecil, to recognise and discuss these quarrelsome, knotty questions, enabled a growing Elizabethan opposition led by Sir Edwin Sandys to turn the Commons once again into a house for the open debate of grievances. James's initial pronouncement 'that this Parliament was not like to be long' was to become one of the understatements of the decade.[1]

The second and third sessions of the Parliament extended from the autumn of 1605 to the summer of 1607. The second session became obsessed with grievances. Members of the Commons debated, in addition to the many questions which dominated the proceedings of the first session, law reform, debtors and the courts, and the fiscal problems of the Crown. Moreover, they began to sit increasingly as a committee of the whole house to determine the course of its business. The third session was devoted to the King's attempt to enact an Anglo-Scots union. In opening this session the Lord Chancellor had warned the members of the 'diversity of spirits' in the House that fed on private gain, and appeared destined to sow disruption in Church and State. The project of union was introduced as a measure to bring together the constructive forces in the country. Unfortunately, the Crown's pursuit of this project was hindered by the lack of an effective working relationship with the Commons. Thus the failure of James to gain constructive progress for a union of England and Scotland by 1607 resulted in Parliament's suspension and a long prorogation.[2]

The fourth and fifth sessions sat from the winter of 1609 to the winter of 1610, and these sessions were highlighted by the debates and negotiations over the Great Contract of Cecil, now Earl of Salisbury. The project was designed to resolve the financial problems of the King by abolishing his feudal rights and profits for an annual parliamentary income. The proceedings over the Contract vacillated from delusions of consensus to failure. At one time James raised the

---

[1] *CJ*, 1, 139–247, the quote at p. 171. See Theodore K. Raab, 'Sir Edwin Sandys and the Parliament of 1604', *Amer. Hist. Rev.* 69 (1964), 646–70; and Notestein, *Commons 1604–10*, 55–140. The Chanc. assisted in drafting the opening procl. – *Eg. Papers*, 384–8; and Bacon, *Letters* III, 173.

[2] *CJ* I, 314–91, the quote at 314; and the *Bowyer Diary* and Notestein, *Commons 1604–10*, 141–254.

price of his request, a move that caused members of the Commons to doubt the wisdom of making the monarch financially independent. They reacted by lowering the price of their offer and declaring that the sovereign could not be trusted. At another time dissension arose from within the Privy Council over the professed wisdom of the Contract. Once the project became questionable within the circles of government an opposition group in the Commons devised a vigorous attack against the 'machinations' of Salisbury and the King that brought the negotiations to a collapse. The lower house saw to it that the monarch 'did not get what they did not want him to have'.[1]

The failure of the Great Contract, the domination of parliamentary deliberations by the Commons, and their attacks on royal ministers and favourites accounted for the King's further prorogation and final dissolution of Parliament on 9 February 1610/11. While James placed the burden of the failure on his chief minister, the Earl of Salisbury, other contemporaries attributed the failure either to the King, his Scots favourites, or to the members of the House of Commons themselves. Chancellor Ellesmere, in composing a tract on this Parliament, placed the blame for the lack of success on the blatant arrogance and pretentiousness of a group of radical members of Parliament who formed a 'rebellious corner in the right hand of the House'. He envisaged their quest for power as a threat to genuine reform, and to the balance and harmony of the Tudor constitution. He believed that the success of the State could be secured only with separate, and effective working relationships between the King and the Council, between the King, Lords, and Commons, and between the monarch and the various courts of law and departments of state.[2]

Ellesmere's observations on the Parliament of 1604–10 are best understood when they are placed within the structure of his legal thought. Parliament, according to Ellesmere, was the highest court of law in the land. Courts not only administered the positive law under the expansive umbrella of the King's absolute prerogative, but they also made law when the necessity arose. Parliament – the court that contained the body of the King and the representatives of the commonwealth – was regarded as the greatest and highest law-making entity. Thus when the judges came before the Court of Parliament to give their ruling on the *Post-Nati*, their decision had

---

[1] J. H. Hexter, *Reappraisals in history* (New York 1961), 137; and the full account in Notestein, *Commons 1604–10*, 255–434.

[2] 'Parl. 1604–10', particularly ff. 1v, 3v–5r, 7r–v.

the authority of a statute that had been engrossed on its rolls.[1] Ellesmere's concept of Parliament was firmly within the general outlines
of the late medieval notion of 'The High Court of Parliament', a
notion that was well regarded by contemporary legal writers.[2]

Although Parliament was depicted as the highest court in the land,
it was also subject to certain judicial limitations. For example,
Ellesmere, as Edmund Plowden and Robert Brooke, believed that
words were the mere images of statutes; that the life of a statute
rested in the minds of its makers.[3] As circumstances changed, the
words of a statute would require careful interpretation in order to
maintain the meaning of its makers. Parliament could of course correct, revise, and repeal its laws. But seldom did this unwieldy body
fulfil such obligations. Thus Ellesmere also believed (with Sir Henry
Hobart and Sir John Croke) that judges, in maintaining the concept
of positive law, were obliged to interpret the past acts of Parliament
in order to keep them relevant to the shifts of time. Placing the interpretation of statutes in the hands of the judges of the common law
and conciliar courts, Ellesmere made no doubt of Parliament's final
omnipotence. The other central courts could except, limit, or revise
statutes, but they could not repeal them. The latter task was the
exclusive responsibility of Parliament.[4]

The division of Parliament into three bodies, according to Ellesmere, represented the participation of the three estates of society in
the most weighty affairs of the commonwealth. His description of
these bodies was fully traditional.[5] The first estate was the King, who

[1] Ellesmere's general views on Parl. were expressed early in his career in the *Discourse*,
108–13, and repeated in the *Post-Nati*, 16–8. The significance he attached to the decisions of the
judges before Parl. is described fully in *ibid*. 18–25.

[2] The notion is ably discussed by Charles Howard McIlwain, *The High Court of Parliament
and its supremacy* (New Haven Conn. 1910), esp. 119–43, 229–36. For some representative
literature see Sir Thomas Smith, *De Republica Anglorum*, ed. L. Alston (Cambridge Mass. 1906),
Bk. II, Chaps. V–VIII; Lambarde, *Archeion*, 123–41; and Richard Crompton, *L'Authoritie
et Jurisdiction des Courts de la Maiestie de la Roygne* (1594), Chap. I.

[3] This was a theme of his earlier *Discourse* and his later 'Brief Chanc.' It is quite similar to
that of Plowden's *Commentaries*. The theme and its literature have been scrutinised by McIlwain,
High Court of Parl. 260–71; and Thorne, *Discourse*, 54–68.

[4] *Post-Nati*, 45, and 'Brief Chanc.' ff. 1r, 5v. His earlier views as to what judges should and
should not do were sketched fully in the *Discourse*, and those views provided the basis of his
later admonitions to judges in *Eg. on Coke, infra* Chap. XV.

[5] See for ex. an ed. of Aristotle's *Politics*, Bks. III–V. Two earlier writers who defined Parl.
similarly were Sir Thomas Elyot (*The Book Named the Governor*, Bk. I sect. 2), and William
Lambarde (*Archeion*, 244–5). A general analysis of this concept of mixed government is that of
Corinne Comstock Weston, *English constitutional theory and the House of Lords 1556–1832*
(1965), 9–22.

was the substitute of God in the British Isles and possessed the absolute prerogative. The second estate was the Lords, who were renowned for their honour and dignity. The third estate was the Commons, who were blessed with ancient privileges and liberties. Each estate required preservation. Together their deliberations made possible the success of the nation-state.[1]

The Lord Chancellor was quite explicit in stating his view of the political danger that confronted England in the early years of the seventeenth century. Adhering to Aristotelian strictures, he stated that the excessive power of the King could lead to tyranny, the excessive power of the Lords to aristocracy, and that of the Commons to democracy. Ellesmere belonged to that sixteenth-century school of thought which believed in the efficacy of mixed government under the leadership of a sovereign King.[2] The danger in England was that a group of men in the Commons was attempting to obtain an enlargement of the power of their House at the expense of the King and the Lords, an illustration that the threat of democracy 'hath grown big and audacious'.[3]

Thus the Chancellor in his later years became increasingly hostile towards the poorer people. This hostility was shown in his letters where he penned statements such as these: 'The blind folly of ye commoners of England, who have followed as captains in seditious rebellion and treason: smiths, cobblers, tailors, carters, tanners, . . . they care not whose the ground, or wood be that makes the fire. And for the future good of the common weal, it falls not in their thoughts.'[4] Ellesmere's preoccupation with the menace of democracy was again a traditional point of view that had been nourished for centuries by the noble class whose ranks he had entered recently.[5]

Ellesmere's concern with the state of the political scene was derived with little doubt from his awareness of England's problems in the later years of Elizabeth. Costly wars against the Catholics in Ireland and on the high seas, together with large bequests to royal

[1] 'Parl. 1604–10', f. 1r.

[2] The view expressed in his copy of R. B., 'Observations Politicall and Civill', Ellesm. MS 1174, ff. 1v-8r. The context is *supra*, Chap. II.

[3] 'Parl, 1604–10', f. 1r–v. But he attacked Aristotle's prejudices on the forms and constitutions of states in the *Post-Nati*, 105.

[4] Ellesm. MS 485 (c. 1605–10), f. 2v; and Ellesm. MS 234 (22 April 1612), f. 1r.

[5] Opinions such as these were not uncommon: see Christopher Hill, 'The many-headed monster in late Tudor and early Stuart political thinking', in Carter, *Ren. to Counter-Ref.* 296–324.

favourites and the price paid for not curbing corruption in the departments of state, had placed the Crown in a perilous economic condition. Moreover, discrimination arising from grants of monopoly, impositions, and purveyance, and an unprecedented rate of inflation, had tarnished the influence and reputation of the Crown.[1] Thus the first essential and inescapable political act of the new King was to call Parliament and hope to win a healthy subsidy. Parliament, however, had long ceased to be a body subservient to the interests of the Crown. Since a number of radical members of Parliament were poised to advance their political ambitions in the House of Commons, Parliament's success in meeting the needs of the new monarch would become a question of genuine concern.

James reacted to this situation with a measure of wisdom. On the one hand he broadened the political base of the Privy Council to make it more representative of the political groupings and regions of the island kingdoms; and on the other hand he developed a 'Working Council' composed of a few select ministers to make the formulation of policy and its administration more efficient. Thus the members of the Working Council who possessed influence and power in the countryside were now in a position to use it more effectively than in the past. They also represented another advance in that historical devolution of political power from the hands of the Crown to those of its ministers. The 'ministerial connection', consisting of a privy councillor's supporters in the Lords and Commons, and his patronees in the halls of government, became a more apparent part of the political reality of the early seventeenth century.[2] The Chancellor and the entourage he had created were now drawn into the vortex of a new pattern of political activity.

Ellesmere developed a significant ministerial connection from the basis of his land, influence, and patronage in the northern Welsh marches and the Midlands.[3] By 1610 almost every one of his estate agents had a position in a department of state.[4] In the Parliament of 1604–10 he had twelve proxies in the House of Lords and controlled eight seats in the Commons. Moreover, in the Parliament of 1614

---

[1] The best summary of England's condition in the first decade of the seventeenth century is that of John Cooper in the *New Cambridge modern history*, vol. IV, ed. J. P. Cooper (Cambridge 1970), 531–47.

[2] Louis A. Knafla, 'The Privy Council, Parliament, and Patterns of English politics, 1603–1621', unpub. paper.

[3] *Supra*, pp. 11–5, 24–7, 30, 30–5.

[4] Hasts. MSS, 'Parl.' box 1; *supra*, 8–14, 24–6, 33–5, 59–60; *infra* Chap. VII; and the Ellesm. MSS *passim*.

he extended his patronage of seats in the Commons to perhaps as many as seventeen.[1] The evidence also indicates that the Chancellor knew how to use the influence at his disposal. In the last Parliament of Elizabeth – when it appeared that the Queen would refuse to act on complaints against monopolies – it was the Lord Keeper's private secretary who breached the silence of the House in an attack on royal policy which eventually forced the Queen to admit that grievances might exist and redress be necessary.[2] Possessing influence such as this, the Lord Keeper made extensive plans in preparation for the Parliament of 1604. Despite apologies for infirmities and physical exhaustion, his considerable work in the Parliaments of 1604 and 1614 was stamped indelibly on their records.[3]

The Chancellor's personal hopes for the Parliament of 1604 were established in a collection of papers which were drafted in the spring as background materials for his address at the opening session. The plans were devoted entirely to that purpose which every member of the ruling class considered as the quintessential responsibility of Parliament: legislation.[4] Ellesmere outlined his assessment of the current state of the country and what had to be done. The structure of the Church and its institutions was secure, Parliament had become the theatre of good government, two British kingdoms had been united under one Crown, and for the first time in decades relations with foreign powers were notable for taking on a peaceful character. There were, however, major problems which required attention. These included the reform of abuses in government, the repeal or rewriting of statutes which had been found to be superfluous, imperfect, or insufficient, acts for local authorities and economic conditions, a

---

[1] Published work on his influence is slight. See the *De L'Isle and Dudley Manuscripts*, H.M.C. III, 142–3; and Lawrence Stone, 'The electoral influence of the second Earl of Salisbury', *EHR* 71 (1956), 388–9. Egerton and Norfolk had 12 proxies, Suffolk 13: *LJ* II, 263, 355, 449, 548, 666. Egerton had a search of proxies made from the reign of Henry VIII: 'A Booke of Proxies', Hasts. MSS, box 1 uncat.

[2] The speech of Downall in the debate on monopolies recorded by Sir John Neale, *Elizabeth I and her Parliaments 1584–1601* (New York 1958), 376–80. Ellesmere's similar views can be found in Ellesm. MS 2610.

[3] While the Chanc's only absences from the Lords for sickness were from 31 March to 7 April 1606, and 27–30 May 1610, he did complain a few times of his 'maladies': *Parl. 1610* I, 38–9, 41–2, 193–4. He worked on several joint committees for the two houses – in addition to those for union – beginning with the first session: *LJ*, II, 303, 309, 332, 367, 371, 399, 410–3, 485; and *Parl. 1610* I, 91, 210–1, 216, 218. His notes on their organisation are in Ellesm. MS 2614.

[4] The concept has been sketched by G. R. Elton, 'Tudor government: the points of contact, I. Parliament', *TRHS* 5th ser. 24 (1974), 183–200.

tightening of the law enforcement system with more vigilance to handle an increasing rate of crime, and the provision of funds for the King.[1]

The Chancellor also seemed to realise the problems which such a programme faced. The notes for his opening address warned against exacerbating the more radical members of Parliament, and stated the necessity of avoiding a conflict between Lords and Commons, and the Commons and the King.[2] In the address itself he referred obliquely to those problems when he warned the members to take concern of the preservation of the legislative process; to use 'godly care and wisdom to foresee, prevent, and provide for dangers, mischiefs, and inconveniences that may ensue. For if ye fail in any of these, you cannot discern truly, judge justly, nor direct your counsels aright.'[3] Perhaps he had in mind that anonymous tract on parliamentary procedure that was drafted to direct inexperienced members of the House of Commons in the skilful and subtle use of tactics in conducting an opposition against the Crown.[4]

Ellesmere's observations on the Parliament of 1604 were an analysis of the proceedings in the House of Commons, and of the relationship of those proceedings to legislation and the governing process. His thesis was that the lower house had become too self-centred, and concerned solely with the political advancement of its individual members. 'The causes of calling of the Parliament, which ought to have been first treated of, were neglected, and some men's private devices preferred.' They began at once to make 'secret and privy conventicles and conferences, wherein they devised and set down special plots for the carrying of business in the house according to their own humour and drifts.' Secondly, they shouted 'very audacious and contemptuous speeches against the King's regal prerogative and power, and his most gracious and happy government'.[5] It appeared that these members of the House sought to destroy the prerogatives of the King, the reputation of the government, the

---

[1] Ellesm. MSS 263, 443, 458, 2613, 35/C/36.

[2] Ellesm. MS 443, ff. 1r–2v.

[3] Ellesm. MS 458, f. 1r.

[4] Catherine Strateman Sims, "Policies in Parliaments," An early seventeenth-century tractate on House of Commons procedure', *HLQ* 15 (1951), 45–58.

[5] 'Parl. 1604–10', ff. 2r, 3v–5r, 6r–7v. Ellesmere complained to the Lords on the refusal of MPs to discuss matters openly in joint conferences: *LJ* II, 495–6. He often expressed his agitation over the failure of the Commons to discuss supply before grievances: *Parl. 1610* I, 13, 169–70, 179, 253.

authority of the courts of law, and the legislative function of Parliament itself.

The cause of the Chancellor's complaints stemmed from his own exertions to direct legislation through the House of Lords and the joint committees of the two houses. He had, for example, expanded the committee system of the Lords under his own chairmanship in order to facilitate the flow of bills from King, Commons, and joint conferences to the full House.[1] With respect to the joint conferences, he had participated in them frequently. He also tried to defend the privileges of the Commons in the debates of his own House.[2] Thus the collapse of the vacillating working relationship between the King's government and the Commons in the fourth and fifth sessions of this Parliament must have been disappointing to a man who had devoted his energies to its success.

The five subjects which Ellesmere regarded as forming the principal business of Parliament were ecclesiastical, economic, and legal reform, Anglo-Scots union, and taxation. His proposals on ecclesiastical matters were largely administrative. These included measures to restrict the entry of Catholic 'spies' into the country, the examination of recusants, and more effective laws and instructions for their detection, prosecution, and punishment.[3] The Chancellor had opened his parliamentary speech with an attack on 'the devilish doctrine of Rome'.[4] Thereafter, he often addressed Parliament, and the assembled lawyers and judges before the Star Chamber, on the need of the governing class to stamp out Roman Catholicism in Britain.[5] Several bills were passed and enacted on religion and the Church, and in-

[1] *Parl. 1610* II, 279–82, 307, 313, 336, 360, 396, 401, 409, 419, 471–3, 503, 519, 528, 587, 601, 611. The development of the committee system in the Lords has been studied by John Louis Beatty, 'Committee appointments in the House of Lords in early seventeenth-century England', *HLQ* 29 (1966), 117–26, esp. 118–21. For procedure, see Elizabeth Read Foster, 'Procedure in the House of Lords during the early Stuart period', *J. of Brit. Studies* 5 (1966), 56–73.

[2] *Parl. 1610* I, 91, 109, 154, 219: *LJ* II, 686–717. The interp. above is also based on the work of Elizabeth Foster, whom the author wishes to thank for discussing these matters with him. An opposite conclusion was reached by Professor Bill Jones, who held that Ellesmere was a sick, lame, and dull man who became more boring and less effective from the turn of the century: W. J. Jones, 'Ellesmere and Politics, 1603–17', in *Early Stuart studies*, ed. Howard S. Reinmuth (Minneapolis Minn. 1970), 11–16.

[3] G. B. Harrison, *A Jacobean journal 1603–1606* (1941), 209–10; Ellesm. MSS 2185–6, 2192; and Ellesm. MSS 2175–7, 7053 ed. by Anthony G. Petti, *Recusant documents from the Ellesmere Manuscripts*, Cath. Rec. Soc. 59 (1968), 145–56; respectively.

[4] Ellesm. MS 459, f. 1r.

[5] *LJ* II, 209–10; G. B. Harrison, *A second Jacobean journal 1607–1610* (1958), 33; and Hawarde, *Reportes*, 322–3, 326–7.

cluded statutes on canon law, ecclesiastical administration, religious observances, and new translation of the Scriptures.[1] Legislation such as this formed a positive note for the Parliament of 1604.

Economically, Ellesmere wanted the reformation of monopolies, impositions, purveyance, and the encouragement of 'local' industry and 'native' commerce.[2] His views on these subjects stemmed from his earlier mining and industrial activities in the northern Welsh marches, and his interest in employment opportunities in the environs of Chester.[3] But his specific proposals were vague; and they failed to constitute a tangible programme. Only later, with the assistance of Lionel Cranfield and others, would the Chancellor assist in directing a programme of economic reform.[4] He did, however, lend the customary support of the Speaker to a number of private bills for particular localities, and public bills of an agrarian and commercial nature, which fulfilled the plans of many individual members of Parliament who had come to serve the specific interests of their constituents.

Judicially, Ellesmere wanted an examination of all the statutes since the reign of Edward I in order to repeal those which were outdated, and to correct and perfect the others.[5] These suggestions were not dissimilar to the later ones which came from the pen of Francis Bacon. Although well sketched, they never advanced beyond the committee stage.[6] The Chancellor's concern for statutes was also revealed in his work in the Lords. He took the initiative in frustrating the passage of poorly drafted bills, and in criticising proposals which were ignorant of the substance of the law with which they were concerned.[7] In other judicial matters he continued his former practice of condemning corrupt lawyers and weak judges, and encouraging the strict application of the law to that world of vagrants, soldiers, sectarians, recusants, and plotters who roamed the countryside as a threat

---

[1] This and other legislation enacted by the Parl. of 1604 is best assessed from the *Stat. Realm*, IV, 1015–1206. The legislation was in fact significant, comprising 96 public acts and 132 private ones. A coll. of petitions for such legislation is in Add. MS 41.613, ff. 1–51, 214–29.

[2] Ellesm. MS 451, f. 1r.

[3] *Supra*, pp. 11–2, 23–5.

[4] *Infra*, Chap. IV.

[5] Ellesm. MS 451, f. 2r–v: 'Statutes to be Repealed', Ellesm. MS 2613; 'Statutes to be considered of', Ellesm. MS 263; and the 'Memorialles', Ellesm. MS 456, his method for re-examining statute law.

[6] Bacon, *Letters*, V, *passim*. His earlier views are stated in his 'Maxims', in *Works*, II, 319–87.

[7] *LJ* II, 279, 412, 565, 576; and Yale Univ. Lib. MS 1610, ff. 201v–3r.

to the established order.[1] It appeared, however, that his ideas on judicial reform were not taken seriously, or at least they were not given much urgency by the King and the Lord Treasurer, who decided on the agenda of business that was to come from the Crown. The Chancellor had been able to convince James to place law reform on the original agenda for Parliament, and several items had been debated in the Commons. But no more was achieved than this.[2] In fact, not even the King's own project for a union of England and Scotland proved to be successful.

Ellesmere was as convinced of the beauty and necessity of an Anglo-Scots union as King James himself, and a draft memorandum for his initial speech to Parliament illustrated his enthusiasm for this project of the King.[3] His reasons, however, were based on different grounds. For James the purpose of union was to enlarge his ultimate authority by consolidating in government and nation that which had been linked only in title.[4] Ellesmere tended to regard union with Scotland in the same light as previous union with Wales: a means to strengthen the regional character of the kingdom. But he also saw the advantages of consolidating the Calvinist forces in the Church, and the island people against future threats of foreign invasion.[5] He had, for example, lost his eldest son and heir, Thomas, in the struggle to defeat Catholicism and the Habsburg interests in Ireland, a struggle which was completed tentatively under General Mountjoy in 1605. A union with Scotland was now regarded as a further step in this direction.

Ellesmere worked hard on the project for a Scottish union. He headed personally the committee of Lords commissioners that met with members of the House of Commons, the joint committee of the two Houses, and the sub-committee in the Lords. The parliamentary

---

[1] Harrison, *Jac. J.* 186–7, 209–10, 281; *2nd Jac. J.* 33. Ellesmere often lumped these groups of people together. As he noted for a Parl. speech: 'Papists, no loyalty, Sectaries, no obedience. Outlaws, no duty but contempt'. Ellesm. MS 451, f. 2r.

[2] James' vague agenda in his *Works*, 270–80.

[3] Ellesm. MS 451, f. 1r-v.

[4] His inaugural speech in James, *Works*, 271–2; and Ellesmere's copy of the procl. – Hunt. RB 145923 (20 Oct. 1604), *ESTC* 8361. His grandchildren used it to draw pictures and practise mathematics. James's corresp. on the subject is in Harl. MS 7189, f. 2r–44v.

[5] George Owens, 'The union of England and Wales', trans. W. Llewelyn Williams, *CymRS* (1909), 47–117; and Folger MS M.b. 42, the 'Wilbraham J.', ff. 139–44. Relevant to this reasoning was his fear of Cath. countries (*supra*, 16–21), his Calvinism (*supra*, 51–6), and his concept of sovereignty (*supra*, Chap. II).

journals reveal his constant attention to the task.[1] No substantial progress, however, was made within the first two years. And by the winter of 1606/7 he was admonishing the members of the joint committee for their failure to work sincerely for the projected union. Despondency had set in.[2] The hearing of the case of Robert Calvin – on the right of a Scots *post-nati* to inherit land in England – came before the courts in 1607/8. Although Calvin and Scottish denizens won the right to inherit, the broader issue was one that had never gained sufficient support.

Thereafter, the Chancellor's active work in the Parliament of 1604 declined significantly in the fourth and fifth sessions, which met through the years 1609–10. He began to restrict his appearances to defending attacks from radical members of Parliament in the Commons on the courts of law. Certain members had refused to leave the House to testify or to be examined before the courts for legal causes in which they were involved. They also attempted to nullify the imprisonment of members by customary judicial processes. Opposition members sought to impeach the authority and jurisdiction of the ecclesiastical and provincial courts. Similarly, they disputed the courts of Star Chamber and Chancery (over which Ellesmere presided), which a number of members of Parliament had termed 'courts of arbitrary discretion'. Some of them even attempted to make the House into a court of original jurisdiction for causes heard before other courts of record.[3] The Chancellor had come to believe that he was witnessing a conspiracy of a group in the Commons against the government and the judiciary which composed a grave threat to the stability of the commonwealth.

The Parliament of 1604 concluded with the débâcle of the Great Contract in 1610. Although the Chancellor had attributed the failure of the King to reach an accommodation with Parliament to an opposition group in the Commons, he himself was never a supporter of the Lord Treasurer's Contract. Ellesmere did desire some

---

[1] Refs. to this committee work from 14 April 1604 to 14 March 1606/7 are in *LJ* II, 277, 287–8, 307, 413, 422, 475, 479, 483, 485, 488. His notes of headings discussed are in Ellesm. MS 1225. A schedule of several of the conferences with some of the Chanc's memoranda is in a small folio ms. entitled 'Touchinge Vnion', L. I. Maynard MS 83.

[2] See, for ex. *LJ* II, 475, 495–6.

[3] 'Parl. 1604–10', ff. 2r–3r, 5r–6v. Exs. of his speeches on the Commons' usurpation of the judicial powers of other courts are in *Parl. 1610* I, 68–9, 137–8. For complaints in the Commons against Ellesmere's judicial proceedings in Wales, see *ibid.* II, 7n, 354–5. He was, however, complimented for his integrity – *Jac. J.* 130.

form of agreement to resolve the monarch's financial problems; but privately he did not accept the terms of Salisbury's proposal.[1] He tried, for example, to avoid the Earl's attempt to have him, the Chancellor, present the speech that would have given thanks for the King's consent to discuss the Contract.[2] He also played a harassing role in Parliament.

Publicly, in speeches to the Lords, the Chancellor offered expert legal advice on the Commons' offer of an annual revenue, but revealed a negative attitude towards the sovereign's relinquishing his feudal rights and profits.[3] And in joint conferences with the Commons he was said to have taken a pessimistic view of the Contract's potential.[4] Ellesmere's distrust of the terms of the Contract was based partly on the importance he attributed to feudal tenures as an expression of the King's absolute prerogatives inseparable from the Crown, a position which had formed the basis of his concept of sovereignty.[5] His distrust was also based, however, on the very practical problem of convincing the monarch to begin to live within his means, and on the practical political problem of thwarting the influence of the Lord Treasurer, which had reached such large proportions. He had in fact been stranded in a middle position that lacked sufficient support in both the Privy Council and the House of Commons.

Although Ellesmere had been a reformer throughout his parliamentary career, he could not accept the growing radicalisation of particular members of Parliament. His peerage had come to insulate him from an awareness of the social and economic basis of a more

[1] The Chanc. had prepared notes on the Contract, and possessed a copy of a memo. supporting the Lord Treasurer's proposals and replying to criticisms of them: Ellesm. MS 1203, ff. 1–6.

[2] *Parl 1610* I, 38–9, 41–2, 193–4. Ellesmere's partial stand against the Contract may have been encouraged by Sir Julius Caesar's opposition. Caesar's role is analysed by Lamar Mott Hill, 'The public career of Sir Julius Caesar, 1584–1614' Ph.D. diss. (Univ. of London 1968), 378–84. Hill also believes that Caesar's opposition was planned with Salisbury, but no evidence has been offered to substantiate the Earl's complicity in the abolition of his project.

[3] *Parl. 1610* I, 199–204; and *ibid.* I, 57, 65, 77, 81, 115, 119. He was, however, willing to allow the King to give up impositions, concealments, and respite of homage – *Parl. 1610* I, 172. His involvement at the committee stage was noted in *ibid.* II, 550, 556, 564–5, 575–9, 671, 678.

[4] The unknown diarist, Yale Univ. Lib. Eng. Misc. MS 1610, f. 201r.

[5] The position was outlined in his speeches before the Lords: *Parl. 1610* I, 42–3, 64, 202, which in turn were based on his ideas in the 'Prerog.' ff. 1–2v. His hesitancy in advancing the disposal of feudal tenures was apparent in his address to the joint conference for the Contract on 14 Nov. 1610. Notes of this address are in the *Hastings MSS* IV, 224–6; and notes of its report to the Commons given in *Parliamentary debates in 1610*, ed. Samuel Rawson Gardiner (1861), 132–4.

intensive political opposition. Thus as a 'rising' lord he did not identi-
fy, as did the beleaguered Sir Walter Ralegh, the decline of the titled
aristocracy with the creation of a significant political vacuum in
which aspiring members of the Commons could press earnestly for
additional privileges.[1] Neither did he realise, as James Harrington did,
that the sharp economic and social development of the Commons
would cause them to demand political power equal to that of their
wealth and prestige.[2] Even though he himself had travelled this
tough path to success. Ellesmere did recognise, however, that the
current dilemma which fed the waters of conflict could not be resolved solely by constitutional means; that it required political
cunning and statesmanship: 'It is time for wise and skilful pilots to
provide for it, and as may be, to withstand and prevent it'.[3]

The second Parliament of James was summoned in the spring of
1614, and marked the Chancellor's return to a major public role in
parliamentary politics. The failure of the Great Contract in 1610
and the death of Salisbury in 1612 had contributed to the reappear-
ance of factional politics based on patronage, ministerial connections,
and the definition of national interests.[4] The conservative faction,
associated with the Howards, had seized the initiative in making royal
policy by Salisbury's death. Their policies were peace abroad,
Catholic toleration, and a minimum of government interference in the
life of the nation. But they also stood for conciliar rather than parliamentary government. The continued lavish expenditures of James
together with mounting royal debts necessitated the King's call for
supply in 1614. Although the conservative faction was not sufficiently
powerful to stop the calling of Parliament, they were clever enough
to nullify any potential success. They set London buzzing with
rumours of widespread interference in elections. Once this interference with elections and parliamentary privilege was debated in
the lower house together with the questions of wardship, monopolies,
impositions, ecclesiastical abuses, and corruption, an almost ir-

---

[1] Walter Ralegh, *The prerogative of Parliaments in England, proved in a dialogue*, in
Harl. Misc. 5 (1813), 192–208.

[2] James Harrington, *The Art of Law-giving* (1659), in *The Oceana of James Harrington and His
Other Works*, ed. John Toland (1771), 390–2.

[3] 'Parl. 1604–10', f. IV. For a discussion of the limitations of constitutional means to
resolve such a dilemma see W. R. Anson, *Law and custom of the constitution* (Oxford 1886), I,
35.

[4] Knafla, 'The Privy Council, Parliament, and English politics, c. 1582–1621', forthcoming
in the *Canadian Journal of History*. The author has introduced the terms 'conservative' for the
pro-Spanish councillors, and 'reformers' for the anti-Spanish.

reconcilable breach appeared between King and Commons. The Addled Parliament of 1614 – convened on April 5 and dissolved on July 7 – had not granted any subsidies, remedied any grievances, or passed any bills.[1]

The parliamentary work of Ellesmere in 1614 identified him as a leader of a new group of moderate reformers. Despite his disgust over the actions of a number of members of Parliament in the last sessions of the previous Parliament, he had maintained his faith in the necessity of parliamentary government. The Chancellor, together with the Archbishop of Canterbury and the Earl of Pembroke, became primarily responsible for convincing the King to call a Parliament in 1614 and to reach a political accommodation with the House of Commons. He also extended his influence in an attempt to contribute to its success. Thus he took few proxies from among his colleagues in the Lords, and devoted his energies to securing the election of favourable men to the Commons.[2] Again, as in James's first Parliament, the Chancellor busied himself in committees of the Lords and joint conferences of the two Houses, and inaugurated the move to reform by committing himself to resolve the dispute over impositions.[3] This was to no avail, as the work of the Howard faction had poisoned the grounds for agreement. However, when James called for the dissolution of Parliament, Ellesmere went so far as to refuse to issue the commission to dissolve the assembly until he could attempt a last-ditch manoeuvre to obtain a compromise.[4]

The Chancellor's final effort at political negotiation was clothed in disappointment, and this time he condemned his colleagues in the Lords (especially the followers of the Howards) for the failure. When attendance in the House was sparse he openly criticised the more lethargic peers for their lack of interest in the crucial questions of state.[5] Moreover, he attempted to humiliate them with accusations of lack of skill and weakness in debate: 'If your Lordships do not look

[1] *CJ* I, 455–506. A complete study of the Parl. is that of Thomas Moir, *The Addled Parliament of 1614* (Oxford 1958). His assessment of the factions is at pp. 24–6, 64–6, 163–9. A full account of why the Howards did not want Parl. to convene – because they were robbing the King of revenue and fearful of parl. investigations – is presented by Anthony F. Upton, *Sir Arthur Ingram c. 1565–1642* (Oxford 1961), 53–82.

[2] Knafla, 'New model lawyer: the career of Sir Thomas Egerton' Ph.D. diss. (Univ. of Calif. 1965), 168–80, 187.

[3] *LJ* II, 686–717; *Hastings MSS* IV, 257–64; and Ellesm. MS 2607.

[4] The technicalities are discussed by Moir, *Addled Parl.* 143–5. See as well Ellesmere's speech to the Lords: *Hastings MSS* IV, 180–3 (6 June 1614).

[5] *LJ*. II, 401, 420, 468–9, 579 for exs. since 1607.

well unto your privileges you will lose them, for as the lower House
are strict in the observing and maintaining of theirs, so we ought to
be of our House.' He even suggested that the leading spokesmen of
the Commons were more learned and knowledgeable than those of the
Lords.[1] Such experiences must also have confirmed his earlier
opinions about the 'court'.[2]

Ellesmere was possessed with a discriminating knowledge of
politics, and with the offices, wealth, and local influence to make a
contribution to national affairs; and his late political career can be
seen as a forerunner of those 'citizen saints' or 'new statesmen' who
formed 'chosen' groups to reform society and its institutions in the
seventeenth century. 'Calvinist politicians', they became the revolu-
tionaries of early modern times.[3] Ellesmere, however, was still more
of a man of the past than of the future. Politically he was more in the
mould of a man who lived essentially to make things work.[4] Representing the aristocracy of the 'country' rather than of the 'court',
he devoted his career on the one hand to the cultivation and exploitation of local interests, and on the other hand to full participation in
the affairs of the nation-state. The nature of his work with the Lords
and Commons revealed the stresses of the English legislature under
James I. His work in the Privy Council was equally revealing of the
dilemmas of James's reign.

[1] Speeches of 28 May 1614 in the *Hastings MSS* IV, 271; and of 25 May 1614 in 'a booke of
remembrances', Hasts. MSS, box entitled 'Parl. Papers 1614', respectively.
[2] *Supra*, 56–9.
[3] Michael Walzer, *The revolution of the Saints* (Cambridge Mass. 1965), Introd. and Chap.
VII; and Paul S. Seaver, *The Puritan lectureships* (Stanford Calif. 1970), 58–63, 292–3.
[4] G. R. Elton, for ex. on 'The political creed of Thomas Cromwell', in *Studies in Tudor
and Stuart politics and government* (1974), II, 193–216, esp. 200–10. The context has been
provided by Arthur B. Ferguson, *The articulate citizen and the English Renaissance* (Durham
N.C. 1965).

REFORMING PRIVY COUNCILLORS: CROWN FINANCES AND THE ADMINISTRATION OF GOVERNMENT

The collapse of the Parliament of 1614 was a hollow victory for the conservative faction in the King's government. The abandonment of Parliament was a tactless measure at a time when the Crown was short of funds and facing a financial crisis. Although the general policies of peace abroad and religious toleration at home were wise ones for the country, the King's government lacked a programme to deal effectively with the immediate problems at hand. The government of King James was not, however, moribund. The monarch had sensed the need to bring new blood into his English Privy Council during and after the decline of his chief minister, the Earl of Salisbury. Thus the years 1611–14 witnessed the appointment of more progressive men to the Council table who had a positive attitude towards the government process.[1]

The appointments of George Abbot, Archbishop of Canterbury, William Herbert, third Earl of Pembroke, Sir Ralph Winwood, Sir Edward Coke, and Fulke Greville, Lord Brooke, were designed to restore royal influence in the country. These men joined councillors like Ellesmere and Caesar in order to resurrect the credibility of the King's government. They were also, however, motivated by the desire of becoming those men who would bring to the country a reformation of the condition, and institutions, of royal government. Some of them formed ministerial connections, and by 1615 these nascent political groups comprised a very loose, but noticeable, political faction in the halls of Westminster. Representing the entry of a newly privileged nobility and knighted gentry into the highest offices of state, they had come to criticise existing royal policies in the pursuit of a new set of 'national interests' which reflected those of their own. They envisaged, however, not an era of strife and civil war, but a return to the 'commonwealth' principles of the mid-sixteenth century. Attempting to change the programme of the King, they sought not his disgrace

---

[1] A masterful analysis of the problems, the men, and their situation is in Menna Prestwich, *Cranfield: politics and profits under the early Stuarts* (Oxford 1966), 158–98.

but the dismemberment of the Howard and Scottish factions who held his ears. They sought nothing less than to secure for their hands the future reins of government.[1]

The reforming privy councillors refused to accept the premise that all policy came from the King. They also refused to believe that the sovereign could continue to resolve his problems by relying on further sales of lands and honours, and an ever-increasing number of schemes to raise additional revenues without striking at the root of the King's wants.[2] Like the Elizabethan Lord Treasurer, Lord Burghley, they believed that expenses must be cut before revenues could be increased.[3] They also believed, with their new financial consultant, Lionel Cranfield, 'that the King's bounty hath caused not only his own but his subjects' poverty'.[4] Thus the reforming councillors began to press for a total retrenchment in Crown spending, a reform of the royal finances, and a new national economic policy. Drawing upon their own resources, they used the institution of the Working Council to establish a committee system that would create a series of proposals to meet the multifarious problems which confronted them.

The Privy Council held extensive sessions in the last week of September 1615 to discuss the measures proposed by the reformers on royal finance, trade, and administration. A majority of the Council had been convinced that only with a measure of financial restraint and reform could the government gain the confidence of a new Parliament and achieve a substantial parliamentary grant,[5] particularly with the failures of 1610 and 1614 fresh behind them.[6] The Lord Chancellor had collected a number of papers on economic and fiscal reform in the years 1611–14. His private tract or memorandum – 'Things to be considered of before a Parliament to be called' – was composed in early September 1614 as a brief for the programme which he would eventually champion at the Council table.[7]

---

[1] Knafla, 'The Privy Council, Parliament, and English politics, c. 1582–1621', forthcoming in the *Canadian Journal of History*.

[2] The various schemes for ex. in D.C.O. 'Ancient Misc.' EM 5 ff. 48–51, 69–74; Petyt MS 538/51/249r–51v, 538/45/132–50; and C.U.L. MS Mm VI 59.

[3] Discussed by B. W. Beckingsale, *Burghley, Tudor statesman 1520–1598* (1967), 236–40.

[4] Sackv. MS M/184, f. 1r.

[5] The financial plight of the Crown had grown significantly since 1610. The P.C. in 1615 pressed for a more thorough exam. of the King's finances than had been made in the Parl. of 1614. The proposals of Sir Henry Neville after the failures of the Addled Parl. in July 1614, appear to have influenced the Council in these matters: SPD 14/74/44–7.

[6] *Supra*, Chap. III.

[7] Ellesm. MS 2610, *infra* Chap. XII.

Ellesmere's memorandum was a reform manifesto that defined the problems of the government and made specific recommendations for their resolution. The general concern which he expressed was that 'the King's state as now it stands is in a consumption, and (as it pleased his majesty to say) in a fever hectic'. The disease was diagnosed as the festering of 'importune suitors . . . who had the charge and husbanding of the King's treasure'. Officers in the Exchequer had abused the King's grace in dispensing royal gifts, in accepting requests for projects whose purpose was to deceive and to defraud the monarch, and in using their offices for private gain. The course of action that he advocated was a direct one: 'wherefor first our duty is to find the true cause of the disease, and then to provide remedy'. Strong measures were required to stop 'the leaks in the cistern of the Treasury'.[1]

The measures which Ellesmere proposed to reduce the ordinary expenditures of the Crown were twofold. Firstly, no new grants were to be given in the future until the King's debts were paid and his budget balanced. If men proffered suits to the monarch for profit, such suits would be acceptable only if the profit went to the Crown. Secondly, a policy of abatement was to be established. This policy would curtail all pensions in the King's government, household, and public works both at home and abroad. It would also strike at the heart of the lavish and uncontrolled spending of the royal court. Once these immediate steps were taken to reduce the ordinary expenditures of the sovereign, a long-term programme could be devised to increase his revenues.[2]

The Chancellor's programme to increase the income of the Crown can be grouped into six general subjects: (1) gifts and offices, (2) imports and exports, (3) foreign merchants, (4) the mint, (5) lands, and (6) profits. The first three subjects could be undertaken more easily than the others. For the first of these, all gifts, offices, and fees which had been recently obtained from the monarch 'upon false suggestions, untrue considerations, and by fraud and deceit' should be investigated. Where evidence could be secured, suits should be instituted for voiding the grants in the relevant courts. The termination of such assignments would raise the revenues of the sovereign and alleviate the commonwealth of grants 'offensive and grievous to the people'.[3]

---

[1] 'Govt. 1615', f. 1. Ellesmere's phraseology here closely resembles that of the opposition group in the H. of C. in 1610. Compare this, for ex. with the speech of John Hoskyns in *Parl. 1610* II, 244–5.

[2] 'Govt. 1615', 2–3.

[3] *Ibid.* 3.

It would also represent an attack on the corruption in the central government which had brought so much ridicule to the Crown.

The second and third subjects in which the King's revenue could be increased were related to trade. For the second, Ellesmere suggested an examination of 'the continual, excessive importation of superfluous and vain wares and merchandizes . . . by which the realm is more and more impoverished and wasted'. He desired a renewal of the book of rates that would tax more heavily the import of gold and silver, and of goods of 'pride, luxury, and excess' such as silks, wines, spices, and tobacco. These policies would help to balance imports with exports, increase revenues, and dampen the fires of consumption. For the third topic Ellesmere suggested an immediate examination of the wealthy strangers, aliens, and merchants who resided in England in order to confiscate their riches for the Exchequer. He requested the draft of a proclamation that would declare the implementation of all statutes concerning foreigners, the commencement of legal proceedings against the most prosperous, and the offer of expensive pardons for the rest.[1] A policy such as this would surely have brought chaos, and the end of the City of London as a growing commercial and financial centre of Europe.

The last three subjects which Ellesmere discussed required a much larger and more time-consuming effort. For the mint, he considered it 'now much amiss', but stated that he lacked the knowledge and understanding to make suggestions for its reform. He had many proposals, however, for gaining additional revenue from Crown lands. The King could sell forests and parks that provided him with little profit or pleasure, sell lands which could be recovered from the sea, enclose great wastes, sell reversions and remainders to estates in tail, grant copyholds and customary lands in fee farms, and sell the monarch's dubious titles to tithes.[2] Many of these proposals, however, would have brought meagre results. Finally, Ellesmere made a list of items which brought profit to the Exchequer and suggested that these could be examined for further gain. The major items were profits from the production of water works, alum, cop-

---

[1] *Ibid.* 4–6. He also commissioned the draft of an elaborate schedule of strangers, aliens, and merchants in London: Ellesm. MS 33/A/34.

[2] 'Govt. 1615', 6–8. The Chanc. spent a large portion of his earlier career in investigating the many areas of the land law on behalf of the Crown as Sol. and Att.-Gen. 1581–94; Rawl. MS C.647, and Lans. MSS 27, 62, 74. See as well *supra*, 11, 14–5, 24–6, 33–4.

per, glass, starch, and tobacco; the goods of outlaws; court fees, and fines from judgments at law; and the sale of trees, woods, and homage.[1]

The Chancellor not only made a general inquiry into the reduction of the ordinary expenses of the Crown and the increase of its revenue, but he also made suggestions on the calibre of men who would be required to implement these proposals. 'Faithful and industrious ministers' were necessary to rate and tax the land wisely, to compound for prices shrewdly, and to conduct the financial affairs of the monarch without seeking private gain. The sovereign could attract such men if he provided them with 'a good future annual revenue', and royalties from the sale of waste lands and the goods of felons. Proposals such as these were indeed progressive ones for the early seventeenth century. Ellesmere warned, however, that the King must act quickly. If he performed according to these guidelines, 'it is not to be doubted but his majesty's good and loving subjects, seeing this course taken by his majesty, will willingly and cheerfully yield large contribution and aid by subsidies, tenths, and fifteenths and otherwise'. [2]

The proposals of Ellesmere's reform manifesto were presented to the Privy Council along with the views of his colleagues in the crucial sessions of late September 1615.[3] Three men in particular presented extensive recommendations: Sir Thomas Lake, Sir Edward Coke, and Lord Ellesmere. Lake's suggestions were designed loosely to stop the flow of royal gifts, to abate spending in the departments of state, to remove impositions to which the House of Commons had objected, to shift the burden of customs duties from exports to imports, to place a

[1] 'Govt. 1615', 8–10. A possibility of potential revenue that he strongly opposed was the sale of pardons. He compiled a brief of his reasons, and noted the views of each councillor on the subject: Ellesm. MS 445, endorsed '1615'.

[2] 'Govt. 1615', 9–11. This theme on the need of the King and his ministers to be revealed to the country and its MPs as men capable of decisive action was put forward more fully in some of Ellesmere's notes for this memo.: 'The reason and wysedome of the parliaments by whome the statutes were made is sufficyent of ytselfe. And yf by the Connivencye, remissenes, or negligence of the ministers, ... they haue not bene executed and obserued; That, theyr faulte, weakens not the strength of the Laws. And the mischiefes and Inconveniences which haue therby ensued, and from tyme to tyme growne more and more, it is too apparent, and the Commen Weale feeles [it']. Ellesm. MS 1216, f. 2v.

[3] Spedding pr. a report of the Council's proceedings and the advice of each councillor in Bacon, *Letters* V, 194–207. The author has checked this against the original: Harl. MS 4289, ff. 224v–30v. The ms. is endorsed 'giuen me by Sir Samuell Sandys'.

surtax on the imports and exports of aliens, to investigate the wealth of foreign merchants, and to provide aid for the cloth industry. The recommendations of Coke and Ellesmere, however, were more severe in both measures and language than those of Lake.

The Chief Justice and the Lord Chancellor took a more trenchant attitude towards the economic and fiscal ills of the government, an attitude that was occasioned by their recent study of these problems. They included most of Lake's suggestions in their proposals, and went further in demanding an investigation of all royal grants and expenses since the King's accession. [1] The report of Ellesmere's recommendations to the Council was similar to that of Coke's. Both men had emphasised previously that new grants must be stopped until the debts incurred for giving previous ones were paid, and that the King must revise his policies on impositions, monopolies, and purveyance, treading at all times 'tenderly and warily'. [2] Only in several minor matters relating to land and fiscal policies did the Chancellor differ from the Chief Justice. Moreover, the general thrust of their proposals resembled that of the other members of the reforming faction. Thus the detailed recommendations of Coke and Ellesmere can be regarded as the essence of the reform programme.

In addressing the Council, the Chancellor began with an attack on his former colleagues: 'That for the matter now in question of preparation, he wished many things now spoken of had been already executed: for they had been so long since and so often spoken of, as ere this time some effect might have been seen, if they had been followed'. [3] Thereafter, he went straight to a factual presentation of the titles of his paper. The reporter of this meeting mentioned that Ellesmere spoke from a prepared paper. Since the titles and organisation of these proposals were identical to those in the tract that is edited here, we can assume that he spoke from this paper or its outline. In fact, a modest outline of the first half of the paper appears in his collected

---

[1] The speeches of Lake, Coke, and Ellesmere are in Bacon, *Letters* v, 195–8, 199–200, and 204–5, respectively. Lake's suggestions were sweetened with a prefatory remark that the cause of the obstacles between the King and his people was the latter's 'misconception of his Majesty's bountiful and magnificent nature'.

[2] *Att-Gen.* vs. *Clerke & others*, Hawarde, *Reportes*, 248–9 (S.C. 15 Nov. 1605). Their previous comments on such matters are in *ibid.* 302–8; 7 *Co. Rep.* 116–8; Ellesm. MS 441; and Coke MS Rep. C, ff. 650–1v, 682v–6r, 688v–94r. Many lawyers of this period were interested in economic and fiscal reform: for ex. Petyt MSS 502/6, ff. 319, 338–42, 362–5, 383, 429, 458, 466, 478–80, 498.

[3] Bacon, *Letters* v, 204.

manuscripts. [1] The significance of Ellesmere's tract is that it was much more frank and detailed than the speech which he delivered to the Council.

The Chancellor in the preface of his tract had penned bitter words against the King, his favourites, royal suitors, and the Treasury officials. Within the body of the paper he was equally vindictive towards foreign and English merchants and the civil service. Such sudden frankness was not out of character. Ellesmere, throughout his law career, had acquired the reputation of an unpredictably outspoken individual. He retained this characteristic even as a privy councillor. [2] The world of political influences, however, required a measure of caution. Although Ellesmere was a leader of the reforming faction, he now exercised some restraint in the public presentation of his more critical proposals.

The economic and fiscal predicament of the royal government was serious by the second decade of the seventeenth century. The country, in spite of the price revolution, was growing appreciably wealthier while the Crown was becoming poorer. The King was being defrauded of his revenues. [3] His grants of monopolies and impositions, customs farms, and licences for the administration of various legal and economic regulations had brought him little income as their aristocratic holders milked the tenants for small fees which were not always paid to the Crown. Many of these men were not office-holders who received grants in appreciation of their gratuitous service in the King's government; they were 'professional parasites' who came to court solely for profit. [4] They were also not new to the reign of James. [5] But by 1614

[1] It is more likely that he spoke from an outline such as Ellesm. MS 1216. This is a brief epitome of pp. 1–5 of his memo. and he refers to his colleagues with equal terseness. In referring to the failure of councillors to enforce the many good laws on the statute books, he concludes: 'But yf we calle to mynde many good and whoalesome statutes latelye made in our owne tyme, yt wyll appeare that those also Lack due execucion, to the great harme of the Commen weale, and this is by the remissenes and neglecte of the ministers' (f. 2v).

[2] *Supra*, 56–64.

[3] The problem of defining fraud and corruption is not as simple as it appears at face value— Joel Hurstfield, 'Political corruption in modern England: the historian's problem', *History* 52 (1957), 16–34.

[4] The general background is ably presented in Christopher Hill, *Reformation to Industrial Revolution* (corr. ed. 1969), 44–118. In particular see Lawrence Stone, *The crisis of the aristocracy* (Oxford 1965), 416–41, 463–76. The quote is Thomas Wilson's: C.U.L. Seligman MS 1625.

[5] For ex. the extensive corruption and financial disorder claimed in the mid-Elizabethan period: B.M. Royal MS 18. A. XLVI, ff. 1–9. A number of tracts were devoted to this general area from the 1590s, and some of them are collected in the Trinity Coll. Dublin Lib. – MSS 802–8.

nearly three-quarters of them were, or were associated with, the conservative faction and the Scots. It is not surprising, therefore, that the reform movement of 1614–15 was launched by the aristocratic office-holders: men such as Pembroke, Ellesmere, and Abbot. The Chancellor himself, who had previously acquired a reputation as pro-Scottish,[1] now turned his venom against the pre-eminence of this world of sycophants 'which may in time ruin the state'.[2]

Ellesmere's address to the Privy Council indicated that he had only recently been genuinely concerned for the economic and financial well-being of the government, and an examination of the sources of his proposals demonstrates that he had acquired some expertise in these areas. The Chancellor had always been keen to examine royal grants since his assumption of the Lord Keepership in 1596. His papers contain many examples of the careful drafting of such assignments and the defiance of suitors who sought grants of monopolies for conducting government services at the expense of Crown and commonwealth.[3] He also was against the sale of Crown lands, even though he had been charged to share the task of arranging their disposition.[4] But Ellesmere had less experience with purely financial and commercial matters.

The Chancellor's slight interest in commercial matters had continued from Elizabethan to Jacobean times,[5] and from the accession of James he began to turn increasingly to the economic problems of the commonwealth. He collected 'A declaration of the decay of her majesty's revenue', and tracts on the condition of Crown finances in 1590 and 1604.[6] Some of this material comprised sections of his notes

---

[1] Their earlier support came from his strong stand on Scottish union: *The register of the Privy Council of Scotland* (Edinburgh 1885), VII, xxx; VIII, 494; and Harl. MS 7189, ff. 2r–44v *passim*.

[2] 'Govt. 1615', f. 1r. Compare this with his initial hope in the ability of James to bring an end to this confluence in 1603: draft letter to Sir Thomas Chaloner, Ellesm. MS 129. Chaloner's tract on the subject may also have been written for Ellesmere; it will be assessed in a forthcoming article by Professor James Cockburn.

[3] His general attitude was expressed in *Salisbury MSS* VII, 359; his memo. on the making of grants in Ellesm. MS 6160; exs. of his drafting grants in *The manuscripts of the Duke of Leeds, the Bridgewater Trust*, ... H.M.C. 11th Rep. App. VII (1888), 132–4; and his obstinate defiance to the King and his favourites in refusing to pass the Uvedall suit: Ellesm. MSS 2943–52.

[4] From at least 1603: Thomas Fuller, *The worthies of England* (rev. ed. 1952), 71; and Ellesm. MS 35/C/37. His participation in the sales is noted in the *CSPD, 1603–10*, pp. 320, 330–1, 335, 379, 420–2, 432, 436–9, 477, 483; and *ibid. 1611–18*, pp. 7, 135, 171–3, 181, 197, 215–6 220, 228–31.

[5] *Supra*, 11–12.

[6] Ellesm. MSS 35/C/37, 1521, and 1170 respectively.

for an address to Parliament in 1604. [1] Thereafter, he spoke frequently in Parliament and the Star Chamber on the need to expand native
industry and commerce, and to lift royal restrictions on commercial
and industrial development. [2] One meeting with Lords Buckhurst and
Salisbury for discussing these problems was held at his own home. [3]
After 1610 Ellesmere began to investigate personally particular areas
of the financial system. He reported to the Privy Council on the discovery of fraud in the farming of the customs, and contributed to
committees for the investigation of exports, imports, and the book
of rates. [4]

The basis of the Chancellor's memorandum stemmed from his close
examination of fiscal and economic matters in the years 1611–15. The
specific proposals which evolved were not solely of his own making,
but were composed with the assistance of two knowledgeable men of
economic affairs in James's government, Sir Julius Caesar and Sir
Lionel Cranfield. The government's economic policy prior to 1611
was Cecilian – to maintain expenses, raise the revenues, and divide
the spoils. [5] This policy, defined in a letter of the Privy Council in
1608, hinged on the exploitation of existing areas of revenue. [6] Salisbury himself had become adept in raping the finances of the Crown
and making profits at its expense. [7] Criticism of the government's
policy and of Salisbury's machinations had been voiced within the
Council as early as 1610, and the necessity to re-evaluate government
policy which emerged thereafter affected Ellesmere significantly.

The papers of Cranfield and Caesar have proven indispensable for
the study of Jacobean economic policy, and Ellesmere's memorandum

---

[1] Ellesm. MS 456, ff. 1r–2r.

[2] *Eg. Papers*, 337–40; *The Manuscripts of Lincoln, Bury St. Edmunds*, . . . H.M.C. 14th Rep.
App. Pt. VIII (1895), 141; Hawarde, *Reportes*, 326–7, 367–8; and Folger MS M.b. 42, ff. 151–65.

[3] *Salisbury MSS*, IX, 93, 143.

[4] Ellesmere had reported to the Council on the discovery of fraud in the farming of the
customs in 1612: *CSPD*, IX, 162; and *Cranfield Papers*, I, 305–8. He sat on committees for the
investigation of exports and imports, and the book of rates in the Parl. of 1614: Ellesm. MS
2614, f. 1r.

[5] Petyt MS 538/37, ff. 55–70; Gardiner, *Hist.* II, 12–5; Prestwich, *Cranfield*, 21–5, 32–7.
A different interp. is that of Joel Hurstfield in his *Queen's wards* (1958), 312–7, 324–5.

[6] Harl. MS 2207, ff. 2r–11v. The letter, signed by the members of the P.C. and attributed
to Salisbury, presented a realistic view of the problems in raising additional revenues at that
time, suggesting politely that James restrict his spending.

[7] Lawrence Stone, 'The fruits of office: the case of Robert Cecil, first Earl of Salisbury
1596–1612', *Essays in the economic and social history of Tudor and Stuart England*, ed. F.J. Fisher
(Cambridge 1961), 89–116.

of 1615 reveals that he had learned much from them. Caesar's brief on how to increase revenues by improving profits from feudal dues and royal lands contained items that were discussed by Ellesmere almost verbatim. [1] Most of these items had been gathered by Caesar in the years 1607–12, and it is not inconceivable that Ellesmere was given access to these early collections. [2] Caesar's suggested policy of a rigid retrenchment in spending for royal favourites, the departments of state, and 'for private mens' gains' was put forward in the years 1611–15. They had become the centre of Ellesmere's views on the economic problems of the Crown by 1615. [3]

Cranfield was primarily concerned at this time with the reform of English trade. His sketch of the major areas of trade which required reform in 1613 could be regarded as a general outline that Ellesmere pursued. [4] Moreover, Cranfield's proposals for a revision of the book of rates were made partially at Ellesmere's request. [5] His major paper on the reform of English trade was sent to the Chancellor in the spring of 1615, and Ellesmere incorporated several of its suggestions regarding the revision of the book of rates, currency reform, and regulations for foreign merchants into his memorandum. [6] Cranfield's papers, moreover, reveal a reciprocal influence with Ellesmere's writings. For example, the merchant banker's later draft proposals for the King were sandwiched between an abstract of the introductory and concluding sections of Ellesmere's tract. [7]

The programme of economic reform that was adopted in the Privy Council in September 1615 was not implemented at that time, even

[1] The brief is an imaginary debate on the Great Contract that puts forward Caesar's ideas. It is pr. in *Debates 1610*, 163–79.

[2] For ex. Add. MS 10.038, esp. ff. 3–4, 6–11, 311–23, 363–70.

[3] The major document containing Caesar's proposals is Lans. MS 165, ff. 138r–9r, dated 5 Jan. 1610/11 and redated 12 Oct. 1611. This is discussed in Lamar Mott Hill, 'The public career of Sir Julius Caesar, 1584–1614', Ph.D. diss. (Univ. of London 1968), 395–8. For a commentary on Caesar's ideas with respect to this subject see Prestwich, *Cranfield*, 42–4, 163–79.

[4] Sackv. MS M/184 (formerly 4074), 4 July 1613; prepared or copied for Cranfield by John Walker (see SP 14/74/23).

[5] Sackv. MS M/99 (formerly 109), Ellesmere to Cranfield, 2 May 1613.

[6] 'Collections to be considered', Sackv. MS M/632 (formerly 4532), dated 25 March 1615.

[7] Sackv. MS 2330, n.d. The typescript list ascribes the ms. inaccurately to the year 1623 (list in the Nat. Reg. of Archives). It could be suggested that Ellesmere's memo. was his own copy of Cranfield's but the evidence does not support this view. The Chanc's outline of the first half of his memo. states, 'the proposicions I haue made, for relieuing the kings present state' (Ellesm. MS 1216, ff. 1r–2v). Cranfield's proposals are an outline of the introductory and concluding sections only (pp. 1–3 and 8–11 of Ellesm. MS 2610), and a few notes suggest a date of *c.* 1616–18. His estimation of Ellesmere was noted by Dr Godfrey Goodman, *The court of James the First* (1839), 282.

though a majority of the body voted for the programme that had been drafted largely on the recommendations of Coke and Ellesmere. James, under the still dominating influence of his favourite, Robert Carr, Earl of Rochester, and the Howard family, allowed these reform measures to lie dormant. Some were adopted in the years 1618–19, but most of them were never seriously considered by the King.[1]

The reforming parliamentary faction had risen in the second decade of James's reign in order to influence the monarch and his favourites. They had attempted to reconcile the breach between King and country by advocating policies of administrative, economic, and fiscal reform. The faction, however, witnessed a subtle change in membership and influence, and failed to gain paramountcy in the private chambers of the sovereign.[2] The conservative and Scottish factions, buttressed by the King's favourites, had prevented any major reforms. It was precisely this situation that motivated the Chancellor to pen the phrase, 'that a good Prince governed by evil ministers is as dangerous as if he were evil himself'.[3]

Although Ellesmere participated in the movement for reform in its infant stages, during the years 1612–15 the reformers did not work in vain. After the failure to implement the programme of 1615 they brought the fall of the King's chief favourite, Rochester, in the following year. Their exposure of corruption in government offices headed by Suffolk, Nottingham, and Lake forced the resignation of these leaders of the Howard faction in 1618.[4] Afterwards, under the leadership of Pembroke, they secured the reform of the navy – the first major reform of the era – and the revival of Parliaments, which was begun in 1621.[5] The underlying basis of this movement for 'good government' was nothing less than the desires which John Milton

---

[1] The rise and death of the Council's proposals, 1612–17, is discussed in Prestwich, *Cranfield*, 108–203. For the reforms of 1618–19, see *ibid.* 205–52.

[2] Knafla, 'Privy Council and Parl.', 24–7.

[3] The Chanc's notes in his autograph copy of Henry Savile, *The Ende of Nero and Beginning of Galba* (1591), Hunt. RB 69625, in the 'preface to the Reader', sig. 3.

[4] Our knowledge of this particular period is hazy because the major individuals, including Suffolk, Nottingham, Lake, and Buckingham, have yet to be studied. Some of the relevant background materials which relate as well to the discussion above are in *Seventeenth-century economic documents*, ed. Joan Thirsk and J. P. Cooper (Oxford 1973), 194–208.

[5] Brian O'Farrell, 'The third Earl of Pembroke's 'Connection'; electoral power and Parliamentary influence in the early seventeenth century', unpub. paper; Prestwich, *Cranfield*, *passim*; and Robert Zaller, *The Parliament of 1621* (Berkeley Calif. 1972). I wish to thank Professors O'Farrell, Roy Schreiber, and A. J. Slavin for their discussions on this subject.

and the commonwealth men of the mid-seventeenth century would come to espouse so poignantly.[1] Those desires were suitably expressed by Ellesmere himself in the midst of the struggles in 1614–15:

To know not only the nature of things, but also the measure of them.

To know not only what is good, but also whether it be possible and feasible, and how and when.

Not to find faults, nor stir doubts and questions, without devising and showing how to amend and clear them.

Fall not out by the way.[2]

Maxims such as these formed a personal perspective not only in Ellesmere's quest for a reform of the Crown's revenues and the economic system, but also in his search for a subject that had been at the centre of his public career from its inception – one that was overshadowed by the more material demands of the early seventeenth century, but which the 'country' Chancellor never lost sight of: law reform.

[1] John Steadman, *John Milton and the Renaissance hero* (Oxford 1967).

[2] Ellesm. MS 456, f. 1v.

THE PROBLEM OF LAW REFORM

In the second decade of the seventeenth century Lord Ellesmere turned not only to the pressing economic and fiscal problems of the Crown and the viability of the government, but also to significant legal problems which had troubled him for some time. At the accession of James the Chancellor had noted irregularities in the usage of the forms of action at common law, and he put forward suggestions for a revision of the statute law. His proposals for the reform of statutes included the abolition or reworking of all enactments which were 'obsolete', 'impossible', 'unnecessary', 'unprofitable', 'contrary', 'confused', or 'multiple'.[1] In more detailed papers he grouped such acts into several categories: statutes to be 'repealed', 'altered', 'enlarged', or created 'anew'.[2] However, these proposals had little impact in the halls of Parliament, and they became dormant by 1610 with the collapse of an effective working relationship between the Crown and the House of Commons. Future progress in the reform of statute law would have to rest with the attempt of the reforming faction in the Privy Council to gain the confidence of the King and seize the initiative in the governing process.

In the meantime, the problems confronting the administration of the law were equally serious. The reform of the common law was a subject which traditionally had been the preserve of the law profession. Changes in common law process came largely from within, and the years of the late sixteenth and early seventeenth centuries were critical ones in its history. What gave this period such a critical nature was the coming together of several complex developments: the rise in prominence of new courts of law, the conflict of jurisdictions, the

---

[1] His written speech for the Parl. of 1604: Ellesm. MS 451, f. 2r. A number of notes on these statutes were prepared for him and bear his endorsement: Ellesm. MS 2616, dated 22 March 1603/4.

[2] Ellesm. MSS 2615–6. He noted James's later public speeches in support of this: *The Kings Majesties Speech* (19 Mar. 1603), Hunt. RB 61876, sig. 4v; and *His Maiesties Speech to both Houses of Parliament* (1607), sig. C.

impact of new social and economic demands, and the growth of litigation. The legal problems which emerged baffled even the most learned
of contemporary lawyers.[1] At the heart of these complexities lay a
fundamental transformation in the law itself – the changing pattern
of litigation. The competition among lawyers for new legal remedies,
their enlargement of legal fictions, the advent of written pleadings,
the shift in personal actions to trial by jury, and the proceeding to trial
by demurrer or special verdict had caused an opening up of legal
procedure that was giving rise to a renaissance in legal thought.[2] The
classical world of the common law where the King's Bench heard
criminal causes and the Common Pleas civil ones, where wrongs were
distinguished from rights, and where there was a meaningful distinction between personal and real actions (if that world ever existed) had
become a world of the past.

Several contemporary jurists, such as Sir Henry Finch and Sir
Francis Bacon, wrote disparagingly of this new state of affairs.
According to Finch the law had become so confused that it could no
longer be defined. The forms of action had swelled beyond recognition, and they were currently obscured with 'a real and general
affection scattered throughout the whole law (as the blood is through
the body)'.[3] Bacon went one step further. He regarded the forms of
action as obsolete, and proposed to resuscitate the elements of the
law by reconstructing them anew.[4] When he did so, he claimed a
victory for making known to all people the certainty of the law.[5] Both
Bacon and Finch looked back to the old law, the law of Littleton and
Fitzherbert. Other jurists, however, accepted the institution of the
common law as sacrosanct, and attempted to understand the changes
which had occurred in a favourable light.

William Fulbeck and Sir John Davies believed that the common law

[1] For ex. the assessment of William Bowyer in a letter to Lord Burghley, 19 June 1592 –
Lans. MS 99, f. 159r; the anon. 'Omne Jus', Add. MS 41.613, ff. 81v–92r; and Thomas
Hunniman's tract in Royal MS 18.A.LXVII, ff. 1r–6v.

[2] There is no actual study of this subject. For general guidelines see esp. S. F. C. Milsom,
Historical foundations of the common law (1969), 67–72, 127–32; and J. H. Baker, *An introduction
to English legal history* (1971), 78–85. Some important insights have been provided by Marjorie
Blatcher, 'The working of the Court of King's Bench in the fifteenth century' Ph.D. diss.
(Univ. of London 1936), 347–52; Samuel E. Thorne, 'Tudor social transformation and legal
change', *New York Univ. Law Rev.* XXVI (1951), 10–23; and L. H. Abbott, *Law reporting in
England 1485–1585* (1973), Chaps. I–II, VII.

[3] Finch, *Law*, 225.

[4] 'Touching the Compiling and Amendment of the Laws of England', in Bacon, *Letters* VI,
61–71. His initial corresp. on the subject is in *ibid.* V, 84–7, and VI, 57–60.

[5] Bacon, *The elements of the common laws of England* (1630), sig. A.4r–v.

had reached its greatest hour. They felt that increased litigation and uncertainty in the law reflected a society of individuals in search of true justice. Thus the old common law was no longer relevant, and legal procedures as well as doctrines were being changed in order to meet the new needs and demands of the governing class.[1] Since there was no tradition of a law commission to deal with law reform, future development for these contemporaries could rise only out of the continuous debate that occurred before the courts as questions came to hand case by case.[2] Sir John Dodderidge and Sir Edward Coke expressed this latter view when they held that, while the common law was becoming increasingly complex, a proper attention to method and reason could reveal the richness and relevancy of this ancient institution.[3]

Lord Chancellor Ellesmere had little confidence in the efficacy of current developments. His past experience in Parliament and the Privy Council had revealed the inability of those institutions to remedy legal problems either through legislation or by administrative fiat. And several common lawyers had made an effort to bring the issue of law reform to Parliament.[4] Neither did Ellesmere accept the current legal practice of promoting legal change through the expansion of legal fictions. Thus he objected to current developments, and sought a solution in the traditional manner: by returning to the past. Ellesmere's past, however, was not the medieval Catholic world, but that mid-Tudor era of Protestantism, Humanism, and Ramism.[5] Like Starkey, Cranmer, and Nicholas Bacon before him, he was in that tradition of legal reform which culminated with the works of William Sheppard.[6]

---

[1] Davies, *Primer Report*, sig. *1r–10r; William Fulbecke, *A Parallele or conference of the civill law, the canon law, and the common law of England* (1601), ff. 59r–61r; and *A Direction or Preparative to the Study of the Lawe* (1600), ff. 5r–9v.

[2] The lines of development that have been used traditionally in the reform of the common law have been assessed by A. K. R. Kiralfy, 'Law reform by legal fictions, equity and legislation in English legal history', *AJLH* x (1966), 3–14.

[3] Sir John Dodderidge, *The English Lawyer* (1631), 240–71; and Coke in 1 *Co. Rep.* sigs. A3–5.

[4] For ex. the coll. of notes, briefs, and papers in the Petyt MSS 502/6/319–533, *passim*.

[5] *Supra*, pp. 39–45, 51–6.

[6] G. R. Elton, 'Reform by statute: Thomas Starkey's dialogue and Thomas Cromwell's policy', *Proceeds. of the Brit. Acad.* LIV (1968), 165–88; Thomas Cranmer, *Reformatio Legum Ecclesiasticarum* (1571); Nicholas Bacon, in Add. MS 32.379, ff. 26–33; SPD 12/105/93; Harl. MS 39, ff. 183v–97v; and William Sheppard, particularly his *England's Balme* (1657). The author wishes to thank Dr Tittler for his suggestions on Bacon, and Dr Nancy Arnsen for allowing him to read her thesis on William Sheppard (Univ. Maryland 1974). The early Tudor background on law reform has been sketched provocatively by G. R. Elton, *Reform and renewal* (Cambridge 1973), Chap. VI.

The Chancellor believed that courts of law must resist the tendency to encroach on the affairs of one another, that the common law must adhere to the meaning and reality of the old forms of action as they had evolved to the mid-sixteenth century, and that legal change itself was a matter that could be resolved only by the highest court in the land – the High Court of Parliament.

Ellesmere's personal response to the seventeenth-century dialogue on the state of the common law was the composition of an informal tract or memorandum in c. 1611–13 entitled 'Memorialles for Iudicature'.[1] The tract was a critique of various aspects of recent common law developments. The Chancellor divided his exposition into two sections. The first part discussed particular inconveniences in the current usage of writs and the forms of action. The second part comprised four general problems which required reformation: the mischievous growth of litigation in society, the increased costs of the courts, the excessive fees of serjeants and attorneys, and the proliferation of dishonest and inexpert men in the law profession.

The first general problem which Ellesmere discussed was the rise of excessive litigation. He attributed this to courts accepting an overlapping jurisdiction, a situation which encouraged a party to initiate action 'in several courts for one and the self same cause'.[2] Such multiple actions brought needless contention and encouraged the profession of the common informer. They also brought considerable expense and inconvenience to the more honest citizens, impeaching the respectability of the legal system. Earlier the Chancellor had written of the need to enforce statutes 'for avoiding trifling suits at Westminster'.[3] Later, as multiple suits continued to increase, he assisted in the drafting of several statutes and brought the matter directly to the attention of the magistrates:

I have noted one thing, that your ancestors though they had no authority, were so painful and careful as soon as they heard of any differences or suits between any of their neighbours, that they would interpose themselves and mediate an end, by which means the expense of time and much money was

---

[1] 'Iudicature', f. 1r. This general proposal also originated from his views on the severity of the law. See his actions discussed *supra*, pp. 16–22, 61–3; and the paper, 'There should be an abatement of severity', Ellesm. MS 1163.

[2] 'Iudicature', f. 1r; and again in 'Prohibitians', 40–1, 45. Attempts to deal with the common informer can be found in the Caesar papers: for ex. 'Mr. Hilles project', Add. MS 10.038, dated 17 April 1607.

[3] Ellesm. MS 2616, dated 22 Mar. 1603/4; and the speech of 29 Nov. 1610 in *Hastings MSS* IV, 229.

saved, and the courts at Westminster nothing near so filled and pestered with causes as now they are.

He then exhorted them to 'spend some time in understanding the faults and grievances in every of your circuits'.[1]

The problem of excessive litigation had become acute with the growth of a new merchant and gentry aristocracy. Their necessity to cope with the problem of inflation (particularly in the late sixteenth century), and then with the problem of recession (the early decades of the seventeenth century) placed a new emphasis on litigation. The law suit became a means to benefit from individuals in a perilous financial condition as well as to forestall impending financial disaster. The expansion of the provincial courts in the north and west, together with the growth of the central courts in London – both developments at the expense of the local courts in the counties – had made possible new and more convenient alternatives to launch suits, or counter suits in several courts for the same matter.[2] Ellesmere's own court, the Court of Chancery, witnessed a significant increase in business from the accession of James.[3] Thus the Chancellor himself was unable to control a situation that was already out of hand. His desire, however, to reduce the litigious nature of society was based on his belief that local institutions provided better remedies than national ones; that men who conducted their affairs in the counties were better off than those who brought their business to the lewd and corrupted city.[4] His views on the dangers of a litigious society, while held partially by some of his contemporaries, presaged the vocal Puritan attacks which would become so prominent in the era of civil war and commonwealth at mid-century.[5]

The second and third propositions concerned an examination of the costs which suitors and clients were assessed in the courts, and of the fees charged by serjeants and lawyers. In both cases the Chancellor recommended that the charges be restored to what they had been in

[1] 'Divers Cases, Speeches, and Presidentes in the High Court of Starre Chamber', Folger MS X.d. 337, f. 16v. The acts were 1 Jac. c. 10 (1604), *Stat. Realm* IV, Pt. 2, pp. 1027; 3 Jac. c. 8 (1604/5), p. 1084; 4 Jac. c. 3 (1606), p. 1141; 7 Jac. c. 5 (1609/10), pp. 1161–2. Other speeches are in *Parl. 1610* II, 348; and *Hastings MSS* IV, 228–9.

[2] Cockburn, *Assizes*, Pt. III.

[3] *Infra*, Chap. VI.

[4] *Supra*, 56–9; and *infra*, Chap. VII.

[5] In particular William Prynne, *A Summary Collection of the Principal Fundamental Rights, Liberties, Proprieties of All English Freemen* (1656); and the anon. *The Exact Law-giver* (1658).

the 1570s.[1] Ellesmere's proposals for an investigation of legal costs and fees stemmed from his general concern for the protection of the individual from the excessive charges of the legal system in an inflationary era. Early in his judicial career he fought against large fees.[2] He participated in a committee of inquiry into court fees, and in 1608 and 1610 he had headed investigations himself.[3] The committees however, were fruitless. King James later acknowledged these failures in 1622 by establishing yet another body for the examination of all fees 'extortionately taken, exacted, and levied'.[4] Nothing was done. Such committees continued to be appointed throughout the 1630s and the 1640s,[5] and they were used ineffectually as a bureaucratic loophole by Stuart government.

The Chancellor's proposals on this subject were unrealistic. Although the increased litigiousness of society no doubt encouraged the rise of expenses both in the courts and the legal profession, a desire to return to the 1570s reveals a lack of concern with the impact of the price revolution, the demands of government, and the intentions of Parliament. The problem confronting the government was a serious one. Crown revenues had failed to keep pace with expenses. Various privy councillors, from Sir William Cecil, Lord Burghley, to Sir Julius Caesar, had noted the necessity of the government to cover the real costs of the courts.[6] The matter of the fees of lawyers was similar, though no less pressing. It should be stated emphatically that the abuses had become notorious from the era of Sir Nicholas Bacon and Lord Burghley to that of Ellesmere itself.[7] But the simple fact was

---

[1] 'Iudicature', f. 1r. Some of the lists of fees which he had prepared are in Ellesm. MSS 1198, 6206B. He made the same argument in his brief on 'Prohibitians', 42–3, 45.

[2] For ex. in Hawarde, *Reportes*, 53–6 at 55; and *Eg. Papers*, 429–32.

[3] Those headed by the Chanc. in 1608 and 1610 are in SPD 14/8/409; Ellesm. MS 2941; and *Cranfield MSS*, 221–2. Earlier commissions are discussed in Jones, *Chancery*, 86–8, 115–6, 143–9, 165–6. Some of the background papers for Ellesmere's commissions can be found in the Caesar coll. – Add. MS 10.038, ff. 424–5. Contemp. papers on the subject include Lans. MSS 35, 169.

[4] *The Copie of His Maiesties Commission, Touching the Fees of the Officers and Ministers belonging to the Courts of Iustice* (1623), 3. Its exams and findings are in Add. MS 34.601, ff. 68r–71v.

[5] Add. MS 34.601, ff. 72–160. For the later commissions and the context, see Stuart E. Prall, *The agitation for law reform during the Puritan Revolution 1640–1660* (The Hague 1966), 50–65.

[6] For ex. in Lans. MS 66, ff. 249r–50r, and Add. MS 10.038, f. 240, respectively.

[7] Bacon's homily in Exeter Coll. Oxford MS 127, ff. 47–8; Francis Alford's petition to Burghley in Lans. MS 44, f. 2; and Francis Bacon's discourse in his *Works* VII, 128. See the discussion in Jones, *Chancery*, 62–8; and the later procls. in *Stuart royal proclamations*, vol. 1 *1603–1625*, ed. J. F. Larkin and P. L. Hughes (Oxford 1973), 512–4, 534–6, 568–70.

that legal fees had failed to keep pace with inflation since the mid-sixteenth century. Parliament itself had set down the original guidelines. That Parliament did not establish statutory controls reflects the importance in the legislature of the members of the law profession, a profession which provided the lower house with its leading members.[1]

Ellesmere's fourth proposition called for a survey and investigation of legal practitioners. The number of entrants to the inns of court had swelled significantly in the late 1560s, and again in the 1590s.[2] Although we lack any genuine study of the law profession, the evidence suggests that the matriculation revolution led to an increased number of practising attorneys in the 1570s and in the first decade of the seventeenth century.[3] The Chancellor had participated personally in the expansion of the inns of court in the 1560s and 1570s. Now, in the 1600s, he became concerned with their continued increases. This concern was matched by that of other contemporary observers, and the views of some of them pre-dated those of the Chancellor himself.

The judges had managed to restrict the number of barristers practising before the courts to the end of the sixteenth century, but they were unsuccessful in holding down the tide which brought swarms of attorneys, or counsellors, by the early seventeenth century. These men, some of whom had scant legal education, made their living by serving clerkships, writing pleadings, and pursuing suits in courts other than that of the Common Pleas. Their numbers quadrupled from the 1570s to the 1630s.[4] Complaints against the 'superfluous number of common attorneys at the law at this day', causing 'great dissensions, disorder, suits and plaints', can be found throughout the records,[5] particularly from the 1570s to the turn of the century.[6] There were several plans to limit their numbers, and

---

[1] The legislative background is discussed in Holdsworth, *HEL* IV, 536–8.

[2] A statistical analysis has been made by Lawrence Stone, 'The educational revolution in England, 1560–1640', *P & P*, no. 28 (1964), 51–64.

[3] Knafla, 'The matriculation revolution and education at the Inns of Court in Renaissance England', in *Tudor men and institutions* (Baton Rouge La. 1972), 234–8.

[4] Michael Birks, *Gentlemen of the law* (1960), 98–110. The growth was from 313 in 1578 to 1,383 in 1633.

[5] Mr Sackford, 'A Note for a letter touching the attorneys of the Kinges Benche and Comen Place', dated 15 Jan. 1585/6. Bearing Burghley's corrections, this states that it was prepared with the help of *CJs* Wray and Anderson, and suggests a full exam. of the number of attorneys practising before the two courts since 1558.

[6] The ex. in Cockburn, *Assizes*, 146; Thomas Wilson's tract in C.U.L. Seligman MS 1625 E.W. 69, Ellesm. MS 1264, ff. 169–72; and the anon. tracts in Lans. MS 44, ff. 8v–12v, and Royal MS 18.A.LXXIII, ff. 2r–7v.

apportion them among the various courts at Westminster.[1] The inns
of court themselves attempted to restrict the growth of attorneys,[2]
but none of these devices succeeded. The number of attorneys 'had
grown great and audacious'.[3]

Despite this criticism the law profession was not wholly negative
towards the growth of the attorney within its prestigious ranks.[4] Some
members believed that the proliferation of attorneys provided a larger
base that would result in the independence of the profession. One
particular writer attributed this growth to the profit motive and placed
it in a positive light: there was no better investment than to buy your
way in and out of an inn of court for a solicitorship, then into the
clerkships of local and central government.[5] Another writer held that
profit was not necessarily a by-product of corruption, and that lawyers
were still among the most honest and worthy men of the governing
class.[6] The evidence, however, certainly suggests that with these
increased numbers patronage had become an important factor in gaining admission to the inns of court and a call to the Bar. Moreover,
barristers once called to the Bar were often expected to buy their way
into the order of Serjeants, and sometimes to the judicial Bench
itself.[7]

The Chancellor agreed with those of his contemporaries who held
that the number of lawyers had grown too quickly, and he demanded
that 'the most expert and honest, discreet and sufficient only to be

[1] The plans in Lans. MS 106, ff. 103v–4r, and Harl. MS 7020, ff. 252r–3v. The author
wishes to thank Mr T. Barrier Clendenin for these refs. Mr Christopher W. Brooks of Linacre
Coll. Oxford is pursuing this subject further in his doctoral diss. and the author wishes to
thank him for his comments.

[2] The refs. to the records of the inns on this subject have been culled by Hugh H. L. Bellot,
'The exclusion of attorneys from the Inns of Court', *LQR* XXVI (1910), 137–45. His conclusions, however, are untenable.

[3] 'Iudicature', f. 1. See also *APC, 1599–1600*, 28–32; and the poem attributed to Sir
Walter Ralegh, 'The Lie'.

[4] It was also beneficial to the Inns of Court and chancery, and to the economy and society
of the Holborn area.

[5] 'Omne Jus', Add. MS 41.613, f. 84.

[6] William Wilkes, *Obedience, or Ecclesiastical Union* (1605), 46–7. The problems of the law
profession at this time have been raised in Holdsworth, *HEL* VI, 431–41, 444–56, 461–74,
477–9, 481–6. The context for the problem of growth has been explored by Mark H. Curtis,
'The alienated intellectuals of early Stuart England', *P & P*, no. 23 (1962), 25–43.

[7] Hyman Henry Anthony Cooper, 'Promotion and politics among the common law judges of
the reigns of James I and Charles I' M.A. thesis, (Liverpool Univ. 1964), 99–143. Important
surveys of the contemp. literature are those of Wilfrid Prest, 'Legal education of the gentry at
the Inns of Court, 1560–1640', *P & P*, no. 38 (1967), 20–39; and J. H. Baker, 'Counsellors and
barristers – an historical survey', *CLJ* XXVII (1969), 205–29.

allowed, and the residue to be discharged and put from the trade'. He also stated that the proliferation of attorneys was closely related to the increase in litigation, for they served 'to stir up suits and so bring water to the mill'.[1] At the beginning of the reign he had made some notes for inquiring into the number and quality of the various ranks of the law profession: barristers, solicitors, scriveners, and clerks.[2] These notes were made preparatory to acts of Parliament which attempted to regulate the law profession.[3] He also utilised his own influence to secure competent appointments to the office of Serjeant-at-law.[4]

Ellesmere was equally concerned with the number and quality of local magistrates, and with their abilities. In addition to sharp addresses which he gave frequently before the justices of the peace assembled in the Star Chamber, in a paper on procedural problems he penned the following endorsement: 'for beginning, proceeding, and executing the law with the least trouble and cost, men learned and of the better sort to be employed as the best ministers of justice'.[5] This kind of statement would be too contentious to make publicly. However, measures stemming from such ideas would blow a chilling wind through the law profession in the days of the Commonwealth and the Protectorate. [6]

The more particular inconveniences of the legal system which Ellesmere disclosed in his tract on law reform were sixteen in number. Although he discussed them at random, the more important ones can be gathered according to two general classifications: problems arising out of the prerogative writs, and problems stemming from legal processes of the forms of action. The three prerogative writs which he discussed were the writs of *certiorari*, *habeas corpus*, and prohibition. The general problems underlying all these writs can be summarised

---

[1] 'Iudicature', f. 1r; and Ellesm. MS 452, endorsed 'Remembrances 4 June 1609', f. 1v.

[2] Ellesm. MS 2616, f. 2v.

[3] Particularly 'An Acte to reforme the Multitudes and Misdemeanors of Attorneyes and Sollicitors at Lawe', 3 Jac. c. 7 (1605/6), *Stat. Realm*, IV, Pt. 2, pp. 1083–4; and 'An Acte to prevent the overcharge of the People', 1 Jac. c. 5 (1604), *ibid*. p. 1022. See also Baker, *CLJ*, XXXII, 56, 72–3.

[4] The list for ex. with his notes and endorsement in Lans. MS 53, f. 120r.

[5] Ellesm. MS 456, f. 2v. His charges to the magistrates are in Hawarde, *Reportes*, 53, 311–2, 314–5.

[6] The important tracts on law reform from 1649–59 have been studied by Prall, *Agitation for law reform*, 50–72, 81–112, 128–43. A representative view of this radical literature was the pointed statement of John Jones; 'Read the Histories of England, and find lawyers the causes of all our Civil Wars in all ages' – *Every Man's Case; or, Lawyers Routed* (1652), 29. The author wishes to thank Dr Prall for this ref.

from the Chancellor's introductory comments on the writ of *dedimus potestatem*. Like any other prerogative writ, a *dedimus potestatem* could be issued by a common law court to empower commissioners to take the answer of a defendant in the country when that person pleaded an inability to come to London.[1] Ellesmere's complaint was that judges no longer inquired of the ability and integrity of the men appointed to such commissions, and that the commissioners were charging defendants excessive fees for the privilege of recording their answers in the country.[2] Complaints such as these had come before him when he was Chancellor of the Exchequer Court of Chester in the 1590s. They continued to come before him as matters of 'equity' in the Court of Chancery.[3]

A writ of *certiorari* was issued by a central tribunal in order to remove to itself the proceedings from a borough, communal, or feudal court. Ellesmere declared that these writs were being issued by clerks in the name of the courts of Chancery, King's Bench, and Common Pleas without consulting the respective judges. A situation such as this caused writs of *certiorari* to be issued on the behalf of several courts for the same matter, resulting in the confusion and inconvenience of the other parties.[4] The Chancellor made the same complaint about the issuance of writs of *procedendo* – writs which forbade appeals to central courts, or cancelled writs of *certiorari*. The basis of his objections was the excessive delegation of responsibilities by the judges of the central courts to their clerks,[5] and the degree to which such actions hindered the work of the local courts in whose hands the effective administration of law and order solely resided.

The privilege of the writ of *habeas corpus* was similarly misemployed. For example, an individual who had been judged and imprisoned for the non-payment of a debt could by a local, provincial, or conciliar court be released on a writ of *habeas corpus*. Ellesmere charged that the judges of the Court of Common Pleas, chiefly in the years when Sir

---

[1] The commissions are assessed in Jones, *Chancery*, 221–5.

[2] 'Iudicature', f. 5r. Ellesmere's order setting down rules for the exam. of witnesses are in G. W. Sanders, *Orders of the High Court of Chancery* (1845), I, 70, 73–4, 78–9; and in Ellesm. MS 2960.

[3] *Supra*, pp. 28–9; Hawarde, *Reportes*, 98 (SC, 28 June 1958); and *infra*, Chap. VII.

[4] 'Iudicature', f. 2v. A very useful study of *certiorari* is that of Edith Henderson, *Foundations of English administrative law* (Cambridge Mass. 1963), 89–98. Ellesmere, however, made no particular mention of the remedy of *mandamus* (writ of restitution) which emerged in the years 1606–15 (*ibid.* 46–80).

[5] For ex. Add. MS 41.613, ff. 84v–6r.

Edward Coke was Chief Justice (1606–13), were allowing convicted men to be released on the privilege of the writ without sufficient process of sureties: 'whereby they take their pleasure abroad in the country, and sometime commit great riots and outrages there, and take no care to pay their debts'.[1] Unfortunately, this alleged abuse of *habeas corpus* is not mentioned in the law reports of the period, nor in the contemporary literature.[2] While Ellesmere's complaint could doubtlessly be justified by individual instances, the parallel which he struck between debtors and rioters was compatible with the harsh attitude he had displayed towards convicted persons, and his opinion of the unemployed members of the lower class which was part of the more reactionary social thought of the period.[3]

The Chancellor also made a critique of prohibitions. The writ of prohibition was being used increasingly by the common law judges in the early seventeenth century to prohibit proceedings in causes before merchant, ecclesiastical, and equity courts.[4] Ellesmere charged that the common law courts were failing to require sufficient witnesses and evidence for the issuance of the writ. This abuse led to the increased number of prohibitions against proceedings in other courts, aiding and abetting the conflict of jurisdiction that was stamped upon the age.[5] He also objected to clerks drafting the writ at great length, thereby impoverishing the subjects through larger fees, and not always properly engrossing them for payment to the Crown.[6] By 1610 the fees themselves could range from twelve shillings to a pound for a single writ.[7]

Ellesmere considered the costly and excessive use of prohibitions to be one of the greatest judicial 'evils' of his time. He demonstrated this concern by devoting some effort to the study and debate of the problem. In one memorandum he made extensive comments on the wording of writs of prohibition which had been lodged against non-common law courts. This document was addressed chiefly to pro-

---

[1] 'Iudicature', ff. 2r–v, 4r, the quote at f. 2v. He made the criticism earlier in 'Prohibitians', p. 45.

[2] For ex. the full ms. report of proceedings in the K.B. in the early years of James: Add. MS 25.218, ff. 66r–7r, 148v–9r, 166v–7r, 190r, 226r.

[3] *Supra*, p. 81.

[4] In Bulstrode's reports of causes in the K.B. there are 44 cases brought by writ of prohibition in the years 1611–14: Bulstrode, *Reports*, Pts. I–III. The pr. reports, moreover, represent merely the tip of the iceberg that is represented by the plea rolls.

[5] 'Iudicature', ff. 3v–4r; and 'Prohibitians', pp. 40–1, 45–7.

[6] *Ibid.* 45.

[7] Cotton MSS Cleopatra F. II, f. 446r.

hibitions against the ecclesiastical and admiralty courts,[1] and became
the basis of Ellesmere's participation in the debates of the Privy
Council in the early years of James's reign, 1608–10. In these debates
he spoke firmly against their excessive application to suits before
ecclesiastical and conciliar courts, and noted their deleterious effect
on provincial and local courts.[2] Later, at a time closer to the composition of this and another tract, he prepared additional notes on the
illegality of common law judges granting writs of prohibition in causes
where the suits could be instituted and determined by an original
writ.[3] Ellesmere's views on prohibitions were couched within his
conception of a legal system where courts observed the abilities of one
another, and were as firmly fixed in their jurisdiction as the stars in the
universe. These views also led him to a confrontation with the judges
of the Court of King's Bench, a confrontation that would bring the
closing years of his public career to a hot conclusion.

The Chancellor's other legal grievances concerned particular
problems which had resulted from the expansion of the forms of action
in the sixteenth century. These problems stemmed from a response to
a worsening situation which had developed by the early sixteenth
century. The proceedings before the common law courts had become
archaic and dilatory, and the judges and practitioners of those courts
felt threatened by a revival of Roman law and an expansion of the
prerogative and conciliar courts which had marked a wave of legal
change in the reign of Henry VIII. The threat was gravest to the Court
of King's Bench, a court that had little original jurisdiction outside
criminal matters and appeals; and many of the criminal causes were
devolving to special commissions, the Assizes, and the Court of Star
Chamber. Thus, in the middle decades of the sixteenth century,
lawyers before the King's Bench experimented with the presentation
of common pleas by allowing plaintiffs to abuse the ancient right of
bringing any civil action against prisoners held in the custody of the
court.[4]

---

[1] 'Prohibitians', *infra* Chap. XIV; and Ellesm. MS 452, endorsed 'Remembrances 4 June
1609'.

[2] A full account is bound to Henry Powle's copy of 'A Treatise of Prohibitions to
Ecclesiastical Courts', L.I. Add. MS G.2 at ff. 97–126v. See also the letter in *Eg. Papers*,
417–8. The substance of the debates has been summarized in *State Trials* II, 131–60. The
major propositions are discussed in the tract, 'In What Cases the Kings Court of Common
Pleas maie grant Prohibitions', Tanner MS 247, ff. 1–24v.

[3] 'Notes for Reformacion', Ellesm. MS 766b.

[4] The best analyses of these developments are those of Baker, *Introduction to legal
history*, 30–5, 182–93; and Milsom, *Historical foundations*, 51–67, 132–8, 297–308.

The King's Bench had original jurisdiction of all men arrested in the County of Middlesex. The device used by lawyers to expand the potential of this jurisdiction was to allege a complaint of trespass against a potential defendant, sue out a writ of *capias* to have him arrested whenever he came into Middlesex, and, once arrested, to bring a bill against him for any common plea. The effective feature of this process was that one who failed to submit could be declared an 'outlaw', and forfeit his lands. The drawback of the device was that a *capias* was an expensive writ purchased from the clerk of a common law court. The first step was to allege a trespass, and the second to have a writ of *capias* issued for the accused's arrest in Middlesex. If the accused was not in Middlesex, but 'lurking' in the country, the court would send another writ of *capias* (called a *latitat*) to where he resided, and then he would be arrested and brought to the court. With this device the plaintiff could sue for any cause or plea once the defendant was a prisoner of the court in Middlesex.[1] The outcry against these tactics was compromised by a letter patent of 1608 that gave the clerks of the Chancery one-half the fee for the writ of a civil action when such an action was lodged in the King's Bench by common bill.[2]

The Court of Common Pleas reacted more slowly to these problems. It possessed, moreover, more business before its court than any other court in the land. However, by the late 1590s it attempted to make its judicial processes more effective by allowing suitors to allege a complaint of trespass, secure the defendant's body with a *capias*, and then proceed by bill instead of original writ. No bargain was struck, however, with the Chancery clerks.[3] How frequent, or successful, this device may have been will not be known until scholars begin to open that mass of legal records which has gone altogether too unused in the study of early modern times.

A second device used initially by the King's Bench, and later by the Common Pleas, was to enlarge the scope of the writ of trespass. A basic distinction in English law had been the difference between trespass (a positive wrong committed), and covenant (something to be per-

---

[1] An interesting but incomplete account is that of Marjorie Blatcher, 'Touching the writ of Latitat: an act of no great moment', in *Elizabethan government and society*, ed. S. T. Bindoff *et al.* (1961), 188–212. The critique is by Baker, *Introduction to legal history*, 34.

[2] The compromise may have been struck even earlier; see the paper in Add. MS 10.038, f. 188, endorsed by Julius Caesar 'Nov. 1607'.

[3] Ralph Sutton held that the abandonment of the traditional process did not bring disadvantage to the defendant: *Personal actions at common law* (1929), 37–45.

formed). The problem arose when one who, in failing to perform his bond, caused wrong or injury. In an instance such as this the plaintiff could argue a 'special case' of trespass instead of covenant. A tortious element, however, would have to exist. The advantage of trespass to the plaintiff was that it brought damages instead of performance. This became the law by the reign of Henry VIII.

The change in trespass occurred in the middle decades of the sixteenth century, when plaintiffs asked for a 'special case' in instances where there was a mere failure to perform (or, a simple breach of contract). Fraud and deceit would be alleged: that the defendant failed to do, or to pay, after good consideration had been given. This 'special case' would be called 'assumpsit', the failure to perform an undertaking. By Slade's Case in 1602 the King's Bench had made every contract for debt a 'promise' to pay, and the failure to adhere to that promise would allow a suit of 'action on the case for assumpsit'. In fact, by 1611 assumpsit could cover almost every kind of debt and covenant.[1]

This same fiction was used in the Court of Common Pleas for expanding the actions dealing with property. The real property actions allowed for the recovery only of freehold land, and the action of ejectment gave leaseholders protection for their leases before the common law courts. By the end of the sixteenth century a great change was occurring in the Court of Common Pleas. Plaintiffs were being allowed to allege fictitious leases in order to sue for the recovery of freehold land by the more simple and inexpensive action of ejectment, rather than by the more expensive and cumbersome action of novel disseisin.[2]

The result of these changes by the early seventeenth century was that common law process no longer had the same kind of certainty and predictability as it had possessed in the past. Ellesmere was a judicial conservative in these aspects of change, and he objected to them in their entirety. He expressed this opposition by noting specific objections to a number of devices used by the common law courts to hasten and expand their abilities to do justice. Thus the list of 'special in-

---

[1] J. H. Baker, 'New Light on Slade's Case', CLJ XXIX (1971), 51–67, 213–36.

[2] The action of ejectment is best described in Sutton, Personal actions, 52–6; for its history see A. W. B. Simpson, An introduction to the history of the land law (corr. ed. Oxford 1964), 135–40. Its extension to copyholders has been studied by Charles Montgomery Gray, Copyhold, equity, and the common law (Cambridge Mass. 1963), 54–92. The origins of legal fictions in the land law have been examined impressively by C. A. F. Meekings, 'Final concords: their history and form', Surrey Rec. Soc. XIX (1946, repr. 1968), ix–lv.

conveniences' noted in his tract included the use or misuse of *capias*, 'outlawry', *latitat*, 'special case', *assumpsit*, and *ejectment*:[1] writs and actions which formed the foundations for the growth of the common law in modern times.

Ellesmere attacked what he called the misuse of the writs of *capias* and *latitat*, and of the process of 'outlawry'. The Chancellor objected to the use of *capias* to attach a person to the Court of Common Pleas, and then allow the plaintiff to proceed against him in any personal action by a simple bill without suing the original writ.[2] This process deprived the Crown of its revenues from the writ, and the defendant of his traditional privileges of defence.[3] The former objection was shared by officials of the King's Treasury and Chancery, and the latter by many common lawyers.

The Chancellor also objected to the King's Bench use of *capias* and *latitat* to bring civil causes under its jurisdiction. This was judged 'a novelty and trick newly devised, and hath no precedent or example in the Register, or in the books of law'.[4] He claimed that such a change — especially the use of *latitat* — would destroy the old, original actions upon which the common law was based.[5] A number of common lawyers agreed with him, and those who wrote tracts on 'the unlawful holding of Common Pleas in the King's Bench' appealed to the Chancellor to use his influence to bring it to an end.[6]

The Chancellor was equally concerned with what he regarded as a fraudulent use of the process of outlawry. He accused the clerks of the common law courts of taking bribes from persons who wished to bring the process of outlawry without issuing first the proper writs of *capias*.[7] By customary right a declaration of outlawry could not be made unless the person served failed to answer the fifth of five such summonses. Ellesmere attributed this misuse to the lack of careful attention by judges, and the unscrupulousness of clerks and attorneys. His criticisms grew out of the unsuccessful attempts to regulate the

---

[1] 'Iudicature', ff. 2r–5r.

[2] 'Iudicature', ff. 3r–4v; and 'Prohibitians', 45. Previously, the *capias* had been issued before, with, or after the original writ.

[3] *Ibid.* f. 4r–v. Additional complaints can be found in Add. MS 10.038, ff. 43r–4r; and Lans. MS 64, ff. 190r–iv. 'Iudicature', f. iv.   [4] 'Iudicature', f. 1v.

[5] 'Prohibitians', 45–6. 'These new writtes, theise latitats, of late much in vse, but in auntiente time neuer knowne nor hearde of, haue done muche hurte and litle good': *Rape v. Girlin & others*, S. C. June 1607, in Hawarde, *Reportes*, 323–7 at 326.

[6] Lans. MS 64, ff. 202v–5v; and Hargrave MS 227, f. 498.

[7] At first in Hawarde, *Reportes*, 113; and later in 'Iudicature'. For the Process see Blackstone, *Commentaries*, III, xvi, 283.

administration of writs in Parliament. His concern, however, was not fully justified. Although there were isolated examples of persons being attacked and suffering the confiscation of their lands and goods, the threat of outlawry had subsided in the second decade of the seventeenth century as parties were allowed increasingly to seek relief through pardons from the Crown.[1] Perhaps the Chancellor himself had become partly responsible for assisting to alleviate the hardships caused by this abuse.

The problems surrounding the development of the actions of *ejectment* and *assumpsit* were equally perplexing, and the only response of the Chancellor was a negative one. His interest in *ejectment* stemmed from his later legal studies in the 1570s and 1580s. At that time he noted in the margins of his new law books the ways in which the action was being applied.[2] Later, in writing on both prohibitions and law reform, he held that the action of *ejectment*, when no longer restricted to leases, so confused the understanding of the real actions that this new usage was contributing to the 'great decay of the true knowledge and learning of the law'.[3] The fiction, however, was fully accepted in all the common law courts by this time, and the ritual of going through the motions had actually been dispensed with in the Court of King's Bench.

The Chancellor also objected to the development of *assumpsit*. Suspicious of the use of the concept in place of the traditional actions of Debt and Covenant, he can be numbered among those jurists who refused to forget the trespassory associations of *assumpsit* and did not want it to lie where Debt was available. But he also wrote complaining of 'a new and common practice' in the Common Pleas: 'to have secret judgments upon confessions of debts and damages'.[4] Earlier the Chancellor had noted examples in his law books of how secret judgments had crept into the conciliar courts as well as those of the common law.[5] Afterwards he criticised this device in his tract on

---

[1] Blatcher, 'Working of the King's Bench', 352–7. Exs. of outlawry in this period are found in the warrant books bearing the King's sign manual: SP 39/4–8.

[2] Ellesm. MS 482, ff. 190–3; and the marginal notes in his copies of Dyer, *Novel Cases*, Hunt. RB 59138, ff. 192r, 309r, 320r, 374r; and William Rastell, *A Collection of Entrees* (1566), Hunt. RB 69108, ff. 243r, 318v, 640r.

[3] 'Iudicature', f. 2r; and 'Prohibitians', 44. As Chanc. he often put this view into practice by accepting injunctions against common law courts that allowed the fictitious leases to be alleged. Exs. of his decisions in such cases are in *Practice Chanc.* 31–4, 43–8. See generally Holdsworth, *HEL* VI, 625–8; VII, 4–23.

[4] 'Iudicature', f. 1r.

[5] Fitzherbert, *Brevium* (but the 3rd ed. 1555 col. 1560), Hunt. RB 59688, ff. 97v, 98v, 99v, 116r; and in Dyer, *Novel Cases*, ff. 168v, 241v, 268r, 339v. Practices such as these are discussed in Holdsworth, *HEL* V, 212–13, 416–17.

'Prohibitians'.[1] At this time he brought these criticisms together in alleging that debtors could procure fictitious creditors and have their debts cancelled without any trial or publicity. Such secret judgments deceived the true creditors who lost the legal title to the funds which were owed to them, 'for they suspect not these secret judgments nor know not how nor where to search for the same'.[2]

Ellesmere's complaints of changing common law processes appear to have been directed to a common law usage that permitted the plaintiff a degree of freedom in setting down his facts, and enabled the judge to allow or disallow them according to his professional discretion. Perhaps he had this usage in mind when he wrote that the judges of the common law were often acting 'as Chancellors to make orders in equity, according to their own discretions, not regarding nor standing upon the strict rules of law ... and so confound the distinct jurisdictions of common law and equity'.[3] He had come to regard matters such as recording judicial business out of term, detention in prison, discretion in awarding costs and damages, and staying an execution of judgment, as 'equitable' practices reserved to courts of equity.[4] Ellesmere was a common lawyer in a conciliar court who was attempting at the same time to apply common law rules to equity; and the situation was not without its paradox.

If there is any one thread that gives unity to this tract, it is the fear of the collapse of the old actions and of the ancient common law traditions. When the Chancellor regretted the demise of the real actions, the multitude of suits in personal actions, and the decay of the old learning, he was expressing a point of view that was not unfamiliar to the judges of the common law. The Chief Justice, Sir Edward Coke, had stated similar but other concerns in the introduction to his eighth report just a few years before the Chancellor had penned his tract.[5] Ellesmere's criticisms, however, give the appearance of being exaggerated. His remedies, had they ever been implemented, would have done more to restrict the ability of the law to change with the needs of a litigious society than to improve it. In this respect Ellesmere was not

---

[1] 'Prohibitians', 47.

[2] 'Iudicature', f. 3r. Although Ellesmere was concerned with Crown fees, he did not note here or elsewhere the non-payment of fines in actions of debt before the K.B. or the non-payment of fines and amercements for all personal actions since the 1590s; see the briefs in Sir Julius Caesar's papers: Add. MS 10.038, ff. 188 and 240, dated Nov. 1607.

[3] 'Iudicature', f. 5r; and Rep. Chanc. 7. These dangers are discussed by Samuel Thorne in his introduction to Edward Hake's Epieikeia (New Haven Conn. 1953), pp. vii, ix.

[4] 'Prohibitians', 43–4; and the later discussion infra, Chap. VII.

[5] 8 Co. Rep. sigs. xxvii–xxviii; and his remonstrances in Ferrer's Case, 6 Co. Rep. 7r (CP 1598), and Blackamore's Case, 8 Co. Rep. 156r (CP 1611).

alone. He was one of those jurists of whom it could be said, 'certainty was the prime necessity of the law'.[1] That quest for certainty was to lead him first into one of the great quagmires of the law, Coke's Reports, and then to one of the most famous judicial disputes of early modern times, the question of the supremacy of the Chancellor's decree.

[1] Samuel E. Thorne, 'Tudor social transformation and legal change', *New York Univ. Law Rev.* XXVI (1951), 10–23, the quote at p. 22.

THE CLASH OF JURISDICTIONS: CENTRAL AND LOCAL AUTHORITIES, SECULAR AND ECCLESIASTICAL

Ellesmere's keen interest in the problems of law reform had placed him in a position where he could no longer agree with some of the current developments in the expansion of the common law. One of the most outspoken supporters of these legal developments was Sir Edward Coke, and his 'Reports' became a landmark for the new common law which was emerging in the late sixteenth and early seventeenth centuries. It was perhaps inevitable that the Chancellor would come to sharp disagreement with the Chief Justice over a number of these issues. Coke's Reports provided the occasion for their disagreements. The Reports, together with Ellesmere's critique, represent in the broadest sense a clash of views on the jurisdiction of courts in the English legal system: central and local, secular and ecclesiastical.

Coke's Reports, published in the years 1600–15, are one of the most important collections of law reports in the early modern period. Recognised as having great authority, they contributed significantly to the development of the common law in the seventeenth and eighteenth centuries; and they rendered their author memorable in the annals of the law profession.[1] Coke was without doubt one of the foremost legal scholars of his generation. He possessed both an infinite capacity for arduous labour and a brilliant mind. The notes which he compiled from the legal record – the plea rolls – reveal a reading and knowledge of the records that was unmatched by contemporaries;[2] and his advice on how to study the law was widely quoted. Coke wrote that the student must search diligently in the Year Books and the plea rolls to discern the issues which were relevant to the development of the law in his time. Although he would have to rely heavily on inference in order to make sense of the legal record, his task was to come to

---

[1] There is, unfortunately, no adequate account of either his life or his career. The ms. colls. in the B.M., the I.T., the P.R.O., and Holkham Hall are very extensive in Coke materials.

[2] Samuel E. Thorne in *A catalogue of the library of Sir Edward Coke*, ed. W. O. Hassall (New Haven Conn, 1950), pp. vi–viii.

conclusions.[1] The relationship between the study of these old sources and modern legal development was cogently expressed in one of his popular aphorisms: 'out of the old fields must come the new corn'.[2]

This man – both as a lawyer and a judge – worked from the time-honoured perspective of individual cases. His idea of the nature of law was based on legal doctrines which had been constructed out of the growth of precedents. No one cause was important, no one case was decisive. The function of the lawyer was to select relevant precedents and compose the most cogent argument for his client. The responsibility of the judge was to make the decision that best accorded with the facts. Common law doctrine was thus the expression of that which had been established.[3]

Coke's Reports are generally known from the printed version. Although he published them from his own manuscripts, few scholars have ever consulted the extant originals. Fortunately, three of the five volumes of his manuscript reports survive, and both lawyers and historians owe a debt to Dr John Baker for piecing together the genesis of Coke's Reports.[4] This extensive collection of cases was compiled between 1579 and 1616. The causes were reported in a more or less chronological fashion, and occasionally he included an analysis of an earlier case he thought to be relevant. Afterwards individual items were selected for publication. Indeed, one is tempted to suggest that they were originally reported for publication. While some of the printed Reports appear to have been published without change, in at least a few instances they were abbreviated, or enlarged with additions or notes from the plea rolls.

The eleven parts of Coke's Reports which were printed in his lifetime appear to have been compiled in three phases. The initial phase concerned selections from his first three manuscript volumes of reports (MS Reps. A–C) for the years 1579–1606. Parts I–III con-

---

[1] Co. Lit. 'The Preface', p. xlii; and 4 Inst. 109.

[2] Yale Law MS G.R. 24, f. 83 (Oct. 1609).

[3] Some of the eably twentieth-century analyses of this subject are still useful. For ex. R. A. MacKay, 'Coke – Parliamentary sovereignty or the supremacy of the law', Michigan Law Rev. 22 (Jan. 1924), 215–47; and the summary in Holdsworth, HEL v, 462–4. Both more stimulating and puzzling is the study of J. G. A. Pocock, The ancient constitution and the feudal law (Cambridge 1957), 35–55. The best critiques are those of Christopher Hill, Intellectual origins of the English Revolution (Oxford 1965), 250–6; and William F. Swindler, Magna Carta legend and legacy (New York 1965), 166–90.

[4] J. H. Baker, 'Coke's notebooks and the sources of his reports', CLJ xxx (1972), 59–86. This supersedes T. F. T. Plucknett, 'The genesis of Coke's reports', Cornell Law Quat. 27 (1942), 190–213. The reconstructed account of Coke's ms. reports, apart from the author's interpretation of the phases, is from Baker, op. cit.

tained the major cases which he reported for these years, and they consisted largely of lengthy accounts of cases on real property law and conveyancing. Parts IV–VI were published in 1604–7 as collections of lesser cases from that same period. The second phase resumed the chronological reporting of major cases from the manuscript reports (MS Reps. D–E) for 1606–11, and this comprised Parts VII–VIII. The third phase, however, marked a new departure in reporting.

Parts IX–XI were published from the reports (lost MS Rep. F) for 1611–15/6, and contained Coke's 'new cases'. These consisted largely of causes which were deliberated before the court in which Coke sat as Lord Chief Justice. Including many controversial decisions – particularly on the royal prerogative, local authorities, and the ecclesiastical courts – Parts IX–XI contained much more commentary than the previous ones. They also included lengthy digressions on issues which the Chief Justice wished to emphasise. These Reports proved to be the most contentious of the printed ones. They did not contain, however, the only controversial cases. Parts XII–XIII, which were published posthumously in 1656–9, included equally debatable cases from Coke's manuscript reports in the third period. Thus, the contents of Parts IX–XIII, in addition to the extant manuscript volume of MS E, demonstrate beyond doubt the controversial character of Coke's reports that was only partially revealed in the printed Reports of Parts IX–XI which caused so much contention in the second decade of the seventeenth century.

Coke's Reports initiated widespread controversy as soon as they were published. The most critical opinions, however, came from self-seeking courtiers of the royal court. Coke was accused of substituting his personal views for the opinions of the Bench, of reporting firm decisions where the judges were divided or the case was not concluded, of inserting long discourses on legal issues that were never argued before the court, and of misinterpreting the past.[1] Charges such as these prompted his personal enemies to capitalise on the opportunity to speak of the Chief Justice as 'a colossal figurehead'.[2] Sir Francis Bacon, his arch-rival, wrote a facetious 'Letter of Advice' from a 'true friend', 'to show you your true face in a glass'. Here Bacon

---

[1] The critical proceedings before the P.C. have been interpreted by C. W. Johnson, *The life of Sir Edward Coke* (1837), I, 318–27. (This work, and that of C. W. James – *Chief Justice Coke*, 1929 – are the best general studies of Coke.) Bacon's account of these proceedings is in the *Letters*, VI, 76–7, 90–6, 397–408.

[2] Anthony Weldon, *The Court and Character of James I* (1650), 123. See also the words of Coke's wife, Lady Elizabeth Hatton: *The lady of Bleeding Heart Yard*, ed. Laura Norsworthy (New York 1936), p. xviii.

accused the Chief Justice of being more pleader than judge: of speaking and not listening, of conversing with books, rather than with men, of being indiscriminate in his use of sources, and hasty in coming to conclusions. 'You make the law to lean a little too much to your opinion; whereby you show yourself a legal tyrant.'[1] While Bacon's known animosity rendered his comments biased and of questionable validity, they were further exaggerated in court gossip to go beyond the boundaries of both historical accuracy and social propriety.

There was also criticism in a non-pejorative sense from within the law profession. Since the Chief Justice was a forceful and controversial advocate throughout his career, reputable judges and reporters often disagreed with his arguments as well as with his decisions. Among them were judges like Altham, Savile, and Walmesley, and reporters such as Croke, Hobart, and Moore.[2] In at least one instance the criticism was weighty.[3] Coke's Reports, however, were a marked improvement over those which preceded them. Although Plowden and Dyer are generally regarded as the first authors of the 'modern report', our knowledge of the legal materials of this period is far too slight to allow such easy generalisations. The great bulk of good law reports were never printed. They are only now being identified, but not until they have been studied will the student of law and history be able to place the works of Coke in their proper contemporary context.[4]

In order to come to an understanding of Coke's Reports, one must look at Coke the lawyer, judge, and politician. Coke was above all an independent man with a mind of his own. As a privy councillor in the years 1613–15, he aided the reformers in proposing measures for fiscal and economic reform. In fact, he indicated the potential of a successful Lord Treasurer.[5] He also attempted to gain recognition of the

[1] 'Witty speeches', Harl. MS 677, ff. 31r and 32r. Baron Altham had expressed a similar sentiment: Ellesm. MS 2184.

[2] The corresp. in Bacon, *Letters* v, 245; *Buccleuch MSS, H.M.C. 10th Rep. App. Pt. IV* (1885), 18; and the *Buccleuch MSS*, 1, 248.

[3] G. D. G. Hall, 'An assize book of the seventeenth century', *AJLH* 7 (1963), 239–45.

[4] A bibliog. of pr. and ms. reports is provided in L. W. Abbott, *Law reporting in England 1485–1585* (1973), Apps. I–II. Some important ms. reports for the late sixteenth and early seventeenth centuries are cited in Baker, 'Coke's notebooks', and in his 'New light on Slade's Case', *CLJ* XXIX (1971), 213–36. Another superb ex. of their use is that of Charles M. Gray, 'Bonham's Case reviewed', *AmPhS* 116 (1972), 35–58.

[5] Coke's genuine ability to perceive economic problems and make suggestions for their resolution has been recognised only recently in the penetrating studies of Prestwich, *Cranfield*, 164–71, 180–2, 192–3, 216–22; and Hill, *Intellectual origins*, 233–43. The origins of that insight came, in the author's opinion, from Coke's years of riding on the circuit; see the background sketched by Cockburn, *Assizes*, 168–83.

necessity for the government and the law courts to work in harmony
with the House of Commons. But in 1616 he fell both from the reforming faction and the Privy Council. Later, as a parliamentarian,
Coke joined with the Earl of Pembroke to force King James to delete
a restraining clause in the patent declaring the elections for the
Parliament of 1621. The clause sought to persuade the electors to shun
'curious and wrangling lawyers' as their representatives in Parliament: those lawyers who formed the backbone of constructive opposition to the Crown.[1] Finally, due to his failures as a moderate reformer
in the second decade of the century he was brought into direct
conflict with the Crown and the Privy Council in the 1620s.

The relationship of the Chief Justice, Sir Edward Coke, to the
Lord Chancellor, Baron Ellesmere, is a crucial one for the understanding of this period. It also reveals the complexity of the age.
Possessed of deeply seated national sentiments, these individuals
aspired to make government more responsible to the new aristocracy
which they represented. Thus both men often joined in zealously to
prosecute persons suspect of treason and non-conformity to the State.[2]
As political allies in the Privy Council, they had sought a reconciliation of Crown and Commons, and worked for fiscal and economic
reform.[3] And in legal matters of great public importance they worked
hand in hand. Hating the sycophants and royal favourites who
dominated the royal court, they helped to expose the Overbury affair
and to secure the fall of the King's favourite, Robert Carr, Earl of
Somerset.[4]

Coke and Ellesmere often displayed a mutual regard for justice and
the rule of law.[5] On one occasion Ellesmere requested Coke to publish
the argument he had just given in the next volume of his Reports, and
on another he hailed the Chief Justice as a man 'who had taken great
pains and delivered many excellent things... and those of great
antiquity, whereof the world never took knowledge before'.[6] The
two men relished, moreover, the opportunity of striking great blows

[1] Bacon, *Letters* VII, 128. The context has been set out by Robert Zaller, *The Parliament of 1621* (Berkeley, Calif. 1971), 47–58, 69–83.

[2] The cases, for ex. in the *Salisbury MSS*, v, 241–4; and Ellesm. MS 250.

[3] Coke reminisced on these experiences when later defining the qualities of a councillor: *Debates in the House of Commons in 1625*, Camden Soc. New Ser. 6 (1878), 115.

[4] Their work on the case is in the *CSPD*, *1611–1618*, pp. 316–37. For the affair and its context see G. V. P. Akrigg, *Jacobean pageant* (Cambridge Mass. 1962), 181–204.

[5] Coke MS Rep. A, f. 318r; and MS Rep. C, ff. 81r, 82v.

[6] Bacon, *Letters* IV, 416 (26 Jan. 1613/4). Other exs. are in Hawarde, *Reportes*, 308; and Ellesm. MS 1281.

at 'evil doers'. For example, when in 1614 a lawyer and his client were exposed in the Star Chamber for blackmail, the Chancellor and the Chief Justice had the attorney disbarred from practice, he and his accomplice pilloried, and their ears cut off. Branded in the forehead with a 'C' for conspiracy, they were then whipped through the streets and fined £500 each.[1] Tough men dispensed tough judgments.

But these two jurists also had their differences, and the differences were not restricted either to their opinions on law reform or to the question of common law and equitable jurisdiction which brought about their open confrontation in 1615–16. Coke was less enamoured than Ellesmere of the monarchy, Church, and local government. When he attacked them directly he was confronted with the solid opposition of the Chancellor. Distinctions such as these increased the competition of both men for patronage in the offices of local and central government.[2] Coke was also less enamoured with Ellesmere's maintenance of the *status quo* in the development of the common law doctrines discussed in the previous chapter. For example, the Chief Justice wanted to expand the uses of action on the case and *latitat*. But the Chancellor, like his beloved poet Samuel Daniel, would have none of this: 'Thou wilt not alter the foundation Thy ancestors have laide of this estate, Nor Grieve thy land with innovation, Nor take from us more than thou wilt collate.'[3]

These differences provide the background for Ellesmere's preparation of a critique of Coke's Reports in the years 1613–16. Although Ellesmere had long regarded Coke as superior in sheer knowledge of the law, the Chancellor had become increasingly dissatisfied with a number of Coke's decisions from *Calvin's Case* in 1608 to those which Coke printed in his Reports from Parts VIII–XI. These decisions had entered the arena of public debate. They also touched on matters which involved the personal activities of both men. Thus from the volumes of Coke's Reports published in 1611–15/6 came fifteen of the twenty-eight cases that Ellesmere discussed in his critique, which was later entitled 'The Lord Chancellor Egertons Observations vpon ye Lord Cookes Reportes'.

Ellesmere's observations focused on Coke's views of three general subjects: the King and the royal prerogative, bishops and prohibitions

---

[1] *Miller v. Reignolds and Bassett* (SC 1614), Godbolt, *Reports*, 205–7.

[2] For ex. the letter of Ellesmere's wife Alice in Hasts. MS 2513 (18 Feb. 1613/4).

[3] Samuel Daniel, *A Panegyric Congratulatory delivered to the King's Most Excellent Majesty* (1603), stanza 30.

against ecclesiastical courts and commissions, and the jurisdiction of local authorities. Of the twenty-eight cases reviewed by the Chancellor, seven were concerned with the first subject, six with the second, and eight with the third. Ellesmere's choice of cases was influenced primarily by the proceedings in which he was directly involved. Thus the Chancellor not only took issue with the arguments used by the Chief Justice, but in some instances he also accused him of misreporting the proceedings and judgments of the court. In more than one-third of the cases, Ellesmere contended that the arguments attributed to the Bench were those of Coke alone, and in some of these instances he charged the Chief Justice with reporting final judgments where the matter had not yet been concluded.

Equally important are the cases in Coke's Reports which Ellesmere did not criticise. The Chancellor, as we have seen, had disagreed previously with the Chief Justice on the evolution of the land law and the forms of action.[1] There is also the possibility that they differed on the law of contracts.[2] Nevertheless, none of these crucial areas in the substantive development of the common law were discussed in Ellesmere's observations on Coke's Reports. The reader will not find here discussions of vexing problems concerning long and short leases, manorial and copyhold customs, ownership and possession, and entails and the common recovery. Problems such as these – in so far as they were ever discussed – were noted specifically in his brief on law reform and indirectly in his tract on prohibitions.[3] Instead, the Chancellor addressed this critique to those current legal debates which concerned important matters of State.

Initially, Ellesmere prepared a common manuscript abridgment of Coke's Reports as they were printed, listing and referencing the cases. His abridgment, however, became more extensive beginning with the publication of the eighth part in 1611.[4] Later, following the appearance of the eleventh part in 1615, Ellesmere drafted a memorandum on Coke's Reports that discussed the prefaces and forty-one cases with citations to many others.[5] This preliminary sketch formed the basis of his final brief. A large portion of this document was organised in

---

[1] *Supra*, pp. 116–21.

[2] Hall, 'Assize Book', 239–45.

[3] Samuel Thorne, 'Tudor social transformation and legal change', *New York Univ. Law Rev.* XXVI (1951), 10–23; and Ellesmere's 'Iudicature'.

[4] 'Abridgement of the Lord Cokes Reportes', Harg. MS 254, ff. 2–31, the change at f. 20.

[5] 'Observacions vpon Cookes Reports', Harg. MS 254, ff. 52r–7r.

four general subjects: the rights of the Church, the power of the King's prerogative, the jurisdiction of courts, and the interests of the citizen. A final, and smaller, section dealt with problems such as Coke's interpretation of the original record, and the reporting of cases in which the issue had not been resolved.[1]

Ellesmere's brief on Coke's Reports was given to the King's legal counsel at some point in the summer of 1616, and it formed the basis of an investigation by the Privy Council. An analysis of the Council's proceedings from 2–21 October 1616 reveals that both the Chancellor and Attorney-General Bacon were made responsible by the King for investigating the Chief Justice with reference to his Reports.[2] In fact, the 'heads of inquiry' which were put to Coke for his 'reconsiderations' came from Ellesmere's brief. The affair appears to have reached a satisfactory conclusion before the Privy Council on 21 October. But it is evident from the correspondence of court gossips that George Villiers, the new royal favourite, was primarily responsible for the King's refusal to accept a conclusion of the matter.[3] Francis Bacon used this opportunity for his own advantage.

Although Bacon had previously spoken of these Reports as saving the common law from utter confusion and collapse, he now prepared a rather presumptuous list of seventeen 'charges' against the Chief Justice's Reports. Many of the Attorney-General's criticisms were unfounded.[4] Another brief, compiled by Henry Yelverton, was far more dispassionate, factual, and substantial.[5] But Bacon was relentless. Seeking political advancement at any cost, he not only continued his campaign to disparage Coke's Reports, but he also concocted a scheme for the 'Reporters of the Law' that would have imposed on legal reporting the tighest rules of censorship that had ever existed in England's history.[6]

Ellesmere's criticism of Coke's Reports was not made for the purpose of political advancement. The Chancellor's critique stemmed from a constant reading of the Reports which developed a life-span

[1] The two sections are 'Eg. on Coke', ff. 32v–46r and 46r–50v, respectively.
[2] The relevant proceedings have been pr. in Bacon, *Letters* VI, 76–97, 397–408.
[3] The accounts of Coke's confrontation with James in 1610 were published by Roland G. Usher, 'James I and Sir Edward Coke', *EHR* 18 (1903), 666–70.
[4] The comment in Bacon, *Letters* VI, 65; and the doc. entitled 'Innovations Introduced into the Laws and Government', *ibid.* 90–3 (Autumn 1616).
[5] Stowe MS 153, ff. 39r–40v.
[6] 'Ordinatio qua constituuntur lez Reporters de Lege', in Bacon, *Letters* VI, 264–8 (Oct. 1617).

of its own. With the publication of Coke's 'new cases' (Parts IX–XI) in 1613–15, the Chancellor's questions became more important. It now appeared that Coke was beginning to attack what Ellesmere regarded as the very basis of the constitution: the King, the Church, and the jurisdiction of local authorities. Thus Ellesmere, regarding himself as the defender of the existing order, composed in 1615 a rough brief of his opinions on Coke's Reports with reference to those three subjects. He then expanded them in his final manuscript, a document which, like his earlier one on the government in 1614, was obviously composed as a brief to bring the matter to the attention of the Privy Council. That it was not brought directly to the judges is an indication that the Chancellor recognised the reputation of the Chief Justice within the judiciary. This strategy of taking the matter to the Privy Council would also draw Coke's bitter enmity.[1]

At the core of this critique lay Coke's failure to accommodate the King. 'Whether they be in point of estate or in point of power, in all his Reports he hath stood so much in praise upon the King's honour, as in his resolutions he hath had no respect to the King's profit.'[2] Coke had attacked the supremacy of the Crown from the Bench. He argued against the right of the monarch to issue letters *in commendam*, and sought to limit prerogative rights in criminal cases and the scope of proclamations.[3] He also refused to consult the King in cases involving royal interests, and to acknowledge the right of the sovereign to consult the judges out of court for their opinions.[4] Initially Ellesmere selected four major cases with which to reveal the errors of the Chief Justice in matters concerning the rights of the Crown. In his final draft he expanded the criticism of these cases and added several others.[5]

---

[1] The C.J. in 'Poyntes Dangerous et absurd opinions affirme devant le Roy per Egerton Chauncellor', in Coke MS Rep. E, points 1–3 at f. 47v.

[2] 'Eg. on Coke', f. 36v.

[3] Respectively: *APC*, XXXIV, 595–609; *Miller v. Reignolds & Bassett* (SC 1614), Godbolt, *Reports*, 205; and *The Case of Proclamations* (PC 1611), 12 *Co. Rep.* 74. Coke's limitations on the King's dispensing powers were explained in a reply to a letter from the Crown which he entitled 'Penal Statutes' (Hill. 1604/5), 7 *Co. Rep.* 35v–6v; and in *The Case of Monopolies* (CP 1602), 11 *Co. Rep.* 84v–8v.

[4] *The Case of Prohibitions del Roy* (CP 1608), 12 *Co. Rep.* 63; and *Peacham's Case* (KB 1615), in Bacon, *Letters*, 120–1. A critique of his report on prohibitions had been made by Usher, 'James I and Coke', 664–75. Later, Coke recanted on several of these issues: *Co. Lit.* 7r–v, 43r–v, 90v, 99r.

[5] *Bonham's*, *Magdalen College*, *Darcy's*, and *Baskerville's* cases in Harg. MS 254, f. 55r; and the additions – including those of the *Prince's* and *Wiseman* cases – in 'Eg. on Coke', ff. 36v–8r. See also Rawl. MS B.432, f. 52.

The Chancellor used two older cases from Coke's Second Report—
the *Baskerville* and *Wiseman* cases (both in 1585) – to demonstrate that
the Chief Justice had sought to embarrass the Crown from the beginning of his Reports.[1] In *Baskerville's Case*, for example, the issue concerned the extent of royal privilege. The Queen had acquired a single
title of presentation to a Church benefice by *lapse*, and in law it was
limited to the very next presentation. Given the right by the patron to
make this, she defaulted. The position of the patron was that if the
Queen could delay her right and exercise it at any time, the inheritance would be injured. The position of the Crown was that the right
could be exercised at the time of its choosing. The court ruled that the
Crown could maintain a title only where its interest was permanent,
perpetual, and unlimited. Ellesmere challenged Coke's report of the
case because the decision was bad, and the interests of the Crown
were too severely restricted in the account. It appears that Ellesmere
agreed with the minority opinion of Judge Francis Rodes in rejecting
the decision of the court as well as Coke's Report.[2]

Ellesmere made a much better critique of Coke's Report of the
Prince's Case (1606/7). The case was full of complexities, and among
the many issues involved was the succession to the Duchy of Cornwall.
Coke, in reporting the case, wrote that the Duchy descended only to
the first begotten son of the monarch (in this instance, Prince Henry).
Ellesmere declared that an examination of the statutes and previous
customs demonstrated that the Duchy belonged to the king's heir
apparent, whoever he might be.[3] Coke's report of the case was
published in 1611, and in the next year Prince Henry died. The un-
foreseen conjunction of these events was apparently responsible for
the circulation of a rumour that Charles could not inherit the Duchy
lands. As a consequence, the Chancellor ordered Sir Edward Phelips,
Master of the Rolls, to draft a special proclamation creating Charles
Duke of Cornwall.[4] Ellesmere's later critique of the *Prince's Case*,

[1] *Baskerville's Case* (CP 1585), 7 *Co. Rep.* 28r; and 'Eg. on Coke', ff. 37v–8r. There is a
rather full report in [William Leonard] *Reports and Cases of Law* (1658), I, 280–1; II, 50–1.
[2] 2 *Co. Rep.* 10r–6r, 'Eg. on Coke', ff. 37v–9r. The author thanks David Yale and
John Baker for their assistance on the complicated issues in this and several other cases.
[3] 8 *Co. Rep.* 14r–6r; 'Eg. on Coke', f. 37v. The major doc. is cited *infra*, Chap. XV,
p. 303, n. 5. Yelverton had the same general objection to Coke's opinions in these three cases:
Stowe MS 153, f. 40r–v; as did Dodderidge: Trin. Coll. Dublin MS 807/3.
[4] *The Declaration of ovr Soveraigne Lord the King* (1613), Hunt, RB 17713 – Ellesmere's
copy with the notes of his son John. Coke later admitted this report to be in error: his letter pr. in
Bacon, *Letters* VI, 77 (2 Oct. 1616).

which raised these issues, displayed a rather vindictive side of his character, since obviously Coke could not have anticipated the untimely death of Charles's older brother.

The Chancellor was on firm ground in discussing another contemporary suit which involved him directly: the *Magdalen College Case* (1615). The college had owed a debt to a Genoese merchant and lacked the liquid capital to redeem it. The resources of the college, moreover, had been restricted by the statute of 13 Elizabeth which had forbidden it to lease land for longer than twenty-one years or three lives. The college discovered a way to avoid the statute by making a separate arrangement with the Crown. It granted a piece of land in Aldgate to the Queen, reserving the rent to itself, with the proviso that within a year she would grant it in turn to the merchant: an ingenious device to honour and pay the debt. In 1580 the merchant sold the land to the Earl of Oxford, and in 1607/8 Dr Barnaby Gooche, the then college Master, attempted to reclaim it after the Earl had erected buildings valued at over £10,000. The college granted a lease to one John Smith, who fictitiously took possession. The Earl's tenant re-entered the land and leased it to one John Warren, who was then fictitiously ejected by John Smith. Warren brought suit against Smith for *ejectment*, and the issue was joined on who had the title to make these leases, the college or the Earl. The issue hinged on the legality of the College's initial grant to the Queen. Coke as Chief Justice declared the view of the Bench that the general words of statutes included the Crown, thus including the Queen within the prohibition of the statute. The grant to the Crown was ruled invalid. The cause was decided for the college in the King's Bench at Easter, 1615, and Coke published his report the same year.[1] The matter, however, was far from over. 'While the arguments were even warm in the judges mouths, the case was likewise warm in the press and published, even though there was a writ of error presently brought upon the said judgment in the Exchequer Chamber which yet dependeth; though by the confidence used by the reporter in setting down the case, the party is much discouraged in his prosecution.'[2]

The parties, as well as the other judges, must have shared in the confusion about the status of the case. Certainly the Earl of Oxford

---

[1] *The Case of the Master and Fellows of Magdalen College* (KB 1615), 11 *Co. Rep.* 66v–79r.
[2] 'Eg. on Coke', f. 47v.

could no longer have much faith in pursuing his claim in the Exchequer Chamber in the light of Coke's strongly worded resolution of the matter in his published report. The Earl, disagreeing with the court's interpretation of the statute and desiring equitable relief for the construction of his buildings, then sued for his value in Chancery. Ellesmere gave him judgment in the famous *Earl of Oxford's Case*.[1]

Ellesmere's arguments in the first section of his critique were sometimes strained as he attempted to impose a symmetry on Coke's Reports that was simply not there. He seems to claim that certain decisions of the Chief Justice involving the royal prerogative were not accurate in law. Furthermore, he disliked entirely the principle of making decisions unfavourable to the Crown the centre of a published law report. Coke and the royal prerogative was not, however, the only subject of these observations. The two major topics were the status and jurisdiction of ecclesiastical and local authorities. In each instance these institutions were being challenged by the courts of common law. The central courts were exercising a decisive influence on the structure of law and authority in the early seventeenth century, and Chief Justice Coke was a major figure in this development. He conceived of the law and legal doctrines as emanating from Westminster. In challenging the autonomy of local, as well as ecclesiastical, institutions, he was not only questioning the existing structure of the courts but also the prerogatives of the Crown upon which they were based. This was especially the case with ecclesiastical jurisdictions.

The ecclesiastical courts of late sixteenth- and early seventeenth-century England were highly diverse institutions. Being represented on the local, diocesan, and metropolitan levels, these jurisdictions formed a significant part of the legal structure.[2] It was largely at the local and diocesan levels, however, that the ecclesiastical courts fulfilled a prominent role in both administration and adjudication. The law of the Church was broad, and it could involve matters ranging from civil actions such as debt to criminal actions involving benefit of clergy, political offences such as non-conformity, religious offences like adultery and heresy, and notarial responsibilities as the ad-

---

[1] *Rep. Chanc.* 1–17; see also Rawl. MS C.917, f. 457. The case is discussed further *infra*, Chap. VII.

[2] The important works of Ronald A. Marchant, *The Puritans and the Church courts in the Diocese of York, 1560–1642* (1960); Christopher Hill, *Society and Puritanism in pre-Revolutionary England* (1964); Paul S. Seaver, *The Puritan lectureships* (Stanford Calif. 1970); and Jay P. Anglin, 'The Essex Puritan movement and the 'bawdy' courts, 1577–1594', in *Tudor men and institutions*, ed. A. J. Slavin (Baton Rouge La. 1972), 171–204.

ministration of wills and testaments. While the precise nature of its influence in the development of law and the legal system is a subject yet unstudied, it can at least be stated that developments of the late sixteenth century increased the prominence of the ecclesiastical courts in English society.[1]

The growth of litigation before the ecclesiastical courts at the local level was a major factor in the legal history of Elizabethan England. Moreover, in some special jurisdictions, as the Bishop's Chancery Court at York, the rise was phenomenal.[2] The reasons for this growth are quite complex, and to some extent they remain unknown. On the one hand, legal process was favourable to the defendant: he could see the written charges against him, certify his answers, call witnesses, and cross-examine those who testified on behalf of the plaintiff. On the other hand, compliance to orders of the courts was weak, and remedies were seldom very tough. In fact, the rate of conviction was even lower than that of the circuit courts of the common law system.[3]

One particular area of ecclesiastical jurisdiction was not, however, generally well regarded: that of the ecclesiastical 'commissions'. Created by royal letters patent under the alleged authority of the Act of Supremacy for certain dioceses and the provinces of York and Canterbury, the commissions were responsible for enforcing the religious policies of the State. Although these commissions had jurisdiction of civil and criminal matters, they did not have the status of courts. Instead, they operated by letters patent without known judicial processes. Their law was often swift, brutal, and more 'politico-religiously' oriented than in the courts. It appears, however, that as long as the commissioners were tied to the localities and staffed with local people, their judicial activities were not the source of significant opposition.[4] For example, in Ellesmere's own area – the diocese of

[1] The author thanks Professor Charles Gray for his comments and criticisms on this subject.

[2] Ronald A. Marchant, *The Church under the law* (Cambridge 1969), tables 8–9 for York; and for Essex, Jay P. Anglin, 'Court of the Archdeacon of Essex, 1570–1609' Ph.D. diss. (Univ. of Calif. Los Angeles, 1966), where the growth was not as large. The major expansion of litigation before eccles. courts and commissions was the thesis of a common lawyer in F-H MS 75, ff. 6v–12r.

[3] The case study of Marchant in *Church under law*, vii-viii, 9–10; and an unpub. paper on criminality by James Cockburn that was read before the Amer. Hist. Assoc. on 29 Dec. 1972. The author thanks Professor Cockburn for the opportunity to read and criticise his paper, and for his comments on matters concerning the circuit courts discussed in this Chap.

[4] Philip Tyler, in his introd. to Roland G. Usher, *The rise and fall of the High Commission* (Oxford 1968 ed.), iii–x.

Chester – both the justices of the peace and the circuit courts appeared to give the commissioners their support.[1] But this was not the situation in London or certain other areas.

The proceedings of the ecclesiastical commissioners in the Court of High Commission, especially in politically oriented matters such as nonconformity, had provided a ground-swell of opposition against ecclesiastical jurisdictions in the late Elizabethan period. Parties could be summoned to the Commission on the information of 'informers', and required to answer questions on an oath *ex officio* before being confronted with any charges. Coming into full power with John Whitgift's accession to the Archbishopric of Canterbury in 1583, the Commission's growing notoriety contributed to the increasing intervention of the central common law courts. They issued writs of prohibition on many kinds of cases involving complicated legal problems on the procedural and substantive scope of the High Commission. Such writs could prevent causes from proceeding further, preclude enforcement once a judgment was rendered, or provide for the release of convicted parties on writs of *habeas corpus*. Besides the defendant's lack of due process before an ecclesiastical commission, no reasons were given for decisions rendered and no record of the arguments was ever maintained.[2]

The judicial activities of the common law and ecclesiastical jurisdictions began to become more interrelated in the 1590s. Substantively, the expansion of common law actions began to involve areas which concerned the customary jurisdiction of ecclesiastical bodies. This included the common law development of remedies for various collateral areas of defamation, slander, tithe, and presentation to benefices.[3] Causes concerning these matters were numerous by the late 1590s. For example, a brief examination of the plea rolls of the Court of King's Bench, civil side, for the years 1595–9, reveals that many prohibitions were issued for such matters against parties who had sued, or were in the process of suing, before ecclesiastical

---

[1] C.R.O. Quarter Sessions Books, and the proceedings of the eccles. commissioners in C.R.O. MS E.D.A. 12/2, for 1562–72. See as well the hearings before the Exch. in P.R.O. E/123/10.

[2] The older study of Mary Hume Maguire, 'Attack of the common lawyers on the oath *ex officio* as administered in the ecclesiastical courts of England', in *Essays in Honour of C.H. McIlwain* (Cambridge Mass. 1936); and the critique of Marchant, *Puritans and Church courts*, 4–8.

[3] Marchant, *Church under law*, 9–10.

commissions.[1] As a result, several collections of 'precedents' were prepared as guide-lines for the future direction of common lawyers.[2]

The evidence indicates that the issue of writs of prohibition by common law courts against causes pending or determined before ecclesiastical courts and commissions had also become quite common by the 1590s. Again, the evidence is found not only in the plea rolls,[3] but also in the collections of common lawyers. Coke himself had gathered such precedents from the years 1585–8, and tracts discussing them were being written by the end of the century.[4] The problem from the perspective of the 'civilians', the Doctors of the Civil Law, was that the ecclesiastical courts were limited in their jurisdiction. Thus the civilians did not take the increased use of prohibitions lightly.

The civilians were the legal practitioners of the ecclesiastical jurisdictions. Educated at Doctors' Commons in London, as apart from the inns of court, they had gained an exclusive practice before the Church and certain conciliar courts since Henry VIII had abolished the study of canon law.[5] The civilians were skilled in law and administration, and devoted to the Established Church and to the institution of monarchy. They gathered bulky collections of arguments to illustrate the customary as well as the statutory basis of the ecclesiastical courts. For example, some of them regarded the law as divided into causes 'ecclesiastical' and 'secular' in distinction to 'civil' and 'criminal',[6] a distinction which bore little reality in the contemporary structure of the law. Others went so far as to state that the common law grew out of the law of the Church, which was derived ultimately from the civil law. Since the civil law was more ancient, they regarded

---

[1] KB 27/1337/246r–7r, 249r–v, 391r–2v, 433r–v, 435r; 1356/156r–7v, 160r–v; 1357/454r–v. This did not occur, however, in the archdeaconal courts: Anglin, 'Archdeacon of Essex', 130–1. The author wishes to thank Dr Anglin for providing him with further refs. and comments.

[2] For ex. Petyt MS 511/16, ff. 1–36; and Rawl. MS B. 202, ff. 1–42.

[3] P.R.O. Docquet Roll (indices) Ind. 1352–3.

[4] Coke in MS Rep. A, ff. 722v, 739r, 741r–v; and the tract on prohibitions and *praemunire* in Cotton MS Cleo. F. II, ff. 450r–64v.

[5] The interpretations of Brian Levack in an unpub. paper on the Civilians of Doctors Commons in London, and of Guy Lytle in an unpub. essay on the Doctors of Civil Law at Oxford and Cambridge. The author thanks both of them for the opportunity to read their papers.

[6] As Petyt MS 538/38, and 538/54; Rawl. MS B.202/105v–13r; Cotton MS Cleo. F. II, ff. 1–37, 262–80; and Trin. Coll. Dublin MSS 532/1, 651, 734, 807.

it as superior to the common law.[1] They also demanded that civilians hold judicial and ceremonial 'precedence' over those trained in common law at the inns of court. This led to a long battle between Doctors and Serjeants for precedence.[2] Since the Church was an ancient institution, civilians did not hesitate publicly to invoke tradition against another segment of the law profession which also appealed to custom for its authority – the common law. Neither did they hesitate to emphasise the new union of Church and State on whose success the existing government unequivocally depended.[3]

The growing interaction, and disputes, between civilians and common lawyers, and hence between the ecclesiastical and common law bodies, was exacerbated with Coke's promotion to the Chief Justiceship of the Common Pleas in 1606 and with Fleming's appointment as Chief Justice of the King's Bench in 1607. The problems also began to be debated openly in the House of Commons and in the press with the circulation of contentious treatises.[4] The years 1607–11 witnessed the great debate between common lawyers and civilians on a number of topics: the jurisdiction of the ecclesiastical courts, and especially of the High Commission; *Fuller's* and *Chancey's* cases; the joint conference of the judges and privy councillors in Michaelmas 1607, Trinity 1608, and Easter and Trinity terms 1609; and the parliamentary debates of 1610/11.[5] The debates culminated in a final conference before the King on 23 May 1611.[6] Both Coke and Ellesmere played prominent roles in these proceedings.[7]

Early in the reign Coke and Ellesmere had agreed on the function of the ecclesiastical courts, and were not far apart in their views of the

---

[1] From a common lawyer's study of the *Institutes* and the *Digest* in Petyt MS 538/55, ff. 188r–212v. See also Thomas Ridley's *View of the Civile and Ecclesiastical Law* (1607), 78.

[2] The rather amusing doc. 'Professors of the Common Lawes . . . in Cases of honor', D.C.O. Misc. MS, the 'Henry Rainsford' vol. ff. 115r–8v; and Barlow MS 9, ff. 1–13.

[3] For ex. George Carleton, *Jurisdiction Regall, Episcopall, Papall* (1610), sig. Ar and pp. 1–10, 44.

[4] The issues were fully expressed in the argument of the common lawyers dated 6 July 1609, and the reply of the civilians dated 7 July 1609 in Rawl. MS B.202, ff. 1–42 and 113–22, respectively. The eccles. side has been fully chronicled by R. G. Usher, *The reconstruction of the English Church* (New York 1910), II, 206–45.

[5] See the notes of Caesar in Lans. MS 160, of Coke in Holkham MS 677, and the debates in *Parl. 1610, passim.*

[6] Usher, *High Commission,* 212–21. The notes of the Clerk of the Council, Henry Powle, are in L.I. Add. MS G.2, ff. 97r–105v.

[7] The arguments here and in the following parag. are taken from some of the fullest accounts: Barlow MS 9, Cleo. MS F. II, Harg. MS 278 ff. 252–407, Petyt MSS 518/1–99 and 538/55/1–36.

commissions. Both stated their positions clearly at the Hampton Court Conference in 1604. Coke asserted that all ecclesiastical commissions should have their jurisdiction severely curtailed, while Ellesmere was concerned to limit the institution of the commission to the diocesan level. He also wished to protect the jurisdiction of the ecclesiastical courts in the dioceses.[1] Later, in the spring of 1609, Ellesmere conferred with Coke and the other judges at York House on the growing areas of conflict. Again the two men advanced similar views. The Chancellor, however, refused to accept the limitations set by the Chief Justice on all ecclesiastical commissions: namely, heresy, schism, incest, polygamy, and recusancy.[2] This disagreement was important, as Coke's arguments were to become the basis of later common law opposition.[3] The problem became acute with the preparation of a defence of the claims of the commissioners by Attorney-General Hobart at the request of the King in the summer of 1609. Coke reacted strongly by preparing a full attack on Hobart's brief, limiting the jurisdiction of the commissions, and declaring that ecclesiastical judges could not interpret statutes.[4] Coke reported many of the relevant cases in his manuscript law reports for these years, but only a few of them were published in his own lifetime.[5]

The two protagonists in the crisis that came before the Privy Council on 23 May 1611 were Chief Justice Coke and Archbishop Bancroft. The Archbishop invoked God, Crown, Church, and Commonwealth in defending the High Commission against prohibitions. The Chief Justice invoked the ancient, immemorial customs of the common law. The most interesting position, however, was that taken by the Lord Chancellor. Ellesmere, due to his common law training, spoke on behalf of the legitimacy of writs of prohibition. But he also contributed some observations on the statutes of Henry VIII, Edward VI, and Elizabeth that pertained to parliamentary sanction for

[1] Holkham MS 677, ff. 252r–5v; Barlow MS 9, pp. 13–22; and Ellesm. MS 2983.

[2] Holkham MS 677, f. 252r–v.

[3] Coke's coll. in Yale Law MS G.R.24, ff. 88r–93v. The major tract was 'In what cases the Kings Court of Common Pleas maie grant Prohibitions', Tanner MS 247, ff. 1r–24v; and Coke's copy in Yale Law MS G.R.24, ff. 71r–82v. Part of Coke's argument was pub. in *Const. Docs.* 156–63.

[4] The brief is in Petyt MSS 511/16 at f. 117, 518 at f. 86, and Stowe MS 420. Coke's attack was pr. in Usher, *Reconstruction of the Church*, II, 241–5.

[5] 12 *Co. Rep.* 19–20, 26–9, 37–50, 58–69, 76–7, 82–6, 93, 109, 112; 13 *Co. Rep.* 4–18, 23, 30–3, 37–47, 58. John Baker is transcribing cases out of Coke MS Rep. E for a possible ed. of a 14th Rep. Controversial opinions which Coke did not publish are for ex. at ff. 16–9, 29–31, 58–62.

ecclesiastical jurisdictions.[1] Ellesmere considered himself as one of the champions of the Reformed Church. This, together with his dislike of controversies between the central courts, led him to speak against the excessive use of writs of prohibition while offering suggestions for reforming both the procedures for issuing the writs and the legal processes of the Court of High Commission.[2]

Ellesmere took issue with the common lawyers on the question of tithes. The jurisdiction over tithes was a specific area in which ecclesiastical and common law authorities clashed, and in preparing for this conference the Chancellor had composed a brief on the jurisdiction of tithes which set out the issues, interpreted the history of the relevant statutes, and came to definite conclusions.[3] According to the civilians, all tithes were under the complete jurisdiction of the ecclesiastical authorities. Statutes had created two kinds of remedy for the collection of tithes: one where a person refused to pay tithes and suffered the penalty of the double value of the tenth part when convicted of non-payment; and another for persons who stole the grain prior to the assessment of the tithe in order to prevent any future attempt at collection. Convictions in the latter instance carried the penalty of the treble value of the tenth. Coke held that the Court of Common Pleas had exclusive jurisdiction of suits in the second instance. He defended this position by arguing that only the common law could interpret the intent of Parliament. Ellesmere acknowledged the jurisdiction of the High Commission in matters of tithe, and denied the supposition that only judges of common law courts could interpret acts of Parliament. On this occasion Ellesmere boldly challenged the arguments of these lawyers. He did not hesitate to make such statements as, 'this new construction is wracked and forced, and is injurious and absurd'.[4]

Following this meeting of 23 May, the Lord Chancellor continued to work for a compromise. On 7 June he was alleged to have visited the judges at Serjeants' Inn. This led to one more conference of the judges

---

[1] He probably spoke from his brief, which was prepared for this occasion: 'Some obseruationes', Barlow MS 9, pp. 13–22. See also Tanner MS 176, f. 261v.

[2] Ellesmere's views are best expressed in Tanner MS 120, ff. 10r–11v. His notes on the procedural aspects are in Ellesm. MS 766b, f. 1r, and Barlow MS 9, p. 48.

[3] The copy of 'Some obseruationes, vpon ye statutes Anno 27 H. 8. Anno 32 H. 8. And Anno 4. E. 6. for payment of Tithes, and construction of the same statutes, concerning the Iurisdiction of the Ecclesiasticall Courtes in suites for this', Barlow MS 9, pp. 13–22. This was endorsed as being delivered by the Chanc. to the Archb. of Cant. Other copies are Barlow MS 24, pp. 40–8, Harg. MS 371, ff. 1r–18v, and Tanner MS 176, ff. 1r–5v.

[4] Barlow MS 9, p. 19.

with the King and Privy Council, where the monarch agreed to reform the High Commission provided that the Court of Common Pleas was more circumspect in the issue of writs of prohibition.[1] The result was the issue of new letters patent on 29 August 1611. These, together with the later patents of 1613 and 1616, stated that the institution of the Court of High Commission was temporary; that it was limited to 'great causes' in defence of the Church; and that it could not fine and imprison except for matters concerning heresy and schism.[2] The great debate over prohibitions and the High Commission was over temporarily. But the issues never died. Writs of prohibition still appear to have been issued following the revised patents. This initial impression is derived from the printed law reports of the period, and it is substantiated by the evidence in the plea rolls.[3] What seems to have occurred is that the partial reform of the High Commission, together with a greater acceptance of ecclesiastical authorities by common lawyers and of prohibitions by civilians, prevented the confrontations of 1607–11 from recurring.[4] Perhaps the work of Chancellor Ellesmere in the years 1611–16 was instrumental in bringing a measure of peace to the relations of Church and society in the early seventeenth century.

Ellesmere's chief concern with Coke and prohibitions was the impact of Coke's Reports upon the Church: 'it is to be observed that throughout all his books, that he hath as it were purposely laboured to derogate much from the rights of the Church, and the dignity of churchmen.'[5] The Chancellor discussed seven cases that concerned the clergy and the ecclesiastical jurisdictions. In three instances he accused the Chief Justice of weakening the lawful authority of the ecclesiastical courts, and attacking the bishops 'as if he took delight a little to lash the clergy, though nothing pertinent to the matter in question'.[6] In these particular cases none of Ellesmere's criticisms

---

[1] 12 *Co. Rep.* 85–6, and Caesar's notes in Lans. MS 160, f. 256. The conf. is reported in SP 14/65/5.

[2] These are discussed in Usher, *High Commission*, 236–46. The letters for these commissions have been pr. in lengthy extracts by G. W. Prothero, *Select statutes and other constitutional documents illustrative of the reigns of Elizabeth and James I* (2nd ed. Oxford 1898), 424–35. The Chanc's notes for drafting these were prepared by 'Holland – Concerning Motions', Ellesm. MS 2983, and endorsed by himself.

[3] The Docket Roll: P.R.O. Ind. 1359. The reports of Bulstrode and Hobart are also relevant.

[4] Laud's movement to bring all eccles. courts under his control and to gain independence from the common law is narrated by H. R. Trevor-Roper, *Archbishop Laud* (2nd ed. 1965), 189–210.

[5] 'Eg. on Coke', f. 32r.

[6] The *Trollop*, *Powlter*, and *Magdalen College* cases; the quote at f. 36r.

was justified. In *Alexander Powlter's Case* (1614), for example, the Chancellor charged the Chief Justice for expostulating on the statute of *praemunire* against bishops and their courts in a cause that was solely concerned with whether a priest who had burned down part of the town of Newmarket should have benefit of clergy. Although the statute was cited in the report, neither the statute nor the subject of *praemunire* was discussed. This polemicism – not in character for the Chancellor – caused Ellesmere to miss Coke's faulty analysis of the statutes of Henry VIII and Edward VI on benefit of clergy in causes for petty treason.[1]

The evidence for three other cases, however, reveals that the Chancellor's research was well done. For example, in the *Bishop of Winchester's Case* (1596), Coke reported a King's Bench resolution that ecclesiastical courts were not sufficient to judge a plea on a prescriptive claim for a discharge of the payment of tithes. The Court, however, never made such a declaration, though Coke did as Attorney-General in prosecuting the case for the plaintiff.[2] In the *Case of Powlett, Marquess of Winchester* (1599), Coke reported as law that where a will contains both land and goods, the probate would be prohibited *in toto* pending litigation about the land before the common law courts. Ellesmere declared that the Bench had adjourned to confer with some of the ecclesiastical judges, where they agreed that only when a will contained land could it be adjudicated before the common law. His account is substantiated partially in the fact that the case has not been found again on the plea roll, and that later law supports the agreement stated here by the Chancellor.[3]

A third prominent case involving ecclesiastical and common law judges was *Specote's Case* (1589–90).[4] This cause concerned three questions: whether the plaintiff held the right of advowson for life by devise, whether a bishop could disturb the presentation of the patron, and whether the devisee was schismatic. The presentee had been refused admission to a benefice because he was charged with being 'schismatic' before the ecclesiastical court of the Bishop of Exeter.

---

[1] 11 *Co. Rep.* 29r–37v; 'Eg. on Coke', ff. 44v–5v. For Coke and his analysis of the statutes see the description in Sir Michael Foster, *A Report of some proceedings . . . and of other Crown Cases* (2nd ed. 1776), 330–6.

[2] 2 *Co. Rep.* 38r–45v; 'Eg. on Coke' ff. 32v–3v. There is also comment in Add. MS 14.030, f. 91r–v. The issues were discussed in Tanner MS 120, ff. 198r–221r.

[3] 'Eg. on Coke', ff. 33v–4v; 3 *Co. Rep.* (1826 ed.), 303; and KB 27/1356–7.

[4] 5 *Co. Rep.* 57r–9r; and 'Eg. on Coke', f. 35v. There were many other reports of this case, and they are cited *infra*, Chap. XV, p. 301, n. 2.

The presentor filed a *quare impedit* in the Court of Common Pleas, where the case was heard on four different occasions in the years 1585–8 before it was finally resolved, Chief Justice Anderson changing his opinion at least twice.[1] In the end, the return of the Bishop was ruled insufficient because the reasoning of the ecclesiastical court was not included in its certificate. The Bishop moved to the Court of King's Bench on a writ of error, and this cause was the subject of Coke's report.

The report of the case in the King's Bench was devoted to Coke's lecture on the need to protect the rights of patrons in 'perilous times', and of the designs of the episcopacy to subvert the historic role of the laity in providing for the Church. He also declared that the Church could not condemn a man as a heretic without making specific charges that could be substantiated with evidence. The judgment in the King's Bench upheld the decision of the Common Pleas. Ellesmere, disagreeing with this review, criticised Coke for debasing the episcopacy and the ecclesiastical courts 'both in their honours and professions', and for making great play of the court's requesting knowledge of the particulars of heresy or schism before accepting the judgment of the Bishop.[2] The Chancellor had always been willing to accept criticism of the Church, and had offered much of his own; but he would never accept an attack on its basic institutions.

The juristic foundations of Ellesmere's criticism of Coke's report of causes involving the Church and ecclesiastical jurisdictions were the Chancellor's conception of the judicial system and his attitudes towards the legal renaissance. Following the Privy Council conference of May 1611, he drafted a tract on prohibitions which presented an assessment of the current problems between ecclesiastical and common law jurisdictions.[3] This tract became the basis of this section of his observations on Coke's Reports. In fact, he appears to have selected cases from the Reports that would illustrate the major points of his work on prohibitions. The tract on prohibitions included four relevant problems: (1) the patronage of benefices, (2) tithes, (3) probate and testaments, and (4) prohibitions. The first of these problems was illustrated by the *Magdalen College Case* (1615). Coke alleged that ecclesiastical courts could not be expected to accept evidence of complaints against churchmen who were non-resident ministers in causes

---

[1] Sir Edmund Anderson, *Les Reports des Mults Principals Cases* (1664), I, 189–91.
[2] 'Eg. on Coke', f. 35v.
[3] 'Prohibitians', pp. 40–8.

concerning pluralities and the patronage of advowsons. For Ellesmere, every court should be the final arbiter of the actions which lay before it. Thus a common law court could issue a prohibition only when the party before the ecclesiastical body was involved in a matter which was actionable by original writ at common law.[1]

The subject of tithes was the second problem which the Chancellor had discussed in his earlier tract on prohibitions. He made a painstaking analysis of the statutes on tithes to demonstrate that ecclesiastical authorities had been given exclusive jurisdiction. Coke, however, in the *Bishop of Winchester's Case* (1596), had argued that spiritual judges were too biased on behalf of the revenues of the Church to protect the interests of the laity, and thus such matters could best be decided at common law. This report provided Ellesmere with a clear example of their differences on this issue.[2] The Chief Justice used a similar argument in discussing the *Marquess of Winchester's Case* on wills and testaments. Here he argued that any will containing land as well as chattels could be determined at common law. Ellesmere had devoted a section of his tract to the probate of wills, and he believed that the ecclesiastical authorities had complete jurisdiction except in cases where land only was bequeathed. He emphasised that if the ecclesiastical authorities were hampered in their duty by the common law, as they were in this instance, there could be no orderly and peaceful settlement of men's estates.[3]

The final topic of Ellesmere's earlier tract concerned prohibitions. The Chancellor held that prohibitions could be issued only when a party applying for the writ could also bring an action by original writ in a common law court. Coke, however, in the *Case of Trollop* and *Specote's Case*, had declared that a court of common law could issue a prohibition against a party who won before an ecclesiastical court when it appeared that such an authority failed to provide justice. Thus a certificate of excommunication would not be recognised at common law unless it included the grounds on which the party was excommunicated. In order that prohibitions were properly granted, Ellesmere suggested that the cause for issuing the writ might be proved in Chancery before the writ would be drawn and served.[4]

---

[1] *Ibid.* pp. 40–1; and 'Eg. on Coke', ff. 35v–6r. The reasoning of Coke seems to make him a defender of pluralism and non-residence. The author thanks Dr Paul Seaver for this suggestion.

[2] 'Prohibitians', pp. 42–3; and 'Eg. on Coke', ff. 32v–3v.

[3] 'Prohibitians', pp. 44–5; and 'Eg. on Coke', ff. 33v–4v.

[4] 'Prohibitians', p. 45; 'Eg. on Coke', ff. 34v–5v; and *supra*, pp. 136–7.

Ellesmere's emphasis in this instance was on the duties and responsibilities of the Chancery as distinct from those of the common law courts. It was after these criticisms that he penned the statement that judges of the common law 'sometimes they take upon them the office of Chancellor', confusing the role of equity and common law, and attempting to gather all jurisdiction and authority into their hands.[1] At issue in the end was what certain common lawyers had come to regard as the supremacy of the common law. Ellesmere, both in his tract on prohibitions and in his critique of Coke's Reports, attempted to make a persuasive case for the preservation of the legal system.[2] This necessitated a defence not only of the ecclesiastical jurisdictions, but also of those local communities of English society which comprised the basic elements of merchants, gentlemen, artisans, and labourers.

The third important subject which Ellesmere discussed from Coke's Reports concerned local and regional jurisdictions. Ellesmere's legal career began in the northern borderlands of England and Wales, and he was from the start a champion of local interests. He carried this perspective with him in the series of promotions which led to the presidency of the Chancery, exercising his considerable public influence on the preservation of local authorities, particularly at the regional level. For example, he had worked continually to preserve and to reform the jurisdiction of the Council in the Marches of Wales. He collected historical notes on its judicial affairs, prepared a list of judges for future appointments, and created his own personal faction of professional lawyers.[3] As late as 1616 he was still actively engaged in attempting to heal internal conflicts.[4] His most prominent efforts, however, lay in the County palatine of Chester.

The Exchequer Court of the County palatine had become a major court of law in the sixteenth century,[5] and its most impressive period of growth was achieved under the stewardship of Robert Dudley, Earl of Leicester, who was Lord Chamberlain from 1565 to 1588. Ellesmere, one of the important lawyers whom Leicester had relied upon in this

[1] 'Prohibitians', pp. 44–6, the quote at p. 44.
[2] The background of this view stems from his earliest legal writings: Ellesm. MS 482, f. 1, and MSS 446, 452.
[3] Respectively: Ellesm. MS 450; Ellesm. MS 1748; and Penry Williams, *The Council in the Marches of Wales under Elizabeth I* (Cardiff 1958), 242, 282–94, 303–7, 315.
[4] Thomas Chamberlayne to Ellesmere, 19 Dec. 1616: Ellesm. MS 396.
[5] The court and the context of the County Palatine has been described by Geoffrey Barraclough, 'The earldom and County Palatine of Chester', *Trans. Hist. Soc. Lancs. and Chesh.* 103 (1953), 34–45.

critical era of the court, assumed the office of chamberlain in 1594. Gaining control of the justices of the peace on becoming Lord Keeper in 1596, he was able to resolve the local jurisdictional disputes between the Exchequer Court, the Council of Wales, and the city of Chester.[1] The Chancellor, a major landowner and official in the area, then developed the Exchequer Court as part of his family fiefdom. He appointed his relative Peter Warburton as vice-chamberlain, and other family relations and estate agents soon made their way into the bureaucracy of this provincial institution. The court dispensed both common law and equity, and Ellesmere used his influence and position at Westminster to prevent the central courts from initiating legal process in the County palatine.[2] Ellesmere's legal experiences were in sharp contrast to those of Sir Edward Coke, a man who devoted his entire legal career to common law jurisdictions in London and its East Anglian environs.

Chief Justice Coke was part of that movement in the legal profession whose aim was to expand the central courts of law – and particularly those administering the common law – at the expense of local and regional jurisdictions. The tentacles of the central courts of common law – the Assizes – had come to exert a decisive grasp on local courts and the justices of the peace by the late sixteenth century.[3] This influence was captured by the Crown in 1595, when Sir Robert Cecil attempted to assert royal control over the role of the Assize judges.[4] In a reorganisation of the circuit system, the Crown inaugurated a new series of Star Chamber addresses to the judges, which were intended to declare publicly policies which they were to enforce on circuit. The judges were then directed more specifically in their work by Privy Council letters. At the Assizes the royal interests were unveiled to those attending under the guise of the Assize sermon, which was similar to those more famous speeches at Paul's Cross.[5]

---

[1] W. J. Jones, 'The Exchequer of Chester in the last years of Elizabeth I', in *Tudor men and institutions*, ed. A. J. Slavin (Baton Rouge La 1972), 123–5, 129–35, 157–63. The background is sketched *supra*, pp. 22–3, 28–9, 33–4.

[2] *Ibid.* 149–54, 163–7; and the Chanc's notes in Ellesm. MS 440.

[3] Cockburn, *Assizes*, 87–93, 101–6, 108–87. The background of this development has been sketched by Sir John Neale, 'English local government: a historical restrospect', in his *Essays in Elizabethan England* (1958), 202–14.

[4] The original thesis of Cockburn, *Assizes*, 6–10, 50–1, 58–9, 67–9, 134–9, 153–4, and esp. 213–31. The role of James I, however, is in the author's opinion, slightly exaggerated at pp. 227–31. Ellesmere later tried to exercise his own influence: Ellesm. MS 2184; and he collected precedents for such action from the records of Sir Nicholas Bacon's presidency: Ellesm. MS 2679, ff. 49–52; and Hasts. MS 1340, ff. 25r–46v.

[5] Millar MacClure, *The Paul's Cross sermons, 1534–1642* (1958).

The extent of this influence, however, will not be fully known until historians have studied English society at the local level with respect to judges, the government, and the courts, both lay and ecclesiastical.

Coke's primary concern from at least as early as 1597 was to restrict the law and authority of the local and regional courts which were under the umbrella of royal, prerogative control, whether that control was real or imaginary. He seems to have been concerned chiefly with the Council in the North, the County Palatine of Durham, and the Council in the Marches of Wales.[1] The two major contests, however, were in the North and Wales, and both the Chief Justice and the Chancellor were fully involved in the latter dispute. The major issue that arose was whether the four English western border counties were subject to the Council of Wales. The particular instance was *Fairley's Case* (1604), where Mr. Fairley refused to obey an order of the Council, was imprisoned, and appealed to the Court of King's Bench for release on a writ of *habeas corpus*.[2] The provincial council refused to release him, and the matter was then sent to the Privy Council for debate and resolution. While the result was never registered in an act of Council or the decree of a court, it appears that this confrontation was won by the King's Bench. The Council of Wales tested it once more in 1608 by imprisoning a man from an English county, and on this occasion the Privy Council ruled in favour of the common law court despite the dissatisfaction of the King.[3]

While Coke worked for the hegemony of the common law, and was concerned with the presence of royal influence as it was exercised through conciliar institutions at the provincial level, as well as with attempts to exert policies of state through common law jurisdictions, Ellesmere's position was more complex. On the one hand, the Chancellor believed in the inalienable rights and privileges of local and regional courts, and he adhered to this belief with the strong conviction of custom and tradition. But on the other hand, the Chancellor does not appear to have supported the policy of Cecil, the Lord Treasurer, to increase the influence of royal policy in the

---

[1] Cockburn, *Assizes*, 38–44. Coke's opinion of these courts was well summed up in the statement that 'there was nothing there but a kind of confusion and hotch-potch of justice' — pub. in Bacon, *Works* II, 166.

[2] *Fairley's Case* (KB 1604), SPD 14/10/84–6; and the background material in Harl. MS 5353.

[3] The debates and copies of relevant papers are in Harl. MS 6797, and Cotton Vitelius MS Ci. The arguments presented by the legal counsel for both sides of the case before the P.C. in 1608 have been pr. in Bacon, *Works* II, 587–611. This contains largely Bacon's brief and his replies.

administration of the legal system. Thus Ellesmere throughout his career was against the device whereby royal favourites were to recommend the appointment of Assize judges. Instead, he held that only the common law judges themselves could recommend judicial officers to travel the circuit courts.[1] The Chancellor also fought royal influence on the behalf of regional authorities. In the marches of Wales episode he broke with his friend Lord Zouch, the President of the Council of Wales, in defending the position of the Court of King's Bench; and he seems to have played an instrumental role in cooling down the dissatisfaction of the King despite support for the royal position from both Cecil and Bacon.[2]

The complexities of the issues in this area of legal history did not, however, preclude the opposition of the Chancellor to certain views and actions of the Chief Justice with respect to local and regional jurisdictions. In spite of their essential agreement on combating the influence of certain royal favourites who intended to undermine the independence of the courts, Ellesmere did not hesitate to challenge Coke on the preservation of the customary authority of non-common law courts. The Chancellor was, after all, a man whose sympathies lay in the 'country', and he demonstrated his belief in the preservation of the whole of traditional law by contesting nine cases reported by the Chief Justice where such activities were called into question. These causes referred to three different kinds of local authorities: private corporations, boroughs, and local commissioners. Since private corporations had a special relationship to the King, issues which concerned the extent of their authority involved political as well as legal questions.

With respect to the privileges of private jurisdictions, Coke had attempted in the *Michelborne Case* (1596) to call into question the King's Court of Marshalsea, relying on a statute of Edward I and alleging precedents from Bracton and Fleta. The evidence was quite slim. The Chief Justice reported that a judgment of the Court of Marshalsea had been overturned in the King's Bench.[3] The Chancellor stated that the record of the Bench never contained a reversal of the judgment in the Marshalsea. An examination of the plea roll substantiates Ellesmere's statement; the case was heard but not ap-

---

[1] I. H. Jeayes, *Letters of Philip Gawdy 1597–1616* (1906), 67–9, 156–7; and Hawarde, *Reportes*, 368.

[2] Folger MS X.d. 337.

[3] 6 *Co. Rep.* 20v–1r; 'Eg. on Coke', f. 44r–v.

parently resolved.[1] However, Coke's report of the plaintiff's brief, that the Marshalsea could not hold pleas of freehold, debt, covenant, or contract, but only pleas of trespass when both parties were of the King's household or within the verge, was an accurate statement of later judicial opinions on the jurisdiction of this court.

The powers of private corporations were at issue, for example, in *Doctor Bonham's Case* (1610/11).[2] The doctor had sought to restrict the College of Physicians in London from exercising exclusive control over the licences of practitioners. The issue was whether the College could imprison as well as fine individuals for practising in the city without its licence. The Chief Justice, however, made speeches on the superiority of medicine at Oxford and Cambridge, and on how the governors of the London College could improve the administration of their institution. He also declared that if the statute of 14 and 15 Henry VIII had intended to give these regulatory powers to the College, the common law could declare that enactment void. The Chancellor and several others condemned the Chief Justice for making what they regarded as extra-judicial speeches, and reporting them as part of the opinion of the court. Ellesmere, like Yelverton, believed that 'acts of Parliament should be corrected by the same pen that drew them'.[3]

The Chief Justice also sought to limit the restrictive powers of boroughs incorporated under royal charter, and the Chancellor contested Coke's report of the decisions in *Clark's Case* (1596), *James Bagg's Case* (1615), and the *Case of the Tailors of Ipswich* (1615).[4] The *Ipswich Case* was particularly contentious. The corporation had attempted to collect a fine from a young man who had engaged in the trade of tailor without a licence from the borough. The man, however, had tailored elsewhere, and in Ipswich he worked solely for the family to which he was attached as a domestic servant. The

---

[1] KB 27/1337/263–4. There was no further entry in the next term: KB 27/1338. For other contemp. comments see Bulstrode, *Reports*, 208–11.

[2] 8 *Co. Rep.* 114r–21r; 'Eg. ⟨ r Coke', f. 40r–v; and Serjeant Hill's comments pr. in *Co. Rep.* (1826 ed.), IV, 176.

[3] Yelverton in Stowe MS 153, f. 39r–v; the quotation at f. 39v. Thorne's view that Coke had no intention of suggesting that judges should declare statutes void, but only of not following statutes in the negative that were unclear, is not supported by Ellesmere: 'Dr. Bonham's Case', *LQR* 54 (1939), ɔmpared with 'Eg. on Coke', f. 40v. That Coke actually said what Ellesmere and others reported has been established by Charles Gray, 'Bonham's Case Reviewed', 35–58.

[4] 11 *Co. Rep.* 53r; 'Eg. on Coke', ff. 40v–2v. The latter case is also in Godbolt, *Reports*, 252–4.

issue was whether in this instance the defendant could practise his trade without a licence, and the statutes of Henry VII and Elizabeth on apprentices clearly excluded domestic servants from this requirement. Coke, however, spoke further. He declared that no man could be prohibited from a lawful trade without cause, and that boroughs had no powers of economic restriction. In fact, his opinion in this case formed part of our modern doctrine of restraint of trade.[1] The Chancellor, however, regarded these extra-judicial remarks as derogatory to the powers of corporations and harmful to the maintenance of the social structure.

The opinions which Coke registered in the *Bonham* and *Ipswich* cases were also based, like those of Ellesmere, on his deep concern for the economic problems of the age. When the price revolution of the late sixteenth century had given way to depression and unemployment in the early seventeenth century, the tensions in English society had heightened. The law could respond either by entrenching local privileges and interests or, as Ellesmere believed, by maintaining the regulatory functions of local corporations and preventing restrictive practices. According to the Chief Justice, every man who became skilled in a lawful trade had the right to work. Furthermore, the right to work was a property right that was part of the inalienable liberty and freedom of a subject. Thus a guild or corporation could regulate the practice of trade to prevent poverty, idleness, social dislocation, or local dissent;[2] but it could not prescribe restrictive penalties against men who were qualified to practise their trade.[3] Coke expounded these views in a number of his reports. But since many modern historians have sought to find the origins of a free enterprise system in the seventeenth century, the thoughts of the Chief Justice have often been misunderstood.[4]

The famous *Case of Monopolies* (1602) revealed how the Chief Justice and the Lord Chancellor could agree on the broader ques-

---

[1] The author thanks Dr John Baker for this information.

[2] For ex. *The Case of the City of London* (KB 1608/9), 8 *Co. Rep.* 121v–30r; and *The Case of Sutton's Hospital* (KB 1612), 10 *Co. Rep.* 23r–35r.

[3] *James Bagg's Case* (KB 1615), 11 *Co. Rep.* 93v–100r; and *Taylor and Shoile's Case* (SI 1607), *ibid.* 11–2.

[4] The problem has been sketched in somewhat different terms by Donald O. Wagner, 'Coke and the Rise of Economic Liberalism', *EcHR* 6 (1935), 31–5; and assessed provocatively by Christopher Hill, *Intellectual origins*, 223–7. The author thanks Dr. T.H.E. Travers for the opportunity of reading his unpub. essay on Coke's analysis of guilds and corporations.

tion of private gain versus public good, even though they could not agree on the role of the monarch in such matters.[1] In this case the monopoly of making playing cards that was given to Darcy by the Crown was ruled invalid by the Court of Common Pleas. The arguments which Coke cited were that the monopoly was against common and statute law, and that it contributed to inflated prices and excessive profits. He concluded that the Crown could not restrict manufacturing unless the prohibition against other parties could be demonstrated to serve the public interest. Ellesmere, however, disagreed that this grant was made against statute law. He held that the judges were concerned specifically with the grounds of the patent and not with the right of the King to issue grants of monopoly. But perhaps more important is the fact that Ellesmere supported the decision of the court and the economic reasoning upon which it was based. This position was consistent with the economic policies which he came to promote in the Privy Council.[2]

In this instance, both the Chief Justice and the Chancellor were concerned with employment and the encouragement of industry and the trades.[3] Just as both men wrote against enclosure and engrossing because those practices led to unemployment in the country (while having used these measures earlier themselves), so they agreed on prohibiting measures which would restrict employment in the cities (where they did not want to live).[4] Thus, a monopoly was held 'bad' if it restricted employment and raised prices artificially for the profit of private individuals who had won a grant at the royal court at the expense of the public good. Neither jurist, however, was necessarily against the institution of monopolies. Ellesmere accepted monopolies but supported the hearing of grievances, while Coke acknowledged them in the Parliaments of 1621 and 1624 in so far as they

[1] All of the pr. reports of the case were pub. with extensive notes in M. B. Donald, *Elizabethan monopolies* (Edinburgh 1961), 196–200, 208–49. The Chanc's critique was in 'Eg. on Coke', f. 37r–v. The errors in Coke's Report were studied by Wagner, 'Coke and economic liberalism', 30–144 at 35–42. The confusion in Coke's mind on the topic was assessed by Hill, *Intellectual origins*, 150–6. Yelverton himself became confused and actually agreed with Coke in criticising him: Stowe MS 153, f. 40r.

[2] *Supra*, Chap. IV.

[3] The role of the C.J. has been assessed lucidly by Barbara Malament, 'The "Economic liberalism" of Sir Edward Coke', *Yale Law J.* 76 (1967), 1343–51. For the background of unemployment and depression see D. C. Coleman, *Revisions in mercantilism* (1969), 92–117.

[4] *CSPD, 1603–10*, p. 541; and for Coke, Holkham MS 746, ff. 1–19. The views of Ellesmere and other privy councillors are cited *supra*, Chap. IV.

contributed to the preservation of quality products and gave encouragement to new industries and employment.[1]

The preservation of the powers of local authorities in the economic life of the community was the third topic in this section of Ellesmere's observations, and the most interesting case that he reviewed was the *Case of the Isle of Ely* (1610).[2] The medieval drainage system for the Fen country of Norfolk and Cambridgeshire had become insufficient by the end of the sixteenth century. Warnings of a breakdown and massive flooding occurred in 1605. The Crown appointed a Commission of Sewers for the River Ouse and the Isle of Ely to draw plans to meet the dangers, and to implement the proposals under the direction of the Privy Council.[3] The commissioners, however, were confronted with a large and rather independent yeoman and freeholder society close to the subsistence level that despised central control. These people launched a petitionary movement against the commissioners each time that body attempted to implement the plans it had proposed: first in 1609, secondly after the flood of 1613, and again in 1618. The purpose of the commissioners was to clean the old drains and rivers, and to construct a new drainage and waterway system. The inhabitants, however, desired only to cleanse and to reopen the existing tributaries. The people appear to have succeeded in winning some of the commissioners over to their point of view by the summer of 1618, and the Commission of Sewers, torn by internal strife, became embroiled in controversies and law suits that eventually brought its efforts to an inconclusive end.[4]

One of the plans of the commissioners in 1609 was to cut a new seven-mile course for the River Ouse in the Isle of Ely, financing the project by having each of the fifteen adjoining towns assess their inhabitants collectively. The people objected both to the new course and the tax, and they petitioned the Privy Council to restrain the commissioners. The Council, in return, sent the matter to Chief Justice Coke and Justices Daniel and Foster of the Common Pleas for their advice. The Chief Justice supported the commissioners,

---

[1] Malament, 'Economic liberalism', 1328–31, 1351–8.

[2] 10 *Co. Rep.* 141r–3r; 'Eg. on Coke', f. 43.

[3] This and the following proceedings are contained in the *CSPD, 1603–10*, pp. 132, 290, 536, 550; and *CSPD, 1611–18*, pp. 212, 413, 536, 552. The proposals are in *ibid.* pp. 514 and 542, respectively.

[4] The general problem is discussed in the *Agrarian history of England and Wales 1500–1640*, ed. Joan Thirsk (Cambridge 1967), 38–41. The controversies are mentioned in *CSPD, 1611–18*, p. 566; and *CSPD, 1619–23*, pp. 13, 38, 96.

and he declared in his report that the Common Pleas held it as good law that the commissioners had no general powers of taxation, and that such powers were never given to them by the statutes of Henry VI and Henry VIII under which they had been appointed.[1] The Chief Justice became the champion of his East Anglian compatriots, but he did not interpret accurately the statutes which were at issue. The statute of Henry VI declared explicitly that such commissioners could not only survey, plan, and construct, but were also 'there to distrain all them for the quantity of their lands and tenements' to meet the costs. The statute of Henry VIII was not only explicit, but it also provided a Chancery process for the collection of unpaid taxes, declaring that the decrees of the commissioners became the law of the land and could be excepted only by Parliament.[2]

Coke's report of his 'advice' appeared soon after the flood of 1613, and it must have upset those members of the Commission who sought to make a final effort to effect a future plan for the Fens. According to the Chancellor, Coke's opinion was never presented judicially, and the plea roll reveals that the case did not appear before the Court.[3] Coke's advice, moreover, was not taken by the Council. While the Chief Justice gave an opinion that was not accepted, and reported as a rule of law that which was never entered in the record of the court, his interpretation of this matter was consistent with contemporary thought on the subject. The early seventeenth century marked a new era of schemes to improve river navigation in England. The draining of the Fens, the cleansing of old channels and the cutting of new ones, were activities necessary for the economic health and growth of the country.[4] Ideas such as these, however, were ahead of their time. More than a century would elapse before they would gain general acceptance.

The Chancellor proved to be most prophetic in those areas of the law which were directly related to his experiences of more than forty years as a student, lawyer, judge, and landowner. His reverence for the northern borderlands of England and Wales and the virtues of

---

[1] 10 *Co. Rep.* 142.

[2] 'Commissions of Sewers', 6 H. VI Chap. 5 (1427), *Stat. Realm* II, 236–8, the quote at p. 236; and 'A general Acte concernynge Commissions of Sewers', 23 H. VIII Chap. 5, *Stat. Realm* III, 368–72, clauses 4–6 at p. 370.

[3] P.R.O. KB 27/1337/263–4. For Ellesmere's encouragement to the local inhabitants see Lans. MS 110, f. 21r.

[4] T. S. Willan, *River navigation in England 1600–1750* (1964 ed.), 2–5; and H. C. Darby, *Draining of the Fens* (Cambridge 1956).

rural society had formed the background of his staunch support of local and regional courts, and his zeal for the Reformed Church lay behind his defence of ecclesiastical authorities.[1] The most recent experience, however, in his long career of public service had been with the Court of Chancery. And by the spring of 1614 he had acquired twenty years of service as Master of the Rolls, Lord Keeper, and Chancellor. The Chancery represented Ellesmere's greatest achievement as an aristocratic office-holder, and his final contribution to the State would be his successful defence of the supremacy of the Chancellor's decree.

[1] *Supra*, Chap. I.

LES ENFANTS TERRIBLES:
COKE, ELLESMERE, AND THE
SUPREMACY OF THE CHANCELLOR'S DECREE

The rise of the Chancery into a prominent court and department of state in the sixteenth century was one of the major judicial and administrative developments of the early modern period. The Chancellor came to preside over a court that had two jurisdictions: a common law and an equity side, which had their own procedures and records. The Chancellor also witnessed the growth of a maze of inner administrative departments and offices, which comprised perhaps the largest bureaucracy in the Tudor State.[1] Conspicuous developments such as these posed awesome problems in comprehending and mastering the responsibilities of the office in the second half of the sixteenth century. And two of the first non-clerical men to preside over the Chancery, Sir Nicholas Bacon (1558–79) and Sir Thomas Egerton (from 1596–1603), were the men who approached, and began to come to grips with, these problems.

For example, both Bacon and Egerton made it a habit to issue regularly administrative directives for processing writs, keeping records, and regulating fees. They also issued numerous orders for the more efficient management of judicial procedures, tightening the rules of evidence, and controlling the form and size of pleadings. These jurists were common lawyers who conceived of equitable relief in terms of common law rules. They also conceived of courts as institutions whose jurisdiction was clearly defined. A broad programme of Chancery reform was initiated by Bacon,[2] but his successors were not equal to the task of fulfilling it. The Chancery drifted towards

---

[1] The best contemp. analyses were those of Hake, *Epieikeia*, 119–44; Lambarde, *Archeion*, 151–66; West, *Symboleog.* ff. 173v–300r; and William Sheppard, *The Faithful Councillor* (1651) 596–703. A full study of the court in the Elizabethan period is that of Jones, *Chancery*. The best studies of the development of equity in this era are those of D. E. C. Yale in *Lord Nottingham's 'Manual of Chancery Practice' and 'Prolegomena of Chancery and Equity'* (Cambridge 1965) 7–27; and Stuart Prall, 'The development of equity in Tudor England', *AJLH* VIII (1964), 1–19.

[2] P.R.O. C.220/15/1–7; and *Orders of the High Court of Chancery*, ed. G.W. Sanders (1845), I, 28–50. Bacon's broader ideas on law reform can be glimpsed in SPD 12/105/93, and B.M. Cotton Titus MS B.VI, ff. 179–80.

less precise judicial doctrines, administrative inefficiency, and corruption in the years following Bacon's death in 1579. Not until Egerton's appointment to the Mastership of the Rolls in 1594, and to the Lord Keepership in 1596, were the plans drawn by Bacon again taken up and translated into accomplishment.[1]

The new Master of the Rolls was resolved to clean up the rot in the offices over which he presided. Encouraged by the sage Lord Treasurer, Lord Burghley, and by his former legal colleagues, Sir John Popham and Sir Edward Coke, Egerton placed a firm hand on the officials in the Rolls Office in the years 1594–6.[2] He invalidated several reversions to offices given by the Queen, and gained personal control over many of the officials. Orders were made to control the work of clerks and under-clerks, to circumscribe the influence of attorneys, and to regulate the issue of writs and the enrolment of records. Egerton's reforms, however, were not fully implemented. Their success depended on the full co-operation of the Lord Keeper, Sir John Puckering. Thus the single most important fact in the history of the early modern Chancery was Egerton's promotion to the presidency of the court in 1596. This move, together with his retention of the office of Master of the Rolls, enabled him to gain control of the court and supervise the offices and records which comprised the foundation of its activities.[3]

The new Lord Keeper was aided in this task by his old friend William Lambarde.[4] Promoted to the keepership of the records at the Rolls Chapel and the Tower, the Kentish legal antiquarian collected ancient precedents, gathered tracts on Chancery procedures and privileges, and kept notes of important recent cases for the use of the Lord Keeper. Lambarde also made many valuable suggestions for

---

[1] That Sir Nicholas was the architect for Chan. reform is the thesis of Robert Tittler: 'Sir Nicholas Bacon and the reform of the Tudor Chancery', *Univ. Tor. Law J.* 23 (1973), 383–95.

[2] Lans. MS 79, f. 83r–v (Egerton to Burghley, 5 June 1595); and *Salisbury MS* VII, 334 (Coke to Robert Cecil, 3 Aug. 1597).

[3] The thesis of Jones, *Chancery*, 50. See *supra*, pp. 28–30, 34–5.

[4] Lambarde's Chancery coll's for Egerton are in Harv. Law MS 1034–5, and they have been analysed by P.L. Ward, 'William Lambarde's collections on Chancery', *Harv. Lib. Bull.* 7 (1953), 271–98. Some of Lambarde's interesting letters to Egerton have been preserved in Ellesm. MS 39, and Hunt. RB 17273 and 62135. The impact of the reforms can be measured from an earlier and later version of Lambarde's account of the Court of Chancery: Harg. MS 227, ff. 193v–8v. The textual problems in Lambarde's historical writings with ref. to the Chan. have been assessed by Paul Ward in the App. of his ed. of the *Archeion*, 145–76. The author thanks Dr Ward for his more recent suggestions that Egerton did not accept the full measure of Lambarde's proposals.

administrative reform in the years 1596–1600. The Lord Keeper was now able to use his influence in the Rolls to shape the progress of the court over which he presided. Orders were issued to regulate the examination of witnesses and to quicken the processes of the court. New schedules of fees were established, and incentives were created to enhance the quality of clerical work. No new offices were instituted, and the authority and prestige of existing offices were raised. Egerton's control of the Chancery became remarkably firm, and this control was demonstrated by his ability to prevent royal grants from passing the great seal if he found them unacceptable.[1]

The influence of the new Lord Keeper was significant in the judicial activities of the court. Receiving advice from common as well as civil lawyers, he aimed initially to settle the procedures of the court and to combat blatant abuses, unnecessary litigation, and clerical incompetence. The law of the Chancery was also to be clear and known. The Lord Keeper gave a sharper definition to equitable concepts by ordering them more thoroughly on the lines of common law rules. Earlier, he had made rules for the better understanding of statutes;[2] now he did the same for equity. The work of the Lord Keeper was not just restrictive in nature. Egerton advanced the theory of trusts and mortgages, and created important legal precedents for the adjudication of contract, debt, deeds, leases, and titles to land; upholding the rights of property owners and creditors while protecting debtors. Developments such as these were facilitated by continuing the tradition of using common law judges to sit in the Rolls with the Masters while the Lord Keeper was engaged at Westminster. Finally, Egerton improved the effectiveness of the court by developing forms of writs and injunctions that would provide the litigant with better remedies and means of enforcement.[3]

Egerton's Chancery became recognised as the high court of equity. It had come to hear many causes by original motions in addition to assuming a supervisory or appellate role for the Court of Requests and lesser conciliar and provincial jurisdictions. The Lord Keeper, however, was careful to define more precisely the relationship of the

---

[1] For the context see W. J. Jones, 'Due process and slow process in the Elizabethan Chancery', *AJLH* 6 (1962), 123–50; and *supra*, pp. 58–65. Reforms that can be attributed to Egerton's initial work are discussed in Jones, *Chancery*, 64–87.

[2] *Supra*, pp. 46–50.

[3] The history of his long Chancellorship is a forbidding task. A useful but inadequate outline is that of Holdsworth, *HEL* v, 231–8. A good perspective on the problems he faced, looking backwards and forwards, is provided by Mr Yale in *Nott's Chanc. Cases*, i, 13–16, 30–3, 65–6.

Chancery to the other major central courts; and especially to narrow the potential areas of conflict with the courts of common law. Whereas he considered the Chancellor's decree as superior to those of other judicial officers, he was sparing in its use. Thus by 1603 the Chancery order and decree books were registering less judicial business than they had prior to his accession in 1596.[1] The programme resulted in an important influence on the judicial record.

Chancery reform came at a critical period in the history of the court. The number of cases that came before the Chancery had more than doubled in the years 1550–70, and it doubled once more from 1570 to 1595. The Chancellor's injunction to prevent parties from appearing in other courts, and to have their causes transferred to the Court of Chancery, was being used more frequently and without a clearly fixed intent. However, the relations between the Chancery and other courts of law, particularly with the courts of Admiralty, Requests, and Wards, and with the ecclesiastical and provincial courts, had been amicable in the Elizabethan period. This spirit of co-operation also seemed to be the keynote of Chancery–common law relations.[2] Common law judges frequently sat in the Chancery to assist in important decisions, and Readers at the inns of court lectured on the antiquity of the Chancery. Among the lectures of famous Readers, Edward Coke called the law of the Court 'time out of mind', and Charles Calthorpe defined its jurisdiction in matters of equity as 'absolute'.[3] Nonetheless, the judges of the common law were becoming increasingly wary of the tremendous growth of litigation before the Court of Chancery, and of its use of the common injunction to disrupt proceedings before the courts of common law.[4]

The question of how far the indistinct jurisdiction of the Chancery was going to develop in the Elizabethan period was resolved by the

---

[1] C.33/89–90, 99–100, 107–8. The decline is in both the pages of records and the number of causes in the order and decree books.

[2] W. J. Jones, 'Conflict or collaboration? Chancery attitudes in the reign of Elizabeth I', *AJLH* 5 (1961), 19–37.

[3] Coke in his Reading of the Statute of Fines (27 E. I) at Lyons Inn in 1580: Harl. MS 5265, f. 165r; and Calthorpe's Reading on copyholds at Furnivall's Inn in 1574: Add. MS 25.215, f. 22v. Coke's refs. to judges sitting and assisting in the Chan. can be found in 1595, for ex. in Coke MS Rep. C, ff. 126r, 134v, 148v, 150r. See also the opinion of the Bench cited by Hobart, *Reports*, 63 (KB 1601).

[4] The thoughts of the judges in *Heal's Case* (KB 1588), in [William Leonard] *Reports and Cases of Law* (2nd ed. 1687), II, 115–16; and the bellicose reaction of Lord Chanc. Hatton: Cecil Monro, *Acta Cancellariae* (1847), 5–8.

judges in the midst of Egerton's Chancery reforms. The issue that developed was whether the Chancellor by virtue of his possession of the King's conscience could still allow a cause against a party who won at common law on the grounds of providing equitable relief; for example, re-examining the party in order to see if he had used fraud in bringing the facts upon which he attained judgment.[1] The issue was referred to all the judges of England informally in 1598 to determine the case of *Finch v. Throgmorton*.[2] The new Lord Keeper was 'omitted and excluded' from participation in this decision,[3] and all the judges but one ruled that the Chancellor could not subpoena parties for causes which had been determined at common law. One of the major grounds of their reasoning was the statutes of 27 Edward III c. 1, and 4 Henry IV c. 23, statutes which provided penalties for suing after judgments at law in another court. The decision was communicated to Egerton by his friend John Popham, and entered into the Chancery's order and decree book.[4] Egerton was then requested by the Queen to reverse officially one of his own decisions in the Chancery that stayed the execution of a judgment at common law on the grounds of providing equitable relief.[5]

The resolution in *Finch v. Throgmorton*, together with Egerton's reforms, must have helped to reduce the number of cases heard by the court and to curtail the use of the common injunction. These factors help to explain the decline in the volume of judicial business that was registered in the Chancery order and decree books by the death of Elizabeth in 1603. But despite these changes the issue raised and resolved in the Finch case was not resolved in the legal profession. Immediately after the decision of 1598, a tract began to circulate claiming that the Court of Chancery could not issue writs of *supersedeas* against the King's Bench in matters of 'peace and good behaviour', reviving the old contest between Sir Nicholas Bacon and Chief Justice Sir Robert Catlyn.[6] A war of tracts ensued, with items appearing for

---

[1] Contemp. disputes on the issue have been discussed by Jones, *Chancery*, 462–73.

[2] The fullest reports are Coke MS Rep. C, ff. 222v–7r; and Petyt MS 538/16/278r–v. Pr. notes are in Bulstrode, *Reports* III, 118; Croke, *Reports*, I, 221, and II, 344; and Moore, *Cases*, 291.

[3] F–H MS 33, f. 2r.

[4] The case was traced in the Chan. order and decree books by John P. Dawson, 'Coke and Ellesmere disinterred: the attack on the Chancery in 1616', *Illinois Law Rev.* 36 (1941), 134–5. The role of Popham was noted in Petyt MS 538/16/278r. Chan. propagandists occasionally stretched the meaning of the key phrase with the translation: 'other courts'.

[5] D.C.O. MS F.M. 5, 'Camera Stellata', f. 180r.

[6] The Bacon–Catlyn dispute is described in Jones, *Chancery*, 345–6.

and against the right of the Chancellor to issue writs of *supersedeas*, and the dispute was enlarged to general statements regarding the 'supremacy' of the courts of Chancery and King's Bench.[1] Several new tracts on the Chancery appeared after this confrontation. Penned by the hands of 'Chancery-men', they argued that the Chancery was the King's prerogative court, the highest court in the realm; and that giving equitable relief to parties after verdict at common law was an 'ancient customary' right.[2]

Judicial conflict existed on many fronts at the turn of the sixteenth century. Whether, for example, the Lord Keeper had accepted the decision of 1598 is a speculative question. We do know that he was fully occupied in reforming the Chancery. However, the number of tracts that begin to appear, penned by the 'Chancery-men' to whom he was restoring privilege and profit, seems more than just coincidental. Perhaps the Lord Keeper objected to the decision of 1598 but was not in a position to fight against it at that time. In any event, the use of the Chancellor's common injunction, and the relations between courts of equity and common law had now entered the arena of public debate. The debate, moreover, came to embrace a wide range of constitutional, legal, and political problems. A brief analysis will enable us to examine in its proper context the history of the conflict which ensued.

Constitutionally, there was little agreement on the structure of the English judiciary in the early seventeenth century. For a lawyer such as Coke, the position of the courts depended on the law which they dispensed. Thus there was statute law (Parliament), common law (King's Bench, Common Pleas, and Exchequer), and equity (Chancery and Requests) in that order, and the Chancery was without doubt 'under' the common law.[3] Sir Francis Bacon, however, held that the authority of a court depended on the nature of the office by

---

[1] The issues were set forth in a tract by Mr Waterhouse, 'A Defence of the Proceedinges in Kinges Benche', dated 10 Feb. 1598/9; and rejoined in an anon. reply 'Obseruations vppon Mr. Waterhouse Defence of the proceeding of the Kinges Benche in matters of peace and good behauiour' (undated). Both tracts circulated widely, and are extant in most major legal colls. Egerton's copies were Ellesm. MSS 2920 and 2986, respectively.

[2] For ex. 'Curia Cancellar', Ellesm. MS 2958, ff. 1r–2r. Also at issue was the use of the injunction by other courts of equity, esp. the Court of Requests. See Caesar's defence in Ellesm. MS 2924, which includes the notes of a Chan. official.

[3] Edward Coke, *The Fourth Part of the Institutes of the Laws of England* (1644), Chaps. I, VII, VIII. A still useful critique of the origins of this Institute is that of William Prynne, *Brief Animadversions* (1669), 'To the Reader'.

which it was convened. Since Chancellors had precedence over common law judges, the Chancery and the Star Chamber were the King's highest courts, and the highest courts in the realm for civil and criminal causes.[1] Dr John Cowell shared this view, but his reasoning was more extreme. He attributed the authority of courts to the closeness they held to the monarch. Thus Dr Cowell believed that the prerogative courts were the most eminent courts in the land.[2]

Ellesmere's views on the constitutional relationships of judicial bodies represented yet another stream of thought. He stated that the English courts could be categorised as central, provincial, and local courts, secular and ecclesiastical. Secular central courts existed for the highest civil and criminal affairs. The most prominent ones were the Common Pleas, Chancery, and Exchequer for civil causes, and the King's Bench and Star Chamber for criminal matters. These courts were all equal in authority, subservient only to what was regarded as the High Court of Parliament.[3]

Questions concerning judicial relationships found their parallel in questions relating to the law of the courts. One of the major subjects of the legal thought of the period was the meaning of 'common law' and of 'equity'. Legal writers such as Edward Hake, Francis Tate, and William West regarded common law as written law, a science based on rules and precedents which stemmed from actions at common law courts. They regarded equity, however, as unwritten law, a moral law that was derived from the law of God. Equity, stemming from divine law, possessed the 'internal sense' of all law. It was described as the 'kernel' of the law and regarded as superior to all other forms.[4] Concepts such as these, however, were too extreme for contemporaries who were fully educated and trained in common law traditions. Christopher Saint-German and Edmund Plowden were two pro-

---

[1] Bacon in the *Case de non procedendo Rege inconsulto* (KB 1615/6), in his *Works* I, 687–725.

[2] Cowell, *Interpreter*, s.v. 'Ch.'

[3] Notes in his copy of *His Maiesties Speach in the Starre Chamber the XX of Iune Anno 1616* (1616), Hunt. RB 61870, f. 12v. See also *supra*, pp. 66–8, 73–6, 79–81.

[4] Hake, *Epieikeia*, 46–8, 56–7, 123–4; and his second letter to Julius Caesar in Lans. MS 161, f. 43v, dated 15 Feb. 1597/8. For Tate, see Lambarde's copy of his tract on 'The Antiquity of the Lord Chancellor of England', Harv. Law MS 1034, ff. 177v–80v. West discusses the subject in his *Symboleog. s.v.* 'Of the Chancery', sects. 3–11. In add. see Thomas Ashe's introd. to *EPIEIKEIA Et Table generall* (1609), sig. Aiiiv-Aiiijr. The analogy between equity as a moral science and common law as a political science was struck by William Fulbecke, *A Parallele or Conference of the Civill Law, the Canon Law, and the Common Law of this Realme of England* (1601), f. 58v.

minent spokesmen on law and equity in the sixteenth century. According to Saint-German there were two kinds of equity, Greek and Roman. The Greek concept was composed of universal principles from which all laws were derived. The Roman form conceived of equity as a principle of the constitution to correct the existing law where it could not provide justice.[1] Whereas Hake saw equity in England in the Greek form, Plowden envisaged it in its Roman form. Equity was the use of the Chancellor's decree to correct or supplement the law where it was deficient. While equity was the meaning, or intent of the law, it could also be a judicial process within the common law system.[2]

The Chancellor's understanding of equity was derived from Saint-German and Plowden. Ellesmere, like Plowden, believed that the concept of Roman equity could be found in the historical development of the English Chancery. Since the two highest forms of law in England were statute and common law, equity was used in the Chancery to supplement the rule of law in civil matters.[3] This conceptual framework lay behind the Chancellor's attempts to design fully the equitable relief of the Chancery according to common law guidelines. In fulfilling the aspirations of his great predecessor, Nicholas Bacon, Ellesmere wrote the modern definition of the equitable jurisdiction of the Chancery into the pages of the later law books.[4] Writers such as Hake, zealous Crown officials as Francis Bacon, civil lawyers like Sir Julius Caesar, peers like Northampton, and court gossips such as Dr Goodman praised the 'High' Court of Chancery in terms which could only antagonise parliamentarians and lawyers who were steeped in the common law tradition. The Chancery, notwithstanding Ellesmere's quiet and effective work, hence became associated in many minds with the growing trend towards royal absolutism. It was often depicted as the highest, absolute court of a King who had 'high-flying' notions about the nature of his supremacy, and propagandists for a pure common law system attacked the Chancery as

[1] Christopher Saint-German, *The Second Dyalogue in Englyshe* (4th ed. col. 1532), ff. 36r–9v. This view was given even further currency by Sir James Dodderidge, *The English Lawyer* (1631), 208–14.

[2] Plowden, *Commentaries*, 465v–6v.

[3] 'Brief Chanc.' ff. 1r–3v. Ellesmere's use of Plowden is illustrated decisively in the marginal notes of his copy, Hunt. RB 62961, for ex. at ff. 360v–6v.

[4] In the words of the modern text, equity: 'a body of rules or principles which form an appendage or gloss to the general rules of law' – *Snell's principles of equity*, ed. R. E. Megarry and P. V. Baker (1960 ed.), 3.

part of their political programme in opposition to the King.[1] Public officials who sat politically to the right of these men were often lumped conveniently under a blanket of opprobrium.

Egerton, raised to the title of Baron Ellesmere and to the status of Lord Chancellor, sat at the beginning of James's reign at the helm of a very popular, reformed court of law. Its remedies could be obtained more cheaply and more quickly, and with better provisions for enforcement than many civil actions at common law. Perhaps this success accounts for the change in the volume of business that occurred at the accession of James. The years 1603–10 revealed a significant rise in judicial activity before the Chancellor in the history of the court. The business recorded in the order and decree books rose nearly fifty per cent in the course of seven years, becoming nearly one-quarter more than it was prior to his accession to office in 1596.[2] It appears that the Chancellor, after reforming the court on firm foundations, was now determined to facilitate the accelerated growth of chancery jurisdiction. It also appears that he considered the common injunction to be no longer restricted by measures other than the rules and procedures which he had established.[3] Thus in spite of the Finch decision, Ellesmere after 1603 resumed the practice of examining parties after judgment at common law. Not only did he employ freely the common injunction, but his use of that legal process became noted in contemporary collections of precedents by the end of the first decade of the seventeenth century.[4]

The common law judges were becoming worried not only about the sudden expansion of this central court of equity, but also of its constitutional and political ramifications. Coke in 1604 condemned the growth of uses, trusts, and other devices of holding land which were being enforced by the Court of Chancery; and later he cited Ellesmere's revival of the injunction in the early years of the century

[1] John Dykstra Eusden, *Puritans, lawyers, and politics in early seventeenth-century England* (New Haven Conn. 1958), 88–110, for some background on the radical lawyers. A draft bill against questioning common law judgments is in H.M.C. *Third report*, App. p. 15. The political programme which they attacked has been discussed fully (but also too rigidly) by Wallace Notestein, *The House of Commons 1604–1610* (New Haven Conn. 1971). Their political context is assessed *supra*, Chap. III.

[2] C.33/107–8, 119–20. This is based on both the quantity of records and the number of cases in the order and decree books. For a number of complex problems which follow, the author thanks Dr Bill Jones for his carefully reasoned comments.

[3] As in the important early case, *Ansin* v. *Twynn* (Ch 1596), Petyt MS 516/5/58v.

[4] For ex. notes on Ellesmere issuing decrees as if the Finch decision had not been made, and on the judge of the K.B. reaffirming it: Add. MS 25.213, ff. 159r, 162r, 185r.

as the occasion that marked the inordinate growth of Chancery juris-diction.[1] Several other judges began to go on record as being 'anti-Chancery'. Yelverton addressed the King's Bench in 1604 with the angry declaration that a legal process in the Chancery 'does not close the mouths of the judges of the common law'.[2] And Coke himself, after Egerton's elevation to the status of Chancellor, appended a note to his account of the Finch case, declaring that for the Chancellor to examine matters in equity after judgment at common law, 'ceo tende al subversion del common ley'.[3]

These were the general sources of discontent which underlay anti-Chancery attitudes in the early years of the seventeenth century, and Ellesmere's 'Breviate for the King's Learned Counsel' was composed in the summer of 1615 as a working paper for the public defence of the Court of Chancery from the attacks of common law jurists against the supremacy of the Chancellor's decree. In the preface, the Chancellor made a plea for a dialogue between the judges, coun-sellors, and lawmakers similar to the plea he had made earlier for a dialogue between lords, commoners, councillors, and the King.[4] The compromise, however, would be on his terms.

The body of Ellesmere's tract was divided into two sections. The first one was devoted to the proposition that the power and authority of the Chancellor was deeply embedded in the ancient constitution. The evidence was drawn from an exposition of the major statutes which concerned the Chancery and other courts of law from the reign of King John to that of Henry IV. The purpose of this exercise was to demonstrate the legitimacy of Chancery jurisdiction under statute law in order to justify its growth. Secondly, the Chancellor proceeded to analyse the statutes of provisors and *praemunire* of Edward III, Richard II, and Henry IV, V, and VI. Two of these stat-utes had been used in the Finch case to attack the supremacy of his decree, and the Chancellor was meticulous in explaining how they applied not to the Court of Chancery interfering with parties in civil actions at common law, but to the interference of the papal courts at Rome. His brief reflected a lifetime's interest in the history of legislation.[5]

---

[1] 3 *Co. Rep.* sigs. A3v–A4v; and in *Commons Debates, 1621*, ed. W. Notestein *et al.* (New Haven Conn. 1935), VI, 63–4.

[2] *Weaver* v. *Clifford* (KB 1604), Yelverton, *Reports*, 42.

[3] Coke MS Rep. C, f. 227r.

[4] 'Brief Chanc.' f. 1r.

[5] The analysis *supra*, pp. 46–51, and *infra*, Chap. X.

Ellesmere's tract included a restatement of well-known procedures for interpreting statutes. The Chancellor had explored this subject in an introductory essay during his law-school days, and later he refined his ideas in drafting a speech on the *Post-Nati*.[1] Ellesmere had long regarded statutes as the major source of the law,[2] and he believed that they must be interpreted strictly according to the words of the act except in cases where the meaning was unclear or ambiguous. In cases such as these he prescribed rules for their understanding. First, the jurist must 'understand and consider what was the mischief at the common law which the Parliament meant to remedy'. Secondly, he had to determine the purpose of the statute at the time in which it was enacted. Thirdly, if any further ambiguities remained, they were to be resolved by a conference of the judges and privy councillors before the King.[3]

Statutory interpretation had become an increasingly important part of common law studies by the late sixteenth century. Edmund Plowden had elevated its study with the publication of his *Commentaries*, in which he wrote a number of fascinating, discursive passages on the problems of understanding statutes.[4] Plowden's ideas had an impact on a generation of law students. It is not unusual to find in the law books of students at the inns of court in the early seventeenth century copious marginal notes on Plowden's interpretation of statute law.[5] This interest was followed in early Stuart times by a number of law reporters and jurists, men who had become fully aware of the problems of interpreting old statutes and framing new ones.[6] Ellesmere himself had patronised the editing, translating, and publication of a new edition of the statutes; and his correspondence with Ferdinando Pulton revealed the problems of making available to lawyers and

---

[1] *Discourse*, and the *Post-Nati*, 46–50, respectively.

[2] For ex. his advice to Sir John Puckering on drafting and interpreting procls. and statutes: Harl. MS 6996, f. 58 (17 Jan. 1593/4).

[3] 'Brief Chanc.' ff. 8r–9r.

[4] Plowden, *Commentaries*, ff. 172–5, 235–8, 465–7. His major concern was in distinguishing between the words and their intent, the body and the soul, and the letter and sense of statutes. Statutory interp. had also, however, been an important topic of study in the Year Books and Readings of the fifteenth and early sixteenth centuries.

[5] Louis A. Knafla, 'The law studies of an Elizabethan student', *HLQ* 32 (1969), 223–8. Ellesmere's notes on statutory interp. in Plowden are in Hunt. RB 62961, ff. 86v–7v, 360v–3r, 396v–8v.

[6] The anon. reporter in Add. MS 25.215, ff. 43r–82v; Bacon, *Elements*, 50–2, 90–3; and Thomas Ashe, *Epieikeia* (1609). An ex. of how different interp's could affect the passage of a statute in clarifying a previous law is that described in a parl. diary: Yale U. L. Eng. Misc. MS 1610, ff. 201v–3r. Francis Bacon had also proposed a scheme to codify statute law.

law-makers an authoritative critical edition.[1] This specialised interest in statute law affected significantly his view of the relationship
of the courts of equity to those of the common law.

The first part of Ellesmere's tract was devoted to a close analysis
of nine statutes of the fourteenth and fifteenth centuries which had
been used by the antagonists of the Court of Chancery, and his account contains the development of three themes which rendered their
arguments impotent: 'common right', the 'law of the land', and the
status of judgments at the courts of common law and equity.[2] According to Ellesmere, 'common right' signified common justice not
common law.[3] The Chancellor held that statutes which referred to
the doing of common right were phrased broadly in order to include
the doing of right by rules of equity as well as by those of common
law. He argued that the common law judges had always accepted the
rules of conscience and equity as comprising the law of the Chancery.
Thus the concept of common right included several different kinds
of legal rules, and was not the special province of any particular court.
'For it standeth with the common law as well that equity and conscience be ministered where the common law cannot help, as that
strict justice be ministered according to the common law, when the
common law may serve.'[4]

In Magna Carta and several later statutes the customs of the land
had been conceived as comprising the 'law of the land'. A number of
jurists began to restrict the scope of this phrase to the common law
courts in the early seventeenth century. A second theme of the initial
section of Ellesmere's tract was an analysis of how such statutes did
not apply, and therefore did not intend to exclude the Court of
Chancery and other courts of equity. The Chancellor had defined
the law of the land as public law, and he regarded equity as a specific substantive body of the public law which the common law was
not legally capable of administering. The particular statutes which
he examined stipulated that no man could be put to answer without
due process of law. His task was to explain the precise manner in
which these statutes were intended to restrict private proceedings

---

[1] The corresp. is in Ellesm. MS 1963–4, 2979. Ellesmere also had a copy of Pulton's earlier
work in which he made notations: *An abstract of al the penall statutes* (3rd ed. 1577), Hunt. RB
61076. See *supra*, pp. 47–51.

[2] 'Brief Chanc.' ff. 1r–6v.

[3] Sir Matthew Hale later regarded common law and common right as the same. This change
in legal thought represents the influence of Cartesianism in the Restoration period.

[4] *Ibid.* ff, 1v–2v, the quotation at f. 2v.

before the King and his Council, 'but not meant to take away the ordinary judicial proceeding and hearing of the causes of conscience and equity in the Chancery', for 'that is *per legem terrae*'.[1]

The relationship of the courts of equity to those of the common law lay at the heart of the objection that courts of equity had no authority over any matters in causes which were brought originally to the courts of common law. Ellesmere's rebuttal of this shaky logic formed his third theme. He began by pointing out that the Chancery did not award injunctions against a common law court, but against a party who had used fraud and deceit in bringing a defendant before it. Secondly, he presented examples of how the common law judges in the past had always obeyed writs of *supersedeas* addressed to them exempting matters of privilege and *rege inconsulto* from their courts, and had themselves sued and been sued in the Chancery. Thirdly, he analysed closely the statute of 4 Henry IV c. 23, which forbade suitors from appealing against civil actions in the common law courts to the King, Council, or Parliament. Ellesmere explained how excessive appeals to those bodies had been a problem prior to the enacting of the statute, and that the act remedied a legitimate grievance. He also pointed out that there was no reference in the statute to proceedings in equity, or to central courts other than those of the common law.[2]

Ellesmere's defence of the origins and expansion of Chancery jurisdiction had been necessitated by the reaction of a number of his common law colleagues against the growth and alleged supremacy of its judicial proceedings. One possible device discussed but never attempted was the use of the writ of prohibition.[3] Although the writ was used with some success against the ecclesiastical courts and lesser courts of equity in the early years of James's reign, 1605–12,[4] there is no evidence to suggest that prohibitions were used against the Chancery. It was due perhaps to this shortcoming of prohibition that a few judges from 1609 to 1616 encouraged the use of *praemunire* in civil actions against parties who applied to the Chancery for injunctions against proceedings at common law. However, since suits of *praemunire* did not appear altogether promising, judges also turned

---

[1] *Ibid.* ff. 1r–v, 1v–3v, 4v, the quotation at f. 1v. An interesting discussion of this question is in C. H. McIlwain, *Constitutionalism and the changing world* (Cambridge 1939), 86–126.

[2] 'Brief Chanc.' ff. 1r–6r.

[3] A relatively rare coll. of precedents to 1612, which suggests the use of prohibitions against the Chan. in the C.P. and K.B. is D.C.O. Misc. MS Godfrey 73–5.

[4] For ex. Godbolt, *Reports*, 208, 216, 219, 243–4; and Rolle, *Reports*, 119, 263, 380. See also *supra*, Chap. VI, and *infra*, Chap. XIV.

to the writ of *habeas corpus*. These were the two devices upon which a direct confrontation emerged between the courts of Chancery and King's Bench in 1614.

The suit of *praemunire* had been expressly created in the fourteenth century to indict, and outlaw, individuals who sued in courts outside the realm without the assent of the monarch. Generally it had been applicable to ecclesiastical causes, but as the penalties were reduced in the Elizabethan period it became tested for a variety of legal actions. For example, the Lord President of Wales attempted to bring suits of *praemunire* against recusants, and a party used it in the King's Bench to prevent a cause from being heard against him in the Vice-Chancellor's Court at Cambridge University for debt.[1] In *Heal's Case* (1588) it was used unsuccessfully in the King's Bench against a decree in equity which overthrew a civil action at common law.[2] Ellesmere himself gave a legal opinion (as Master of the Rolls in 1595) that *praemunire* could lie against brokers who drove hard bargains in contracting for usurious interest.[3] Gradually the phrase of the statute which brought a civil action of *praemunire* against appeals 'to another's court' began to be interpreted as appealing against a party before the King's Bench or Common Pleas. The action became prominent in the early years of the reign of James I, particularly against debtors who sought to avoid the payment of their debts. One popular treatise on law reform alleged that debtors throughout the land had become threatened by actions of *praemunire* if they were released from gaol by commissioners for debtors or gaol delivery.[4] A petition from Edward Lytelbury to the Privy Council in 1609 was a plea to prevent his creditor from pursuing five indictments of *praemunire* against him for a debt of £30 from which he sought relief.[5] Although no evidence has been found on the conclusion of such matters, *praemunire* appears to have been one of the scare tactics used by creditors in the early seventeenth century to recover their debts.

The other device used against the Court of Chancery from 1615

---

[1] Lans. MS 111; C.U.L. Corpus Christi Coll. MS 106, pp. 600, 605–6, respectively. Dr John Baker has seen exs. from the reign of H. VIII in his study of Spelman's Reports.

[2] *Heale's Case* (KB 1588), Leonard, *Reports*, II, 115–16. That it had become an inflammable topic can be seen in Cockburn, *Assizes*, 220.

[3] Letter to Robert Cecil, *Salisbury MS*, V, 362–3 (5 Sept. 1595).

[4] James Dackambe, 'To the Highe and Mightie Monarche James', B.M. Royal MS 18.A. 36, ff. 6v–12r. There is also a coll. of exs. in Thomas Ashe, *Le Second Volume del Promptuarie* (1614), ff. 221v–2v.

[5] Lans. MS 91, f. 110r (20 June 1609).

was the writ of *habeas corpus*, an ancient writ of process to release men imprisoned by the Chancellor for refusing to surrender the awards of verdicts obtained at common law. The writ, however, was used with discretion in special instances, not for general situations. A cursory examination of printed and manuscript law reports fixes the crucial date for its prominence in the Court of King's Bench for men imprisoned by the Chancery to the years 1614–16. For example, in Bulstrode's reports of cases in the King's Bench for the years 1609–16, fifteen instances of hearings for the issue of the writ of *habeas corpus* are cited, and thirteen date from 1614–16.[1] Among the fuller and more comprehensive manuscript reports, two collections list numerous *habeas corpus* proceedings from 1610 to 1616, and at least five such causes were heard in Trinity term 1615,[2] in the midst of Coke's last major attack on the supremacy of the Chancellor's decree.

The questioning of the extent of the Chancellor's decree came from parties before the Court of King's Bench, and it began under the presidency of Sir Thomas Fleming, Chief Justice from 1607 to 1613.[3] Fleming not only encouraged the suit of *praemunire* to check the supremacy of the Chancellor's decree, but lawyers began to question the record of the court in protecting the interests of their clients. Many lawyers, like Coke, distorted medieval authority to argue that the Chancery was not a court of record because it could imprison but not fine, and its proceedings were written on paper and not parchment.[4] In *Doughty vs. Fawn* (1612), a plaintiff who had sued and lost in Chancery on a bond for the performance of a will appealed to the King's Bench, and one of his allegations for the repeal of the Chancery decision was that its 'orders are but in paper and not of record to be tried by the record'.[5] The case was reported

---

[1] Bulstrode, *Reports* I, 186, 201; II, 10, 139, 259, 268, 300–1, 308; III, 27, 48, 109, 115, 146, 213. Many of these were directed on the behalf of parties imprisoned by the Council in Wales.

[2] Rawl. MS C.382, ff. 56v–7v, 63r–4r, 71r–v; and with a few others, Add. MS 25.218, ff. 42r–v, 64r–6v, 166v, 190r, 226r.

[3] As he said unequivocally: 'There are too many causes drawn into the Chancery to be relieved there, which are more fit to be determined by trial at common law'–*Gollow* v. *Bacon* (KB 1611), Bulstrode, *Reports* I, 112.

[4] Samuel E. Thorne, 'Courts of record and Sir Edward Coke', *Univ. Tor. Law J.* 2 (1937), 24–49. The initial premise of Coke's position is stated in 4 *Co. Rep.* sigs. B3–4. There are many other contemp. refs. in ms. colls.

[5] *Doughty* v. *Fawn* (KB 1612), in Yelverton, *Reports*, 226–7, the quote at 227. See also Bulstrode, *Reports*, 19; and R. Brownlow and J. Goldesborough, *Reports of divers choice Cases in Law* (1688 ed.), 117–18.

by several observers, and the plea of the plaintiff was rejected by the court.

This questioning was continued when Coke succeeded Fleming as Chief Justice of the Court of King's Bench in October 1613. Upon taking his seat in the Michaelmas term, a Chancery ruling that denied the Finch decision of 1598 came to the attention of the court.[1] Within the following year numerous attempts were made by parties to use *habeas corpus* or *praemunire* to challenge the supremacy of the Chancellor's decree.[2] The year also witnessed an attempt in Parliament to pass a bill that would prevent other courts from 'questioning' judgments at common law.[3] Challenges such as these represented an attempt by more earnest common lawyers to reduce the non-common law courts of the realm to a more subsidiary role in the system. These men spoke of the supremacy of the common law. They sought direction of judicial proceedings in local and provincial courts, and certain discretionary jurisdiction over the ecclesiastical courts and the courts of Admiralty, Requests, and Wards and Liveries. Living in an era of political and economic tension, they were as concerned with political and constitutional issues as they were with judicial ones.[4] The alleged supremacy of the Chancellor's decree was particularly offensive, and their only recourse was in the restoration of the Finch decision of 1598 under the guidance of the new Chief Justice. He was only too ready to comply.[5]

The Chief Justice released his first thunderbolt in *Heath vs. Ridley*, where he refused to regard a common injunction that was served to prevent the execution of a judgment at common law. Affirming the Finch decision of 1598, he declared that no court of equity could

---

[1] *Browne* v. *Heath* (KB 1613), Add. MS 25.213, f. 159r.

[2] For ex. *Jenoar and Alexander's Case*, *Bradley and Jones' Case*, *Wright's Case*, *Heath* v. *Ridley*, *Miller* v. *Reignolds*, *Glanvill* v. *Courtney*, and *Allen's Case*. These are cited as discussed *infra*.

[3] H.M.C. *Third report, Appendix*, 15.

[4] Sir Charles Ogilvie, *The king's government and the common law 1471–1641* (Oxford 1958), 118–60; Eusden, *Puritans, lawyers, and politics*, 41–63, 88–113; J. G. A. Pocock, *The ancient constitution and the feudal law* (Cambridge 1957), 30–69; and Margaret Judson, *The crisis of the constitution* (New Brunswick N.J. 1949). However, none of these works is satisfactory on this subject.

[5] Coke's coll. of precedents for this matter has been preserved in Yale Law MS G.R 24, ff. 3r–19r, 44r–137v; and Holkham MS 677. Two major papers have been written on this conflict: Dawson, 'Coke and Ellesmere disinterred', and J. H. Baker, 'The common lawyers and the Chancery: 1616', *The Irish Jurist* 4 (1969), 368–92. Both are pioneering efforts and, together with the work of Dr Jones, are essential reading for the legal history of the early seventeenth century.

interfere with any case or verdict at common law, and that such an infringement was a violation of the statutes of *praemunire* of Edward III and Henry IV.[1] Thereafter, there seemed to be no lack of lawyers seeking *praemunire* and *habeas corpus* on the behalf of clients. In the Michaelmas term of 1614 Coke released Mr Glanvill – a notorious, fraudulent London jeweller who had been imprisoned for refusing to obey a Chancery decree – on a writ of *habeas corpus*. Glanvill's agent, Robert Davies, had sold Mr Courtney four jewels for £400, and Courtney gave a bond for £600 as security for his payment of the debt. The jewels, however, were only worth £60, and with Courtney's refusal to pay the debt Glanvill won an execution of the bond in the King's Bench. Courtney then sued Glanvill in the Chancery for fraud. Glanvill, having refused to appear, was imprisoned. Chief Justice Coke, in releasing Mr Glanvill, declared unequivocally that he would never allow such actions against parties who obtained judgment at common law 'so long as I have this coif on my head'.[2]

Glanvill now appeared to be the figure on which the supremacy of the Chancellor's decree was going to be resolved. That, at least, is the way Ellesmere regarded it. The Chancellor committed Glanvill to prison once again in May 1615. But again the Court of King's Bench released him on a writ of *habeas corpus*, claiming in a unanimous decision that the return of the Chancery was not sufficient because the reasons for the return were not given.[3] In the same Easter term the Apsley and Ruswell cases – which involved the application for writs of *habeas corpus* after imprisonment by the Chancellor – were adjourned to the following session. Apsley and Ruswell were released in the Trinity term, and a number of requests for new hearings on writs of *habeas corpus* came forward to the court.[4]

In the meantime two other controversial cases had emerged: the *Magdalen College Case*, where the Earl of Oxford had been deprived of £10,000 of land and construction because he had believed in the

[1] *Heath* v. *Ridley* (KB 1614), Bulstrode, *Reports* II, 194; Croke, *Reports*, II, 335–6.

[2] The pr. reports of *Glanvill* v. *Courtney* (KB 1614), are Bulstrode, *Reports* II, 301–2; Croke, *Reports*, II, 343; Moore, *Cases*, 838; and Rolle, *Reports*, 111, 218–19, the quote at 111.

[3] The case can be followed accurately only by using the fuller ms. reports. These are the Sir Arthur Mainwaring report in Add. MS 11.574, ff. 43r–9r; Tourneur MS Rep. ff. 2v, 54v; Sir Robert Cotton's in Folger MS V.b. 48, ff. 12v–13r; Sir George Cary's in Harv. Law MS 1034, ff. 122v–4v; and Arthur Tourneur's in Harv. Law MS 111, ff. 47v–8v.

[4] *Apsley's Case* (KB 1615), Moore, *Cases*, 839–40; Rolle, *Reports*, 192–3, 218; and Rawl. MS C.382, f. 63r. *Ruswell's Case* (KB 1615), Rolle, *Reports*, 218–19; Tourneur MS Rep. f. 82; and Rawl. MS C.382, f. 63r–v. The requests were noted in *ibid.* ff. 56v–7v, 63r–4r, 71r–v; and in Add. MS 25.218, ff. 42r–v, 64r–6r.

strength of his title, and *Sir Anthony Mildmay's Case*. In the former cause the Earl applied to the Chancery to receive equitable relief.[1] In the latter cause Coke struck against a lower court by accepting an action of *praemunire* against Mildmay for committing a party to the Fleet – on behalf of a Commission of Sewers – in contradiction to a decision made in King's Bench.[2] He also continued to accept such actions against other courts of equity.[3] The Chief Justice was challenging openly the supremacy of the Chancellor's decree.

Ellesmere responded promptly in the Michaelmas term, and he had no lack of motive. His returns to the King's Bench to account for the imprisonment of Apsley and Ruswell had been rejected, and at least one action for *praemunire* had achieved its desired end.[4] Thus the *Earl of Oxford's Case* in the Michaelmas term of 1615 was used by Ellesmere as the occasion for his first major address on the question of the supremacy of the Chancellor's decree. He presented a lengthy speech in which he defended the historic jurisdiction of the Court of Chancery and the absolute supremacy of the Chancellor's decree in providing equitable relief to parties who had suffered unjustly from decisions at common law; a speech that was copied into many contemporary law reports of the period.[5] The defendants in this case, Dr Googe and Mr Smith, had refused to appear for trial, and were imprisoned for declining to answer the charges which had been made against them. They then petitioned the Court of King's Bench to be released on a writ of *habeas corpus*.

Chief Justice Coke and Justice Dodderidge spoke strongly of the relevance of the statutes of 27 Edward III and 4 Henry IV for *praemunire*, and of the necessity for the defendants' release. On this occasion, however, the return by the Chancellor specified fully the reasons for committing the defendants, and it appears that Coke and Dodderidge did not carry a majority of the King's Bench for their release.[6] The cause continued in the Chancery, where the plaintiff won unopposed. Meanwhile, Glanvill and others were attacking the

---

[1] *The Case of Magdalen College* (KB 1615), 11 *Co. Rep.* 66v–79r; and *supra*, Chap. VI.

[2] *Sir Anthony Mildmay's Case* (KB 1615), Rawl. MS C.382, f. 61v. Earlier stages of the case are reported in Bulstrode, *Reports* II, 197; and Croke, *Reports*, II, 336.

[3] These have been fully doc'd by Dawson, 'Coke and Ellesmere', 135, 148–51. See also *CSPD, 1611–18*, 290 (June 1615).

[4] The tortuous course of the *Ruswell* and *Apsley* cases in the order and decree books has been charted by Dawson, *ibid.* 141–4.

[5] *Rep. Chanc.* 1–16. It appears in most of the ms. Chan. colls referred to *infra*, Chap. VIII.

[6] According to the accounts of *Dr. Googe's Case* (KB 1615), in Bulstrode, *Reports* III, 115, 278; and Rolle, *Reports*, 277–8.

Chancellor's decrees in the halls of London's prisons, urging more men to seek their freedom by applying for writs of *habeas corpus*. Glanvill himself prepared a bill of *praemunire* against the attorney and legal counsel of the party who had defeated him earlier in the Chancery. Brought before a grand jury, the bill was thrown out as insufficient. [1]

In Hilary term 1615/6, Glanvill made one more attempt to curb the Chancellor's decree. Allied with Allen, an unscrupulous money-lender who had been imprisoned by the Chancellor in 1613, they preferred a bill of *praemunire* against the officials of the Court of Chancery for disturbing judgments at common law. Moreover, they secured the aid of a crooked scrivener named Levesay who had obtained a seat on the grand jury. Once again a jury failed to find the bill true. Coke was furious by this time, and twice he sent the jury back to reconsider the matter. At one point, witnesses later testified, he told the jury that they could now go forward and indict the Chancery officials because the Lord Chancellor had just died. The jury, however, appeared to be just as obstinate as the Chief Justice. In a final vote it returned a finding of *ignoramus* by 17 to 2. Coke, undeterred, delivered a stirring speech to the largely gathered crowd which brought an abyss of silence followed by an early adjournment of the day's proceedings: 'That whosoever shall set his hand to a bill in any English court after a judgment at law, we will preclose him from the bar for ever speaking more in this court; I give you a fair warning to preserve you from a greater mischief. We must look about or the common law of England will be overthrown. [2]

Praemunire was no longer a viable suit against the Chancellor's decree, and *habeas corpus* had proved to be inadequate to deter its exercise. The matter for all practical and theoretical purposes was at an end. Not, however, for the Lord Chancellor. He had Glanvill and Allen arrested for an appearance before the Star Chamber in the Easter term for questioning the Chancellor's decree. Refusing to answer for their actions, Ellesmere ordered 'that they should be put in irons, and so more and more clogged till they answered'. [3] He then proceeded to have the supremacy of his decree entered officially into

---

[1] Add. MS 11.574, f. 43r.

[2] The reports of the final stage of both the *Glanvill* and *Allen* cases are in the ms. reports cited on p. 171, n. 3. It is discussed in Baker, 'Common lawyers and Chancery', 379–81. The allegations of Coke's actions that were prepared for the Chanc. are in Ellesm. MSS 5971–3, the quote in 5971, ff. iv–2r. See also Ellesm. MSS 5935–6.

[3] Hobart, *Reports*, ff. 160–1, the quote at f. 160v. This may seem severe, but it was in character: *supra*, pp. 16–21, 61–3.

the records by the King and the Privy Council. The Chancery reforms which he had achieved, together with the growth of the court in its new guise, were accomplishments which Ellesmere regarded as just-ifying his long tenure and influence in the history of the English judiciary. And he sought to preserve them. The evidence indicates that by the autumn of 1615 he had set his mind to construct an un-impeachable case for the supremacy of the Chancellor's decree.

The second half of the tract that Chancellor Ellesmere had com-posed in the late summer of 1615 was an analysis of six statutes of provisors and *praemunire* which had been used before the Court of King's Bench against the Chancery since Coke's decision in *Heath* v. *Ridley* in the spring of 1614. Commencing with the two statutes of 25 Edward III on provisors, the first statute declared that any man who purchased deeds from the Court of Rome for abbeys and priories in England would be regarded as an enemy of the realm and outlawed. The second noted the continued practice of purchasing such deeds from the Court of Rome, and repeated the punishments for the viol-ations. 'Both these statutes were specially provided to restrain the usurpation of the Pope and Church of Rome in those cases of provis-ions and reservations.'[1] The Chancellor then devoted considerable attention to the statutes of 27 Edward III c. 1 and 16 Richard II c. 5 on *praemunire*.

The statute 27 Edward III alleged that many people were still being drawn out of England for suits before the papal curia notwith-standing the former statutes, and that such actions were 'in prejudice and derision of the King and his Crown and of all the people of this realm, and the undoing and destruction of the common laws'. The Chancellor then gave a lengthy analysis of the statute in order to demonstrate that it sought to curb the removal of judicial suits from the kingdom, and that it did not consider the hearing of causes in courts within the country as falling within that prohibition. The course of his analysis consisted of an investigation into the mischief complained of, the form of proceeding used against the offenders, and the remedy. The mischief was clearly the drawing of men out of the realm. Ellesmere maintained that this grievance could not possibly pertain to the Chancery because it was 'one of the King's supreme courts of justice, and as much or more grieved by the inordinate usur-pation of the Pope and his courts, as any other of the King's courts'.

[1] 'Brief Chanc.' ff. 6v–7r, quoted at f. 7r.

Further, both the form of proceeding against offenders and requests for remedy were provided by the act, and actions were to be taken specifically before the King, Council, Chancery, King's Bench, or Common Pleas. Thus this law could never include the Chancery within its prohibition, 'Sith they have designed the Chancery to be a special and prime court to punish offenders against the statute'. [1]

Ellesmere used the same form of analysis with the statute of 16 Richard II c. 5. The act complained of the Pope's transfer of presentments to ecclesiastical benefices without the assent of the King, making the monarch 'subject to the Pope in perpetual destruction to the King and his Crown, and all his realm'. It enacted that any person who pursued such presentments should forfeit his benefices and be outlawed. The Chancellor made a lengthy study of the statute to demonstrate that it sought specifically to prevent 'the ambitious usurpation by the Pope and Church of Rome'. Although it prohibited appeals to Rome, in no way did it refer to the jurisdiction of the Court of Chancery or to any other court of equity. 'The intent of all these Parliaments was only to punish offenders who maintained the usurped and pretended authority of the Pope and Church of Rome, and prosecuted any action by virtue of the same in any case whereof the cognisance and final discussion pertained to the King and his courts.' [2]

Ellesmere's brief was addressed to the Privy Council, and it formed the basis of his move to ensure the supremacy of the Chancellor's decree. Dated September 1615, it was composed prior to Coke's final assault on the Chancery and is a document full of learning and reason. When the Glanvill and Allen bills were brought to the King's Bench against the Chancery officials in February 1615/16, the Chancellor wrote a formal letter to the Privy Council and to Attorney-General Francis Bacon requesting an investigation of the precedents concerning the supremacy of the Chancellor's decree. The letter, dated 19 March, included his brief of precedents on the equitable jurisdiction of the Chancery and of parties brought to that court after judgment at the common law. It also recommended the Solicitor, Attorney-General, and the King's serjeants to peruse and correct his evidence. [3] A judicial committee was struck to prepare a report, and their brief – which was filed within one week – covered much of the

---

[1] *Ibid*. ff. 7r–9r, the quotes at ff. 8v and 9r, respectively.
[2] *Ibid*. ff. 9v–11v.
[3] C.33/129/1151.

groundwork of the first half of Ellesmere's tract, affirming his position. A week later, on 27 March 1616, the Chancellor wrote a second formal letter to the Council requesting an investigation of the understanding of the statutes of *praemunire*. A similar judicial committee was struck, and its report substantiated the second part of Ellesmere's tract.[1]

The movement to have Coke dismissed from the Privy Council and the King's Bench came not from Ellesmere but from Sir Francis Bacon and Archbishop George Abbot. There is little doubt that Bacon wanted Coke dismissed. His letters to James and Buckingham that begin on 12 February 1615/16 are striking testimony of his animosity towards the Chief Justice. As he wrote on one occasion in his inimitable style: 'Fame hath swift wings, specially that which hath black feathers.'[2] Abbot's opposition to Coke stemmed from the Chief Justice's constant attacks on bishops and the ecclesiastical courts throughout his career on the Bench. Abbot's letters to colleagues soliciting their support for the dismissal of the Chief Justice date from 21 January 1611/12.[3] Thereafter, Coke's problems in the Glanvill and Allen cases gained the attention of court gossips. Drawing political opposition for his stand on the *commendam* and *rege inconsulto* debates, the Chief Justice began to lose the support of his friends at the royal court.[4] But Coke's nadir on the Bench as well as at court seems, on the basis of contemporary correspondence, to have occurred in the month of June,[5] when James made his famous speech in the Star Chamber that affirmed the supremacy of the Chancellor's decree. The King begged for an end to 'changes from court to court: for he that changeth courts, shows to mistrust the justness of the

[1] The best of the pr. versions are in Cary, *Reports*, 163–83; *Rep. Chanc.* III, 1–45; Sanders, *Chancery orders*, 89–98, 1038–41; and Bacon, *Letters* V, 385–95. Two ms. copies are fuller: Bacon's original at Folger MS V.a. 121, 96–128; and Cary's in Harv. Law MS 1035, ff. 77v–140r.

[2] Folger MS V.b.132, pp. 45–6, 71–3, the quote at p. 45. Their antagonisms have been portrayed nicely by Catherine Drinker Bowen, *The lion and the throne* (1957), in Chaps. VII, XXV–XXX. Her later biog. of Bacon is derived largely from this work, and both books should be ignored for discussions of legal matters.

[3] Ellesm. MS 2183–4, and *CSPD, 1611–18*, p. 370.

[4] For the *Case of Commendams* (PC 1616), see Bacon, *Letters* V, 357–69; APC XXXIV, 595–609; and Gardiner, *Hist.* III, 14–19. The *Case of the Rege Inconsulto* (KB 1615/6), is in Bacon, *Letters* V, 223–36.

[5] Letters from the royal court are in *CSPD, 1611–18*, pp. 373 (14 June 1616), 381 (13 July 1616); in add. see the evidence collected by Lucy Aiken, *Memoirs of the court of King James the First* (1822), II, 32–46. Letters from the Bench are in *Buccleuch MS*, H.M.C. (1885), 18 (16 and 26 June 1616); and *Buccleuch MS*, H.M.C. (1926), I, 248 (26 June 1616).

cause';[1] a statement which in normal times could have applied to the Chancery as well as to the King's Bench.

In July Ellesmere had the monarch's decision and his own arguments for the supremacy of the Chancellor's decree entered into the second copy of the order and decree books in brightly coloured letters with flourishing illumination.[2] The dispute was apparently over except for the swollen ambition of Attorney-General Bacon. The Attorney-General, who earlier had written of a speedy death for the Lord Chancellor and named himself as successor, now seemed to have taken up the knife for Coke's scalp. The evidence suggests that Bacon linked dissatisfaction with Coke's use of *praemunire*, and certain 'offences' in his famous reports of his contentious speeches to the King, in illustrating the danger of Coke's continuation in office and the necessity for his dismissal. While Ellesmere wrote off the episode as 'a ridiculous pageant of a new play', Bacon reopened the wounds inflicted in the spring of 1616 in the following autumn.[3] Coke was brought before the Privy Council on 17 October, made to answer questions to the dissatisfaction of the King, and was finally dismissed from his offices on 10 November. Bacon had not only written the brief for Coke's dismissal, but he had also prepared the warrant for his release from office.[4]

The actions of Bacon and the flood of pro-Chancery literature that stemmed from the offices of the Chancery in the years 1616–17 contributed immensely to a popularisation of the final contest of Ellesmere's public career, a popularisation that has stamped its impact on historical writing and coloured our understanding of law and politics in the early seventeenth century. And it began with the controversy over the Glanvill and Allen cases in 1615/16. A platoon of witnesses was allegedly shepherded under the guidance of the Lord Chancellor's son John into the Court of King's Bench in Hilary 1615/16, to witness the proceedings in the Glanvill and Allen cases. The group consisted of relatives, estate agents, and Chancery officials, and they gave written testimony relating to Coke's behaviour towards the jury and the court that was given to the Privy Council and used for the

---

[1] *His Maiesties Speach in the Starre Chamber*, sig. E4. The speech had been repr. in James, *Works*, 326–45.

[2] C.33/130/1173r–9v.

[3] The docs and corresp. illustrating Bacon's role are pr. in Bacon, *Letters* VI, 79–96. The statement of Ellesmere is in Add. MS 19.402, f. 110r.

[4] Bacon, *Letters*, VI, 97–8.

initial suspension of the Chief Justice.[1] The testimony, however, was highly biased; and outside of this group there was no common agreement as to precisely what transpired. Among the private correspondence and notes of councillors who sought Coke's dismissal, Sir Julius Caesar agreed with the testimony but Bacon did not.[2] Coke himself admitted much to the Privy Council in his later examination, but not the alleged threats to the jury and the court.[3] The many Chancery office-holders and servers who were beholden to their patron must have been determined to leave nothing in doubt, and their energies did not stop with the dismissal of the Chief Justice.

Numerous collections of tracts and cases were gathered by Chancery officials after 1616 to make the expansion of the jurisdiction of Ellesmere's Chancery a historical fact.[4] In one of these, by William Tothill, the law of the land was conceived of in terms of causes which were 'usually' relieved in Chancery, and those which were 'best sued elsewhere'.[5] Or, in the words of another collector, 'cases where there is help in Chancery' and 'cases where there is no help in Chancery'.[6] This preoccupation with the preservation of the expansion of the Chancery caused one nineteenth century antiquary to transcribe volumes of material out of the Chancery archives which focused on Ellesmere's tenure of office.[7] It also had a clear parallel

---

[1] Ellesmere's copies of the bills of *praemunire* are Ellesm. MS 5971, endorsed by John, 'My fathers breviate for the K Counsell'. This item was pub'd by Samuel Thorne in the *HLQ* 2 (1938), 85–8. The lists of witnesses in which several individuals certify each major statement of the Chief Justice, are Ellesm. MS 5972–3, endorsed by John: 'Prooffes of the proceedinges the last daye of Hillary Terme'.

[2] Cæsar's summary of the proceedings is in Add. MS 11.574, f. 47r–v; his opinion of the testimony is noted in Lans. MS 162, ff. 5r–6v. Bacon's view was expressed in Folger MS V.b. 132, p. 74. The account for the P.C. is in *APC* XXXIV, 644–8.

[3] B. M. Sloane MS 1710, ff. 137v–8r. His formal denial is in *APC* XXXIV, 647–8.

[4] The collections of cases which fall into the period 1604–14 are those of Sir Julius Cæsar, Lans. MS 1110, ff. 1r–33v; Sir Matthew Carew, Harv. Law MS 1035; and William Tothill, Harl. MS 4265, ff. 1–34. The latter was pub'd with additions as *Transactions of the High Court of Chancery* (1649). Perhaps the most prominent colls of Chan. materials gathered after 1616 were those of Cæsar (Lans. MS 174), Sir Robert Cotton (L.I. Add. MS B.3), John Selden (Hale MS 47), Arthur Tourneur (Harv. Law MS 111), Francis Vaughan (P.R.O. SP Misc. 9/12), and the anon. but valuable Camb. MS Gg.2.31.

[5] Harl. MS 4265, ff. 27v–34v.

[6] A rather popular work: Add. MS 25.245, ff. 16r–26r; Add. MS 25.246, ff. 14r–21r; Harl. MS 6809, ff. 52r–60r. This was alleged to be 'out of a book of the late Lord Chauncellor Baron Ellesmere', for which there is no evidence. What is interesting is that one generally finds only the section for 'cases where there is no help in Chancery': as in Harl. MS 39, ff. 262r–7v; Harg. MS 281, ff. 12r–7r; B.M. Stowe MS 216, ff. 43r–50r; and P.R.O. SP Misc. 9/12/ 17r–22r.

[7] The transcripts of Cecil Monro are now Harv. Law MS 2027, vols. I–VI. Extracts from Ellesmere's decisions in the Chan. are in vol. IV, 81–1261.

in the zeal for affirming the supremacy of the Chancellor's decree.

In the years 1615–16 several tracts were composed on aspects of Ellesmere's brief for the Privy Council on the relationship of the courts of Rome to those of England in the medieval period, on the statute of 27 Edward III c. 1, and on the interpretation of the statutes of *praemunire* in the fourteenth and fifteenth centuries, and also in the seventeenth.[1] Moreover, nearly every important collection of Chancery proceedings in the seventeenth century included the full text of the case against Coke in the spring of 1616, the King's Star Chamber speech in June, and the proceedings which led to Coke's eventual dismissal in November.[2] Few historical controversies have been so well documented on one side as that of the 'Chancery-men' against Coke and the Court of King's Bench. In fact, the only brief for a defence of Coke's interpretation of the statutes of *praemunire* has been written by a modern historian.[3]

The contemporary defence of Coke's position can be found in a few manuscript law reports and legal diaries which until recently have gone largely unnoticed.[4] The authors of these writings were fully aware of the unprecedented growth of Chancery business since 1604, a growth that continued unchecked after Ellesmere's death, and was not arrested until the accession of Sir Thomas Coventry to the Woolsack in 1625. Their view was that the principle of the supremacy of

---

[1] The powers of the Bishop and Court of Rome: Yale Law MS G.R. 24, ff. 55r–70v. 'That the Court of Chauncery cannott be intended within the Statute of 7 E. III. ca. 1' – Lans. MS 174, ff. 226r–35v; Lans. MS 613, ff. 16r–31v; Harg. MS 240, ff. 312r–28v; Harl. MS 4265, ff. 50v–67r; B. M. Stowe MS 296, ff. 51r–7r; Hale MS 47, ff. 243r–54r; Hale MS 83, ff. 272–94; Folger MS V.b. 48, ff. 6v–8r; Harv. Law MS 1035, ff. 97v–114v. 'Mr. Anthony Ben his discourse touchinge the Præmunire': Lans. MS 174, ff. 205r–15r; Stowe MS 177, ff. 190r–98v; Beds. Rec. Off. Countess of Cowper MSS. 'Certaine Extravagante Reasons proveinge the Assertion «no *præmunire* against temporal courts» for further consideracion' – Harv. Law MS 1035, ff. 109v–14v. 'Of Præmunire' by Francis North, Baron Guilford: Add. MS 40. 160, ff. 17r–25v; Tanner MS 459, ff. 74r–88v.

[2] The official draft of evidence collected against proceedings that challenged the Chanc's decree, was pr. in Cary, *Reports*, 115–35; and *Rep. Chanc.* 163–83. The evidence, however, was copied into several colls at early dates, and it is not always the same: Harl MS 4265, ff. 83r–99v; Harl. MS 5191, ff. 6r–14v; Lans. MS 174, ff. 118v–51r; Stowe MS 298, ff. 178v–84r, 217r–28r; P.R.O. SP Misc. 9/12/158–67; Tanner MS 74, ff. 43r–7r; Folger MS V.b. 48, ff. 6v–8r, 13v–8r; Harv. Law MS 111, ff. 54r–63v; and Harv. Law MS 1034, ff. 130v–40r. Bacon's notes for assembling this are in Folger MS V.a. 121, ff. 96–128. The proceedings against Coke exist only in fragments. For ex. Harg. MS 240, ff. 306r–9v; Lans. MS 162, f. 6r–v; B. M. Sloane MS 1710, ff. 137r–8r; Bodl. Ashmol. MS 830, f. 125r–v; and Tanner MS 304, ff. 64v–6r.

[3] Dawson, 'Coke and Ellesmere', 132–6.

[4] Baker, 'Common Lawyers and Chancery', 383–4.

the Chancellor's decree was alien to the common law; that it would only encourage people to take their civil suits to the Chancery even if the cause was actionable at common law. Thus the decision of the King and Privy Council could cause the overthrow of the common law. It could also lead 'the whole nation under a few into that slavery which it now labours'.[1]

The departed Chief Justice was no less critical of the decision of 1616. He too felt that it would lead to the subversion of the common law. The key point in Coke's opposition was the manner in which the decision was made. In an unusual manuscript from his reports that was circulated after his death in 1634, Coke chastised the King for not soliciting the legal opinions of the judges, and in accepting the evidence of the Chancellor and 'Chancery-men' for an issue that involved the supremacy of the Chancellor's decree.[2] This was the equivalent of allowing a party to judge his own cause. In the complementary opinion of one of his keen supporters, 'disgrace of the judges and professors of law is done to the law itself, for without them the law is but a dead letter'.[3]

The fears of Coke and others, however, were never justified. Although the business of the Court of Chancery had reached overwhelming heights which even the officials of the court could not handle adequately,[4] the court under the long tenure of Lord Ellesmere was no longer a threat to the common law. It had become a court of record staffed with common lawyers that would grow in harmony with the courts of common law. What it required after 1616 was a younger man who would utilise Ellesmere's reforms and eschew growth at the expense of judicial process. This was provided by Coventry, who reduced the level of court proceedings to the size that had been attained by Ellesmere in his early years.[5] Afterwards, the Chancery was threatened in the 'Puritan Revolution', and again in

---

[1] Tourneur MS Rep. f. 55v.

[2] 'Dangerous & absurd opinions affirme de part le Roy per Egerton Chauncellor', Coke MS Rep. E, 1 f. The copy was also inserted into a ms. copy of what became the 12th and 13th parts of Coke's reports: I.T. Misc. MS 21, points 1–3, 8, 11 at f. 36r. Another copy is in Univ. Coll. London, Ogden MS 29, f. 569.

[3] Tourneur MS Rep. f. 55v.

[4] N. E. McClure, *The Letters of John Chamberlain* (Philadelphia 1934), II, 36 (16 Nov. 1616); *Commons Debates 1621*, VI, 63–4; and Tourneur MS Rep. f. 79v, for good criticism.

[5] C.33/129–30, 139–40, 149–50, 159–60. For Coventry, for whom a study is long overdue, see the contemp. assessment in B. M. Sloane MS 3075, f. 8r–v.

the 'Glorious Revolution', but on each occasion it survived easily on the shoulders of the precedents of the early seventeenth century.[1]

The history of the Chancery in the late sixteenth and seventeenth centuries mirrors many of the facets of the life of its Chancellor. Ellesmere was a man who had learnt not only to survive, but also how to win. Tough and egregious, he throve on hard work and competition. Dogged to the very end, he had the intellectual acumen and the political *savoir-faire* to master a situation, and at times the historical perspective to make a lasting contribution. He was devoted to the accumulation of influence and power, and public life was in his veins. Although he might have written of retirement as early as 1612, on the eve of the common law–Chancery debate, the great outpouring of activity in legal and political affairs that characterised the last stage of his career suggests that he was a man who throve on the challenge of life in Whitehall and Westminster.[2] One of his ardent critics suggested that he could not live without 'the smell of yellow wax'.[3] Perhaps, unwittingly, this critic provided a fitting epitaph to the career of Chancellor Ellesmere.

[1] Holdsworth, *HEL* I, 463–5; *Nott's Chanc. Cases* I, 73–4; and *The manuscripts of the House of Lords 1690–91*, H.M.C. 13th Rep. App. Pt. 7 (1892), 128–41.

[2] His earliest petitions for retirement are Ellesm. MS 236–7, dated 17 Aug. 1612 and 8 Feb. 1613. His political, social, and legal enemies wrote disparagingly of his alleged feebleness and debility, together with his known dislike of urban London and the life of the royal court, in order to force his retirement; and it has caused most modern authorities to regard him as senile or hypochrondrial. A rep. sample of their propaganda can be obtained from *CSPD, 1611–18*, pp. 168, 174, 227, 272, 275, 279, 349, 354, 436–7.

[3] Tourneur MS Rep. f. 63r. (The wax for sealing documents in the Chan.)

THE PROVENANCE OF ELLESMERE'S TRACTS

THE ROYAL PREROGATIVE

A printed tract entitled *An Essay of a King, with an explanation what manner of persons those should be that are to execute the power or ordinance of the Kings Prerogative*, was published in an anonymous, miscellaneous collection of essays in 1642.[1] It was published without an editor or an acknowledgment of the source. A different version of the same work was published in 1648 as part of *The Remaines of the Right Honorable Francis Lord Verulam*.[2] This version, in contrast to the former one, contained drastic stylistic changes in addition to minor material differences. In the nineteenth century, James Spedding reprinted the 1642 edition of this tract as a 'Spurious Essay', an addendum to his scholarly edition of the papers of Sir Francis Bacon.[3] Both Spedding and Dr Rawley were convinced, however, that Bacon had not composed the tract.[4] But 'Baconians' could not be so easily denied. In 1939, Professor Wormuth attributed this work – without evidence – to Bacon, and many scholars since then have maintained that unwarranted attribution.[5]

A manuscript tract on the royal prerogative in the Harvard Law Library appears to be an earlier copy of the two essays published in 1642 and 1648. Its full title is 'A Coppie of wrytten discourse by the Lord Chancellor Ellesmere concerning the Royall Prerogatiue, and what manner of persones that should be and are to execute the power and ordinacion of the Kinges Prerogatiue'.[6] The attribution, in addi-

---

[1] The B.M. copy, pp. 5–8.

[2] It is noted uncritically in R. W. Gibson, *Francis Bacon, a bibliography of his works and of Baconiana to the year 1750* (Oxford 1950).

[3] Bacon, *Works* II, 390–4.

[4] *Ibid.* 383–6.

[5] Francis D. Wormuth, *The royal prerogative, 1603–1649* (Ithaca N.Y. 1939), 58–60. The exception is Margaret Judson, who used the Harvard Law MS to write a penetrating analysis of royal power and the public good: *The crisis of the constitution* (New Brunswick N.J. 1949), 29–31.

[6] Harv. Law MS 4006.

tion to the internal evidence, ascribes its authorship to Chancellor Ellesmere. The manuscript is a sole copy, and perhaps came to Harvard as part of the William Lambarde papers, thereby accounting for its early presence in North America.

A second manuscript copy of this tract is in the Northamptonshire Record Office. It is entitled 'Prerogatiue Royall, shewinge what manner of persons those should bee that are to execute the powre or ordination of the Kings Prerogatiue'.[1] This copy is also ascribed to Ellesmere. An isolated item in the Finch-Hatton manuscript collection, it was probably a copy belonging to one of Ellesmere's family relations through his wife Alice. Both her estate records, and copies of several of Ellesmere's parliamentary and legal papers, became part of the collection of the family's Midland estates at Ashridge House, some of which eventually came to rest in the Northamptonshire Record Office. The only other relevant manuscript is an anonymous fragment on the royal prerogative in the British Museum, which seems to be an abridgment of the first two paragraphs of Ellesmere's tract.[2]

The importance of the Chancellor's tract has been brought to the author's attention in the admirable study of the seventeenth-century constitution by Professor Judson.[3] This tract was one of the few attempts by a lawyer-statesman to deal in detail with the thorny problem of sovereignty in Jacobean England.[4] The edition of the work that follows in Chapter 9 attempts to collate the two manuscript versions with the printed editions of 1642 and 1648. It also seeks to explain the relationship of its contents to Ellesmere's other writings – especially his speech on the *Post-Nati*.

Our text of Ellesmere's tract on the royal prerogative is at least one step removed from the original. An attempt to chart the evolution of the manuscript could be made as follows:

orig. → copy X → Harvard Law 4006 (A)
N.R.O. Finch-Hatton 578 (B) → (cont.)
1642 ed. (C) → Spedd. ed. → 1648 ed. (D)

---

[1] 'Prerogative Royall', N. R. O. Finch-Hatton MS 578, ff. 1–2r (*c.* Restoration period).
[2] 'Prerogative Royall', Harl. MS 250, f. 154r–v (copied *c.* Chas. I).
[3] Judson, *Crisis of the constitution*, 29–31.
[4] Discussed *supra*, Chap. II.

Since both the Harvard and Northampton manuscripts (referred to here as copies A and B) are divorced from the original, this edition of the tract is based on manuscript copy A, which seems to be closest to the unlocated original and probably its nearest descendant. Deviations in manuscript copy B are noted throughout the textual apparatus. The edition also incorporates material from the 1642 and 1648 editions (copies C and D) when those versions supply a defect to copy A that was lost in the early evolution of the tract, and notes their own significant omissions. Full disclosure of these revisions is also incorporated into the textual notes, which are designated by italicised letter references. The Spedding version has been omitted for consideration because it is a not altogether accurate copy of the 1642 edition (copy C).

CALVIN'S CASE: THE *POST-NATI* AND ANGLO–SCOTS UNION

The only work which Ellesmere published in his lifetime was a long and scholarly tract comprising *The Speech of the Lord Chancellor of England, in the Eschequer Chamber, touching the Post-Nati* (London, 1609).[1] Although James VI of Scotland never succeeded in his ambitions to unite the two countries of England and Scotland after his accession, the difficulties of individuals born in the reign of the new monarch in inheriting land in both realms were sufficient to cause a test case to be brought before the Exchequer Chamber in 1608. The question of the *post-nati*, like the questions about Anglo-Scots Union, was debated fully in Parliament and throughout the country from 1604. Numerous tracts appeared in these years, ranging from thorough, scholarly analyses such as the study of Sir John Dodderidge,[2] to flowery, sycophantic writings like the essay of Sir Francis Bacon.[3] The large number of extant speeches and tracts has led some writers to make hasty attributions. Professor Mosse, for example, finding a copy of Bacon's tract in the Ellesmere collection without Bacon's name attached, attributed it — without a scrap of

---

[1] The Hunt. Lib. copy, RB 269696, STC 7540.

[2] 'A breif consideration of the union of twoe Kingdomes in the handes of one Kinge', Sloane MS 3479, ff. 59r–67v. A digest of the views of other lawyers and judges are in L. I. Maynard MS 83.

[3] 'A Briefe discourse touchinge the happy union of the Kingdomes of England and Scotland', Ellesm. MS 34/B/45, ff. 1–12. Another copy is in a Bacon collection: Add. MS 4263, ff. 106–9. Bacon's speech was reported in *State Trials* II, 575–606.

evidence – to Lord Ellesmere.[1] He then made it the centre of a discussion on sovereignty and Anglo-Scots Union.

The Chancellor's speech in *Calvin's Case* (called here the *Post-Nati*) was no routine decision from the Bench. The Chancellor's presentation was a lengthy study of English law and history. Composed in 1608 from copious notes,[2] it was published with the encouragement of King James.[3] The book was unusually well received. Even judges and lawyers who disagreed with the Chancellor on judicial questions praised the learning that he evinced in this cause.[4] Ellesmere's personal view of the speech, however, was typically self-denying. As he wrote to Lord Salisbury in presenting him with a gift copy: it was 'an idle tale, ill told, which you heard with much patience but not without weariness'.[5] One could well have sympathised with the Lord Treasurer, as according to an observer the Chancellor was 'almost four hours in his arguments'.[6] The final proceedings were one of the most protracted experiences in the history of the judiciary. Fourteen judges gave their opinions over the course of eight days. The Chief Justice made no exaggeration when he exclaimed 'that never any case in man's memory was argued by so many judges'.[7]

The Chancellor's tract circulated among many of the legal collections of the period. His arguments were copied into commonplace books, and at least one student copied out the whole work.[8] In succeeding centuries parts of the tract were pirated by writers interested in Anglo-Scots union and the problem of sovereignty.[9] Many of these became popular works on the eve of the actual legislative union of England and Scotland in 1707. The tract, however, was not a best seller. Lionel Cranfield purchased a copy in the year of publication for 1s. 6d.; but fourteen years later Sir Simonds D'Ewes bought a remaindered, or second-hand copy for sixpence.[10]

---

[1] George Mosse, *The struggle for sovereignty in England* (East Lansing Mich. 1950). Mosse's reply to the author's inquiry was that he could no longer find his notes.

[2] Ellesm. MSS 1873 (3 May 1608), 1872 (4 June 1608), 451, and 1215.

[3] Ellesmere to James, 28 Nov. 1608, in *Miscellany of the Abbotsville club*, I, 220–1.

[4] Coke in 7 Co. Rep. 3v; and the notes of anon. lawyers in the copies of the *Post-Nati* in B. M. 518. i. 2 (2), and in Hunt. 269696.

[5] Ellesmere to Salisbury, 3 Feb. and 9 March 1608/9, in *Salisbury MSS*, XXI, 13, 28.

[6] Hawarde, *Reportes*, 366.

[7] 7 Co. Rep. 'The Preface'.

[8] For ex. Tanner MS 75, f. 16r–v, and Harl. MS 5346, ff. 66–92, respectively.

[9] For the anon. ed. of *The Famous Case of Robert Calvin a Scotsman* (Edinburgh 1705); and R. Austin, *Allegiance not impeached* (1944), respectively.

[10] *Cranfield Papers* I, 179; and the notice in Andrew G. Watson, *The library of Sir Simonds D'Ewes* (1966), 231.

The edition of Ellesmere's speech in Chapter 10 is a transcription of one of the two, and only, printed editions of 1609. The marginal notes have been incorporated into the text with brackets, and the sole additions to the text are chapter numbers that have been inserted to designate a suggested list of headings. These suggested titles have been included in order to give the reader a clear indication of its lengthy contents. The notes attempt to assess the Chancellor's use of sources, both original and secondary, and to point out the collected briefs in his personal library which he consulted.

PARLIAMENT, GOVERNMENT, AND LAW REFORM

Three important tracts were left by the Chancellor in his private collection of papers, and each was a holograph: an analysis of the Parliament of 1604–10 (Chapter 11), a critique of the state of the King's government and finances in 1615 (Chapter 12), and a brief on law reform (Chapter 13). These tracts were briefs which he prepared for the Privy Council, although only the tract on government was noted by contemporaries as having been seen and discussed. They were formal briefs which explored their subjects in considerable detail. All three works were composed with similar characteristics. These included brief and concise analyses carefully, and in general neatly written. Each work was closely organised into sections, and within each section the sentences were set out as series of independent clauses which contained lists of facts or thoughts. These briefs contained the core of Ellesmere's observations on English politics, government, and and the law.

The Chancellor's 'Speciall obseruacions touching all the sessions of the last parlement anno 7 Regis' 1604–10,[1] has been edited by Elizabeth Read Foster, and is contained in her admirable collection of diaries and papers from the fourth and fifth sessions of the Parliament of 1604.[2] It is one of the most interesting accounts of the Parliament to come to hand. The edition that follows in Chapter 11 makes full use of Miss Foster's collection, and of her annotations on the measures and speakers to which several of the Chancellor's comments were addressed. It also, however, incorporates references to the Commons and Lords Journals for Ellesmere's participation in the

[1] Ellesm. MS 2599.
[2] *Parl. 1610* I, 276–83. The ed. has been modernised.

matters which he discussed, as well as references to his parliamentary papers and speeches that formed the basis of this tract.[1]

His tract on the state of the royal government – 'Thinges to be considered of before a parlement to be Called' – was written as a brief for the debates before the Privy Council in the autumn of 1615.[2] This was a highly detailed anatomy of the Chancellor's proposals for reforming the King's finances, and for restoring the breach between King and Commons that had widened with the failure of the Addled Parliament in 1614.[3] It comprised the measures of the reform programme of the new aristocracy to restore confidence and respectability to the royal government. This edition of the brief in Chapter 12 provides references to the papers of other councillors which Ellesmere used directly, and to his own collections on the subject. It is also keyed to the rough paper which he drafted that was probably an outline for the preparation of his formal brief to the Council.[4]

Ellesmere's manuscript containing 'Memorialles for Judicature. Pro Bono Publico' differs from these other two papers in both purpose and composition.[5] The tract, first of all, was not composed for any specific occasion. No closer date can be ascribed than the general one of 1609–14. Secondly, very few memoranda relevant to the brief are extant from his later career. This fact – although one which has been determined more by the migration of manuscripts than by the historical record – would account for the reactionary character of the tract. It was based on the Chancellor's reaction to new legal developments in the common law courts, whose potential he might not always have seen.[6] Thirdly, the tract was hurriedly prepared and never properly completed. Beginning with folio four there are many corrections, and from folio five to the end the writing is quite sloppy.

The annotations in Ellesmere's brief on law reform were very extensive. Since his corrections were numerous, the italicised, alphabetical notes provide references to material which had been deleted or revised. These textual notes also specify words and phrases that were added at a later time. Although these changes and additions were

---

[1] Discussed *supra*, Chap. III.

[2] Ellesm. MS 2610.

[3] Discussed *supra*, Chap. IV.

[4] With the editorial note: 'The proposicions I haue made for relieving the kings present estate as it now stands.' Ellesm. MS 1216.

[5] Ellesm. MS 2623.

[6] Discussed *supra*, Chap. V.

significant, they appear to have been made at the same time of the original composition of the tract. The other, numerical notes attempt to establish from his earlier papers some of the sources of the tract. The Chancellor's brief on law reform edited here in Chapter 13 was a critique of the evolution of the procedure and forms of action at common law, and it provides us with an interesting assessment of the legal problems of the age.

PROHIBITIONS AND THE ECCLESIASTICAL COURTS

Related to Ellesmere's tract on law reform was a complementary manuscript of 'Some Notes, and Remembrances, concerning Prohibitians, for staying of suites in the Ecclesiasticall Courtes, and in the Courts of Admiraltie'.[1] This tract was composed specifically as a brief to the Privy Council for the debates on prohibitions in May 1611. The problem of common law courts prohibiting suits before ecclesiastical and admiralty jurisdictions became a public issue in the years 1607–11. Ellesmere was doubly concerned with the ramifications of this clash of jurisdictions; it threatened not only the existing structure of the legal system, but also the public image of the Reformed Church.[2] His brief was an attempt to reach a compromise, and in this instance the efforts of the Chancellor were successful.

The copy of Ellesmere's tract that has come down to us and is presented in Chapter 14 is a document from the Barlow manuscripts of the Bodleian Library. Written clearly in a clerk's hand, it can be dated at approximately 1611–13. Ellesmere had become Chancellor of the University of Oxford in 1610, and this and several other collections in the Bodleian contain copies of a number of his papers related to the Church, patronage, and university affairs. Although the manuscript is attributed to the Chancellor, the internal evidence is in itself convincing. The discussion of judges and politics is similar to that in his earlier tract on 'Parliament 1604–10', and his later 'Brief on Chancery';[3] The critique of common law actions looks as if it was taken from his tract on 'Iudicature' (or vice versa);[4] and the com-

---

[1] Barlow MS 9, pp. 40–8, endorsed, 'written by the Lord Chancelor Ellesmere'. There is a copy of this in Hargrave MS 371, entitled 'Some Notes and Remembrances concerning Prohibitions for staying of suits in the Ecclesiastical Courts'.

[2] *Supra*, Chap. VI.

[3] Respectively: 'Prohibitians', p. 47 with 'Parl. 1604–10', f. 1; and 'Prohibitians', p. 45 with 'Brief Chanc.' ff. 6v–11v.

[4] 'Prohibitians', pp. 45–6 with 'Iudicature', ff. 1r–3v.

ments on prohibitions and the ecclesiastical authorities are compatible with his notes and arguments in the debates of 1611.[1] In addition, his detailed analysis of the problem of prohibition supplies the theoretical, juristic framework for the cases which he was noting and criticising from the publications of Coke's Reports in these years.[2]

The brief on 'Prohibitians' covered a number of topics, some of which overlapped with Ellesmere's other tracts. The major subjects were the payment of tithes, rights of patronage, probate of testaments, prohibitions against ecclesiastical and admiralty jurisdictions, and the fixing of costs and damages in such proceedings. The Chancellor was particularly concerned, however, with the attitude of Chief Justice Coke towards bishops, Civilians, and the Church courts.[3] The notes assess Ellesmere's use of sources, and place those topics of discussion within the provenance of his other writings, and of his actions as Chancellor and privy councillor.

OBSERVATIONS ON COKE'S REPORTS

The Lord Egerton's Observations on the Lord Coke's Reports was published in the 1650s by George Paul for Bernard Lintott between the two Temple gates in Fleet Street.[4] Although most modern writers, from Sir Frederic Pollock and Sir William Holdsworth onwards,[5] have denied Ellesmere's authorship, the evidence for his authorship is – short of the original manuscript – conclusive. Firstly, we have the opinions of Francis Hargrave and Lord Hardwicke that these observations were composed by Chancellor Ellesmere.[6] Secondly, we have the Chancellor's copy of Coke's *Fifth Report*, which contains marginal notes on statutes and the jurisdiction of ecclesiastical courts that were referred to and discussed in the tract.[7] Thirdly, there is a manuscript volume in the British Museum which contains (1) Ellesmere's

---

[1] *Supra*, Chap. VI, p. 138 nn. 4–7, p. 139 nn. 1–3, p. 140 nn. 1–4.

[2] For ex. 'Eg. on Coke', ff. 33v–4v.

[3] *Ibid.* ff. 32r, 36r.

[4] It was undated. The vol. used here is the B.M. copy.

[5] Holdsworth, *HEL*, v 234–5, 478. This has been accepted at face value by all later legal historians.

[6] Hargrave's endorsement on the bound vol. of the ms. and pr. versions in the B.M. – Harg. MS 254; and the notes of a late seventeenth-century lawyer in a pr. copy in L.I. – Add. MS L, sigs. i–iv.

[7] Edward Coke, *The Fifth Part of the Reports of Sir Edward Coke Knight* (1605), Hunt. 60778.

'Abridgement of the Lord Cokes Reportes', (2) a copy of 'Observacions vpon Cookes Reports made by the Lord Chancellor Egerton taken by me out of his owne papers written with his owne hand', (3) a copy of 'The Lord Chancellor Egertons Observacions vpon ye Lord Cookes Reportes', and (4) an unbound copy of the printed edition.[1]

A study of these papers suggests that the volume which became Hargrave 254 was the collection from which Ellesmere's tract was published. The manuscript copy of the 'Observacions' was a finished product, written in the Chancellor's style. It contains, moreover, internal evidence of Ellesmere's authorship. The chief topics of the cases analysed – the royal prerogative, the Church and writs of pro- hibition, and the jurisdiction of local courts – were precisely those topics in which the two jurists fell into dispute, and several of the matters at issue stemmed from cases in which both men were publicly involved. In addition, the Chancellor's criticisms were based on issues of which he had personal and verifiable knowledge.[2]

Ellesmere penned a prologue of brutal sarcasm to his initial outline of observations on Coke's Reports:

That as your lordship is *Lex loquens* out of whose mouth like Oracles proceed Laws to posterity, that as you are Licurgus in prescribing Laws for the Common wealth, so you will be a means in protecting Literature for their necessary use; that as you are *a lato* in counselling for the good of all, so you will be a Hercules in defending that which is for the good of all.[3]

This short brief probably served as Ellesmere's model for the composition of the final work. The manuscript copy of his Observa- tions is edited here in Chapter 15. The textual notes refer to errors in the published copy of the tract. Since the errors in the printed edition are not substantial, pagination is given for both the manuscript (italicised numerals) and the printed copies. The other notes to the tract provide references to the cases in Coke's Reports, and to the significant accounts of other reporters. They also draw attention to relevant manuscripts in the Chancellor's papers. Coke's Reports, together with Ellesmere's Observations, consist of a variety of inter- pretations on some of the more important legal problems in the late sixteenth and early seventeenth centuries.

[1] Harg. MS 254, ff. 2–31r, 52r–4r, 32r–51v, and the pr. copy at the end, respectively.
[2] Discussed *supra*, Chap. VI.
[3] Harg. MS 254, f. 52r.

THE BRIEF ON CHANCERY

The most critical legal problem which the Chancellor faced at the conclusion of his career was the question of the supremacy of the Chancellor's decree. 'A breviate or direccion for the Kings learned Councell collected by the Lord Chauncellor Ellesmere' was a tract that attempted to thwart Coke's attack on the Court of Chancery in the years 1614–16.[1] Dated September 1615, it formed the basis of the Council's investigation of Coke's charges and actions that led to his dismissal from the Privy Council and the Chief Justiceship of the Court of King's Bench in the following year.

Ellesmere's brief was actually composed in the summer of 1615. He began with a general statement of the relationship between judges, councillors, law-makers, and the King. Then in the first part he made a detailed analysis of the statutes which supported the ancient authority and equitable jurisdiction of the Court of Chancery. In the second part he wrote a careful exposition of the medieval statutes of provisors and *praemunire* that had formed the foundation of Coke's criticism of the Chancery. Ellesmere's skilful analysis demonstrated how these acts were not pertinent to the jurisdiction of the Court. Besides providing an exercise in statutory interpretation that recalled his first precocious paper on the subject in the 1570s, his defence of the equitable proceedings of the Chancery became a landmark in the history of English law.[2]

Although Ellesmere's authorship of this tract has never been confidently asserted, the lack of an original text and the presence of hundreds of extant manuscript copies has precluded any definite ascription. Most legal historians have used the printed version of 1641, which was pejoratively entitled *The Privileges and Prerogatives of the High Court of Chancery*.[3] However, once the manuscript copies are examined, it appears that a pedigree of the earliest copies can be drawn; and at least one, if not two copies, can be suggested as being closest to the original and thus the most authentic of the extant copies. The Folger Library manuscript noted above, which will be called copy

---

[1] Folger MS V.b. 190, ff. 1r–11r.

[2] *Supra*, Chaps. I, VII.

[3] It is also significant in its barbarous composition for the press. Ellesmere was declared its author in Simeon Theoloal, *Le Digest des Briefes Originals & des choses concernants eux* (1671 ed.), 82–3.

A, and a Cambridge University Library manuscript, which will be called copy B,[1] provide the primary basis of this edition of the tract.

The manuscript edited here is the Folger one, and the textual notes carry a commentary on every important difference between it and the Cambridge copy. The differences, fortunately, are minor ones. The other manuscripts derivative from these earliest copies fall into three different sections, each section having characteristics common to itself: copy E, which was Robert Cotton's summary of copy A;[2] copy F, from Roger Twysden's collection which had begun a new series;[3] and copies C–D, from William Lambarde's and Arthur Tourner's collections, which formed another series from the Cambridge manuscript (copy B) noted above.[4]

Based on this analysis, a pedigree of Ellesmere's tract on 'Prohibitians' would be as follows:

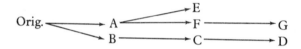

The differences in these copies form the basis of the textual notes.

The necessity of establishing a text for this tract becomes apparent once one realises that the printed copy noted above, which will be regarded as copy G, is a document that has been used throughout the centuries as a bona fide one when it is nothing more than a corrupt derivation of copy F. Sentences and lines have been transposed or omitted, whole paragraphs deleted, and the style changed. Such a situation helps to explain why Sir William Holdsworth had reservations in attributing it to anyone. So too did the antiquarians of the nineteenth century.[5] It is only when one examines the manuscript closest to the original that the many references and statements from Ellesmere's personal and public writings reveal its authorship. The numerical notes in the text are designed to illustrate these instances.

[1] C.U.L. MS Gg. 2.31, ff. 194r–200v.

[2] Folger MS V.b. 48, ff. 6v–8r.

[3] Folger MS G.b.7, ff, 74r–81r.

[4] Harv. Law MS 1034 ff. 77v–92r, and MS 111 ff. 1r–16v, respectively.

[5] Holdsworth, *HEL* v, 272–3; and *Notes and Queries*, Ser. 5, V, 68–9, 116, 218, 436. Like Holdsworth, they thought that the *Certaine Observations Concerning the Office of the Lord Chancellor* (1651), was Ellesmere's. There is no internal evidence to support this suggestion.

There were, however, many additional manuscript copies of this tract. Many of them are poor ones, but those closest to the manuscript traditions noted above, and still useful to study, will be cited.[1] With regards to the provenance of copies A and B, the Folger manuscript appears to have been at one time with the More of Loseley family papers, and thus came with the deposit of the papers of the descendants of Ellesmere's second wife, Elizabeth Wolley. Copy B is in a Cambridge volume of Chancery materials that was prepared by a clerk, and the volume represents perhaps the best collection of Chancery materials for Ellesmere's presidency of the Court.

[1] Namely: Add. MS 25.246, ff. 40r–7v; Hale MS 47, ff. 233r–42v; Lans. MS 613, ff. 2r–16r; Harg. MSS 227 ff. 247v–51v, 240 ff. 290r–356r, and 249 ff. 121r–34v; Harl. MSS 39 ff. 97r–115v, 1767 ff. 1r–14r; 4265 ff. 35r–67r, and 5191 ff. 25v–30r; SP Misc. 9/12, ff. 141r–55r; SPD, 1623–25 & Addenda, 8/142; Stowe MSS 177 ff. 177r–98r, and 298 ff. 163r–78v; Tanner MS 244, ff. 2r–22v; and Trin. Coll. Camb. MS 757.

PART TWO

ELLESMERE'S TRACTS

The texts have been transcribed in the original with three exceptions: abbreviations have been extended except in Ellesmere's notes; the first letters of words beginning new sentences have been capitalised; and punctuation has been added where it has appeared to be absolutely necessary (for example, to separate lists of items). All case titles are printed in roman type.

Brackets [ ] denote page numbers of the tracts, and are also used to set off Ellesmere's own footnotes to his text.

Angular brackets ⟨ ⟩ have been used for conjectured readings.

Double angular brackets ⟪ ⟫ have been used for additions of my own where such clarification seems essential.

Textual footnotes are identified by notation with italic letters.[a] The author's instructions regarding textual variations are in italic.

General notes are identified with cardinal numerals.[1]

Finally, I wish to thank the following libraries and archives for allowing permission to transcribe and edit these manuscripts: the Harvard Law Lib. and Northamptonshire Rec. Off. for the 'Royall Prerogatiue' (Chap. IX); the Henry E. Huntington Lib. for 'Speciall Observacions' (Chap. XI), 'Thinges to be considered' (Chap. XII), and 'Memorialles for Iudicature' (Chap. XIII); the Bodleian Lib. for 'Prohibitians' (Chap. XIV); the British Museum for 'Observacions vpon Cookes Reports' (Chap. XV); and the Folger Shakespeare, and Cambridge Univ. Lib. for 'A breviate' (Chap. XVI).

'A COPPIE OF A WRYTTEN DISCOURSE BY THE LORD CHAUNCELLOR ELSEMORE CONCERNING THE ROYALL PREROGATIUE'[1]

(c. 1604)

That absolute prerogatiue which according to the Kings pleasure ⟪is⟫ revealed by his lawes,[2] maie be exercised and executed by any Subiecte to whome power may be giuen by the King in anie place of Iudgment, or Comission which the King [1] by his law hath ordeyned, in which the Iudge subordinate Cannot wrong the people; the law layeing downe a measure by which[a] euerie Iudge shall gouerne and execute, against which law if anie Iudge proceed he is by the lawe questionable, and punishable for[b] his trangression. In this nature are all the Iudges and Comissioners[c] of the land noe otherwise then in therie Courts, in which the King in person is supposed to sitt.[3] [2r] ⟪They⟫ whoe[d] Cannot make that trespas, fellonie, or treason, which the law hath not made soe to be, neither Can punish the guiltie by other punishment then the lawes haue apppinted. This prerogatiue or power, as it is ouer all the Subjects, soe being knowne by the Subjects they are without excuse if they offend, and suffer noe wrong if they be iustlie punished. By this prerogatiue the King gouerneth all sorte [2v] of people according to his knowne will.[4]

The absolute prerogatiue[e] which is in Kings according to therie priuate will and Judgment, Cannot be executed by therie[f] sub-

---

[a] the *canc. before* which *as in C and D.*

[b] for *inserted for* by *as in C and D.*

[c] and Judges *canc. after* Comissioners *as in B, C, and D.*

[d] *No sentence break in B, where* whoe *refers to* King.

[e] *No new paragraph in A or B.*

[f] Any *in B, and no following break in sentence.*

[1] Harv. Law MS 4006. The title continues: 'and what manner of persones that should be and are to execute the power and ordinacion of the Kinges Prerogatiue'.

[2] A coll. of precedents and laws concerning the K. and the exercise of his prerog. was prepared for Ellesmere with a note 'done to haste' – Ellesm. MS 1169, 'A Colleccion of notes out of the Recordes in the Towre'. The sections in ff. 1–18 are esp. relevant.

[3] Ellesmere's concept of the K. as the source of all laws was formulated in the *Post-Nati*, 104–8; in fact, the ideas on kingship that are expressed in the 'Prerog.' seem to assume those which were set down in the *Post-Nati*.

[4] Statutes, procls. and legal judgments concerning offences against the sovereign were coll'd for the Chanc. in Ellesm. MS 446. It appears that Sir George Carew, a Chanc. Master who served him for many years, compiled most of these.

iecte 《s》.[1] Neither is it possible to giue such power by Comission, nor is it fitt to subiecte the people to the same. For the King in that he is the Substitute of god ymediatelie; the father of his people; and the head of the Common wealth;[2] [3r] hath by participacion with God, and with his Subiectes, a discretion, Iudgment, and feeling of loue to-wardes those ouer whome he raigneth, onelie proper to himselfe, and his place and person; whoe seeing he Cannot into others infuse the wisdome, power,[a] and guifts which God in respect of his place and Charge hath enabled him with all, Can neither subordinate any other iudge to gouerne by that [3v] knowledge which the King Can noe otherwaies then by his knowne will participate vnto him.[3]

And if anie such subordinate Iudge[b] shall obteyne Commission according to the discretion of such iudge to gouerne the people,[c] that iudge is bound to thinke that to bee his sound discretion[d] which the law (which is the Kings owne[e] will) sheweth vnto him to be that Iustice which ought[f] to be administred; otherwise he might[g] well esteeme himselfe to be aboue the Kings lawes, whoe will not gouerne [4r] by them but as haueing[h] a power deriued from other then the Kinge, which in[i] the Kingdome will administer Iustice Contrarie to the Iustice of the land. Neither[j] Can such Iudge or Comissioner[k] vnder the name of Kinglie authoritey shroudd[l] his owne high offence, seeing the Con-science and discretion of euerie man as particular and priuate to himselfe, soe as the discretion of the Iudge Cannot be properlie, [4v] or possiblie be the discretion or Conscience of the King; And if not

---

[a] *Added from C. Read* his wisdome *in B for the* wisdome *in A.*

[b] *No new paragraph in A or B.*

[c] Kings *inserted before* people *in B.*

[d] of such iudge to governe ... his sound discretion *added before* which the law *from B and C.*

[e] owne] knowne *in B.*

[f] not *canc. after* ought *as in C and D.*

[g] not *canc. after* might *as in C and D.*

[h] but as hauing] to haue *in B.*

[i] which in *inserted for* within *from C and D.*

[j] lawe and neither] land. Neither *in B and C.*

[k] *The tense is altered to the singular as in B, C, and D.*

[l] can *canc. before* shroudd *as in C and D.*

[1] This concept was also expressed by Ellesmere in a speech before the S. C.: Hawarde, *Reportes,* 188.

[2] In a speech to Parl. he used this position to argue that the new monarch could also by virtue of his unique nature 'restrain thinges against the common weal'; notes for the Parlia-ment of 1604 in Ellesm. MS 456, f. 2r.

[3] The location of the source of the K's power and auth. in the word of God, and its influence in framing a concept of royal sovereignty was sketched in the *Post-Nati,* 105–8 and 72–6, respectively.

discretion, neither «is» the iudgment his which is ruled by another mans onlie. Therefore it may seeme they rather desire to be Kings, then to rule the people vnder him, whoe will not administrate Iustice by lawe but by therie owne willes.[a]

This administracion of a Subiecte[b] is derrogatorie to the Kings prerogatiue, for that he administrates Iustice [5r] out of private directiones, being not Capable of generall direction «in» how to vse the Kings pleasure in Cases of particular respecte; which yf other[c] then the King himselfe Can doe, how Can it be that anie man should desire anie thing which is vnfitt or impossible, but that it must proceed out of some exorbitant affeccion;[d] the rather seeing such places are full of trouble, and being altogether vnnecessarie, noe man will [5v] seeke to thrust himselfe thereinto but for hope of gaine.[1] Then is not prerogatiue oppugned but maineteyned, though it be desired that euerie subordinate Magistrate maie not be made supreame,[2] whereby he maie seal up[e] the hearts of the people, take from the King the respecte due unto him onelie,[f] or Iudge the people otherwise then the King doth himselfe.[g] For though the King be not bound to [6r] render any accompt to the Law for the iustice which in person hee doth administer yet euery subordinate iudge must[h] render accompte to the King (by his lawes) howe he hath administred[i] Iustice in the place which he is sett.[3] But if he hath power to rule by his priuate direction, for which there is noe lawe, how Can he be questioned by the lawe if in his priuate Censure he offend.[4]

---

[a] C and D contain many differences in this paragraph; B merely several.

[b] No new paragraph in A or B. Read in for of in B.

[c] noe canc. before other as in B, C, and D.

[d] This clause runs into the next one in B, C, and D.

[e] steale of] seale up in B, C, and D.

[f] due respecte onelie] respecte due unto him onelie in B, C, and D.

[g] he himselfe doth] the Kinge himselfe doth in B, the King doth himselfe in C and D.

[h] render any accompt ... subordinate iudge must added before render accompte to the King as in B, and slightly different in C and D.

[i] maie administrate] hath administred in B, C, and D.

[1] The argument here and in the parag. above appears in the Chanc's notes in Ellesm. MS 465.

[2] A contemp. copy of this tract, entitled 'Prerogatiue Royall' (Harl. MS 250, f. 154r–v), ends at this point.

[3] The accountability of judges to the Crown formed a key element of Ellesmere's attack on corruption and favouritism in the courts as well as in the depart's of state. For ex. see his earlier copy of a brief for the reform of practices in the Court of Wards and Liveries: Ellesm. MS 3001.

[4] That private requests are not masked by public presence, and that judges should rule strictly according to the precedents of the law without private direction, was the theme of his speech to Parl. in 1601: Sir Simonds D'Ewes, The Journals of All the Parliaments during the Reign of Queen Elizabeth (1682), 619. The theme became a dominant feature of his speech on the Post-Nati, 16–42, 50–4.

Therefor,[a] it should seeme that in giueing authoritie the King ordeyneth noe subordinate Magistrates, but absolute Kings; and what [6v] doth the King leaue to himselfe, who[b] giueth as much to another as himselfe hath?[c] Neither is there a greater bond to tye the subiecte to his Prince in particular then when he shall haue recourse vnto him in his person or in his power for releife of the ⟨wrongs⟩ which from Priuate men shall be offered, or for reformacion of the oppressions[d] which [7r] anie subordinate Magistrate shall impose vpon the people.[1]

But against the wrong Committed against the Iudgments (the Iudge haueing power from the King to Iudge according to his owne discretion),[e] though there be manifest danger and damadge[f] to the people[g] there Can be noe offence to the Iudge who hath power to execute according [7v] to his discretion, when the discretion of anie Iudge shall be thought fitt[h] to be vnlimited. And therefore there Can be therein no reformacion, but whereby[i] the King useth his prerogatiue to giue his oppressed Subiects right. The Subiecte is bound to suffer helplesse wrong, and the discontente of the people is Cast vppon the King ⟪when⟫ the lawes ⟪are⟫ being [8r] neglected,[2] which with therie equitie in all other Courses of Iudgement interpose themselues and yeeld remedy.[j]

And to conclude,[k] Custome Cannot allow that which is vnreasonable in it selfe; Wisdome will not allow that which is anie waie dan-

---

[a] Therefor *inserted for* theirof *from B, C, and D. No new paragraph in A or B.*

[b] who *inserted for* which *from B, C, and D.*

[c] *C and especially D contain many differences in the three sentences above.*

[d] oppressions *inserted for* apprehencions *from B, C, and D.*

[e] discretion] sence *in B.*

[f] danger and *omitted before* dammage *in B.*

[g] *The paragraph through* people *is omitted in C and D.*

[h] thought, vnfitt] thought fit *in B, C, and D.*

[i] *In C and D whereas inserted for* whereby, *and this clause runs on into the next one. In B read* reformacion, whereby *in this . . .*

[j] and yeeld remedy *added after* themselves *from C and D. Most of the two sentences above have been omitted in C and D.*

[k] And to conclude *added before* Custome *from B and C. No new paragraph in A or B.*

[1] Or, as he said earlier, courts administer justice, but only the monarch can give mercy to the people–Hawarde, *Reportes* (SC 1589), 164. Elsewhere, Ellesmere described eloquently that the strongest personal bond which existed in the country was that between the K. and his individual subjects: *Post-Nati*, 76–83, 98–104.

[2] The neglect of the laws formed a major stream in his public speeches in the S.C., which are noted at length in Hawarde, *Reportes*, from 1596 to 1608. He had also begun to prepare drafts of papers on reforming the laws, and a major consideration was the restoration of the toughness of the ancient laws: Elles. MS 2936, endorsed '8 Iune 1604', and Ellesm. MS 452, endorsed '4 Iune 1609'.

gerous and noe waie proffitable. Iustice neuer approued that Gouerment wherein it Cannot be but wrong must be Committed.[1] Neither Can there be anie rule [8v] by which to trie it, or meanes for reformacion. Therefore whoesoeuer desireth gouerment must seeke such as he is Capable of, not such as seemeth to himselfe most easy to be executed; for in appearaunce it is easy to him whoe knoweth noe lawe nor Iustice to rule as he listeth, his will neuer wanting a power to itselfe. But it is safe [a] and blamelesse both for the Iudge and [9r] people, [b] That Iudges be appointed whoe know the lawe; and that they be lymited to gouerne according to the law,[c] is a thing of necessitie and of extraordinary Care.[d] Elsemere. [9v]

[a] wanting to it selfe but is safe] wanting to it selfe: But it is safe *in B*, wanting a power to itselfe. But is safe *in C*.

[b] and honour to the King *added after* people, *in C and D*.

[c] *B ends here.*

[d] *The paragraph in C and D reads quite differently.*

[1] The Chancellor believed strongly that custom and reason formed the only-unimpeachable basis for the interp. and course of the law: *Post-Nati*, 33–6, 59–72, 84–98.

'THE SPEECH OF THE LORD CHANCELLOR OF ENGLAND, IN THE ESCHEQUER CHAMBER, TOUCHING THE *POST-NATI*'[1] (1608)

Suggested chapter equivalents

《INTRODUCTION》

My Lords, mine age, mine infirmitie, and indisposition of health, my decaie and weakenesse of memorie, and *Desuetudo*, and long discontinuance from this maner of Legall exercise (above foureteene yeares) have bereaved mee of the meanes and helpes that should inhable me to speake in so great a Case. [1]

I feare therefore that it will bee deemed presumption (if not worse) that I adventure to speake heerein at all; specially after so many learn-

---

[1] (1609). Repr. here from the author's personal copy.

ed and judicious Arguments of so many grave, learned, and reverend Judges.[1]

To say the same that hath beene saied, must needes be unpleasaunt, wearisome, and loathsome to the hearers; and not to say the same is to speake little to the purpose: for, what more can be saied than hath bene?

Yet, for the Case is depending in Chancerie, and adjourned hither for difficultie in Law, and there I must give judgement according to the Law; Whether the Complainant bee inhabled, by, Lawe, to maintaine his suit in that Court or not: I hould it more fitting to deliver the reasons of my judgement heere, where others have beene heard, than there, before a few, which have not heard that which hath bene so learnedly argued, and largely debated heere. [2]

And therefore the Case standing thus, I will speake what I thinke: And I must say as one of the grave Judges saied, I can tell no newes; But some old things which I have read and observed I will remember, but I can not divine, or prophesie *de futuris*, I leave that as Justice Yelverton did.[2]

I am free and at libertie *Nullius addictus jurare in verba Magistri*, and therefore I will speake ingenuously and freely.

In the arguing of this Case, some things which are of great weight with mee, have (in mine opinion) beene passed over too lightly; and some other thinges which seeme to me but light, have beene overweighed, as I thinke.

Halfe an howers time longer or shorter I meane not to strive for,[3] and therefore I will presume on your patience, and assume to my selfe such convenient time as others have done: And yet I will husband time as well as I can.

I will not be abashed to strengthen my [3] weake memorie with helpe of some scribled papers,[4] as others have done: for I accompt it a point of wisedome to follow wise mens Examples.

---

[1] Fourteen judges delivered speeches on the case in the final two law terms of Easter and Trin., 1608, and the speeches consumed eight days. The Chanc's was the last to be given on June 7.

[2] According to Coke, Yelverton spoke on the fourth day, but the author has not found a record or report of his speech – 7 *Co. Rep.* f. 2r–v.

[3] According to one observer, he was 'allmoste 4 howres in his argumente' – Hawarde, *Reportes*, 366.

[4] The Chanc's briefs for the prepared speech are Ellesm, MSS 1872 and 1873; the latter is dated 3 May 1608. It appears, however that he may have spoken from the text for this book. According again to Hawarde, he 'reade muche in his booke' – *Reportes*, 366.

Other *Exordium,* Insinuation, Protestation, or Preface for the Matter it selfe, either to prepare attentive and benevolent auditors, or to stirre offence or mislike against either partie, I meane not to use; it is fit for Orators, I never professed the Art, I had never skill in it:[1] And it is not *Decorum* for Judges, that ought to respect the Matter, and not the humors of the Hearers.

The *Exordium* the Civilians use in their Sentences I like well; *In Deinomine Amen, & Deo primitus invocato;* other *Exordium* I care not for.

«CHAPTER I» THE CASE.

The Case now depending in Chancerie which is adjourned hither, is thus.[2]

Robert Calvine, sonne and heire apparant of James L. Calvine of Colcrosse in the Realme [4] of Scotland, an Infant of three yeares of age, borne in the said Realme of Scotland, maketh title by his Bill to a Messuage and Garden with the appurtenances in the parish of Saint Buttolph without Bishops-gate in the Citie of London: and complaineth against John Bingley, and Richard Griffin, for detaining the Evidences concerning the same Messuage and Lands, and taking the profits thereof.

The Defendants pleade, that the Plaintife is an Alien, and that in the third yeare of his Majesties raigne of England, and in the nine and thirtieth yeare of his Majesties raigne of Scotland, hee was borne in the Realme of Scotland, within the ligeance of his said Majestie, of his Realme of Scotland, and out of the ligeance of our soveraigne Lord the King of his Realme of England.

And the Defendants say further, That at the time of the birth of the Complainant, and long before, and ever sithence, the said Kingdome of Scotland was, and still is, ruled and governed by the proper [5] Lawes and Statutes of the said Kingdome of Scotland, and not by the Lawes and Statutes of this Realme of England; And

---

[1] It was, according to a contemp. lawyer, a powerful performance: marginal notes in a pr. copy, Hunt. RB 269696, p. 5.

[2] The only full report of the case before the Exch. Ch. is in *State Trials* II, 562–695. This contains an abstract of earlier discs. on the subject in the joint com. of the two houses of Parl, a schedule of hearings before the Exch. Ch, the speech of Bacon for John Calvin, and the decisions of Coke and Ellesmere. There is, however, a very interesting account of the speeches in Hawarde, *Reportes,* 349–66.

therfore the Defendants demaund Judgement Whether the Complainant ought to be answered to his said Bill, or shall be received to prosecute the said suite against the Defendants, being for, and concerning the title of Inheritance, and evidence touching the same.

Hereupon the Complainant hath demurred in Law.

This is the speciall Case now depending in the Chancerie; in which, and touching all like Cases in generall, mine opinion is, and since the question was first mooved hath beene, That these *Post-nati* are not Aliens to the King, nor to his Kingdome of England; but by their Birth-right, are liege subjects to the King; and capable of estates of Inheritance, and freehould of Lands in England; and may have and [6] Maintaine as well Reall as Personall actions for the same. And that therefore the now Complainant Robert Calvine ought to be answered.

This opinion I did first conceive upon those rules and reasons in Law (as well the Common law of England, as the Civile law) which heereafter in the course of my speech I will remember. And in this opinion I have beene since confirmed by many great and weightie reasons.

《CHAPTER 2》THE PROCEEDING IN THE GENERALL CASE OF POST-NATI.
[Stat. 1 Jac. 19 Mart. 1603][1]

First, in the Statute made in the first yeare of his Majesties raigne of England, authorizing the Treatie betweene the Commissioners for both the Kingdomes, it is said (as Justice Warbarton noted well) That both the famous and ancient Realmes of England and Scotland, are now united in allegeance and loyall subjection in his royall person, to his Majestie, and his posteritie for ever.

Here wee have the Judgement of the Parliament, that there is a Unitie in allegeance [7] to one Royall person; And therefore I see not how wee may out of imaginarie conceipts, and by subtile distinctions straine our wittes to frame severall allegeances to one and the same Royall person, contrary to so plaine a declaration made by Parliament.

---

[1] I James I, chap. 2, *Stat. Realm* IV.1018–9. The Chanc's notes on the statute, used perhaps for framing it, are in Ellesm. MS 455, f. 2v.

The Proclamation, 2 Jacobi
[20 Octobr. 1604.]¹

Next followeth his Majesties Proclamation 20. *Octobris* 1604. by which hee assumed to himselfe the Name and Style of King of great Britaine: In which Proclamation, among many other weighty reasons, this is added for one, 'We have received from those that bee skilfull in the Lawes of the Land, That immediately upon our succession, diverse of our auncient Lawes of this Realme are *ipso facto* expired; as namely, that of Escuage, and of the naturalization of the Subjects.'² This was not done sodainely nor lightly; but upon grave, and serious deliberation, and advise: And therefore seemeth to mee to be a Matter of great importance, and not to be lightly regarded. [8]

The same twentieth of October these Commissioners began their Treatie. [The Commissioners authorized by parliament, did begin 20 October and did continue untill 6 December, 2 *Jacobi*.] Of the grave and judicious Course which they held, in debating of the Matter then propounded, I will forbeare to speake: But for this point of Naturalization now in question, their resolution in the end was thus:

The Resolution of the Commissioners.

That it shall be propounded to both the Parliaments at the next Sessions, that an Act be made containing a declaration, as followeth: 'That all the Subjects of both the Realmes, borne since the decease of Elizabeth the late Queen of England of happy memorie, and al that shalbe borne hereafter under the obedience of his Majestie, and his royall Progeny, are by the common Lawes of both the Realmes, and shal be for ever, inhabled to obtaine, succeed, inherite, and possesse all Lands, Goods, and Chattels, and etc. as fully, and amply as the Subjects of either Realme respectively might have done, or may doe in any sort within the Kingdome where they were borne.'³ [9] This, after long debating, and grave, and deliberate consideration, was, in the end, the resolution of the greater part of the Commissioners, not one openly gainesaying it. And diverse of the principall Judges of

---

¹ STC 8361.

² Ellesmere's two copies were Hunt. RB 172605 and 145923, the quote at p. 2. The latter copy was used by one of his grandchildren to practise arithmetical tables. The procl. and James's speech are pr. in *Const. Docs.* 32–7.

³ The act for the commissioners, with Salisbury's corrections and the order for their appointment, are in SP 14/8/61–3, 100–1.

the Realme were present at all times when the point was debated. And herein I note the wise and judicious forme of that resolution, which was not to propound to the Parliament the making of a new Lawe; but a declaration of the common Lawes of both the Realmes in this question.[1]

Now, if we consider who these Commissioners were, what Lords of the higher House, and what persons of the common House, selected of all degrees, most eminent for their learning and judgement, aswell in Civile and Common Law, as in knowledge, and experience other waies, being assisted by the grave Judges of the Realme:[2] If this, I say, be well considered, then this Resolution must be accompted and esteemed as a matter of [10] great and weighty importance, and much to bee regarded in the deciding of this question.

The Judges opinion in Parliament.

According to this Act of the Commissioners, the Case was propounded in the next Session of Parliament. In the higher House, the Judges were required to deliver their opinions. There were then eleaven Judges present; whereof tenne did with one uniforme consent affirme the Lawe to be; That the *Post-nati* were not Aliens, but naturall Subjects (one onely dissenting.) After this, the Question was debated in a solemne Conference betweene both the Houses of Parliament at severall times, and at great length, and with much liberty. Nothing was omitted that Wit or Art could invent to object against this opinion; And that was done by men of great learning, and singular judgement in the Common Lawe, and Civile Lawe; and by some other Gentlemen of the Common House, of rare [11] gifts for their learning, knowledge, elocution and experience.

At this Conference the Judges were present; who, after they had heard all that was, or could be said, did confirme their former opinions, which they had before delivered in the higher House: Three of the chiefe of them declaring their reasons, and all the rest (saving one alone) concurring in the same. So, here was now a generall resolution by all the Judges of the Realme (one excepted) and that deli-

---

[1] The heads for these debates were set down by the Chanc. in Ellesm. MS 1225. The resolution to proceed in this manner, however, did not accord well with precedent. See the disc. of William Lambarde in *Archeion*, 118–31.

[2] On the contrary, the commissioners were not particularly distinguished. There were only two privy councillors, six lawyers, and one merchant among the 27; most were country gentlemen: Moore, *Cases*, 790.

vered not privately, but in Parliament; which without more adoe
had beene sufficient to have decided and determined this question.

The force and strength of the Kings proclamations.[1]

Touching the Proclamation, it was discreetely and modestly saied by
a learned Gentleman of the lower House, That it was of great
respect, and much to be regarded; but yet it was not binding, nor
concluding: for, Proclamations can neither make, nor declare Lawes.
And [12] besides, that this Proclamation was not grounded upon
any Resolution of the reverend Judges; but upon the opinion of
some skilfull in the Lawes of this Land.

Of the strength of Proclamations, being made by the King, by the
advise of his Counsell and Judges, I will not discourse, yet I will
admonish those that bee learned and studious in the Lawes, and by
their profession are to give counsell, and to direct themselves,
and others, to take heede that they doe not contemne or lightly
regard such Proclamations.[2]

And to induce them thereunto, I desire them to looke upon, and
consider advisedly these few Proclamations, Provisions, or Ordinances, which I will point out unto them; and of what validitie and
force they have beene houlden to bee in construction of Lawe, albeit
they be neither Statutes, nor Acts of Parliament.

M. 4. H. 3. in Dower [Fitzh. Dower 179], the Defendant
pleaded, '*Quod petens est de potestate Regis Franciae, & residens in
Francia; Et provisum est* [13] *à Consilio Regis, quod nullus de potestate
Regis Franciae respondeatur in Anglia antequam Angli respondeantur de
jure suo in Francia.*' This the Plaintifes Atturney could not denie;
and thereupon the Judgement was, *Ideo sine dic.*

Anno 20. H. 3. certaine Provisions and Ordinances were made
which were called *Provisiones Merton*, where the King assembled his
Archbishops, Bishops, Earles, and Barons for the Coronation of the
King, and his wife Queene Elenor; and the words be, '*Provisum est
in Curia Domini Regis apud Merton coram Wilihelmo Cantuariensi
Archiepiscopo, & Coepiscopis, Suffraganeis suis; Et coram majori parte
Comitum & Baronum Angliae ibidem existentium pro Coronatione*

---

[1] This was composed not only with reference to the procl. on p. 206 above, but also to two
other procls: one for equal justice to Scots and Englishmen (STC 8326), and another for the
commissioners (STC 8359).

[2] The account is based on his earlier discussion of proclamations in the *Discourse*, 103–7.
A contemp. lawyer noted his strong opposition to Ellesmere's view in his own copy of the *Post-
Nati*: B.M. RB 518.i.2 (2), pp. 12–3.

ipsius Domini Regis & Helionorae Reginae, pro qua omnes vocati
fuerunt: Cum tractatum esset de Communi utilitate Regni super arti-
culis subscriptis. Ita provisum fuit & concessum, tam à praedictis
Archiepiscopis, Episcopis, Comitibus, & Baronibus, & aliis. De viduis
primò &c.[1] [14]

Fitzherbert citeth a Provision made *Anno* 19. H. 3. in these words
[Fitzherbert Nat. Br. 32], '*Et provisum fuit coram Domino Rege,*
Archiepiscopis, Episcopis, Comitibus, & Baronibus, Quod nulla Assisa
ultimae praesentationis de caetero capiatur de Ecclesiis, Praebendatis
nec de Praebendis.' This Provision was allowed and continued for
Lawe, untill W. 2. *Anno* 13. Edw. 1. ca. 5. which provides the contrary
by expresse words.

Anno 6. Ed. 1. the King and his Judges made certaine Explanations
of the Statute of Gloucester, which are called, *Explanationes statuti*
Gloucestriae: And these be the wordes, '*Postmodum per Dominum*
Regem & Justiciarios suos factae sunt quaedam Explanationes quo-
rundam articulorum superius positorum.' Which Explanations have
ever since been received as a Law.

There is a Proclamation by King Ed. 3. bearing Teste at Westminster *Anno* 15. Ed. 3. And Judge Thorpes opinion Pa. 39. E. 3. 7,
both which I will now forbeare to report, and wish the Students to
read the same [15] in the printed Bookes, where they shall see both
the effect and the reason and the cause thereof; They are worth their
reading, and may informe and direct them what judgement to make of
Proclamations.

How the Judges opinion delivered in parliament ought to be regarded.[2]

Object. Touching the opinion of the Judges, some have objected (yet
modestly, and I suppose, according to their conscience and understanding) That there is not like regarde to be had of Judges opinions
given in Parliament, as ought to bee of their Judgements in their
proper Courts and Seates of Justice: for, in those places their Oath
bindeth them; but not so in the other.

Respons. 1. To this I answer: The reverence, and worthinesse of
the men is such, as is not to bee quarrelled and doubted of, if there
were no Oathe at all: for, if men of so great and eminent places feare

---

[1] 'The Provisions of Merton', 20 Henry III. This is a faithful transcript of the original:
Stat. Realm I, 1.

[2] A contemp. lawyer considered this section of the speech (through p. 24) as one of the more
valuable ones: anon. notes on Ellesmere's speech in Tanner MS 75, f. 164r–v.

not God and his Judgements, even out of a [16] religious conscience, which is *Fraenum ante peccatum, & flagrum post peccatum*, it may be doubted that the externall ceremonie of adding a Booke will little availe.

2. Their Oath doth bind them as much in the Court of Parliament, as in their proper Courts: for, that is the supreme Court of all; and they are called thither by the Kings Writ, not to sit as Tell-clockes, or idle hearers; but *quòd personalitèr intersitis nobiscum, ac cum caeteris de Consilio nostro super dictis negotiis tractaturi, vestrumq; Consilium impensuri*: And those *Negotia* be *Ardua & urgentia negotia Regni &c*. And their Oath, amongst other things, is, That they shall counsell the King truely in his businesse.

3. This Exception may serve against the Judges, as well in Cases when they sit and give Judgement, as Justices of Assises, *Nisi prius*, *Oyer* and *Terminer*, and Gaole Delivery, as in this Case of Parliament: for, there they have none other Oath but their generall Oath. [17]

4. It becomes us to esteeme of Judges now, as our forefathers esteemed them in times past; for as they succeede them in Time and Place (I thanke God, and the King, I have neither cause to feare any for displeasure, nor to flatter any for favour: wherefore I will neither be afraid, nor abashed to speake what I thinke:) I say therefore, that as our Judges now succeed the former Judges, in Time and Place; so they succeede them, and are not inferior to them in Wisedome, Learning, Integritie, and all other judicious and religious Vertues.

The judgement of the parliament, of Judges opinions delivered in parliament.

Then let us see what the wisedome of Parliaments in times past attributed to the Judges opinions declared in Parliament; Of which there bee many Examples; but, I will trouble you but with two or three.

I wil not remember Richard the seconds time (of which some of our Chroniclers doe talke idlely, and understand little) where power and might of some potent [18] persons oppressed justice, and faithfull Judges, for expounding the Law soundly, and truely. The first that I will remember, is this.

《1.》 In the Parliament 28. H. 6. 16. *Januarii*, the Commons made suite, That W. de la Poole Duke of Suffolke should be committed to prison for many treasons and other hainous crimes committed by him. The Lords in Parliament were in doubt what answer to give; They demanded the opinion of the Judges: Their opinion was, That hee ought not to be committed; And their reason was, for that the Commons did not charge him with anie particular offence, but with generall slaunders and reports; And therefore because the Specialties were not shewed, he was not to bee committed. This opinion was allowed; And thereupon 28. *Januarii*, the Commons exhibited certaine speciall Articles against him, *viz.* That hee conspired with the French King to invade [19] the Realme and etc. And thereupon hee was committed to the Tower.[1]

2. In the parliament *Anno* 31. H. 6. in the vacation (the parliament being continued by prorogation) Thomas Thorpe the Speaker was condemned in a thousand pounds dammages in an action of Trespasse, brought against him by the Duke of Yorke, and was committed to prison in Execution for the same. After, when the parliament was re-assembled, the Commons made suite to the King and the Lords, to have Thorpe the Speaker delivered, for the good exploite of the Parliament; whereupon, the Duke of Yorkes Counsell declared the whole case at large. The Lords demaunded the opinion of the Judges, whether, in that case, Thorpe ought to be delivered out of prison by priviledge of Parliament: The Judges made this aunswer, That they ought not to determine the priviledge of that high Court of parliament; But for [20] the declaration of proceeding in lower Courts, in cases where Writtes of *Supersedeas* for the priviledge of the parliament be brought unto them, They answered: 'That if any person that is a Member of the Parliament be arrested in such cases as bee not for treason or felonie, or for suretie of peace, or condemnation had before the parliament, it is used that such persons be released; and may make Atturney, so as they may have their freedome and libertie, freely to intend the parliament.' Hereupon it was concluded, 'That Thorpe should still remaine in prison according to the Law, Notwithstanding the priviledge of parliament, and that he was the Speaker.' Which resolution was declared to the Commons by Walter Moyle, one of the Kings Serjeants at Law. And then the Commons were commaunded in the Kings name, by the Bishop of

---

[1] *Rotuli Parliamentum*, 28 Henry VI (1449), 176–83. The back-ground for this and the following case is discussed in J. Enoch Powell and Keith Wallis, *The House of Lords in the Middle Ages* (1968), 491–5.

Lincolne (in the absence of the Archbishop of Canterbury then Chauncellor) to choose another Speaker.[1] [21]

3. In the parliament *Anno* 7. H. 8. a question was moved, whether spirituall persons might be convented before temporall Judges for criminall causes; There, sir John Fineux and the other Judges delivered their opinion, that they might and ought to be so. And their opinion was allowed, and maintained by the King and the Lords: And D. Standish, who before had houlden the same opinion, was delivered from the Bishops. And it is worth the noting, what words passed in that Case betweene the Archbishop of Canterbury, and that worthie Judge Fineux.[2]

Writs of Errour sued in parliament

4. If a writte of Errour bee brought in parliament upon a Judgement given in the Kings Bench, the Lords of the higher House alone (without the Commons) are to examine the Errours; But that is by the advise and counsell of the Judges, who are to informe them what the Law is, and so to direct them in their Judgement. And if the Judgement be reversed, [22] then commaundement is to be given to the Lord Chancellour to doe Execution accordingly. And so it was in *Anno* 17. R. 2. in a writte of Errour brought in parliament by the Deane and Chapiter of Lichfield, against the Prior and Covent of Newport-Panell, as appeareth by the Record. But if the Judgement bee affirmed, then the Court of the Kings Bench are to proceede to Execution of the Judgement, as it appeareth in Flowerdewes Case P. 1. H. 7. fol. 19. But it is to bee noted, that in all such writtes of Errour, the Lords are to proceede according to the Law; and for their Judgement therein they are informed and guided by the Judges; and doe not follow their owne opinions or discretions otherwise.[3]

This extravagant Discourse touching Proclamations, and Judges opinions delivered in parliament, and how they ought to be regarded, I have thought materiall and necessarie, both in respect [23] of the time wherein we live, and the Matter which we have in hand: And these be things which I thinke have beene too lightly passed over: But if you condemne it as impertinent, I must then

[1] Speaker Thomas Thorpe and the famous case of parl. privilege: Bryce Lyon, *A constitutional and legal history of medieval England* (New York 1960), 608–11.

[2] *Standish's Case* (Parl. 1515), Robert Keilway, *Reports d'Ascuns Cases* (1688), 184–5.

[3] His notes on the medieval precedents were made chiefly in his copies of Littleton's *Tenures* (Hunt. RB 62234) and Fitzherbert's *New Natura Brevium* (Hunt. RB 59688).

confesse I have presumed too much upon your patience; I pray you beare with mee, it is but my labour lost, and a little time misspent, if it seeme so unto you: You are wont to pardon greater faults; Call it either a Passe-time, or Wast-time, as pleaseth you. Now, to returne to the Case we have in hand.

The processes and forme of proceeding in the Case of R. C. now in question.

The generall Question having had this passage (by Proclamation, by Commission, and by debating in Parliament) remaineth yet without conclusion or judgement: And as every man abounds in his owne sence, so every one is left to his owne opinion; Specially those that were not satisfied with the grave Resolution of the Judges in Parliament, which (although some may tearme & accompt [24] as bare opinions) I must alwayes valew, and esteeme as a reall and absolute Judgement. Now, I say, this generall Question is reduced to two particular Cases, and is judicially depending in two «of» the highest Courts of justice in this Realme; and that is by one Complainant against severall Defendants for the freehoulde and inheritance of severall parcells of Land; and (as M. Solicitor said well) is a Case, not fained, nor surmised, but a true Case betweene true parties: And being *Quae stio juris, non facti*, is by both these Courts adjourned hither to be decided, and determined by all the Judges of England, as the rarenesse of the Case, and the weight and importance of it, both for the present and the future doth require.[1]

And the Case being of this nature and qualitie, it is not amisse to observe the proceeding in it: for, it is woorth the observing, and not to bee forgotten. The Defendants counsell, men of great learning, and in their profession inferiour to [25] none of their qualitie and degree, men conversant and wel exercised in the Question, and such as in the great conference in parliament, most of them were specially selected and chosen (for so they wel deserved) as most sufficient, able, and fit, as well for Learning and Knowledge, as for all other giftes of Witte and Nature, to handle so great and rare a Question. And although it hath pleased them of their good discretion to use the paines but of a few in the debating and arguing of the Case at the Barre: yet no doubt that was done upon mature deliberation and conference with all the residue: And whatsoever the Spirites, the

[1] The case was not a 'true case betweene true parties'; the parties, including the Crown, seem to have shaped the matter in order to bring it forward as a rare case.

Learning, the Wisedome, and Knowledge of all the others, upon long studie could affoorde, was put into the mouth of those few to serve as Organs and Instruments to deliver it unto us; which they have so well and sufficiently performed, that they deserve great praise and commendation: For, in my poore opinion, the witte of man could not [26] devise to say more touching this Question in Lawe than they have said. And whatsoever hath been sithence spoken for that part, it is for the Matter, but the same in substance, which the counsel at the Barre did deliver; though it hath beene varied in forme, and amplified with other wordes and phrases, and furnished with shew of some other strained Cases and authorities.[1]

The handling of it by the learned and reverend Judges, hath beene such, as it may appeare to the world, that every one hath spoken his owne heart and conscience; and hath laboured by long studie to search out the Law and the true reason of the Law in this rare Case; and so they have spoken, as *Coram Deo & Angelis*: None with desire to seeme popular; for nothing ought to be *tam populare quam veritas*. None to seeme to be Time-servers, or Men-pleasers; for the King (whome under God they serve) being *Pater patriae*, and soveraigne head of both these great [27] united Kingdomes, is to them both like as the head of a naturall body is to all the Members of the same, and is not, nor can not be partiall more to one than to an other. He deliteth in trueth, and desireth it; and without trueth hee cannot bee pleased. Hee ruleth by his Lawe, and commaundeth his Judges to minister to all his Subjects Law and Justice sincerely and truely; and equally and indifferently, without any partiall respect.[2]

It was never seene, but that in all rare and difficult Cases, there have beene diversitie of Opinions; but yet without breach of Charitie, which is the Bond of Unitie. So it hath happened in this Case. The Case hath beene argued at large by foureteene learned Judges; twelve of them have concurred in judgement, but upon severall reasons: for, as many waies may leade to one end of the journey; so diverse and severall reasons may conduce to one true and certaine conclusion. [28]

---

[1] The disenchanted lawyer agreed that the defence had done all that was possible in presenting its case: Hunt, RB 269696, pp. 10–11, 27.

[2] Ellesmere's statement of the K's views on the role of the judges was taken from a speech of K. James that was delivered to Parl. on 19 March 1603/4, where the Chanc. had bracketed the K's statement in his copy of the speech: *The Kings Majesties Speech* (1604), Hunt. RB 61876, sig. 4v.

And here I may not omit the woorthie memorie of the late grave and reverend Judge, Sir John Popham, chiefe Justice of the Kings Bench deceased (a man of great wisedome, and of singular learning and judgement in the Law) who was absolutely of the same opinion, as he often declared, as well in open Parliament, as otherwise.

The Apostle Thomas doubted of the Resurrection of our Saviour Jesus Christ, when all the rest of the Apostles did firmly beleeve it: But that this doubting confirmed, in the whole Church, the Faith of the Resurrection.

The two worthie and learned Judges that have doubted in this Case, as they beare his Name,[1] so I doubt not but their doubting hath given occasion to cleare the doubt in others; and so to confirme in both the Kingdomes, both for the Present and the Future, the truth of the Judgement in this Case. [29]

Thus, my Lords, have you hitherto nothing from me but Amen, to that which all the Judges (saving two) have said; and much more you cannot expect from mee: Yet, since I must give Judgement in this Case; and I said in the beginning, that I would render the reasons of my Judgement: (for that is the course of argument I must houlde) I will now deliver unto you, what are the speciall and principall reasons that first have induced mee, and still moove mee to houlde the opin-ion that I doe: And as I goe, I will indevour to cleare some doubts and questions, that partly in the conference in Parliament, and partly otherwise, I have heard made; not onely touching this Case it selfe, but also touching the forme and maner how it is to be decided and judged.

How this Case is to be judged, and by what Law.

The Case is rare, and new (as it hath beene often said) it was never decided, *Terminis terminantibus*; It was never judged by any Statute Law, which is a [30] positive Law; nor by Judgement of the Judges of the common Law.

Now, the first Question is (as some would have it) How it is to be Judged, and by what Law; and have wished that it might have staied untill the Parliament, and so bee decided by Parliament. They that make this doubt, I will let them demurre, and die in their doubts: for, the Case being adjourned hither before all the Judges of England, is now to be judged by them according to the common Law of

---

[1] Being Thomas Walmesley and Thomas Foster.

England; and not tarry for a Parliament: For, it is no transcendent Question, but that the common Lawe can and ought to rule it, and over-rule it, as Justice Williams said well.

⟪CHAPTER 3⟫ WHAT IS THE COMMON LAW OF ENGLAND: AND WHETHER IT BE JUS SCRIPTUM.

But then this Question produceth another; That is, What is the common Law of England; Whether it be *Jus scriptum*, or *non scriptum*; and such other like niceties: For, wee have in this age so many Questionists; and *Quo modo*, and *Quare*, are so common in most mens [31] mouthes, that they leave neither Religion, nor Lawe, nor King nor Counsell, nor Policie, nor Government out of question.[1]

And the end they have in this Question, What is the common Lawe? is to shake and weaken the ground and principles of all governement: And in this particular Question of the Law of England, to overthrow that Law whereby this Realm hath many hundred yeeres beene governed in all honour and happinesse: or at least to cast an aspersion upon it, as though it were weake and uncertaine. I wil therefore declare mine opinion in this point plainely and confidently, as I thinke in my conscience, and as I finde to be sufficiently warranted by auncient Writers, and good authorities voide of all exception.

The ground of the common Law.

The common Law of England is grounded upon the Law of God, and extendes itselfe to the originall Law of Nature, and the universall Law of Nations. [32]

When it respects the Church, it is called *Lex Ecclesiae Anglicanae*, as *Magna Charta ca.* 1. *Ecclesia Anglicana habeat omnia sua jura integra & illaesa.*[2]

When it respects the Crowne and the King, it is sometimes called *Lex Coronae*, as in Stat. 25. Edw. 3. *ca.* 1. *Lex Coronae Angliae est & semper fuit &c.*[3] And it is sometimes called *Lex Regia*, as in *Registro*

---

[1] This ultra-conservative stance was out of character for the Chanc. See his earlier attitudes (Knafla, 'The Law studies of an Elizabethan student', HLQ, 32 (1969), 227–39), and his later ones as illustrated by his tracts on 'Govt. 1615' and 'Iudicature'.

[2] 'Magna Carta Regis Johannis', 17 John (1215). The meaning here is close to the original: 'Anglicana ecclesia libra sit & hat Jura sua integra, & libertates suas illesas' – *Stat. Realm* I, 9.

[3] The Statute of Provisors of Benefices', 25 Edward III (1350/51), stat. 4, chap. 1. The Chanc. has twisted the words and meaning of the statute, which is this: 'que desicome le droit de la Corone Dengleterre & la loi du dite Roialme sont tieles' – *Stat. Realm* I, 317.

fo. 61. *Ad jura Regia spectat*: And, *Ad Conservationem jurium Coronae nostrae, & ad jura Regia ne depereant &c.*

When it respects the common subjects, it is called, *Lex Terrae*; as in *Magna Charta ca.* 29. *Nisi per legale judicium parium, vel per legem Terrae.*[1]

The common Law is not originally Lex scripta.

Yet, in all these Cases, whether it respects the Church, the Crowne, or the Subjects, it is comprehended under this generall tearme; The common Lawes of England: Which although they bee for a great part thereof reduced into writing; yet they are not originally *Leges scriptae.*

This I learned of the late Lord Treasurer [33] Burleigh (whose Honourable memorie England can never forget) and hearing it from him, I indevored by my private studie to satisfie my selfe thorowlie in it.[2] And, whosoever shall well consider the Lawes of England, which were before the Conquest (whereof wee have some Remenants, and Patches) or since the Conquest untill *Magna Charta, Anno* 9. H. 3. will make little doubt of it.

In H. 2. time, Glanvile writeth thus, '*Leges Anglicanas licét non scriptas, leges appellari non videtur absurdum.*'

And in H. 3. time Bracton writeth thus; '*Cúm autem feré in omnibus Regionibus utantur legibus & jure scripto, sola Anglia usa est in suis finibus, jure non scripto & consuetudine; in ea quidem, ex non scripto Jus venit, quod usus comprobavit.*'[3]

But I may not agree with Bracton, that '*Sola Anglia usa est jure non scripto*': For I find that the gravest, and the greatest learned Writers of the Civile Lawe, both auncient [34] and of this our time, doe hould the same opinion, touching the Civile Lawe it selfe; for thus they write: '*Ex non scripto Jus venit, quod usus approbavit.*' And thus; '*Jus Civile dictum ex non scripto natum est.*' And, '*Jus non scriptum dicitur Consuetudo, non quod scripto perpetuó careat, hoc enim falsum est. Nam & Consuetudines in memoriam constantiorem reducuntur in Scripturam, ut caetera quoque quae sine scriptura perficiuntur: Sed non scriptum jus est: id est, quód á scriptura vis eius non*

---

[1] 'Magna Carta Regis Johannia', 17 John (1215). An exact quotation with the exception of 'suorum *deleted after* parium' – *ibid.* 11.

[2] His concept of the positive law had changed since his law-school days. Compare this and what follows with his earlier treatise ed. by Thorne, *Discourse*, 103–13.

[3] Probably from his copy of Bracton, Hunt. RB 97059. Ellesmere's definition of the common law was quoted by that zealot of the 'common law mind', Sir John Davies, in the introd. to his *Primer Report*, sig. 2r. The views of Davies, however, differed from those of the Chanc.

coepit nec pendeat.'[1] So, hereby it may appeare how in this we concurre with the Civile Law.

⟪CHAPTER 4⟫ HOW THE COMMON LAW OF ENGLAND MAY BE KNOWNE.

Object. But hereupon these Questionists move an other Question,
viz. If the common Law be not written, how then shall it be knowen?

Respons. To this I answer; It is the common custome of the Realme
(as Bracton saith, '*Jus venit quod usus comprobavit*'): And it [35]
standeth upon two maine pillers and principall parts, by which it is
to bee learned and knowen.

Maximes and Principles.

⟪1.⟫ The first, is certaine knowne Principles and Maximes, and
ancient Customs, against which there never hath been, nor ought
to bee any dispute. As in Cases of Subjects; an estate in Fee-simple,
for life, for yeeres, Dower, Curtesie, and etc.[2]

In cases of the Crowne, the Female to Inherite: The Eldest sone
to be preferred: No respect of Halfe Blood: No Tenant in Dower, or by
the Curtesie of the Crowne: No disabilitie of the Kings person by
Infancie and etc.

Responsa prudentum.

⟪2.⟫ The second is, where there be no such Principles, then, former Judgements given in like Cases: And these be but *Arbitria Judicum, & Responsa Prudentum*, received, allowed, and put in practise and
execution by the Kings authoritie. [36]

Of these Bracton speaketh; '*Ego H. de Bracton animum erexi ad
vetera Judicia justorum perscrutanda; facta ipsorum, Consilia, &
Responsa in unam suminam redigendo compilavi.*'

And before the Conquest, King Ethelbert caused a Booke to bee
made, which was called *Decreta Judiciorum:* And King Alured
⟪Alfred⟫ did the like, as Master Lambard a judicious and learned
observer of Antiquities [Lambard *in explicatione verbi Hyde*], doth
remember.[3]

---

[1] Although the quotation cannot be located, it could have come from Ellesmere's copy of a
tract dedicated to him by Dr William Wade on the civil law, which views Civil law origins and
development in a manner that is similar to that noted here: Ellesm. MS 34/B/44, dated Nov. 1598.

[2] For more exs. of this philosophy of the law see his tract on 'Iudicature'.

[3] The citations in these parags. are to the Year Books, and were probably derived from his
bulky commonplace book: Ellesm. MS 496.

Of these also the Judges speake H. 33. H. 6. Moyle, fo. 8. 'Wee rule the Law according to the auncient course.' Ashton, fol. 9. 'All our Lawe is guided by use, and by Statute.' And Prysot saieth, fol. 9. 'There cannot be a positive Lawe, but such as was judged or made by Statute'. Wherein I note also that hee equalleth a Judgement with a Statute.

In 36. H. 6. fol. 25. Fortescue reasoneth thus; 'The Lawe is as I have said, and so hath beene alwaies since the Lawe began.'

In 37. H. 6. f. 22. Ascue reasons thus; 'Such a Charter hath beene allowable in the time of our [37] Predecessours, which were as sage and learned as we be.'

In H. 4. Edw. 4. fol. 41. Markham reasoneth thus; 'It is good for us to doe as it hath beene used before this time, and not to keepe one way one day for one partie, and another day the contrary for the other partie: And so the former Precedents be sufficient for us to follow.' And Judgement was given accordingly.

And in the former Case 36. H. 6. Fortescue saith further; 'Wee have many Courses and Formes which be houlden for Law.'[1]

Also everie one of these foure principall Courts, The Chancery, Kings Bench, Common-plees, and Eschequer, have in many things severall courses and formes which are observed for Law, and that not onely in that proper Court, but also in all Courtes through the Realme; whereof many Examples bee remembred in the Case of the Mines in Plowdens *Commentaries*.[2]

In novo casu novum remedium.

3. But if there bee no such former [38] Judgements, nor direct Examples or Precedents, then this Rule hath a further extention, which is this.

There is a Rule in the common Law, That *in novo casu novum remedium est apponendum. Et concordent Clerici de Breve faciendo, ita quod nullus recedat a Cancellaria sine remedio*: For the Chauncerie is properly *Officina Justitiae & Aequitatis*; where all originall writs (which in ancient times were the Grounds of all Suites) are devised and framed. And these *Clerici* were grave and ancient men; skilful, and long experienced in the course of the Chauncerie; and called *Clerici de prima forma*: And of late time *Magistri Cancellariae*; who

---

[1] In William Lambarde, *Apxaiouomia sive de priscis anglorum legibus libri* (1568), ff. 82r–9r and 18v–44r, respectively. The Chanc. was fond of citing the old laws, particularly of Ethelbert and Egbert, in his speeches. For ex. Hawarde, *Reportes*, 44–5, 65–6.

[2] They are given extensively in *The Case of Mines* (Exch. 1565), 313–40.

in new and strange cases, besides their owne knowledge and experience, had oftentimes conference with the grave Judges for the
devising and framing of new Writtes when neede required. And
this I take to bee the same which is in the Statute W. 2. ca. 24.
[*Anno* 13 Ed. 1]. '*Et quotiescunque de caetero evenerit in Cancellaria,
quod in uno casu* [39] *reperitur breve, & in consimili casu, cadente sub
eodemjure & simili indigente remedio, non reperitur, Concordent Clerici
de Cancellaria in brevi faciendo, vel atterminent quaerentes in proximum Parliamentum: Et scribantur casus in quibus concordare non
possunt, & referant eos ad proximum parliamentum: Et de consensu
Jurisperitorum fiat Breve, no contingat de caetero, quód Curia Regis
deficiat conquerentibus in Justicia perquirenda.*'[1]

Wherein I note these three things: First, The Clerkes are to agree;
and if they agree, that is an end, and standes for Lawe, and then no
referment to the Parliament. Secondly, If the Clerks agree not, and so
the case be referred to the Parliament; Then *De Consensu Jurisperitorum fiat Breve*; So *Consensus Jurisperitorum* is the Rule, and not the
multitude of vulgar opinions. The third is, That Justice faile not them
which complaine: Which will often faile, if you stay untill a Parliament: For Parliaments are not to be called for the wrong of a few
private Subjects; but for [40] the great and urgent affaires of the King
and the Realme.

I find also a like Rule in the Civile Lawe; *Ubi non est directa lex
standum est arbitrio Judicis, vel producendum ad similia.* And another
saith, *De similibus ad similia judicium & argumentatio recipiuntur.*

Rex solus judicat, &c.

4. Besides these, there is an other generall and certaine Rule in the
Civile Lawe, which I reserve to the last parte of that which I meane to
speake in this Matter.

So, leaving that unto a more proper place, I will hereupon conclude,
That if there bee no former Judgements, nor Examples, nor Precedents
to bee found, then *Concordia Clericorum*, and *Arbitrium Judicum* is to
seeke out the true and solide reason; and thereupon to ground their
Judgements in all new cases: For it was truely said by a learned
Gentleman of the lower House, '*Deficiente lege recurrendum est ad
consuetudinem: Deficiente consuetudine* [41] *recurrendum ad rationem.*'
And so from the Judges wee shall have *Responsa prudentum* to decide all

---

[1] 'Statutes at Westminster', 13 Edward I (1285), chap. 24. This is an exact transcription
except for a few typographical errors – *Stat. Realm* I, 83–4.

such new cases and questions. And according to this Rule, all such new doubts and questions have been resolved and decided by the grave Judges in former times.[1]

A request to the professors of the civile Lawe. But here, before I proceede fruther, I am to make a suite, which is this:

That whatsoever I have spoken, or shall happen to speake of the Civile Lawe; or whatsoever I shall cite out of any Writer of the Law, I pray favour of my Masters that professe it. I acknowledge that Law to bee ancient and generall in many parts of the world; and I reverence the professors of it, as men of great learning, wisedome, and judgement. I professe it not; I have learned little of it; but in that little I have found that in the reall and essentiall partes of Justice, the Civile and common Lawe doe in many things concurre, though they differ much in the [42] forme and maner of proceeding. And that which I shall have occasion to produce of that Law, will bee to shew how the common Law and Civile doe agree in one reason and judgement in those things which I shall speake of.[2]

Yet I must take liberty to say, That neither in Spaine, nor in France (those two great Monarchies) it is not generally received nor allowed as a concluding and binding Law.

They take there the reason of it onely as a direction to their proceeding and Judgement: But to produce or alleadge it as a concluding or binding Law, was no lesse than *Capitis poena*.

This I make not of my selfe; for, besides common practise and experience, I have an honest and substantiall witnesse, Master Adam Blacwood a Scottishman, a man of singular learning in the Civile Lawe, who defendeth in like maner the Lawes of Scotland, as appeareth in his learned Booke intituled *Pro Regibus* [43] *Apologia* [Blackwood ca. 10] written by him against a seditious Dialogue or Libell made by George Buchanan, *De jure regni apud Scotos*,[3] where hee tells him, '*Aliud Sceptrum aliud plectrum*'. But it is not amisse to recite his owne wordes, which are thus; '*Philippus cognomento Pulcher,*

---

[1] His attitude towards the creation of new law through *arbitrium judicium* and *responsa prudentum* dates from his early legal career, and can be explored in his briefs of law cases in the 1570s in Ellesm. MS 482.

[2] Ellesmere had patronised several Civilians, and received a number of dedicatory ms. treatises on the Civil law. A contemp. lawyer noted in his personal copy of the *Post-Nati* the Chanc's dilemma in comparing the common and civil laws: B.M. RB 518.i.2 (2), pp. 42–3.

[3] George Buchanan, *De iure regni apud Scotos dialogus* (Edinburgh 1579). This popular work had appeared in three additional eds. by 1581; cf. H. R. Trevor-Roper, 'George Buchanan and the ancient Scottish constitution', *EHR* Suppl. No. 3 (1966).

*cúm Lutetiae supremae jurisdictionis curiam institueret, eam Romano
jure solutam esse declaravit: in eámque sententiam vetus extat ejus Curiae
decretum, ne causarum patroni Romanarum Legum auctoritatem patriae
legibus opponant. Sed cúm illae bono & aequo niti videntur & probabilem
utilitatis publicae causam continere, nos earum utimur haud imperio, sed
ratione, cui omnes homines naturae praescripto subijciuntur. Quin et si
quid adversus rationem legum Romanarum perperám ac temeré judicatum
est, id earum multis poenis haud aestimatur, sed vel Principis, vel superi-
oris magistratus arbitratu. Nam cúm in publici muneris partem admittimur,
& conceptis verbis inauguramur, solemni sacramento regiarum & munici-
pialium legum atque morum observationem, nulla Romani juris mentione,
spondemus. Apud Hispanos* [44] *capitis poenam ijs indictam legimus qui
Romanarum legum auctoritatem vel in foro laudarent, vel in pulvere
scholastico profiterentur. Sed si quid occurreret patriis legibus ac moribus
indefinitum quod judicanti religionem adferret, unicum erat eximendo
scrupulo regis consulendi remedium. Alaricus Tolosae regnans idem
Gothis imperavit, ut si quis adversus ipsius leges, Civile Romanorum jus
citaret, temeré factum morte lueretur.'* [1]

Recurrend. ad Rationem, &c. Now to returne to that which I have
touched before, I say, that when there is no direct Lawe, nor precise
Example, we must *Recurrere ad rationem, & ad responsa prudentum*:
For, although *Quod lego, non credo*, may be a true and certaine
rule in Divinite; yet for interpretation of Lawes, it is not alwaies so:
For wee must distinguish betweene *fidem moralem*, and *fidem divinam*,
or else wee shall confound many things in the civile and politike governement of Kingdomes and States. For, the first Precedent which we
have now, had no precedent when it began; But as Tacitus [45] saith,
'*Quae nunc vetustissima creduntur nova fuerent, & quod hodie exemplis
tuemur, inter exempla futurum est.*'* [2] And to those that hould, that
nothing is to bee done but by former examples, Horace speaketh thus;
'*O imitatores servum pecus*': And Cicero saith, '*Non exempla majorum
quaerenda, sed consilium est eorum à quibus exempla nata sunt explican-
dum.*'

Thus hath Justice beene duely administred in England, and thereby
the Kings have ruled, the people have beene governed, and the Kingdome hath flourished for many hundred yeeres; and then no such
busie Questionists mooved any quarrell against it.

---

[1] Adam Blackwood, *Adversvs Georgii Bvchanani Dialogvm* (Pictavis 1581). The Chanc. took
several extracts from this, and another Blackwood book, which now comprise Ellesm. MS 2538.

[2] From his endorsed copy of Henry Savile, *The Ende of Nero and Beginning of Galba. Fower
Bookes of the Histories of Cornelivs Tacitvs* (1591), Hunt. RB 69625.

Exposition of Statutes.[1] Thus have all doubts growing upon *Magna Charta*, and *Charta de Foresta*, made in King Henry the thirds time, and upon the Statutes of *West.* 1. *West.* 2. *West.* 3. and many other Statutes made Ed: 1. time: And upon *Prerogativa Regis*, and many other Statutes made in Edw. 2. time, beene from time to time [46] expounded; and so of later times, the Statutes of Fines, of Uses, of Willes, and many moe.

<CHAPTER 5>> EXPOSITION OF LAWES

Thus, also have all doubts and Cases, whereof there was no Statute or positive Law, beene alwaies expounded: for such are most of the cases which wee have in our Yeere-Bookes, and Bookes of Reports, which are in effect nothing but *Responsa prudentum*, as Justice Crooke did truely say.

Lawes obsolete. Upon this reason it is, that some lawes, as well Statute Law, as common Law, are obsolete and worne out of use: for, all humane Lawes are but *Leges temporis*: And the wisedome of the Judges found them to be unmeete for the time they lived in, although very good and necessary for the time wherein they were made. And therefore it is said, '*Leges humanae nascuntur, vigent, & moriuntur, & habent ortum, statum, & occasum.*'[2]

Lawes changed. By this Rule also, and upon this reason it is, that oftentimes ancient Lawes are [47] changed by interpretation of the Judges, as well in Cases criminall as civile.

In criminall cases the lawe was *Voluntas reputabitur pro facto*; but it is not so now, saving in Treason onely.

In an appeale of *Maime* Britton fol. 48. saith, '*Soit le Judgement, que il perde autiel member, come il aver tolle a le plaintife*'; but it is not so now.[3]

In auncient time, one present, aiding, comforting, and assisting to a murder, was taken to be no principall, but an accessorie, as it appeareth M. 40. Edw. 3. fol. 42. & 40. *li. Ass.* p. 8. & p. 25. But now in that case hee is judged a principall. And so it was ruled by all the Justices M. 4. H. 7. 18. and so Plowden affirmeth the Lawe to be, in his *Commentaries* fol. 99. and 100.[4]

[1] This and further sections on the interp. of statutes were cited as auth. in 'a Discourse of ye high courte of parlyment and of ye authoritye of the same' – Add. MS 22.591, ff. 125v–6r.
[2] The basis of his ideas on obsolete law is discussed in Knafla, 'Law Studies', 230–7.
[3] This accords with the original: *Britton*, ed. Francis Morgan Nichols (Oxford, 1865), I, 122–3; and with Ellesmere's own copy, which is Hunt. RB 60508.
[4] 'Matters of the Crown happening at Salop' (GD, 1553), in Plowden, *Commentaries*, 97–101.

In civile causes in ancient time, the lawe was houlden, That he in Remainder in Taile could not have an action of Waste, nor bee received upon default of Tenant for life: But afterwards, the Law was often judged otherwise; and so is [48] the common experience and practise at this day.

In *Anno* 40. Ed. 3. 28. Finchden, chiefe Justice of the common place, saith, that in ancient time the Vicar could not have an Action against the Parson; But hee saieth the contrarie is used at this day, which is the better.

In ancient time a Disseisee could not enter upon the feoffee of the Disseisor, for saving of the warrantie; but for many yeeres the Lawe hath beene houlden otherwise, and so the common practise yet remaineth.

Construction of words. By this Rule it is also, that words are taken and construed, sometimes by Extension; sometimes by Restriction; sometimes by Implication; somtimes a Disjunctive for a Copulative; a Copulative for a Disjunctive; the present tense for the future; the future for the present; sometimes by equity out of the reach of the wordes; sometime words taken in a contrary sence; sometime figuratively, as *Continens pro* [49] *contento*, and many other like: And of all these, examples be infinite, aswell in the Civile lawe as Common lawe.[1]

Judges consulted with the privie Counsell.

And oftentimes the reverend Judges have had such a grave regard in their proceeding, that before they would resolve, or give judgement in such new cases, they desired to consult with the Kinges privie Counsell; as appeares in diverse cases in king Ed. 3. his time.

R. W. assaulted Adam Brabson in presence of the Justices of Assise at Winchester, [39 Ed. 3. li. as. p. 1], for which A. B. complained by Bill before the saide Justices, alledging this offence to bee in despite of the King and his Justices, to his dammage of an hundred pounds. R. W. pleaded, Not guiltie; and was found guiltie, and dammages taxed to tenne pounds. Thereupon the Judges awarded him to prison in the Sherifes keeping. And for the Fine, and that which should be further done for the King, for the assault done in the presence of the Judges, they would have the [50] advise of the Kings Counsell: For in a like case, [M. 19 Ed. 3. Judgement 174], because

---

[1] Based on the *Discourse*, 123–9.

R. C. did strike a Jurour at Westminster, which passed in an Enquest against one of his friends, It was adjudged by all the Counsell, 'that his right hand should be cut off; and his lands and goodes forfeited to the King'. These bee the words in the Booke.[1]

In this case I note three things.

1. The Judges consulted with the Counsell.

2. They had a like Case before when the Counsell was also consulted with, *vis. Anno* 19. E. 3. and yet they would not proceede in this case before they had againe consulted with the Counsell.

3. That before *Anno* 19. Ed. 3. there was no like case nor precedent for such a Judgement; And therefore the Judges would not of themselves pronounce that heavy Judgement before they had conferred with the Counsell touching the same. And after they had the opinion [51] and advise of the Kinges Counsell, they proceeded to that Judgement.

Thomas Ughtred Knight, brought a *Forme-done* against a poore man and his wife; [M. 39 Ed. 3. 35]. They came and yeelded to the Demaundant, which seemed suspitious to the Court: whereupon they examined the Matter, and staied Judgement, because it was suspitious. And Thorpe saied, that in the like Case of Giles Blacket it was spoken of in Parliament:'And wee were commaunded, that when any like Case should come, we should not go to judgement without good advise. Wherefore sue to the Counsell, and as they will have us to doe, wee will; and otherwise not, in this Case.'

Greene and Thorpe were sent by the Judges [M. 40 Ed. 3. 34] to the Kings Counsel (where there were 24. Bishops and Earles) to demand of them, whether by the Statute 14. Ed. 3. *ca*. 6. a word may be amended in a Writ, [52] aswel as a letter or a sillable: for, the statute speakes but of a letter or a sillable; and it was answered, That it may well be amended; For, there can not bee a Word without a Sillable; and that it was a nice Question of so sage men.[2]

Thus *Arbitria Judicum*, and *Responsa prudentum* have beene received, allowed, and reverenced in all times as Positive Lawe; and so it must be still; For, otherwise much mischiefe and greate inconvenience will ensue: for new cases happen every day: No lawe ever was, or ever can be made that can provide remedie for all future cases; or

---

[1] The cases out of the plea rolls cited here and below are probably extracted from his commonplace book, Ellesm. MS 496.

[2] 'Statute the First', 14 Edward III (1340), chap. 6. The statute was quite explicit – only a syllable or a letter: *Stat. Realm* I, 283.

comprehend all circumstances of humane actions which Judges are to determine: Therefore, when such happen, and complaint is made; what shall Judges doe? Shall they give no remedie to the partie grieved? Shall they stay for a Parliament? *Interim patitur justus.* They must therefore follow *Dictamen rationis*; [Judges to be directed by reason and discretion]; and so give speedie justice. And in [53] many matters of materiall circumstances they must guide themselves by discretion.

As in judging upon Presumptions; To discerne which be *Praesumptiones temerariae*, which *Probabiles*, which *Violentae*.

So for Time; what is a convenient Time, and what not.

So for Waste; what is Waste punishable, and what not.

So for Tenders of money; what is a convenient place for tender of mony, and what not: and what is a lawfull Tender, and what not.

So for Disparagement; what is a disparagement, and what not: And so of other the like cases, which are infinite.

That the common Lawe is uncerten

Object. If it be said (for so some have said) That if this be thus, then the common Lawe of England is uncerten; and so the rule of Justice, by which the people are governed, is too pliable, and too weake, and uncerten. [54]

Respons. By the same reason it may be said, That all the Lawes of all nations are uncerten: For, in the Civile Lawe, which is taken to be the most universall and generall Lawe in the world, they hould the same rule and order in all cases which be out of the direct words of the Lawe; and such cases bee infinite: For, as I saied, new cases spring every day as malice and fraude increaseth. And since the Roman Empire beganne, most of their Lawes be either *Edicta Principum*, or *Arbitria Judicum*, or *Responsa prudentum*. And in their Judgements they are guided by Arrests and former Judgements, as may appeare in the books of many that have collected such Arrests. And they attribute so much to such former Judgements, That as Prysot equalleth them to a Positive Lawe, so they hould, That *Sententia facit Jus, & res judicata pro veritate accipitur, & legis interpretatio legis vim obtinet.*

Nay (which is more uncerten) sometimes they relie upon Doctours opinions [55] delivered in their Prelections and Treatises. And when they finde them varying, and differing one from another (as sometimes they doe) then they preferre that which is *Communior opinio*: And so in good reason they may: For, *Pluralitas idem sentientium semper superat*; *quia facilius invenitur quod à pluribus quaeritur.*

But to conclude this point, I would aske of these Novelists, what they would have done in Sibill Belknappes case, if they had lived in Henry the fourths time?[1]

Sir Robert Belknappe, that reverend and learned Judge, of whome sundrie noble and worthie persons, and some now of great and eminent place in England are descended, was banished out of the Realme, (*Relegatus in Vasconiam,*) not for any desert or offence of his, but by the might of his potent enemies, and malice of the time. The Lady his wife continued in England; she was wronged; she brought a Writ in her owne Name alone, not naming her Husband. Exception was taken against [56] it, because her husband was living; and it was adjudged good, and she recovered: and the Judge Markeham said: '*Ecce modo mirum quòd foemina fert Breue Regis, Non nominando virum conjunctum robore legis.*' [M. 2 H. 4. 7.]

Here was a rare and a new case, yet it was not deferred untill a Parliament: it was judged, and her wrong was righted by the common Law of England, and that *Ex arbitrio Judicum & ex responsis prudentum*, and yet it was counted *Mirum* with an *Ecce.*

Now to applie this to R. Calvines case: his case is rare and new; so was that: There is no direct Law for him in precise and expresse tearmes: There was never Judgement before touching any borne in Scotland since King James beganne his happie raigne in England: Hee is the first that is brought in question: So there was no direct Lawe for Sibill Belknap to sue in her owne name without her husband, who [57] was then living: nay rather there was direct Lawe against it; yet by the Lawe of England shee had Judgement to recover with an *Ecce modo mirum*: So by the Lawe of England Judgement ought to be given for Robert Calvine, but not with an *Ecce modo mirum*; but upon strong Arguments deduced à *similibus*, and *ex dictamine rationis.*

«CHAPTER 6» NOTE FOURE FORMES OF INTERPRETATION OF LAWES.

But before I come to those arguments, I wil use a few words more touching some Rules which I have read, for the interpretation of Lawes.

---

[1] *Rotuli Parliamentorum*, 1 Henry IV (1400), 442.

There is a grave and learned Writer in the Civile Lawe that setteth downe foure wayes and formes of interpretation of Lawes: That is, first, *Interpretatio historica*; secondly, *Etymologica*; thirdly, *Analogica*; fourthly, *Practica*.

In the Argument of this Case all these formes have been used, and largely handled: and the two first be those that seeme but light to me, and therefore in mine [58] opinion have beene too much stood upon, and over-weighed.

Historica.

For the Historicall Interpretation, it is alwaies darke, obscure, and uncerten, of what kingdome, country, or place soever you speake; I doe alwayes and onely except the divine Histories written in the Bible.[1]

Livy saith, '*In tanta rerum vetustate multi temporis errores implicantur.*'

Saint Augustine speaking of the supposed bookes of Henoch, saith, '*Libri isti ob nimiam antiquitatem reijciuntur.*'

Wherefore, for this part let this suffice, whether in the beginning there were one or severall kingdomes in great Britaine; or one or severall Monarchs and Kings of these two great and famous King-domes in great Britaine. The King our Soveraigne is lawfully and lineally descended of the first great Monarchs and Kings of both the Kingdomes; [Fergus. Inas.] and that by so long a continued line of lawfull discent, as [59] therein hee exceedeth all the Kings that the World now knoweth; and therefore to inquire further of Historicall knowledge in this Case, I hould it needlesse.[2]

Etymologica.

For the Etymologicall Interpretation, there hath beene very much said, even as much as Wit and Art could devise: There have beene alleaged many Definitions, Descriptions, Distinctions, Differences, Divisions, Subdivisions, Allusion of wordes, Extension of wordes, Construction of words; and nothing left unsearched to finde what is

---

[1] This statement does not accord with the facts. Ellesmere had collected several histories and occasionally annotated them. Two of the most prominent were his autog. copies of Henry Savile's *The Ende of Nero* (1591), Hunt. RB 69625; and a ms. history of Eng. from the beginnings to 1591 that lacks a title page: Ellesm. MS 34/B/26.

[2] He noted the history of the royal descent in a brief for this speech dated June 1608: Ellesm. MS 1872, f. 3r.

Ligeantia, Allegiantia, Fides, Obedientia, Subjectio, Subditi; And who be *Aborigines, Indigenae, Alienigenae, Adventicii, Denizati &c*. And much of this hath beene drawne out of some Writers of the Civile Lawe; amongst whom the Etymologicall Interpretation of the words *Ligeus*, and *Ligeantia*, is as uncerten and doubtfull, as it is with our common Lawyers; And so upon any of these there cannot be any certen Rule found for [60] Judges to judge by, especially in new and rare Cases.[1]

As for Definition, Ulpian teacheth us, '*Ominis definitio in jure Civile est periculosa:*' and it is said, that '*Definitio est duplex: Propria, quae constat ex genere, & differentia: Impropria, quae & descriptio vocatur, & est quaelibet rei designatio:*' So Definition and Description are often confounded, and both uncerten. Then, since both be uncerten and dangerous, I will leave both and seeke a more certen Rule to judge by.

As for Etymologie of words, I agree with him which saieth, It is *Levis & fallax, & plerumque ridicula*. It is a Pedant Grammarians fault. Marcus Varro and others have beene noted for it. And if you examine the Examples which some doe bring, you will perceive how ridiculous and vaine it is: So this Rule will not serve to finde out that which wee seeke for: These bee but *Tendiculae verborum, & Aucupationes syllabarum* as one calleth them:[2] It may have some use and [61] serve a turne in Schooles, but it is too light for Judgements in Lawe, and for the seates of Justice.

Aquinas setteth downe a more certen Rule, '*In vocibus videndum, non tàm à quo quàm ad quid sumantur.*' And wordes should bee taken *Sensu currenti*: for Use and Custome is the best Expositor both of Lawes and Wordes; *Quem penes arbitrium & jus & norma loquendi.*

Wherefore, of the many and diverse distinctions, divisions, and subdivisions, that have beene made in this Case, I will say no more but, *Confusum est quicquid in pulverem sectum est*: and will conclude with Bishop Juel; 'A man may wander and misse his way in Mists of Distinctions.'

Ligeantia sensu currenti est vinculum fidei &c. Then leaving these Historicall and Etymologicall Interpretations, and these curious and

---

[1] He had examined much of this at length in his *Discourse, passim*.

[2] The Chanc. appears to be referring to the caution and advice of John Florio, who dedicated two of his major works to him: *Florio's Second Frutes* (1591), and *A Worlde of Words* (1598). See esp. the dedicatory ms. letter that is quoted in full in Sotheby and Co., *Catalogue of the remaining portion of the Bridgewater Library* (1951), 20.

subtile Distinctions and Divisions, I say, *Ligeantia*, or *Allegiantia* understood *Sensu currenti*, is '*vinculum fidei & obedientiae*,' as Justice Daniel said well. And [62] hee that is borne in any of the Kings Dominions, and under the Kings obedience, is the Kings liege subject, and borne *Ad fidem Regis* (for that is the proper and ancient word which the Law of England hath used; *Ad fidem Regis Angliae, Ad fidem Regis Franciae*) and therefore hee can not bee a Stranger or *Alien* to the King, or in any of his Kingdomes; and by consequence is inhabled to have lands in England, and to sue, and be sued in any Reall action for the same.[1]

And *Ligeantia* hath sometimes a more large Extension: For, hee that is an *Alien* borne out of the Kings Dominions, under the obedience of another King, if hee dwell in England, and be protected by the King and his Lawes, hee oweth to the King the duetie of Allegeance; and so he is *Ligatus Regi*, and *Ligeus Regis*: and if hee commit treason, the Indictment shall be *Contra ligeantiae suae debitum*, as it was in Shirley the French-mans case: yet is hee not the Kings subject: for, hee was not borne [63] *Ad fidem Regis*; But, this is not that Ligeance which wee must finde: For, in a true and lawfull subject, there must be *Subjectio, fides, & obedientia*; and those cannot be severed, no more than true Faith and Charitie in a true Christian. And he that hath these three *à Nativitate* is *Ligeus Regis*, and can not be a Stranger or *Alien* to the King, or in his Kingdomes. And that it is so, may be proved by the Rule of the other two Interpretations of Lawe; That is, *Analogica, & Practica*.

Analogica.

King James hath now the Kingdomes of England, Scotland, and Ireland, and the Isles of Gernsey, and Jersey by discent; all these bee his Dominions, and under his subjection and obedience.

King Henry the second had England and Normandy by discent, from his mother Mawd the Empresse; and Anjow, and Maine by discent from his father Geffery Plantagenet; and Ireland by conquest.

Henry the third had England and Ireland [64] by discent from his Grand-father Henry the second: and Aquitany by discent from his Grand-mother Queene Elenor wife to king Henry the second, and daughter to the duke of Aquitany.

---

[1] The Chanc. gave considerable time to the problem of aliens because several legal opinions held that aliens could not inherit land in England. For ex. the tract often falsely attributed to Robert Cotton, a copy of which is in Harl. MS 293 at f. 179r.

Edward the first had all the same by discent; and part of Scotland by Conquest.

Edward the second, and Edward the third had all the same by discent also: and besides, Edward the third claimed all France by discent from his mother Queene Isabell, and had the most part of it in possession; and so had Henry the fift and Henry the sixt also.[1]

Now if in these kings times, Subjects borne in those Countries, being then under their obedience, were no *Aliens*, but capable of Lands in England: And if at this time subjects borne in Ireland, or Gernsey, and Jersey be no *Aliens*, but capable of Lands in England; then, by an Analogicall Interpretation, why should not subjects borne in Scotland be at this time in like [65] degree? For, in proportion, and in likenesse, and conveniencie, there can bee no difference at all.

⟪CHAPTER 7⟫ PRACTICA: & SIC AD SIMILIA.[2]

But whether the subjects borne in those Countries in the time of those kings were then capable of Lands in England as naturall subjects; or were deemed *Aliens*, is the Question: and therein *Interpretatio Practica* is to be considered; and so the case is brought to be examined *per similia*. And in Divinitie, *Praxis sanctorum est interpres praeceptorum*.

Now then the Question is, Whether the Kings Subjects of England and Scotland, that be *Post-nati*, may be resembled to the Kings subjects of Ireland, and the Isles of Gernsey, and etc. as now they bee: and to the Subjects of Normandie, Anjow, and Gascoyne, and parte of Scotland in former times, when the same were the Dominions, and under the obedience of the king of England: (for I speake alwaies, and would be understood of kingdomes and [66] dominions in possession, and under obedience, and not of those whereunto the King hath right, but hath no possession or obedience.) I hould, that in all points materiall concerning this Question they are alike, thogh not in all

---

[1] The history and genealogy of this period, if not Ellesmere's account, is quite accurate. The source for much of it was probably Francis Thynne, whom the Chanc. had patronized from an early date. The ms. copies of Thynne's histories that were presented to Ellesmere are Ellesm. MSS 1137 and 34/B/12.

[2] The major source for the historical precedents concerning France, Normandy, Anjou, Gascony, and Ireland (pp. 231–41) appears to be a treatise on 'Vnions of states be of different natures', L.I. Maynad MS 83, item. no. 3. Ellesmere's notes from this appear on two separate loose leaves lodged between ff. 6–7. The issues were outlined by a clerk for the Chancellor in Ellesm. MS 1215, and the Chanc. noted his objections on each issue in the margins of the paper. Notes on the historical args. are at f. 1r–v.

things: (for, then it were *Idem*, and not *Simile:*) and this can not be
better understoode, than by examining the Objections to the contrarie: which in substance may be reduced to foure in number.

Ireland. Object. I. [1] First for Ireland, it was gotten by Conquest,
and the Conquerour may impose what Lawes hee will upon them:
But it is otherwise of kingdomes comming by discent.

Respons. This is a conceipted difference, and lacks the foundation of Reason, and hath not the true parts of a difference: for those
that are borne in Ireland, and those that are borne in Scotland, are
all alike for their birth within the Kings Dominions, and [67] are
borne under the like subjection and obedience to the King, and have
the like bond; Nay, even the same bond of Allegiance; That is, they
are borne *Ad fidem Regis*.

Besides, where it is said, The Conquerour may impose what Lawes
hee will: Then consider how it was in the *Interim* before king John
gave Lawes to Ireland.

Nay, which is more, I aske whether the Conquerour of Ireland can
give new Lawes to England, and make Irishmen to be as naturall
borne subjects in England (if their birth-right doe not give it them)
which before the Conquest they were not? for, that is properly the
Question: But if any difference be, the Case of descent is the stronger:
For, (as Justice Yelverton said) That is by an undoubted Title made
by lawe; the other by a doubtfull Title wonne by the Sword.

France. [2] But leave Ireland gotten by Conquest; what say you to
the great kingdome of [68] France; which Edward the third had first
in right by lawfull descent, and after in possession by triumphant
Conquest; and which Henry the sixt held after in possession by
descent? Was ever doubt made, whether the subjects borne there so
long as it was in subjection and obedience to the king were capable of
Lands in England?

I will now turne the Case, and aske an other question; If King
James our Soveraigne had first beene king of England by lawfull

---

[1] Ellesmere's outlines of the four objections which are presented and answered here at pp.
232–5, are in Ellesm. MS 1215, ff. 1–3v.

[2] The Chanc's interp. of the status of the inhabitants of the Continental lands of the English
monarch (pp. 233–8) were derived perhaps from Sir John Dodderidge: 'A brief consideration of
the vnion of twoe Kingdomes in the handes of one Kinge', Sloane MS 3479, ff. 59–67. The
theme, however, was that of K. James himself. It formed the basis of his arg. in his first speech to
Parl. on 19 March 1603/4 (James, *Works*, 269–80), a copy of which the Chanc. obtained for his
library: Hunt. RB 145923. James also spoke on the subject at length in his 'contemptuous' speech
to Parl. of one and a half hours on 18 Nov. 1606: *Bowyer diary*, 185.

descent (as now hee is) and after Scotland had descended unto him, should not the Subjects of Scotland (I speake still of *Post-nati*) have beene judged as Naturall subjects in England, as those of France were in Ed. 3. time?

Then, he having now both kingdomes by lineall, true, and lawfull descent, it can make no difference touching the capacitie of subjects, which kingdome descended to him first, and which second; but both are to him alike. And it is cleere, [69] *Post-nati* in England are now capable and inheritable in Scotland, though some have made a causelesse and needelesse doubt of it: and so on the other side those of Scotland are in England.

Normandy, and Aquitany. Object. 2. It is saide Normandie and Aquitany were no Monarchies or Kingdomes, but Dukedomes or Seigniories in Fraunce, and holden of the Crowne of France, and therfore not to be resembled to Scotland, which is an ancient and absolute kingdome.

Respons. This Objection reacheth not to the reason of our Question: For, bee they kingdomes, be they Seigniories, yet the subjects borne there, were borne out of the kingdome of England, and so in that respect Aliens: But in that they were borne within the kings dominions, and under his subjection and obedience, they were no Aliens, but liege and naturall borne subjects to the King; and so capable and inheritable in England. [70]

I say besides, the dukes of Normandie and Aquitany were absolute Princes, and had soveraigne power in those countries, although they did not beare the name of Kings; as at this time the duke of Savoy; the duke of Florence; the duke and state of Venice; and of late, the great duke of Russia; the duke of Burgundy; the Archduke of Austria, and etc.

So the difference in Stile and Name makes no difference in Soveraignty: For, king Henry the eight had as absolute soveraignetie in Ireland, when his Stile was Lord of Ireland, as when hee changed his Stile, and was called King of Ireland.[1]

And to say, That the Tenure of the Crowne of Fraunce should give any priviledge to them of Normandy and Aquitany in England is a strange conceipt; It might rather be objected against them. But, as I

---

[1] The question of style hinged on the concept of sovereignty, and it was one of the more contentious areas of debate. See the account, for ex. of the debate in Parl. and among the commissioners in Harl. MS 292, f. 136r–v, and the short treatise in Harl. MS 1300, ff. 147–50r.

saide before, they were borne within the Kings dominions, and under his obeisance, and therefore as subjects borne in England. [71]

And if men may beleeve some ancient Stories, Aquitany and Normandy had sometimes kings, and were kingdomes of themselves: and not depending nor subject to the Crowne of France: and the kingdome of France was then a small portion of Gallia, and but a little one, in comparison of that which it is at this day. And some say, that there were foure and twentie kings in Gaule: But as the kings of France increased in power and strength, they subdued their neighbor-Princes, and so that kingdome grew to that greatnesse that now it is at; even as the Heptarchie in England was dissolved, and made an intier kingdome, when one of the kings mightier than the rest subdued his Neighbours.

The Crowne and great seale of England. Object. 3. [1] It is said further, that Normandy and Aquitany, were subjects to the Crowne of England; and to the great Seale of England; but so is not Scotland: *Ergo* and etc.

Respons. This standeth not wel with that which [72] was objected before; That they were but Seigniories houlden of the Crowne of Fraunce. And it is true, that before Edward the thirds time, those kings of England that held those great Seigniories, did acknowledge, that they held the same of the Crowne of Fraunce.

But these Objections be light, and not worth the time that hath beene spent about them. The Soveraignety is in the person of the King; the Crowne is but an Ensigne of Soveraignty; the Investure and Coronation are but Ceremonies of honor, and majestie: the King is an absolute and perfect king before he be crowned, and without those Ceremonies. [2]

The Seale is to be altered and changed at the will and pleasure of the King: hee may have one, hee may have many, as pleaseth him. The King did use Queene Elizabeths Seale, for diverse moneths after his comming into England. Queene Elizabeth used king Philips and queene Maries seale for a time; and queene Marie [73] used king Edwards seale: And all that was so done, was well and lawfully done. Many things were done by ancient kings of England before the Conquest by their signature, and signe manuell without anie seale at all; and some such since the Conquest also: as Graunts made by Maude the Empresse to Albericke de Vere, and others. [3]

---

[1] This section was expanded in his tract on the 'Prerog.'
[2] The absolute aspect of the K's person was developed in the 'Prerog.', ff. 3r–4r.
[3] Probably from John Kitchin's *Le Covrt Leete, et Court Baron* (1580), STC 15017.

The King may by his great seale commaund all his Subjects that bee under his obedience wheresoever they bee in the world: So he did in Normandy; so he did in Aquitany; so he did in that part of Scotland that he had in possession: And in 24. Edw. 1. his Judges kept ordinarie Courts of justice there: and I have seene the Records of *Placita Exercitus Regis apud Edinburgh, Apud Roxburgh, Apud S. Johns-Towne, &c. in Scotia.* So hee may commaund his subjects, if they be in France, Spaine, Rome, or Turkie, or the Indies. And for severall seales, the Earle of Chester had a speciall seale for that his ancient County Palatine: The Duke of Lancaster had a speciall seale [74] for his new County Palatine. And after, when these Countries came to the kinges possession, the Kinges continued severall seales in them both for the administration of justice; but as subordinate to the great seale of England.[1]

And I make little doubt, but if the King shall now command any of his subjects of Scotland under his great seale of England, they will (as they ought) duetifully obey him: As in Edward the 1. Edward the 2. and Edward the 3. times they commaunded many of the Lords of that parte of Scotland which then was under their obedience.

I finde, that in 13. Edw. 2. *quarto die Junii*, the King *Constituit Adomarum de Valentia comitem Pembrochiae Custodem Regni sui; ac locum suum tenentem quamdiu Rex in partibus transmarinis moram fecerit.* And the next day, *viz. Die Jovis quinto die Junii Rex ordinavit, quod magnum Sigillum suum remaneret clausum in aliquo loco securo, dum Rex esset in partibus* [75] *transmarinis: Et ordinavit quoddam aliud paruum Sigillum interim pro regimine Regni, ad brevia, &c. Consignanda, sub Teste Adomari de Valentia Comitis Pembroch. Nota,* heere was a petty seale *pro regimine Regni,* wherein are comprised Commissions for Justice, *Mandatoria, & ad brevia consignanda*; which is for *Remedialia* as they are tearmed.

Several Laws. Object. 4. It is saide, that Scotland hath Lawes that are proper for that kingdome, and that they are not subject to the Lawes of England, and so *è contra.*

And lastly it was saide, that in England every person was within the jurisdiction of some Leete, and at the age of twelve yeeres every one is to bee sworne in the Leete to be Foyall and Loyall to the King of England; That is, to the Lawes of England, (for so hee understoode

---

[1] The distinction made between the Crown and the seal was applauded by one observer as a very important distinction: Tanner MS 75, f. 16v. The subject is developed further *infra*, pp. 244–5, 254–8.

Loyall:) But *Post-nati* in Scotland can not be so; and that they have another forme of Oath in Scotland: *Ergo, &c.* [76]

Respons. For this last part, of the oathe in the Leete, the Lord chiefe Baron did cleare it so plainely, as more needes not to be saide. This is '*Legalis ligeantia*', It is not *Alta ligeantia* by birth, which is that which we have now in Question.

The Historicall discourse that hath bin made of Leetes, of Law-dayes, of *Decenna, Decennarii*, of the Tenne-mens Tale, and the Oathe of all Male children of twelve yeeres, and etc. taken at the Leete, is no newes indeede, it is very olde.[1]

Master Lambard hath it all, and more too, at large *in Explicatione verborum* in the word *Centuria*; It was before the Conquest.[2]

But it maketh nothing to this naturall Allegeance and subjection of birth; it is not *Alta ligeantia* by birth-right; it is but *Legalis ligeantia* by Policie. And Fitzherbert calleth it 'Swearing to the Lawe'.

And if that were the onely Bond and Marke of Allegeance, many are out of it, and so at libertie: As, children under [77] twelve yeeres; yet sometimes they may commit treason and felony; where, *Malitia supplet ætatem*; So women of all sortes; yet they may be shrewd and dangerous traitours; and if they bee women nobly borne, or widowes that were wives to noble men, they shall be tried *per pares*:

Also Noble men of all sortes, who are neither bound to attend the Leete, nor to take that Oathe, as appeareth by Britton cap. 29. treating of the Court called *The Shirifes Turne*, out of which the Leete seemeth to be extracted: For, whatsoever is not presented in the Leete may be presented and punished in the Shirifs Turne. And M. Kitchin citeth Britton in this point for the Leete; and alleadgeth also the statute of *Marlebridge* cap. 10. to the same purpose.[3]

And at this day the view of Francke-pleges and the putting in of Francke-pleges, and the *Decennarii*, are but bare names of things past, the use and substance is obsolete and gone. [78]

And, as it was saide, few in this place have put in such Pleges, or taken that Oath, and yet I trust wee are good subjects, and beare true faith and allegeance.

But this hath beene so fully answered and cleared by the Lord chiefe Baron, and the Lord Coke, chiefe Justice of the Common pleas, as I doe wrong to spend time in it.

[1] Probably from Kitchin, *Le Covrt Leete.*
[2] William Lambarde, *Apxaionomia sive de priscis anglorum legibus libri* (1568), *s.v. Centuria.*
[3] Kitchin, *Covrt Leete.*

But touching the severall Lawes; I say, that severall lawes can make no difference in Matter of Soveraignetie; and in the bond of Allegeance and obedience to one King: And so it concludeth nothing for the point in question.[1]

Normandy and Aquitany had severall lawes differing from the lawes of England: so had France in king Edward the 3. and Henry the 6. time.

Ireland, before king Johns time continued their ancient lawes, and so, for the most part, have done ever since.

Gernesey and Jersey have yet at this day [79] severall lawes, which, for the most part, were the ancient laws and customes of Normandy.

Wales had, and in many things yet have severall lawes: so for the Countie Palatine of Chester also.

Yet these never were, nor must not be cancelled and cut off from their allegeance and obedience to the King; nor the Kings subjects borne there be incapable of Lands and Inheritance in England: for where there is but one Soveraigne, all his subjects borne in all his Dominions be borne *Ad fidem Regis*; and are bound to him by one bond of Faith and Allegeance: And in that, one is not greater nor lesser than an other; nor one to bee preferred before an other: but all to be obedient alike; and to be ruled alike; yet under severall lawes and customes. And as Saint Gregorie saieth of the Church, *In una fide nihil officit Ecclesiae sanctae diversa consuetudo*. So I will conclude for this point, That diversitie of Lawes and Customs makes no [80] breach of that unitie of obedience, faith, and allegeance, which all liege subjects owe to their liege King and Soveraigne Lord. And as none of them can be aliens to the King, so none of them can bee aliens or Strangers in any of his kingdomes or dominions; nor Aliens or Strangers one to another, no more than a Kentish-man, to a Cheshire-man; or *è contra*.

And therefore all that have bin borne in any of the kinges Dominions since he was kinge of England are capable and inheritable in all his Dominions without exception.

Defect of Triall.[2] And as to the other part of the Objection, that there will be defect of triall; for, things done in Scotland, cannot bee

---

[1] The discussion which follows (pp. 237–45) on the customs and laws of Normandy and Aquitaine; Jersey, Guernsey, and Ireland; and Kent, Cheshire, and Wales accords rather closely with our historical understanding of them today.

[2] This too was a contentious issue, and the Chanc. appears to have discounted the actual problems. That the differences were not great was shown by a later tract: Sloane MS 1786, ff. 100–4v.

tried in England; I say, that that maketh little to our present Question, whether *Post-nati* in Scotland bee Aliens in England, and not capable of landes in England: but it trencheth to cast some aspersion upon the common lawe of England; That [81] it is not sufficient to give justice to the kinges subjects for lacke of sufficient meanes of triall of questions of fact: but to this baron Altham gave so full an answeare, as more cannot bee saied: And so he did both cleare the doubt, and did uphould the sufficiency of the lawe of England in that behalfe. And it seemeth strange, that this should now bee found out to bee objected against Scotland, since it was never heeretofore objected for France, Normandie, Aquitany, nor is at this day for Ireland, Gernesey, and Jersey and etc. whereas all stand upon the same reason for the point of Triall. But the wisedome of the lawe of England hath beene such, as there never failed certen rules for triall of all questions in fact; and those were fitted and adapted to the Matter which was to bee tryed. And therefore, whosoever doth diligently observe it, he shall finde in the course and practise of the lawes of England above twenty severall formes of Trialls: as by Battell; by Jurie, and that [82] in diverse kindes; by Wager of Lawe; by Proofes; by Examination; by Inspection; by Certificates of diverse kindes; and by manie other waies: And lest there should bee any defect in that behalfe the lawe hath provided severall formes of joining of issues; and in that, hath speciall regarde of things done out of the Realme, as every Student may see in the bookes of Reports.

Thus I have passed these foure Objections, and therefore for this part I conclude, That if *Argumentum à simili* were ever good and concludent in Lawe, my Lords the Judges have prooved this Case by so many plaine and direct Examples, and like Cases; and by so many stronge arguments and solide reasons drawne out of booke Cases, out of Statutes, out of the true rules and forme of pleading, and out of ancient Records and Precedents, some produced by M. Atturney, and many moe remembred by the Judges, as no [83] one thing can be more plainely exemplified, nor appeare more like to an other, than this Case is to those Cases which they have remembred.

《 CHAPTER 8 》 ARGUMENT BY REASON

Recurrend. ad Rationem. But if examples and arguments *à simili doe faile*, then it remaineth *Recurrere ad Rationem*; and what reason that ought to bee, and how to bee understoode, is to be considered: for, it

---

[1] In add. see Ellesmere's copy of T. B., 'Obseruations Politicall and Civill', Ellesm. MS 1174, ff. 46–85.

is said, that '*Lex est ratio summa jubens ea quae facienda sunt, &
prohibens contraria*'. So it must be the depth of reason, not the light
and shallow distempered reasons of common discoursers walking in
Powles, or at Ordinaries in their feasting and drinking, drowned with
drincke, or blowne away with a whiffe of Tobacco. Lucretius noteth,
that in many there is '*Rationis egestas*': And saint Gregory saith, '*Qui
in factis Dei rationem non videt, infirmitatem suam considerans cur non
videat, rationem videt*': For, although Reason and Knowledge bee
infinite, yet no man can have more of it than he is capable of: Every
man must receive it, and keepe it [84] in his owne vessell; he cannot
borrow his Neighbours braine-pan to put it in. And therefore it is not
without cause, that one of the gravest and best learned lawyers of our
age, and a privie Counsellor to one of the greatest Monarches of
Europe, describeth those that should bee Interpreters of lawes by
foure speciall qualities [*Hopperus de vera Juris prudentia*. pag. 118],
That is 1. *Aetate graves*, 2. *Eruditione praestantes*, 3. *Usu rerum
prudentes*, 4. *Publica authoritate constituti*: So, there must be gravitie,
there must be learning, there must be Experience, and there must be
authoritie: and if any one of these want, they are not to bee allowed
to bee Interpreters of the lawe.[1]

How all these qualities concurre in these reverend Judges, whome
wee have heard in this present Case, I will spare to speake what I
thinke: For, Chrysostome teacheth mee, '*Qui laudatur in facie,
flagellatur in corde.*'

In seeking out this depth of Reason, [85] the same Author giveth a
caution, which is this; '*Vitium quod in hoc genere fugi debet est, ne, si
Rationem non invenias, mox legem sine ratione esse clames.*'[2] [*Hopperus*
ibid. pag. 119]. And in 36. H. 6. Fortescue saieth the same in effect,
which is thus; 'Wee have many Courses and Formes which bee houlden for Lawe, and have beene houlden and used because of Reason;
and notwithstanding the reason bee not ready in memory, yet by
studie and labour a man may finde it.'

Now when wee come to examine by reason, whether *Post-nati* in
Scotland shall be disabled as aliens, or shall bee capable of lands in
England, as naturall borne subjects there;[3] wee are first to consider
what is the reason why aliens in the Dominions, and under the

---

[1] Taken accurately from Joachim Hopper, *Sedvardus, sive De Vera Ivrisprvdentia* (Antwerp
1590); more generally, see pp. 117–24 of Hopper.

[2] *Ibid.* 119.

[3] A source for this subject appears to be a small tract entitled: 'That those born in England
and Scotland before the Kings coming to this crown are by law naturalized in either Kingdom',
L.I. Maynard MS 83, item no. 8.

obedience of other forraine Princes, are not capable of lands in
England: And surely the true reason is, that which was noted by baron
Altham; and hath since bin ofte remembred, *viz.* The danger that
might thereby come to the King and the common-weale: Specially
[86] by drawing hither too great multitudes of them: for so the
Treasure of the realme might be transported by them into other forraine Kingdomes and Countries; whereby it might bee used against
the King, and to the prejudice of the State. And besides, they might
under-hand practise Sedition and Rebellion in the kingdome, and
cause many other dangers and inconveniences: but that reason cannot
serve against *Post-nati* in Scotland, now that there is but one king of
both the kingdomes, no more than it can serve against those that are
borne in Ireland, or Gernesey, or Jersey: and therefore in reason they
are as capable of landes in England as the kings subjects of Ireland,
and Gernesey, and Jersey are.

Objections.[1]   Against this, there have also been many Objections
made, and Reasons devised that seeme witty, and have some shew
of probabilitie to prove that *Post-nati* in Scotland are Aliens, and
ought not in reason [87] to bee capable of landes in England, *videlicet*:

1. That England and Scotland were two ancient severall kingdomes under severall Kinges, and severall Crownes.

2. That they continue yet severall kingdomes.

3. That they have yet severall Lawes, severall Seales, severall
Crownes, and severall Kinges: For, it is said, though King James
be king of both, and hath but one naturall bodie, yet in judgement
of lawe, hee is in respect of his two severall kingdomes, as two severall
kinges, and the subjects of eche several kingdome are bound to him by
distinct allegeance, according to the severall lawes of the kingdome
where they were borne.

And all this is grounded upon this rule of fiction in Lawe: *Quando
duo jura concurunt in una persona, aequum est ac si essent in diversis.*

And upon this ground, is this new form of pleading devised, which
the [88] Defendants have used in this Case: such as cannot be found
in any Record, ever to have beene pleaded before; and may as well
serve against the Kinges subjects of Ireland, as against the *Post-nati*
of Scotland. And sithence in former times the like forme of pleading

---

[1] These objections were first summarised by James in a speech to Parl. 31 March 1607 – *His
Maiesties Speech to both the Houses of Parliament* (London 1607), Ellesmere's copy being Hunt.
RB 91517.

was never seene against any of the kings of Englandes subjects, which were borne in any of his dominions out of England, as in Normandie or Aquitany, or in France (I meane such part of it as was in the kinges possession, and in subjection and obedience to him, and not in that parte of France which his Enemies helde) it may be probably inferred, That it was then generally houlden, that neither such a forme of pleading, nor the Matter it selfe was sufficient in Lawe to disable any such plaintife: for, against French-men that were not under the kinges obedience wee finde it often pleaded. And as those that were not subjects to the Kinge, nor borne under his obedience, did then presume to bring suites, [89] and actions in England. So it can not bee thought, but that the King having then so large and ample Dominions beyond the Seas, as Normandy and Aquitany, and many other parts of France, some of his subjects borne there, had cause to have, and did bring the like suites in England. And sithence no such Plea is found to have beene then used against them, it can not in Lawe and Reason bee now alowed against the *Post-nati* in Scotland; For, I may say as Ascue said in 37. H. 6. 'Our Predecessors were as sage and learned as we be.'

And I see not, but that in this Case a good argument may bee reasonably deduced from the Negative, as it was in the Case reported by the great learned, and most grave and reverend Judge sir James Dyer chiefe Justice of the Common pleas, *Anno* 23. Elizabeth. [P. 23 Elizab. Dyer. 376].[1] The question there, was Whether an erronious Judgement given in Rie ⟨⟨Rye⟩⟩, which is a member of the Cinque portes, might bee reversed in the kinges Bench, or Common place at Westminster; [90] And it was thus resolved; '*Sed pro eo quod nullum tale breve in Registro nec in aliquibus Praecedentibus Curiarum praedictarum inveniri potverat, dominus Cancellarius Bromley per opinionem Capitalium Justiciariorum utriusque Banci denegavit tale breve concedere.*' And so Justice Fenners argument houldeth well, *viz.* 'There is in this Case no lawe to exclude the Complainant, *Ergo* he is a liege and a naturall borne subject.'[2]

But the forme of pleading in the time of king Ed. 1. in Cobledickes case, which was cited out of Hengam, (and the booke shewed here by the Lorde chiefe Justice Coke) is so direct and plaine for this our

---

[1] The Chanc. did not consider Dyer's reports, however, to be worthy of the man; for there were 'strange things printed, which detract greatly from the authority of Diers book' – Hawarde, *Reportes*, 127.

[2] Dyer, *Novel Cases*, 376, which Ellesmere noted from his own copy: Hunt. RB 59138.

Question, as nothing can be more plaine: and therefore I thinke it not amisse to report it againe.[1]

That Case was in effect and substance, thus:

A woman brought a Writ of *Ayell* against Roger Cobledicke, and declared of the seisin of Roger her Grand-father, and conveied the discent to Gilbert her father; [91] and from him to the Demaundant, as his daughter and heire. The Tenant pleaded, that the Demaundant was a French-woman, and not of the ligeance nor of the fidelitie of England; and demaunded Judgement if shee ought to have the action against him. This plea was houlden to bee insufficient; and thereupon the Tenant amended his plea, and pleaded further, That the Demaundant was not of the ligeance of England, nor of the fidelitie of the king; and demaunded Judgement, and etc. And against that plea none exception was taken, but thereupon the demaundant prayed licence to depart from her Writ. By this it appeareth plainely, that the first plea, alledging that she was a French-woman, and not of the ligeance, nor of the fidelitie of England, was insufficient (and so declared by Berreford the chiefe Justice) For, there can bee no fidelitie nor allegeance due to England, respecting the land and soile without a Soveraigne and King. But the second Plea [92] alledging, That shee was not of the ligeance of England, nor of the fidelitie of the King, was good and sufficient: for, to the King fidelitie and allegeance is due; and therefore, since shee failed in that, she was not to be answered: and thereupon shee praied licence to departe from her Writ, and so shee left her Suite.

Now for the reasons which have been drawne and strained out of the Statute *Anno* 14. Ed. 3. [Stat. 14. Ed. 3. That the realm of England shal not be subject to France.] If they bee well examined, they serve little for this point which wee have in hand.[2]

It is to be considered, at what time, and upon what occasion that Statute was made. King Edw. 3. beeing right heire to the Crowne and Kingdome of France by descent from his mother, and having spent many yeares for the recovering of the same, resolved to take upon him the Name and Stile of King of France; beeing advised thereunto by them of Flanders: Hereupon he did take the Stile of King of [93] Fraunce; and altered his Seale and his Armes; and after a while, placed the Armes of France before the ancient Armes of England,

---

[1] This could not be found in *Radulphi de Hengham Summae*, ed. William Huse Dunham (Cambridge 1932). Perhaps, as the passage suggests, he took the ref. from Coke.

[2] 'Statute the Third', 14 Edward III (1340), *Stat. Realm* I, 292.

as they are borne at this day. This gave occasion for the making of this statute: for some people (*Ascun gentes*, saith the statute) seeing this change, and considering the large and ample Extent, and magnificence of that great Kingdome, began to doubt that the King would make his Imperiall seate there; and conceived thereby, that the kingdome of England, beeing the lesser, should bee in subjection of the king and kingdome of France, beeing the greater, and to be governed and ruled by a Vice-Roy, or Deputy, as they sawe Ireland was. And though in the kinges stile England was placed before France, yet they sawe the Armes of France marshalled before the Armes of England; though at first hearing thereof some say it was not so.

To cleare this doubt, and to take away this feare from the subjects of England, [94] was this Statute made, as doth plainely appeare by the wordes of the Statute it selfe.[1]

Now if you will make an apt and proper application of that Case then, between England and Fraunce, to this our Case now, betweene Scotland and England, it must be thus:

1. Ed. 3. then king of England (beeing the lesser) had afterwards the kingdome of France (being the greater) by descent, and tooke the Stile of King of France.

King James king of Scotland (beeing the lesser) hath afterward the kingdome of England (beeing the greater) by descent, and taketh the Stile of King of England.

2. King E. 3. altered his Seale, and his Armes, and placed the Armes of France before the Armes of England.

King James hath changed his Seale and his Armes in England, and hath placed the [95] Armes of England before the Armes of Scotland.

3. It was then doubted, that King Edw. 3. would remoove his Court out of England the lesser, and keepe his Imperiall seate and state in France the greater.

King James hath indeede remooved his Court out of Scotland the lesser; and doth in his Royall person (with the Queene and Prince, and all his Children) keepe his Imperiall seate in England the greater.

4. In all these the Cases agree; but yet one difference there is, and that is in the Stile: For king Edw. 3. in his Stile placed England

---

[1] The statute which is assessed here at length received much contemp. discussion, and copies of the args. can be found in most large colls. of legal papers dating from the period. See, for ex. 'Certaine errors uppon the statute made 25 E. 3. of children borne beyond the sea conceived by Serjeant Browne and confuted by Serjeant Fairfax in manner of a dialogue' – Hale MS 80, ff. 150r–71r, and Sloane MS 2716, ff. 1r–37v.

the lesser, being his ancient kingdome, before France the greater, beeing newly descended unto him.

But King James in his Stile placeth England the greater, though newly descended unto him, before Scotland the lesser beeing his ancient kingdome. [96]

5. Now this being thus; perhappes Scotland might out of this Example have conceived the like doubt against England, as England did then against France: But as there was then no doubt made, whether the kings subjects borne in England should be capable of lands in France; so, out of this statute, and upon this example no doubt can bee inferred, whether the kings subjects now borne in Scotland shall be capable of lands in England.

But, all these Objections, and the ground whereupon they are framed, *viz. Quando duo jura, &c.* have beene so thoroughly and profoundly examined, and so learnedly and fully answered and cleared by the Judges, as I make no doubt but all wise and indifferent hearers be wel satisfied therein.

And if there be any so possessed with a prejudicate opinion against Truth, and Reason, that will say in their owne hearts *licèt persuaseris non persuadebis*; and so, either Serpent-like stop their eares, or else [97] wilfully absent themselves, because they would not heare the weakenesse and absurdities of their owne conceipts laied open and confuted: If there bee any such I say (as I trust there bee but few, and yet I feare there bee some) I would they had learned of Tertullian, That, *'Veritas docendo suadet, non suadendo docet.'* And I wish that they be not found among the number of those to whome Saint Paul saieth, *'Si quis ignorat, ignoret:'* And Saint John in the Apocalips, *'Qui sordidus est, sordescat adhuc.'* And I will exhort with Saint Paul, *'Qui tenet teneat,'* and not waver or doubt by such weake arguments and objections.

A dangerous distinction betweene the King and the Crowne.[1]

But in this new learning, there is one part of it so strange, and of so dangerous consequent, as I may not let it passe, *viz.* that the king is as a king divided in himselfe; and so as two kinges of two several kingdomes; and that there be severall allegeances, and several subjections due unto him respectively in regarde of his [98] severall kingdomes, the one not participating with the other.

---

[1] Ellesmere's views on faith and allegiance were commonplace, and the tone of his arg. (at pp. 245–52) resembles that of William Tyndale's *The Obedience of a Christian Man* (eight eds. 1528–61), and Sir John Cheke's *The hurt of sedicion* (four eds. 1549–76).

This is a dangerous distinction betweene the King and the Crowne, and betweene the King and the kingdome: It reacheth too farre; I wish every good subject to beware of it. It was never taught, but either by traitors, as in Spencers Bill in Ed. 2. time (which baron Snigge, and the Lord chiefe Baron, and Lord Coke remembred) or by treasonable Papists, as Harding in his *Confutation of the Apologie*,[1] maintaineth that kinges have their authority by the positive Lawe of Nations, and have no more power, than the People hath, of whome they take their temporal jurisdiction; and so *Ficlerus Simanca*, and other of that crew.

Or by seditious Sectaries and Puritans, as Buchannon *De Jure Regni apud Scotos*, Penry, Knox, and such like.[2]

For, by these, and those that are their followers, and of their Faction, there is in [99] their pamphlets too much such traiterous seede sowne.

Absurdities in this dangerous distinction.

But leaving this, I will adde a little more, to proove, that in reason Robert Calvine, and other like *Post-nati* in Scotland, ought by Lawe to be capable of landes in England: and for that, I wil remember one rule more which is certen and faileth not, and ought to be observed in all Interpretation of Lawes; and that is, *Ne Quid absurdum, ne quid illusorium admittatur.*

But, upon this subtile and dangerous Distinction of Faith and Allegeance due to the King, and of Faith and Allegeance due to the Crowne, and to the Kingdome (which is the onely Basis and fundamentall maine reason to disable the Plaintife, and all *Post-nati*) there follow too many grosse, and fowle absurdities, whereof I will touch some few, and so conclude, that in Lawe and reason this subtile, but absurd and dangerous, distinction ought not to be allowed. [100]

《CHAPTER 9》 SOVEREIGNTY AND ANGLO-SCOTS UNION

This bond of Allegeance whereof we dispute, is *Vinculum fidei*;[3] it bindeth the soule and conscience of every subject, severally and

---

[1] Thomas Harding, *A Confutation of a book* [by Bishop Jewell] *intituled An Apologie of the Church of England* (Antwerp 1565), STC 12762.

[2] George Buchanan, *De iure regni apud Scotos dialogus* (Edinburgh 1579).

[3] The subject of allegiance formed the second half of his objections in his critique of a tract against union: Ellesm. MS 1215, ff. 2r–3v.

respectively, to bee faithfull and obedient to the King: And as a Soule or Conscience cannot bee framed by Policie; so Faith and Allegeance can not bee framed by Policie, nor put into a politike body. An oathe must be sworne by a naturall bodie; homage and fealtie must bee done by a naturall bodie, a politike body cannot doe it.

Now then, since there is but one king, and soveraigne to whome this faith and allegeance is due by al his subjects of England and Scotland, can any humane policie divide this one King, and make him two kinges?[1] Can *Cor Regis Angliae* be *in manu Domini*, and *Cor Regis Scotiae* not so? Can there bee warres betweene the king of England and the king of Scotland? or betweene the kingdome of England and the kingdome of Scotland, so long as there is but one kinge? Can the kinge of England now send [101] an Army royall into Scotland against the king of Scotland? Can there bee any Letters of Marke or Reprisall now graunted by the King of England, against the subjects of the king of Scotland? Can there bee any Protections now, *Quia profecturus in exercitu Jacobi Regis Angliae in Scotiam?*

Nay shortly, Can any man bee a true subject to king James as king of England, and a traitor or rebel to king James as king of Scotland?[2] Shall a foote breadth, or an inch breadth of ground make a difference of birth-right of subjects borne under one kinge? Nay, where there are not any certen bounds or limits knowne at all, but an imaginary partition wall, by a conceipted fiction in Lawe? It is enough to propound these and such like Questions, whereof many more might bee remembred: they carry a sufficient and plaine answeare in themselves: *Magis docet qui prudentèr interrogat.*

As the King nor his heart cannot bee [102] divided, for hee is one intier king over all his subjects, in which soever of his kingdomes or Dominions they were borne, so hee must not bee served nor obeyed by halves; hee must have intier and perfect obedience of his subjects: for, *Ligentia* (as baron Heron saied well) must have foure qualities; It maust bee 1. *Pura & simplex*: 2. *Integra & solida*: 3. *Uniuersalis non localis*: 4. *Permanens, continua, & illaesa.*[3] Divide a mans heart, and

---

[1] This and the following two parags., strong in conception and eloquence, were developed out of a section of the Chanc's speech to Parl. in 1603/4: Ellesm. MS 451, fol. 1r.

[2] James, in addressing Parl. shortly after this speech, put the analogy the other way: 'ye know if the King of Scotland prove a knave the King of England can never be an honest man' – *Works*, 235.

[3] A thesis that he explored as a legal concept in the 'Prerog.', ff. 3r–4r. The matters in this parag. and the following one were queried by a lawyer in his copy of the *Post-Nati*: B.M. RB 518.i.2(2), pp. 103–4.

you lose both parts of it, and make no heart at all; so hee that is not
an intier subject, but halfe faced, is no subject at all; and hee that is
borne an intier and perfect subject, ought by Reason and Law to have
all the freedomes, priviledges, and benefites pertaining to his birth-
right in all the Kinges Dominions; and such are all the *Post-nati* in
England and Scotland. And the inconvenience of this imaginary lo-
call allegeance hath beene so lately, and so fully declared by the
Lorde chiefe Justice Coke, as more needes not bee said in it. [103]

In some speciall cases there sometime may be a king of subjects
without land in possession, as Justice Fenner noted in the governement
which Moses had over the people of Israel in the wildernesse; and as
in the case which sir John Popham the late Lord chiefe Justice did
put in the Parliament: If a King and his subjects bee driven out of
his kingdome by his enemies, yet notwithstanding hee continueth still
king over those subjects, and they are still bound unto him by their
bond of allegeance, wheresoever hee and they bee: But there can not
bee a king of land without subjects: For, that were but *Imperium in
belluas*, and *Rex & subditi sunt relativa*.

Rex solus/judicat, and etc.

I saied there was an other generall rule for expounding of Lawes,
which I reserved to bee last spoken of, I will now but touch it; for, I
will not stand to examine by humane reasons, whether kings were
before Lawes, or Lawes before kinges; nor how kings were first ordained; nor [104] whether the kings, or the people did first make
Lawes; nor the severall constitutions and frames of states and
common-weales; nor what Plato or Aristotle have written of this
argument.

They were men of singuler learning and wisedome, but wee must
consider the time, and the countrie in which they lived, and in all
their great learning they lacked the true learning of the knowledge
of God. They were borne and lived in Greece, and in popular States:
they were enemies, or at least mislikers of all Monarchies; yet one
of them disdained not to bee a servant or mercenarie hireling to a
Monarch.[1] They accompted all the world barbarous, but their owne
Countrey of Greece: their opinions therefore are no Cannons to give
Lawes to kinges and kingdomes, no more than sir Thomas Moores
Utopia, or such Pamphlets as wee have at everie Marte.[2]

---

[1] Other refs. are in Ellesm. MS 485.

[2] The Chanc. looked upon More as he did Knox, Barrow, and Penry. These were extremists, and Ellesmere loathed 'popular' men: *supra (Past-Nati)*, p. 99.

I beleeve him that saieth, 'Per me Reges regnant, & Principes justa decernunt;' [Prou. ca. 8]; And [105] I make no doubt, but that as God ordained kings, and hath given Lawes to kings themselves, so hee hath authorized and given power to kings to give Lawes to their subjects; and so kings did first make lawes, and then ruled by their lawes, and altered and changed their Lawes from time to time, as they sawe occasion, for the good of themselves, and their subjects.

And this power they have from God almighty; For, as Saint Augustine saieth, 'In hoc Reges Deo serviunt sicut eis Divinitùs praecipitur, in quantum sunt Reges, si in suo Regno bona jubeant, mala prohibeant, non solum quae pertinent ad humanam societatem, verumetiam quae ad divinam religionem.'

And I hould Thomas Aquinas his opinion to be good, 'Rex solutus à Legibus quòad vim coactiuam, subditus est legibus quòad vim directiuam propria voluntate.' And for this opinion there is a stronger authoritie, even from God himselfe in Ecclesiastes, ca. 8. ver. 2. 'Ego os Regis observo; Et praecepta juramenti [106] Dei: & ver. 4. Sermo illius potestate plenus est: Nec dicere ei quisquam potest, quare ita facis?'

Now beeing led a little from the Common Lawe to the Civile Lawe, I finde in the civile Lawe a direct Text, warranting that generall Rule which I reserved to this place, which is this; 'Inter aequitatemiusque interpositam interpretationem nobis solis & licet & oportet inspicere.' [Cod. li I, Tit. 14. le. I.]

And another like Text in these words, 'Sententia Principis Jus dubium declarans, Jus facit quòad omnes.' [Ibidem le. 12.] And some grave and notable Writers in the civile Lawe say, 'Rex est lex ɩ nimata:' Some say, 'Rex est lex loquens:' Some others say, 'Interpretantur legem consuetudo & Princeps:' Another saieth, 'Rex solus judicat de causa à jure non definita.'[1]

And as I may not forget Saint Augustines words, which are these; 'Generale pactum est societatis humanae regibus suis obtemperare:' So I may not wrong the Judges of the common Lawe of England so much as to [107] suffer an imputation to bee cast upon them, That they, or the Common lawe doe not attribute as great power and authoritie to their Soveraignes the kinges of England, as the Romane lawes did to their Emperours: For, Bracton the chiefe Justice in the time of king Henry the third, hath these direct wordes, 'De Chartis Regiis & factis regum

---

[1] Although his copy of the Digest cannot be found, the ascriptions are relatively accurate when compared to the modern ed. He made notes out of the Digest for other matters in Ellesm. MS 465.

non debent nec possunt Justiciarii nec privatae personae disputare. Nec etiam, si in illa dubitatio oriatur, possunt cam interpretari. Et in dubiis & obscuris, vel si aliqua dictio duos contineat intellectus, domini Regis erit expectanda interpretatio & voluntas; Cum ejus sit interpretari cujus est condere.' And Britton in the time of the king Ed. I. writeth as much in effect.[1]

So as now if this question seem difficult, that neither direct law, nor Examples and Precedents, nor application of like Cases, nor discourse of reason, nor the grave opinion of the learned and reverend Judges, can resolve it, here is a true and certen Rule, how both by the Civile Lawe, [108] and the ancient Common lawe of England it may and ought to be decided: That is, by sentence of the most religious, learned, and judicious king that ever this kingdome or Iland had.

But this Case is so cleare as this needeth not at all.

And in this I would be mis-understoode, as though I spake of making of new Lawes, or of altering the Lawes now standing; I meane not so, but I speake only of interpretation of the Lawe in new questions and doubts, as now in this present case: neither doe I meane hereby to derogate any thing from the high court of Parliament; (farre be it from my thought) It is the great Councell of the kingdome, wherein every subject hath interest. And to speake of the constitution or forme of it, or how, or when it was first begunne, is for busie Questionists; It ought to bee obeyed and reverenced, but not disputed; and it is at this time impertinent to this Question. [109]

But certen it is, it hath beene the wisedome of the Kinges of this Realme to reserve in themselves that supreame power to call their Nobles, Clergie, and commons together, when they sawe great and urgent Causes; and by that great Councell to make Edicts and Statutes for the weale of their people, and safetie of the Kingdome and State, as in *Anno* 10. Edw. 3. the Assembly at Nottingham for the great wars in France: And in *Anno* 20. H. 3. *Provisiones Merton*, which I remembred before.[2]

Object. of Inconveniencie and frugalitie.

There have beene made some Objections of inconveniencie, as for bearing of Scot and Lot, and such other charges; and some out of frugalitie, that the king shall lose his profit of making Denizens, and

---

[1] From his copy of Henry Bracton, *De Legibus & Consuetudinibus Angliae* (1569), Hunt. RB 69059.

[2] *Supra*, pp. 208–9 and n. 1 on p. 209.

such like: These are so light as I leave them to the winde; They are neither fit for Parliament, nor Councell, nor Court.

Object. upon diffidence. Another argument and reason against the *Post-nati* hath beene lately made out [110] of diffidence and mistrust, that they will come into England sans number, and so as it were to surcharge our Common; and that this may be in *secula seculorum.* I know not well what this meanes. The Nation is ancient, noble and famous; they have many honourable and woorthie Noble men and Gentlemen, and many wise and woorthie men of all degrees and qualities; they have lands and faire possessions in Scotland: Is it therefore to bee supposed, or can it in reason bee imagined, that such multitude sans number will leave their native soile, and all transport themselves hither? Hath the Irish done so? Or those of Wales, or of the Isles of Man, Gernesey, and Jersey? Why should we then suspect it now more for Scotland?[1]

Nay, doe you suppose that the Kinge of England will ever suffer so great a parte of his Dominions, and so great and famous a Kingdome as Scotland is to be dispeopled? It is a doubt imagined without any foundation or ground of reason. [111] But if it were to bee doubted, the twelve Judges that have concurred in opinion, and that late worthy Judge Popham had as great cause to feare it as any others: They are wise, they are learned, they have faire possessions and good estates, They have posteritie to care for, as others have.[2]

Yet, admit it bee a matter worth the doubting of, what is that to the yoong *Post-nati* that are not like in many yeares to come hither in such number? Shall we upon this causlesse feare deprive them of their lawfull Birth-right?

Have wee seene in these five yeeres past anie moe of them than this one alone that have gotten any Lands in England? And this little that he hath is so small and poore a portion, that his purchase is not great, and therefore no just cause of offence to any.

Ante-nati.

Nay, if you looke upon the *Ante-nati*, you shall find no such confluence hither, but some few (and very few in respect [112] of that great and

---

[1] Ellesmere was at first very congenial to the Scots. This opinion changed drastically by 1614, when he attacked them indirectly throughout his tract on 'Govt.'

[2] The Chanc. believed that union would bring econ. prosperity, although he was careful to avoid confrontation by not emphasising that opinion here. Earlier, when some merchants composed a list of econ. args. against union for the joint com. of Parl., 'they were roundly shaken by my Lord Chancellor': *Bowyer Diary,* 209 (14 Feb. 1606).

populous kingdome) that have done long and worthie service to his Majestie, have, and still doe attend him, which I trust no man mislikes: For, there can bee none so simple, or childish (if they have but common sense) as to thinke that his Majesty should have come hither alone amongst us, and have left behinde him in Scotland, and as it were caste off all his ould and worthie Servants.

And if these Noble and worthie Gentlemen of Scotland, I meane the *Ante-nati* be lovingly and brotherly entertained amongst us, with mutuall love and benevolence, that so we may *coalescere*, and be united together, by marriage, and otherwise (as in some particular cases wee see it already happily begunne) no doubt God will blesse this Union of both these Nations, and make them, and the King, and great Britaine to be famous through the world; and feared and redoubted of our enemies, and of all that wish us ill: For, *Vis unita* [113] *fortior, & concordia multos facit unum.* But what may follow upon such arguments of diffidence and suspition, which seeme but to hinder Union, and to breede discord and dissention I will not speake; Let every wise man consider it well: For, *Humana consilia castigantur ubi coel estibus se praeferunt.* And remember Saint Paules caution, 'Si invicem mordetis, videte ne ab invicem consumamine.'[1]

And for the resemblance that hath bin made of this Case of *Post-nati* (but indeed for the Union of both Kingdomes) with the houswife cutting of her cloth by a threede, I will say but this, That if shee cut her peece of cloth in length aswell as in breadth, all the threeds will bee cutte, and the cloth marred. And this cutting in this our Case, is, to cutte all aswell in length as in breadth, even through all the Kinges Dominions; and so will rent asunder the whole frame of the [114] Union; and cut in peeces all the threeds of Allegeance.

A question, how long this suspition and dis-union shall continue?

But now I will aske this question: How long shall this suspition and doubt continue? Shall there bee a dis-union for ever? If it bee saied, No, but untill the Lawes, and Customes of both Kingdomes bee made one and the same: then I aske; how, and when shall that be done? And it may bee, that the Constitutions of the Countries bee such as there can hardly in all things bee such an absolute and perfect reconciling or uniting of Lawes as is fancied. Is it yet so betweene

---

[1] The Scots had been energetic in their desire for the project at the beginning, and had considered the Chanc. correctly as 'their man'. See, for ex. the letter of the Scottish P. C. to Ellesmere in *Acts of the Privy Council of Scotland* (1887), VIII, 494 (10 March 1608).

England and Wales? or betweene Kent and Cornewall? or betweene many other parts of this Kingdome? I say no; and I speake it confidently, and truely it is not so; nor well can be so. Therefore let England and Scotland be in like degree now, as England and Wales were for many hundred yeeres, and in many things are yet still; and yet let Union and Love increase amongst us, [115] even *in secula seculorum*. Let us not be such as Saint Bernard noteth, '*Amant quod non decet, timent quod non opertet, dolent vane, gaudent vanius.*' And let us no longer make question, whether severall Lawes and Customes bee markes of seperation and dis-union, or of severall Allegeances; for certainely they are not.[1]

Objection upon Divination.

One other Reason remaines against these *Post-nati*, and that is out of a provident foresight, or as it were a prophesying: What if a seperation of these Kingdomes fall hereafter?

Respons. Of this I can say but *Absit omen*. It is *Potentia remota* (as Justice Williams saied) and I trust in God *Remotissima*: And I will ever pray to God that it never fall so, untill the King of all Kinges resume all Scepters and Kingdomes into his owne hands. And let us take heede of sinnes of Ingratitude and Disobedience; and remember, that Adam and Eve were punished, *Non* [116] *propter pomum, sed propter vetitum.* And for such Prophets, let the Prophet Ezechiel ca. 13. answer them, '*Vae Prophaetis insipientibus qui sequuntur spiritum suum, & nihil vident.*' And the Prophet Esay speaketh to all such with an other '*Vae, Vae illis qui dispergunt.*'

Now then, as M. Solicitor beganne with seeking out the truth; so I will conclude with Esdras words, '*Magna est Veritas & prævalet.*' And with this further, '*Eatenus rationandum donec veritas inveniatur: Cùm inventa est veritas, figendum ibi Judicium: Et in victoria veritatis, soli veritatis inimici pereunt.*'[2]

《CHAPTER 10》 THE CONCLUSION

Thus I have heere delivered my concurrence in opinion with my Lordes the Judges, and the reasons that induce and satisfie my con-

---

[1] This was the objection of perhaps a majority of the legal prof. The laws of Eng. that were 'offensive and repugnant' to union were diagrammed in Harl. MS 292, ff. 137v–8r.

[2] The prophecies, which he used often in his writings, were noted in Ellesm. MSS 456, 482, 485; and in the margins of his copy of Fitzherbert, *Brevium*, Hunt. RB 59688.

science, That Ro. Calvine, and all the *Post-nati* in Scotland, are in Reason, and by the Common Lawe of [117] England naturall borne subjects within the allegeance of the King of England; and inhabled to purchase and have free-hould and inheritance of land in England; and to bring reall actions for the same in England.

For, if they have not this benefit by this blessed and happie Union, then are they in no better case in England, than the king of Spaines subjects borne in Spaine, and etc. And so by this Union they have gotten nothing: What they have lost Justice Yelverton did well note.

And therefore I must give Judgement in the Chancerie, That the Defendants there ought to make direct answer to Ro. Calvines Bill for the Lands and Evidences for which he complaines. [118]

XI

'SPECIALL OBSERUACIONS TOUCHING ALL THE SESSIONS OF THE LAST PARLEMENT ANNO 7 REGIS AND ETC.[1] (1611)

In a parlement in Englande, Three states, and in three Degrees are alwayes to be specially regarded: and Care to be taken, that no one Incroche too farre vpon the other.

1. The Kinge is to haue his Regalitye, and supreme Prerogatiue and Soueraignytye, Inviolable preserued.

2. The Nobles, Prelates, and Lordes, to haue theyr honour and dignitye maynteyned.

3. The Commons to haue theyr auncient Liberties and priueleges, Contynued and kept wythout breache or preiudice.

1. Yf the first be extended and strayned too highe, yt tendes to Tyrannye.

2. If the 2⟨⟨nd⟩⟩ presume too much, and challenge ouer great power and authoritye, yt wyll aspire to Aristocracy.

3. Yf the thyrde by suffred to usurpe and incroache too farre vpon the Regalitye, yt wyll not cease, (yf it be not stayed in tyme) vntil yt breake out into Democracy.[2]

In this present state, there is no cause to doubte either the first, or the seconde; for of late yeares they haue rather[a] declined and decayed, then increased. [1r] But the Popular state, ever since the begynnynge of his maiestes gracious and sweete gouernement, hath growne bygge and audacious. And in euery session of Parlement swelled more and more. And yf waye be stylle gyven vnto yt, (as of late hath bene) yt is to be Doubted what the ende wyll be.

Saynct Barnardes caution ys good: '*Cavendum est ne dum versus subditos nimia seruetur humilitas, regendi frangatur authoritas.*' And yt was longe agoe obserued by Liuye, '*Vulgus aut humiliter seruit, aut superbe dominatur.*' And yt is dayly founde true, *Plebis Importuni-*

---

[a] increased *crossed out after* rather.

[1] Ellesm. MS 2599.

[2] Notes on these strictures were contained in his copies of Fitzherbert's *Brevium*, Hunt. RB 59688, the title page; and of *Littletons Tenures*, Hunt. RB 62234, rear fly leaves. See also his copy of T. B., 'Obseruations Politicall and Civill', Ellesm. MS 1174, ff. 2v–6r.

tas Cedendo accenditur. And often tymes exhortacions and persuasions, thoughe neuer so wyse, learned, eloquent and Religious, prevayle Litle with a headdy multitude; for certen yt is, *Malitia non Instruitur sermonibus, sed incenditur*; and grant wylfull foly what it desireth, yt wyll neuer be satisfyed.[1]

Yt is commenly seene that the waters swell before a boysterous storme, and then yt is tyme for wyse and skyfull pylottes, to prouide for yt, and as much as may be, to wythstande and prevent yt. Great and daungerous Inundacions, happen for the moost parte, by reason that smalle breaches, are neglected and not looked vnto, and stopped in the begynnynge. [IV]

Before the 4th Session of the Late parlement somme breaches were made vpon the Regalitye and supreme prerogatiue of the Crowne, vnder pretext of lawfull Libertie, and auncient priuileges.[2] And these were eyther willingely allowed, or wyth connivencye tollerated, althoughe indede the same are directely agaynst Lawe and Iustice, and not warranted by the true and auncient rules and precedentes of Parlement. Of which sort these fewe maye serue for example.

1. The Causes of callinge of the parlement, which ought to haue bene first treated of, were neglected, and somme mens private devices preferred, and therin much tyme mispent.[3]

2. Ordinary Iustice was delayed, by reason that somme of the parlement house, being warned or sommoned by the Kynges wryttes, either to answere in sutes agaynst theym, or to be examyned as wytnesses to testyfye the truth of theyr knowledge, dyd carelesly make defaulte or dyd wilfully contemne. And this was grounded vpon pretence of a new Inuented and supposed priuilege and libertye, not warranted either by [2r] Lawe or reason, or by any auncient precedent or example. For that priuilege of parlement ought not by Lawe, to be extended any further but to secure and protecte those of the

---

[1] Taken from his address to the third session in the *CJ* 314–5.

[2] A ref. to 'The Form of Apology and Satisfaction, to be presented to his Majesty', 20 June 1604, in Yelv. MS 59, ff. 99r–117v. See also the copy in the State Papers that has been analysed by G. R. Elton, 'A high road to civil war?' in *From Renaissance to Counter-Reformation*, ed. C. H. Carter (New York 1965), 325–47.

[3] The Chanc. was writing of the programme put forward by the K. and his lengthy account of what should be accomplished in his opening speech. His address to the Parl. – of which a copy in his own hand exists – was devoted primarily to the urgency of proceeding to a union with Scot., and only secondarily to econ. and legal reform: Ellesm. MS 451, and the slightly different version in Ellesm. MS 458. Composed in 1603/4, some of his drafts of papers for this session are Ellesm. MSS 2613, 2615–16, 456.

parlement house from any attachement or arrest of theyre persons.¹

3. Also persons outlawed were receyued, allowed, and Iustified to be Lawfull members of the parlement, and therby were priuileged and protected from the ordinary course of Lawe and Iustice. Wheras by lawe they are vtterly disabled to be Jurors or wytnesses, and haue neither Landes or goodes of theyr owne, nor libertye of theyre persons, And are therfore vnfitte to be of so graue a senate and Counsell, and can not be deemed to be mete to be Lawe Makers.

4. They dyd also lately take vpon theym to Iudge of the sufficyency and insufficiencye of Shyreffes returnes of writtes, for electinge and somonynge knightes for shyres, and Citizens and burgesses for Cityes and boroughes, to serue in parlement, and presumed to allowe and disallowe of such returnes at theyr pleasure.² [2v] Which by Lawe, they ought not to doe. For the Lower house ys not any Courte of recorde, Nor haue the recorde of any wryttes or Returnes, or any other recorde remaynynge wyth theym, whervpon theye maye Iudge. And the examples of former tymes be herinᵃ directely to the Contrary. As appereth specially in the parlement *anno* 5 Henry 4. *Rotuli.*

5. They haue also by pretence of theyr priuileges, discharged somme persons out of execucion, which were Imprisoned before the Somons or warnynge of the parlement. And to countenaunce and maynteyne theyr priuilege to doe so in Lyke Cases herafter, they procured an acte to passe in *anno* 1. of his maiestes raigne, By whose meanes I meane not to remember.³

Of Lyke sorte, more particular Cases might be remembred, but these be too many. For they be such as can not be exemplified out of any recordes of former parlements, that be extant to be sene since the Conquest, or out of any bokes of the Lawe.⁴ [3r]

But this is not all; for besydes this rare and straunge forme of theyr

---

ᵃ be herein *crossed out after* be herin.

¹ He delivered a speech on this before the H. of L. in 1614: *LJ* II, 714–15; *Hastings MS*, IV, 270–1.

² *Sir Francis Goodwin's Case*, in *State Trials* II, 91–114; and *CJ* 149–52, 156–60, 162–4. For a disc. of the docs. see Bacon, *Letters* III, 163–72, which embroiled Ellesmere in a controversy with a number of MPs. At one such session he accused them of using abridgements of statutes rather than the statutes at large in drafting and interpreting warrants: *Bowyer Diary*, 217–18 (5 March 1606/7). The Chanc's position on this subject was similar to that of James: the K's letter of 1 April 1604; SPD 14/7/1.

³ *Thomas Shirley's Case*, 1604, in *CJ* 155–6, 167, 171–3, 198–209, 213–15, 242, 245–6. See also the disc. of G. W. Prothero, 'The parliamentary privilege of freedom from arrest and Sir Thomas Shirley's Case, 1604', *EHR* 8 (1893), 733–40.

⁴ Esp. in the third session: *CJ* 331–9, 342–6, 352–3, 368–75, 379–90.

procedinges, Somme particular persons (desirous to be remarkeable and valued and estemed aboue others, for theyr zeale, wysedome, Learnynge, Iudgement, and experience) haue presumed to vse in the Lower house publickely, very audacious and Contemptuous speches, agaynst the Kinges Regalle prerogatiue and power, and his moost gracious and happy gouernement. And this hath passed with applause of many others there, and wyth litle or no reprehension at all. And so hath bene stylle contynued and more and more increased, wyth great animosity and Insolencye. Of this kynde these fewe particulars folowinge wyll not be forgotten in this our age.[1]

A. Yt was sayed by one of theym (a man of great Lyvelyhood and abilitye, and houdinge a good and gaynefull place, vnder his maiestie) That theye came to deliuer grieffe and sorowe. That the tymes paste were goulden dayes, and the late tyme a goulden tyme, and that ⟨then⟩ Subiects had iuste cause to reioyce. That they had promyse and hope of Reformacion, But all was worse and worse. That Pharaoes frogges were comme amongest us. [3v] That the Case was miserable, and that the losse of Subiectes loue, was full of perille and daunger. Wyth further[a] mynatorye and threttenynge wordes, That yt was only the profession of the Gospelle, which conteyned and stayed the People.[2]

B. Yt was sayed by an other, That there was not *Pax sed Pactio Seruitutis.* That they had not any cause eyther of feare or hope. And mocion made by hym to breake uppe and sytte no more vntill they had relieffe of theyr grievances; and whylest[b] they contynued together, to chuse a Speaker of theym selues, *De die in Diem.* And that in theyr Conferences wyth the Lordes, they shoulde not stande bare headed, but to sytte wyth the Lordes, and theyr heades Couered. Which mocion touchinge theyr Conferences with the Lordes, was after renewed by somme others.[3]

C. And in the matter of vnion, yt was sayd by an eloquent and learned gent, That yt was but voluntary, and not necessarye. That yt woulde be our wracke and ruiyne. That our bountye woulde be our bane. That the blysfulnes of the Receyuer woulde be the bane of the gyver. [4r] And that *Nimia amicitia causam dat odii*, and therfore good

---

[a] further *inserted above.*   *Read as* wished *in Foster, Parl. 1610, I, 278.*

[1] Particularly in the second session: *CJ* 396, 399–402, 405, 408–11, 422–3, 430–2, 435–9, 452–3.

[2] According to Elizabeth Foster, this was spoken by John Hare, Clerk of the Court of Wards.

[3] Discussed in *Bowyer Diary*, 158, 232–5.

to remember the oulde sayinge 'Loue me Litle, Loue me Longe.'[1] And in this poynt touching vnion somme professing the lawe added, that yt woulde eyther be uniust or unsaffe.

[Session 4] D. And in the Later Sessions, many of these, and other matters of lyke nature were propounded and passed verbally in theyr Consultacions and debates. And this specially, That the same parlement (beinge so well affected, and a body so well Compounded) shoulde be contynued and houlden euery fyue yeares certenly, wythout any other or new Sommons. But somme not contented with that which was so treated of in publicke, dyd single theym from the others, and kept secrette and priuye Conventicles and Conferences, wherein they devised and sett downe speciall plottes, for the Caryinge of businesse in the house, accordinge to theyr owne humour and driftes, and that in the waightest and moost Important Causes, as namely touchinge the great and Royall Contracte which was then intended and in handelinge. And for the stayinge of grantinge of any subsidyes and fyftenes.[2]

E. To which purpose yt was devised that Syxe of theym, who had great [4v] contenaunce, and dyd beare great swaye in the house, shoulde be prepared to speake at large agaynst the grauntinge of any Subsidy at all, and shoulde sette furth all the argumentes and reasons that might be obiected or pretended agaynst yt; And that after[a] those theyr speches the residue shoulde be silent,[3] and not to speake any thinge therin at all, vntille the bylle shoulde be put to the question, and then to ouerthorowe yt wyth a generall NO.

And besides they studyed and laboured much to contriue and sett furth many supposed grievances in the state and gouernement. In the moost parte wherof, they dyd not so much indeuour to seke remedy and reformacion of mischiefes or inconveniences in the Comen weale, as to quarrell and Impeache his Maiestes prerogatiue, and his regalle Iurisdiccion, power, and authoritye.[4] As these specially:[b] touching

---

[a] after inserted above.   [b] these especially inserted above.

[1] Sir Edwin Sandys, 14 March 1607, in ibid. 239. The Chanc's refutation of those args. was made in the Post-Nati, 110–17.

[2] Ellesmere was reported to have given a bold speech in 1606 against the refusal of such individuals to communicate publicly, declaring 'that silence in consultations affecteth nothing': Speech of 26 Nov. 1606 before the com's of both houses, in Bowyer Diary, 191–2.

[3] Which prompted the Chancellor to remark in Parl. that 'Yt is now so as yf I haue taken anie notes, I haue not light to reade them': Hastings MS, IV, 225.

[4] That is, an approach in marked contrast to that of the Chanc., who could draft eulogies to the sovereign (Ellesm. MS 443), while he prepared a catalogue of mischiefs for remedy (Ellesm. MS 456).

his highenes Proclamacions, Touchinge his right and power of Imposi-
cion, and rates of Merchandizes, and etc. Touchinge the hyghe
Commissions Ecclesiasticalle, Touchinge the Prouinciall Conselles in
Wales and the North. Touchinge the Court of starre chamber, and
all Courtes of equitye, which they termed Courtes of arbitrary Discrecion, (Inuolvinge therin also the authoritye of the priuye Counsell).
Touchinge the staynge of sutes in the Courtes of Admiraltye, and all
[5r] ecclesiasticall courtes, and all Courtes of equitye, whatsoeuer by wryttes of Prohibicion.[1]

[Session 4] And albeyt the Lower house be not a Court of recorde
as before ys sayed, Nor haue any power or Lawfull Iurisdiccion to
examyne witnesses, or to minister any oathe at all to any person; yet
in somme of theyr late Sessions, they dyd challenge and vsurpe
a[a] juditiall power and forme of procedinge in diuers seuerall Cases:
as in examyninge a Iudgement gyven in a Courte of the commen lawe,
vpon a Demurrer in lawe. And therin they proceded so fare, as that
they passed a bylle declaringe the Lawe to be contrary to the former
Iudgement. And this they dyd, wythout having the aduice, or hearinge
any of the Iudges of the lawe.[2]

They dyd Lykewyse examyne a sentence gyven in the Admiralle
Courte in one Pontis Case. And in that also they passed a Bylle to
Inable hym to haue an appealle from that sentence; whereas the
Appeale was formerly denyed, aswell for that it appered that it was
not grauntable by Lawe, as also for that the lords of the Priuy Counsell, havinge often hearde the Cause debated, resolued vpon graue
consideracion of matter of state, that yt ought not to be graunted
in that Case.[3]

They dyd also examyne in poynt of Equitye and Conscience,
diuerse decrees made in the Chancerye. They dyd also convente before theym Sir Stephen [5v] Proctor Knight, and henry spyller
esquire, vpon priuate informacions and suggestions.[4] A Case of rare
example, and yf it be drawne to a president, maye haue a Daungerous
Consequence.

[a] usurpe; a] usurpe a
[1] These items were contained in the petitions of grievances of 7 July 1610: *Parl. 1610*
II, 254–71. The debates, and Ellesmere's role in them, are noted in the Wilbraham MS J.,
151–61.
[2] The Chanc. believed that any legal body which sought to change the area of its auth.
was usurping the royal prerog. and the liberties of the people: 'Prerog.', ff. 1–2r.
[3] *An Act for the relief of Robert Pennington and John Holinshed, prisoners in the Marshalsea,
and William Pountis, prisoner in the Compter of the Poultry, London.*
[4] The case, but especially Sir Stephen Proctor, is discussed throughout the docs. and
commentary in *Parl. 1610.*

They dyd also take vpon theym to graunt Iniunccions to staye suites in the Chauncerye, as in Pelhams Case, Gargranes Case, Sandys Case,[1] and so lykewyse in somme other Courtes.[2]

And for the better Countenauncynge of these theyr doinges, and to strengthen theyr pretensed Iurisdiccion in lyke cases herafter, they passed twoo bylles, so strang both in forme and matter, as in former tymes haue not bene sene.

The one of those bylles, ys thus Intitled: An acte agaynst Taxes and Imposicions vpon merchantes and other the Subiectes of this realme, or vpon theyr wares, goods, and chattells. In the preamble[b] of this bylle, yt is affirmed directely and precisely, That the proprietye of any mans gooddes or chattelles, can not nor ought not, to be alterred or changed, Nor any waye charged, by any absolute authoritye of the Kinges Maiestie, wythout assent of parlement. And in the body of the bylle, they propounde to be Inacted as a certen and absolute lawe, That all Imposicions paste in the tyme of the Kings Maiestie, or of any his predecessors, and all that shall herafter be Imposed by the Kinge his heyres or Successors, wythout assent of [6r] Parlement, shall be adiudged in lawe to be voyde. Addinge a penaltye, that he that shall levye any such, shall be dishabled to beare[c] any such office, and shall forfaicte 40 lb to the partie grieued.[3]

The other of those bylles ys thus Intitled: An acte for better attendance and tryalle of Causes in the Commons house of Parlement. In which bylle, Three thinges are proponded to be Inacted for Lawe.

1. That yf any member of that house, departe or absent hymselfe, without Licence of the house first obteyned, Or such sufficyent Cause alleged, as the house shall allowe, he shall forfaicte such fine, not excedinge XX lb, as shall be assessed by that house, and to be Imployed to such vses as that house shall appoynt. Wyth a Prouiso that the said house maye acquite and discharge the offenders of such fine before yt be levyed.

2. That yt shall be lawfull aswell for the Speaker of that house syttinge in the house, as for a Committee of the same house, being

---

[a] *This should read* Abergavenny.   [b] yt is *crossed out* after preamble.

[c] beare *read as* have *in ibid.,* I, 281.

[1] Concerning Edward Aldford: *CJ* 423–5; *Lord Abergavenny's Case: CJ* 446–51; LJ 613–28; and Sir Edwin Sandys in *Parl. 1610* II, 323.

[2] In none of these instances, however, were their attacks as constant as on the eccles. courts: see the *CJ*, 173, 226–9, 345–7, 374–5, 382–4, 418–21, 425–37, 446–53.

[3] The text of the bill is in *Parl. 1610* II, 410–12.

Seven at the leaste, to take any examynacion or affidauit vpon oathe in any Cause dependinge or commynge before them, yf so to theym yt shall seeme good.[1]

3. A Prouiso, That yf any person shall ⟨by⟩ vertue of this acte be punyshed by fine or otherwyse, or acquited or [6v] discharged, Then the same person shall not be punyshed for the same offence, in any other Court or place what soeuer.

[Session 5] This irregular and Insolent Course of theyr procedinge, was hoately and egerly pursued in the Last Session. For when report was made in the Lower house, of that which was propounded by the Lord Treasurer, at the meetinge of the Committees for bothe houses, for the renewinge and further procedinge in the great Contracte; Somme of theym affirmed openly That it was neuer meant that the Contracte shoulde procede and take effecte, and that there was no hope to haue any securitye for the same, because they sawe that theyr grievances were not answerred, and Lawe and Iustice was denyed theym.[2]

E. An other goinge further dyd speake more audatiouslye, Saying that this Parlement was accompted a wyse and a stoute Parlement, But theyr Contreyes and posteritie coulde not accompt theym so, Synce they coulde not obteyne Lawe and Iustice to redresse theyr grievances. Addinge further that the Last Session, they were promysed that matters shoulde procede *Pari gressu, et aequis passibus*, But yt was not so meant, nor performed vnto them; for when the Kynge had obteyned his purpose, nothinge was effected or graunted which they desired.[3]

F. And further more, where[a] his maiestye out of his great and [7r] gracious fauer, sent for somme selected persons of the Lower house, to conferre with theym vpon somme necessary and Important matters; and that, not as wyth members of parlement, but as priuate persons and his Lovinge Subiectes,[b] This was quarelled at; and thervpon it was moued by somme in the open howse, That in theym that so dyd attende his maiestye, yt was an offence that deserued the Tower. And yt was moued by somme others, That the offenders shoulde be called to the barre to answerre yt. Some

---

[a] *Read as* when *in ibid., I, 282.*   [b] F *appears in the margin next to this line.*

[1] Actions such as these would, in Ellesmere's opinion, be the exercise of the king's prerog. for private gain and not for the public good: 'Prerog.', ff. 3r–6v.

[2] These problems also existed in joint com's of previous sessions: *CJ* 347–54, 394–415.

[3] The Commons debate of 16 Nov. 1610 in *Parl. 1610* II, 332–6.

others sayed that herafter they were to be estemed but as vnsauery salte.[1]

G. And one affirmed Confidently and bouldely, that by the Lawe, the Kinge had no power to calle any of that house, in such sorte before hym; and that the priuilege and Iurisdiccion of that howse dyd exempte theym from beinge so called, for yf any of theym were sued Iudicially in any of the Kinges Courts, and called by the Kynges wrytt vnder the great seale, they were priuileged and ought not to answere, and therfore *A fortiori* were to be priuileged for attendinge vpon such a verballe Commandement.[2] And this was vrged so fare that a Committee was appoynted to consider of the matter, and to sette downe an order to be obserued in Lyke Cases. Who resolued that albeyt any were so called thereafter, yet they ought not to reveale to the Kinge, any thinge that was debated or treated of in the house. Not regardinge that the Kinge assembled theym, and ys headde of that Counsell, wythout whome they ought not to consulte of any thinge.[3] [7v]

---

[1] Nicholas Fuller's speech, 23 Nov. 1610: *ibid.* II, 407. For the debate, see *ibid.* II, 337–8, 342–3.

[2] Elizabeth Foster suggests that this probably refers to the speech of William Holt in *Debates 1610*, 140–1.

[3] The Chanc's belief in the necessity of free and open conf's to resolve difficult problems was emphasised in the *Post-Nati*, 50–4.

XII

'THINGES TO BE CONSIDERED OF BEFORE A PARLEMENT TO BE CALLED' (1615)[1]

The Kinges state as now it standes, ys in a Consumpsion, and (as it pleased his maiestie to saye) in a feuer hecticke.

The disease.

Wherfore first our duetie ys, to fynde out the true Cause of the disease, and then to prouide Remedye. [2]

The Kings bountie abused.

Yt is apparent that his Maiesties gracious bountie hath bene abused by too Many, who as Bernarde sayeth, are '*Importum vt accipiant, Inquieti donec accipiant, Ingrati Cum acceperint*' [Importune sutors].

Gayne made by sutors.

And too much waye hath bene gyven to these Importune suitors, by those who had the Charge and husbandinge of the Kinges Treasure, and therfore should haue withstoode and stopped such sutes, and haue better informed his Maiestie. But theye, for the moost parte, made theyr owne gayne therby, and so abused and deceyued bothe the kinge and the suitors. [3]

Tully sayeth, They be '*sordidi homines qui benefitia Caesaris vendebant*' [Li. 13 Epist. 37]. And amonge the Lawes of the Emperors Carolus and Ludonicus, yt is ordeyned: '*Vt nullus de Consiliariis nostris propter benefitium a nobis impetrandum munera accipiant*' [Le. 224 pa. 966].

---

[1] Ellesm. MS 2610. Dated 18 Sept. 1615, and endorsed again at the end: 'Collections to be Considered'.

[2] The Chanc. had become increasingly aware of the economic and financial problems of the Crown in the course of his first decade in the P.C., and this concern was reflected in his S.C. addresses to the magistrates, 1597–1608: Hawarde, *Reportes*, 78–9, 161–2, 186–9, 326–7, 367–8. After 1610 he went back to his brief for a parl. speech of 1604 to note the kinds of problems for which no com's had been planned (Ellesm. MS 2614), which he then explored in this tract.

[3] This attack on the favourites is stronger than that at f. 1, and in sharp contrast to his earlier praise of the Scottish favourites of King James in 1608: *Post-Nati*, 110–17.

For remedy.

Now what remedy there may be, for so great and daungerous a consumpsion (which maye in tyme ruyne the state), and how his Maiestes present debtes maye be spedilye payed, ys first and speciallye to be regarded.

To equalle the ordinary receiptes and expences.

For thys, Consideracion ought to be had of his Maiestes ordinary honorable expences, and of his ordinary Revenewes and Receiptes: And according to the proporcion of hys receiptes to rate and stablish his ordinary Expences, and to reduce the same into a perfecte and Certen Compasse, To be herafter, by his Maiestes wysedome, and gracious goodnes, inviolablye kepte. And from hence furthe the Leakes in the Cisterne of the Treasurye to be stopped by his Maiestie.[1] [1]

The effectinge of thys, wylle stande in these twoo partes.

1. *For the future: To stay granted.*

For the future tyme, To foresee and preuent, That herafter no graunte be suffred[a] to passe of any thinge that maye abate or diminysh any parte of his Maiestes ordinary revenewes or receiptes, vntill his Maiestes debtes be payed and his ordinary Receiptes and expences be equalled.

And yf any person shall make any proiecte or offer of any sute wherby profitte may be made, Then the same to be conuerted to the increase of his Maiestes Revenew, so fare furthe as maye stande with Iustice, honour, and Conscience, And may be wythout inconvenience, grevance, or offence to the people. For that is a poynte to be in all such sutes specially regarded.

2. *For the present: Abatement.*

For the tyme present, To establysh this even proporcion and equalitye betwene the Receiptes and Expences, Consideracion ys to be had what abatementes May be made of any parte of the moderne expences and charges, As Namely in these herafter mencioned, and the Lyke. [2]

In pencions aswell foreyne as within the Kyngedome.

---

^a made *crossed out before* suffred.

[1] Ellesmere was attempting to overcome the criticism that was expressed in the Commons on supply in 1614: *CJ* 461–3, 467, 472–5, 506.

[2] Some of the details of the items in the following list are in Ellesm. MS 1216, f. 1r, an early draft of the Chanc's tract. 'First for abatinge' formed the initial section.

In the Realme of Irelande, and vnited prouinces.

In his Maiestes househoulde, by retrenchinge of new tables or otherwyse.

In the Offices of the Navye.

In the Offices of the Stable.

In the Office of the Wardrobe.

In the Office of the Robes.

In the seuerall Offices of his Maiestes buyldinges and workes. [2]

And in the moost of these, There is to be considered.

The quantitye of that which is prouided.

The qualitye, *viz.* the goodnes or badnes of yt.

The Necessitye, as whether it be nedefull of superfluous.

The price whether Excessiue or Reasonable.

The vse, Imployment of that which is prouided.

Also in fees for kepinge of Castells, fortes, and houses which are ruyned and decayed, Or wherof there is no vse.[1]

Whatsoeuer shall be thus abated, As yt wyll serue for proporcion and equalitye to be kepte herafter, betwene the Receiptes and Expences, So for the present yt wyll be a helpe towardes the payment of his Maiestes present debtes.

To increase the reuenew.

Besydes, Syth it is too manifest, That the auncient revewes of the Crowne haue bene much dimynished of late yeares; Consideracion is to be had how the same may be supplyed and increased, by Lawful, Juste, and honorable meanes.[2]

To examyne lavysh gyftes and etc.[3]

And herein yt standeth with honour and Iustice to examyne what Lavyshe gyftes and grantes haue bene obteyned from his maiestie,

---

[1] The first half of Cranfield's outline of Ellesmere's tract is a close abstract of these opening two and a half pages, ending with this sentence: Sack. MS 2330, f. 1r–v. This lengthy list for an inquiry into the K's govt. is as extensive as the demands of the Commons which Ellesmere had criticised five years earlier: 'Parl. 1604–10', f. 5r.

[2] Namely, by restoring the ancient laws with respect to the abuses concerning feudal rights, and the corruption and inefficiency of officials in the K's govt. – The basis of a brief prepared for him in Ellesm. MS 35/C/37.

[3] This section, together with the one below beginning 'What gaine hath bene made', formed the second part of his earlier draft: Ellesm. MS 1216, f. iv. The details, however, were omitted in the composition of this version.

vpon false suggestions, untrue consideracions, and by fraude and deceipte, and by whome and for whome. And such of those as maye be Iustely avoyded, either by stricte rules of Lawe, or by Iudiciall proceedinge in Courtes of Equitye, or in the Starre chamber, to be called in question, and yf Juste cause shall appere, to be made voyde.[1]

So for new offices.

And the same course to be houlden for grauntes of new offices wyth new fees, which for the mooste parte are nedeles,[a] or inconvenient, and chargeable to the kynge, and offensiue and grievous to the people. [3]

This maye be soone performed, and yt wyll be very profittable to his Maiestie; For it wyll be a great increase and supplye of his revenewe, and a good helpe towarde the payment of his debts, and very gratefull to all his good and honest Subiectes.

What gayne hath bene made by sale of his Maiesties Bontie and grace.

To this might be added, That Inquirye be also made, what gayne somme haue made, by Portesale of his Maiestes favour, bountie, and grace: And that gayne to be called for towarde the payment of his great debtes. But of those that haue made such gayne, shoulde be demed *sordidi homines*, yt wyll be a *Noli me tangere*.[2]

To equall the Exportacion and Importacion.

An other thinge of greattest Importance, ys the Contynualle excessiue Importacion of foreyn, superfluous, and vayne wares and merchandizes, farre Excedinge the Exportacion of the Ryche and Royall commodities of this Kyngedome. By which the Realme ys daylye more and more Impouerished and wasted, and yf it be not remedyed in tyme, the state can not longe subsyste. This requyreth great Consideracion, care, and Industrye of men skylfulle in the trade of merchandize; But such as feare God, and Loue the Kinge and the Commen Weale, and wylle not preferre theyr private gayne for

---

[a] and are nedeles *written and crossed out after* are nedeles.

[1] The Chanc's interp. of the role of judges had not changed: 'Prerog.', ff. 1-2.

[2] The subject of the sale of the K's grace was debated fully before the P.C., and the Chanc. later noted the views of each councillor in his notes on that session: Ellesm. MS 445, dated Dec. 1615. His position is noted on f. 2v.

the present, before the Kinges welfare, and the publicke state of the Realme.[1]

The Boke of Rates.

Amongest other thinges, I houlde yt convenient, that the laste boke of Rates be reviewed, and in Many thinges alterred, and many of the late Imposicions to be taken awaye, And somme to be Lefte and increased: And those to be Layed vpon thinges which serue for delicacies, pryde, Luxurye, and Excesse, and to corrupte the people, as these specially: Clothe of goulde and siluer, Sylkes of all kyndes, Wynes of all kyndes, Lawnes and Camerickes, Venice goulde and siluer, Spices of all kyndes, Frutes of all kyndes, Tobacco and etc. [4]

Yf this poynte for equallinge the Exportacion and Importacion be not effectuallye and spedilye dealte in, whatsoeuer else shall be attempted for abatinge or supplye, wyll be to Litle purpose: for this is a Consumynge Canker.[2]

Aliens and Straungers.

And for the better effectinge of this, Consideracion is to be taken what number of straungers and aliens, aswell merchantes as of other trades, are in the Kingedome, and specially, In and nere London, what Course they houlde in theyr trafficke and tradinge, To what excessiue wealthe many of theym are Latelye growne, and by what meanes.[3] And thervpon to consider what Lawes and statutes standinge now in force, are mete to be put in Execucion. And speciallye those herafter mencioned.

Statutes to be put in execution.

1. The statutes for Imployinge of money receyued for merchandize.
2. The statutes concernynge the Exchange of Goulde and syluer Coyned, and receyued more in value and etc.
3. The statutes agaynst transporting of goulde and syluer, in money, plate, or Bullyon.
4. The statutes prohibitinge to paye or deliuer by Exchange, to any person borne out of the Realme, any goulde, plate, or Bullyon and etc.

[1] This parag. formed the third section of his earlier draft, which is highly abridged here: Ellesm. MS 1216, f. 2r.

[2] None of these concerns can be found in his extant papers.

[3] The Chanc. had a survey taken for the London area, but it does not appear that anything was done with it: Ellesm. MS 25/A/17.

5. The statutes concernynge Exchange to be made to Rome or elsewhere, The merchantes to be bonden to bye merchandizes of the staple, and etc. to the value, wythin 3 monethes.

6. The statutes Concernyng Aliens dwellinge in Englande. *Ne forte per tollerantiam longiorem periculum maius Immineat.* As is sayde in the oulde acte anno Edward I, which is intitled *statutum de moneta paruum.*[1] [5]

A premonicion.

A premonicion to be gyven by Proclamacion or otherwyse, That these Lawes and statutes, or somme such of theym as shall be thought to be moost expedient, and best fyttinge to the present tyme and state, *Rebus stantibus*, shall be put in execucion herafter, more strictely and seuerely, from a certen daye to be prefixed.

A present legalle procedinge and etc.

And neuerthelesse presentlye, without delaye or differringe of tyme, a legalle proceedinge to be commenced and prosecuted, agaynst somme of the greatteste, wealthyest, and vyehest of the Offendors, for their Contempts and offences paste. They wyll be herby excited to sue for pardons, and to paye well for the same, and so wylle many other Lykewyse by theyr example. And by this meanes somme Competent summes of money may be presently levyed, for payment of his Maiestes debts, And these Lawes be herafter better Loked vnto and executed, for the good and weale of the kyngedome, and increasinge of his Maiestes treasure.[2] And so his highenes shall haue the Lesse Cause (his debtes beinge payed) to calle vpon his Subiectes for ayde or Contribucion.

The mynte.

The matter of the mynte and coynage is also to be seriouslye considered of, by those that haue knowledge and vnderstandinge therin.

---

[1] Ellesmere drew these out of his list of proposals for the reform of statutes that was prepared for the Parl. of 1604: Ellesm. MS 456, f. 2r–v. They formed the fourth section of his initial draft of this tract in 1615: Ellesm. MS 1216, f. 2v.

[2] The problem of recovering fines and sums due to the Crown in order to meet its own debt was discussed in the Chanc's copy of a tract on financial reform: Ellesm. MS 1170. His rather tough attitude to using the full rigour of the law in these civil matters was analogous to his attitude towards criminal offences: the S.C. decrees, for ex. In Hawarde, *Reportes*, 222–30 at 229, and 367–72 at 371.

For yt is now much amisse, To the Manifest great preiudice of his Maiestie, and Impoueryshing of his Kyngedomes.

Many proiectes.

Somme other thinges haue bene grauely and Iudiciously taken into Consideracion, for the supplye and increase of his maiestes revenewe, as Namely these:[1]

1. To alien and selle in fee ferme, some of his maiestes forestes, Chaces, parks, Lyinge fare of, and remote from any of his highenes Royall houses of accesse, and of which his Maiestie hath neither pleasure nor profitte.[6]
2. To inclose and Improue somme of his great wastes and Commen groundes, and to graunte the same in fee ferme.
3. To Infranchise and graunt in fee ferme his auncient Copyhoulde and customary Landes.
4. To selle Reuercions and Remaindors, dependinge vpon estates in tayle, wherof there be many issues Inheritable lyvinge.
5. To sell in fee ferme surrounded groundes to be recouered from the sea.
6. To selle Tythes of groundes not lyinge in any knowne paryshes.
7. To prepare and maynteyne Royall fyshinge in the seas belonginge to his Maiestie.[a]

All these be very good for supplye and increasynge of his Maiestes yerely reuenewe, and wyll in tyme helpe towarde the payment of his debtes.

The King payeth usury to his owne subiectes.[2]

But these wylle requyre longe tyme, and faythfulle, diligent, and industrious ministers. And in the meane tyme the debtes wyll remayne vnpayed and wyll increase by Iewish bytinge and growinge vsurye, which his Maiestye ys inforced to paye to his owne Subiectes, and perhappes for hys owne money. A thinge, in this kyngedome, neuer seene before his gracious Raigne. And yet moost of his progenitors and predecessors haue borowed great summes of money of theyr Lovinge Subiectes. And sometymes haue so borowed to lende to

---

[a] *Point seven was added later.*

[1] These points were in contradiction to his opinion – voiced frequently after 1603 – that it would be dangerous for the Crown to sell further land, rights, and privileges.

[2] The views expressed here were obviously influenced by those of his old friend, Sir Thomas Challoner, whose ms. treatise 'Agaynst vsurye' is Ellesm. MS 2468. The Chanc. was vicious in sentencing a 'usurer' in the S.C. in 1605: *Warren's Case, in Reportes,* 236–7.

somme other Princes theyr Neighbours and allyes. As Kinge Henry 8. borowed of his subiectes, and leante to the Emperor Charles 5. Quene Mary borowed to maynteyne Kynge Phillippes warres agaynst France. Quene Elizabeth borowed and leant to the states of the vnited provinces, and to the Late french Kynge Henry 4. But none of theym dyd ever paye vsurye for the same as his maiesty doeth. These matters are of such great Importance, as ought to be taken in hande spedylye, and dealte in effectually. For so Longe as thinges stande thus, the Inequalitye betwene [7] the Receiptes and expences wylle stylle contynue and growe more and more, which hathe bene suffred too Longe alredye.

Somme other proiectes haue bene, or may be made, which are not to be neglected, but to be Imbraced and putte in practize as tyme and occasion shall serue.

By whome these proiectes shall be Executed.

When these proiectes for (1)[a] alienynge forests and etc, (2) for improvinge of Wastes and etc, (3) for Infranchisinge of Copyhouldes and etc, and (4) for sale of Reuercions and Remeynders and etc, shall be putte in force,[b] Speciall regarde is to be had, not only of the sufficiencye, but also of the Integritye and fidelitye of the Ministers, to whome so great a charge and truste shall be committed. For otherwyse those that shall haue power and author[t]ye, to taxe and rate the value of the Landes, and those that shall Compounde for the price, are Lyke to gayne more by the bargayne, than the Kynge or the Crowne, And so *Nouissimus Error* wyll be *Pereior[c] priori*.[1]

Consider the late Courses.

And for the better vnderstandinge and direccion in this, yt is not amisse to Loke backe vpon the Course which hathe bene lately houlden; In sale of the Kinges landes, to (1) selected Contractors and etc, (2) and for assertes, (3) and for defectiue tithes, (4) and for surveyes and sale of wooddes, and (5) for leases in Reuercion and etc.

---

[a] *The numerals within sentences found in this and the following paragraphs were sometimes separated by slashes, sometimes by a parenthesis, and at other times by a period; the author has inserted parentheses throughout.*

[b] sore *should be read as* force.   [c] Pereior] Percior.

[1] On the relation of the ministers to the sovereign, see the Chanc's copy of 'Obseruations Politicall and Civill', Ellesm. MS 1174, ff. 15v–21v.

And to Inquire who hath gayned by such and other the lyke shyftes and bargaynes. And who soever haue so gayned by defrauding the kynge, They are theire heyres and executors, may lawfullye be questioned for yt, and Called to answerre.

The moost spedy and redy waye for payment of the Kinges debtes.[1]

Whylest these proiectes for supplye and increase of his Maiestes yerelye revenewe, (servinge rather for the future, than for the present, and which wyll be longe in doinge) shall be in deliberacion and handelynge, The other thinges which require mature and spedy despatche, must not be neglected nor differred, as namely the payinge of his Maiestes debtes. [8] Which can not be any waye so spedilye effected, as by (1) abatinge of somme parte of his present annuell expences and charges, (wherof some particularities are before specified). By (2) examynynge and Makinge voyde, somme such fraudulente gyftes and grauntes, as are before mencioned. By (3) amendinge the boke of rates, and taking awaye Many of the smalle and vnprofitable (but yet offensive) Imposicions, and by contynuynge and increasinge the Imposicions vpon other merchandizes and wares of greatter worth, seruinge for Delicacye, Luxurye, and Excesse, as is before declared.[2] And so by reducing the balance of Exportacion to a more equalle and better forme. By executing the statutes. By levyinge of debtes since 30 Elizabeth.[a]

Distribucion of the businesse to seuerall persons.

Which beinge well distributed to seuerall industrious and apte persons, maye all be in action, and handeled, at one and the selfe same tyme. And at the same tyme also, the other proiectes for supplye and increasinge of the Annelle Revenewe, maye lykewyse be proceded in, and the one not to be any Impediment or hyndrance to the other.

Many other meanes for paying the debts.

And for the more spedye payment of his Maiestes debtes, and to rydde and deliuer hym from this consumynge Canker of borowinge

---

[a] by executing... since 30 Elizabeth *was added later.*

[1] The second half of Cranfield's outline of Ellesmere's tract abstracts pp. 8–11, from here to the end, in a loosely worded fashion: Sack. MS 2330, f. 1r–v.

[2] Ellesmere had prepared a brief on impositions in May 1614, where he noted the ambivalence of the judges in Parl. and made several suggestions for attacking the problem: Ellesm. MS 2607.

vpon usurye, Speciall care is also to be taken; That (1) debtes owinge to his Maiestie synce *anno* 30 Elizabeth be Levyed with all diligence. And (2) reasonable fines to be payed by those that haue made buyldinges, or receyved Inmates, agaynst the Lawe or the proclamacions. Besydes (3) consideracion is to be had, that the profittes of his Maiestes wardes and Lyueries, and wardes Landes be fullye and trulye answerred.[1] [9]

And furthermore the Lyke Consideracion ys to be had what (1) profitte ys or may be made of his Maiestes Allume workes,[a] (2) Battery workes, water workes, (3) Copper as works, (4) Glasse workes, And of (5) Starche, (6) Tobacco, (7) Of the newe Company of Merchantes, (8) of the issues Roiall in the Exchecker, (9) Of the goodes and chattells of outlawes, (10) Of fines vpon sutes by *Latitat* and *quo minus*, (11) Of Dotarde trees to be soulde, *Quere et Caue*, (12) Of leases to be made of Coppice woddes and vnderwoddes *Quere et caue*, (13) Of byrentes as hennes, Capons, egges and such lyke, (14) Of perquisites of Courtes (not medlinge with fines for Copihouldes), (15) Of sale of Castelles and oulde houses to be demolyshed, (16) Of the profittes of the Clerke of the Mercates office, (17) Of the profittes of *Anno diem & vastum*, (18) Of the profittes *que Catalla felonum et fugitinorum*, (19) Of the profettes of Respite of homage.[2]

Meanes for future reuenewe.

And as of all, or of the moost parte of these, somme spedye profitte and gayne may be made, to serue for the present, yf the busynesse be well handled by faythfull and industrious ministers;[3] So of diuers of theym maye be levied a good future annelle revenewe. And yf it shall be thought good, that his Maiesty discharge his subiectes of payment of Respite of homage, and to grant to Lords of Maners, these Royalties of yeare, daye, and waste, and the goodes of felons and fugitiues, yt is Lykelye that many wylle purchase the same, at a good

---

[a] *The numerals in this and the following sections sometimes precede, or follow the prepositions and/or articles; the numerals have been placed in front.*

[1] With ref. to the brief on the reform of the Court of Wards and Liveries that was prepared possibly by Egerton, Lord Burghley, and others in the late Elizabethan period: Ellesm. MS 3001.

[2] This list is different from the one he had prepared in 1604: Ellesm. MS 456, f. 2v.

[3] And *infra*, f. 1. The Chanc. placed much of the blame for the state of the K's govt. on the royal ministers. Earlier, he had noted the maxim of Henry Savile: 'a good prince gouerned by euill ministers is as dangerous as if hee were euill himselfe': his copy of Savile's *The Ende of Nero* (1591), Hunt. RB 69625, 'To the Reader', sig. 3r.

rate. But that wyll aske Longe tyme, and to be handled by litle and litle.[1] [10]

When to calle a Parlement.

When all, or somme of the thinges before mencioned shall be begunne and in doinge, As Namely: (1) The abatinge and etc, (2) The examynynge of gyftes, and grantes and etc, (3) The amendinge of the boke of Rates, (4) The reformynge of the Imposicions and etc, (5) The putting in execucion of somme of the statutes before mencioned, Then yt wyll be requisite to calle a parlement;[2] And yt is not to be doubted, but his Maiestes good and Lovinge subiectes, seinge this Course taken by his Maiestie, wylle wyllingely and cherefullye yelde large contribucion and ayde, by Subsidies, Tenthes, and fyftenes and otherwyse.[3]

Mature Consultacion and spedy execucion.

This beinge the state of thinges as now they stande, Tyme is not to be spent and consumed with talke and discourse, as yt hath bene too longe, wythout resolvinge, or concludinge any thinge certenlye, But that which vpon mature conference and deliberacion shall be resolued vpon, to be presently put in execucion. For yt is moost true and certen which Demosthenes sayed, *'Rerum occasiones tarditatem, nostram etignauiam non Expectant.'*[4] [*ora* 1 Con. Philipp.]. [11]

---

[1] The corruption of officials in the depts. of state, and their responsibility for 'ye decaye of her maiestes revenue', was the theme of a tract on the decay of feudal revenues acquired by the Chanc.: Ellesm. MS 1521.

[2] Compare this with the Commons grievances in 1614: *CJ* 458–9, 462–9, 473–4, 491–3, 506.

[3] Ellesmere's programme was one full of substance, and in some ways it was a reply to the demands made by the Commons in the fifth session of Parl. 1610/11, to which he had written such harsh words: 'Parl. 1604–10', f. 7r. Yet he also seems to have felt like his judicial friend and colleague Henry Yelverton; that the king, by securing his estate, could then 'bridle the Impertynencie of Parliamentes': Yelverton's paper to James on 'The Proposicion', Stowe MS 153, f. 41r.

[4] The Chanc's appeal for conference and debate at the conclusion of this tract resembled that at the conclusion of his former brief: 'Parl. 1604–10', f. 7r–v. He now wished to pursue the parl. programme which had been abandoned in 1614: Hunt. Hastings MS, box noted 'Parl. Papers', speech of 5 April 1614.

XIII

'MEMORIALLES FOR IUDICATURE. PRO BONO PUBLICO'[1] (*c.* 1609)

GENERALL PROPOSICIONS.

1. To propounde to the Iudges howe the Incertentye of Iudicature maye be reformed and reduced to more certentye,[2] and how[a] the Infinite multiplycitye of sutes maye be avoyded, with which the people are intollerablye reped, and put to excessiue charge, as[b] by verditte agaynst verditte, and by Iudgement agaynst Iudgement, and by manifoulde[c] sutes in seuerall Courtes for one and the selfe same Cause.[3]

2. A viewe to be taken of the fees which sutors and Clyents paye, in all the Courtes of Iustice,[4] and to cause the same to be abated, and reduced to that rate and stinte, as was permitted and allowed before 30 yeares last paste,[5] and not to[d] allowe such new incroched fees and charges[e] as haue synce that tyme, bene extorted or exacted of the subiectes.

---

[a] not *deleted before* how.   [b] as *inserted before* by.

[c] manifoulde *inserted before* sutes.   [d] to *inserted before* allowe.

[e] new incroched fees and charges *inserted after* such.

[1] Ellesm. MS 2623. Written above this is the endorsement 'Pro Rege/ Memoriales pro Rege'.

[2] The uncertainty of the common law was a subject which the K. was delighted to expose. See Ellesmore's copy of *His Maiesties Speech to both the Houses of Parliament* (London 1607), Hunt. RB 91517, sig. C. The Chanc. noted a few of the uncertainties in Ellesm. MS 451, f. 2r. The background to this proposition was formed in his tract on 'Parl. 1604–10', ff. 5r–6v.

[3] These same subjects were put forward at the same time by Sir John Davies – whom Ellesmere had patronised to an Irish judgeship. Davies came to opposite conclusions: *Primer Report*, sigs. 3v–10r. The background of the problem – that parties who go to several courts require several different lawyers – was disc'd in the 1580s, and was defined succinctly in Francis Alford's recommendations to Lord Burghley on law reform: Lans. MS 44, f. 2r–v.

[4] The basis of this proposition lay in the Chanc's proposals for the exam. of fees and grants in all the depts. of state: 'Govt.' 2–3. He had a book of fees prepared for all courts, and depts. of state and household in *c.* 1596 (Ellesm. MS 6206B), and again in James's reign (Ellesm. MS 1198).

[5] The early 1580s, precisely the period in which the av. price of all arable crops begins to rise dramatically: *The agrarian history of England and Wales, Vol. IV 1500–1640* (Cambridge 1967), 819.

3. The fees of serieantes and lawyers to be moderated accordinge to former orders hertofore taken in that behalfe, which were sett downe in tables in euery Court,*a* and the same tables doe yet remayne.[1]

4. A view to be taken of the Number of Attorneyes in euery Court, specially in the kinges bench and commen place,[2] and thervpon a competent number of the moost expert and honest, discrete and*b* sufficyent only to be allowed, and the resydue to be discharged and put from that trade.

5. None of the Iudges servantes to be allowed to be attorneyes or solicitors of Causes*c* in those Courtes were theyre maisters bee Iudges.

[1r]

SPECIALL, A NOTE OF*d* SOMME MORE PARTICULAR INCONVENIENCES.

A. 1. That accions*e* upon the Case, upon false surmises and fictions in Lawe [*videlicet*f that Corne, haye, leade, Tynne, woode, and etc. which was growing in Cornewalle or Yorkeshyre, and was loste and founde in London or Middlesex and etc.],[3] be not herafter suffred for tryall of the estate, right, or title of Landes Lyinge in foreyn Countyes [*vie* Coke 6. ferredes Case fo. 7].[4] For this is a noveltye and a*g* tricke newlye deuised, and hath no precedent or example in the Register, or in the bokes of the Lawe, and is contrary to the auncyent institucion, and true groundes of the Lawe, and is the occasion of infinite sutes.*h*

---

a And the same tables doe yet remayne *added after* Court.
b honest, discrete and *inserted before* sufficyent.
c or solicitors of Causes *inserted after* attorneys.
d A note of *added before* somme.   *e* in *deleted before* accions.
f videlicet *inserted before* that.   *g* true] noveltye and a.
h and is the occasion of infinite sutes *added after* Lawe.

[1] He had sat on a com. of the P. C. to investigate the fees in the Courts of S. C., Chan., K. B. and C. P. in 1610: *Cranfield MSS*, 221–2.

[2] In add. see his earlier speech before the Court of S. C. in Hawarde, *Reportes*, 20; and his notes in Ellesm. MS 456.

[3] He is referring here to the writ of *latitat* and the eventual abandonment of the prelim. *capias*. The complaint began in the 1590s, and was expressed in a tract that received considerable circulation: 'Of the unlawfull holding of common pleas in the Kinges Benche', Lans. MS 64, ff. 202v–25r.

[4] This was not precisely the issue in *Ferrer's Case* (CP. 1598), where the purpose of the judges was to declare that when one was barred in a personal action the bar is perpetual except for action by Error or Attaint: 6 *Co. Rep.* f. 7r–v.

B. 2. The generall practize of the accion of *Eiectione firme*,[1] as of late tyme it hath bene vsed, is one other[a] of the greatest causes of incertentye of Iudicature, and of multiplicitye and infitenes[b] of sutes. There is no example to be founde of yt, in such sort, as of[c] late yeres it is commenly practized,[d] before *anno* 14 Henry 7, and verye rare many yeares after that tyme, and alwayes mislyked by many of the Reuerende and best learned Iudges, as Sir Anthonye[e] Fitzherbert, Sir James Dyer, and etc.[2] Yt hath bene a[f] great decaye of the true knowledge and learninge[g] of the lawe in reall accions, and hath almoost utterlye ouerthrowne, all accions realle that be possessory,[h] as assises of *Nouell Disseisin*, and writtes of entre and etc.[3]

C. 3. Persons that be in execucion, upon Iudgementes for debte or damages, ought[i] by the Lawe to be kept in *salue & arcta Custodia*, and not to be inlarged vntill the partie be satisfied. But of late yeares, there[j] hathe bene practizes devised[k] to gyue theym libertye to goe abroade [2r] with a keper, or otherwyse to in Large theym for a tyme, by writtes of *Habeas Corpus*; wherby they take theyr pleasure abroade in the Contry, and somtyme committe great ryottes and outrages there, and take no care to paye theyr debtes, or satisfye the Iudgmentes agaynst theym[l] as by Lawe and Iustice they ought to doe.[4]

D. 4. Accions and sutes in inferuor Courtes, are commenly stayed and[m] remoued by writtes of *Cerciorari*, graunted out of the Chauncery, the Kinges bench, and the commen place. And this is done for the

---

[a] other *inserted after* one.
[c] is of] as of.
[e] Sir Anthonye *inserted before* Fitzherbert.
[g] and learninge *inserted after* knowledge.
[h] as assises of . . . and etc. *added after* possessory.
[i] not to be inlarged, but *crossed out after* ought.
[j] yt] there.
[k] devised *inserted after* practizes.
[l] as by Lawe . . . to doe *added after* theym.
[m] stayed and *inserted before* remoued.

[b] *read* infiniteness.
[d] used] practized.
[f] the] a.

[1] His early annotations on *ejectment* are cited *supra*, Chap. V, 118–20.

[2] The development had its successful origins in *Sladès Case* (KB, 1597–1602), where the plaintiff recovered in debt on an action on the case for *assumpsit*. This occurred after Dyer's career (d. 1582, *Novel Cases* published 1585). Cf. J. H. Baker, 'New light on Slade's Case', *CLJ* xxix (1971), 51–67, 213–36.

[3] The Chanc's view that developments such as this had rendered the law confused and obscure was a theme of his speech to Parl. in 1604, where his notes were appended with the comment 'Nota bene': Ellesm. MS 451, f. 2r.

[4] The evidence for the use of *habeas corpus* to release debtors is cited *supra*, Chap. V, 113–15, Chap. VII, 168–71.

moost parte, by the Clerkes, without warrant or knowledg of the Iudges;[1] and therby yt often Commeth to passe, that one sute is remoued into seuerall Courtes, and sometyme by seuerall writtes into one and the selfe*a* same Court, wherby Iustice is hyndred, and the parties put to great and excessiue expences and charges.[2] Wherfore ordr shoulde be taken that no such writtes of *Cerciorari* shoulde be so *b* granted, but upon good and probable cause *c* serued to the Iudges. And the Lyk ordr to be for writtes of *Procedendo*, when such sutes be lawfully remoued.

E. 5. Also writtes of *cerciorari* for removinge of Inditementes haue of late bene more frequent [murders, felonies, Recusants, vitailers],[3] then in former tymes, wherby the proceding against many notorious offendors hath bene stayde, and often tymes the offendors haue escaped with out punyshment. [2v]

i. 6. Of late there is growne a new and commen practize, To haue secrett Iudgements upon confessions of debtes and dammages; and somtymes defesances are made upon the same, and somtymes colludinge and secrette trust,*d* without any defesance at all. Wherby many true creditors, and honest true purchasors are deceyued and vndone.[4] For they suspecte not these secrett Iudgmentes nor *e* know not how, nor where to serche for the same. Wheras yf any such debte were by Statute or Recognusance, yt might be founde in the office which was specially ordeyned for that purpose, by a late statute *f* *anno* 27. Elizabeth touching fraudulent conveyances.[5]

---

a selfe *inserted before* same.   *b* so *inserted before* granted.

c cause *inserted after* probable.

d and defesances are upon the same, and secret trust] and sometymes defesances are made upon the same, and sometymes colludinge and secrette trust.

e they suspecte not *deleted before* nor.

f in the office ordeyned by a late statute] in the office which was specially ordeyned for that purpose, by a late statute.

[1] The problem of the delegation, or misuse, of the seals of the courts was examined for the Chanc. by Mr Murray – one of his officials – in Ellesm. MS 2980.

[2] What Ellesmere had principally in mind was the complaints of conciliar and provincial courts against the use of the writs of *certiorari* and prohibition. These were spelled out by his relative Sir Roger Wilbraham, a Master of Requests, in Wilb. MS J. f. 164–5.

[3] He had commented on the different ways in which the writ of *certiorari* had come to be used in the *Earl of Hertford's Case*, Ellesm. MS 482, ff. 171r–2r.

[4] Ref's to his earlier notes on 'secret judgments' and fines have been given *supra*, Chap. V, 119–21.

[5] 'An act against covenous and fraudulent conveyaunces', 27 Eliz. cap. 4 (1584/5), in *Stat. Realm* IV, 709–11. The purpose of the act was to protect the Crown and lawful purchasers, leasees, and heirs.

ii. 7. Of late also there is an other new practize growne in the Commen place; That is, to sue an originall wrytte of *trespasse quare vi & armis*, which is no*a* finable writte, and to cause the defendant to be taken by a writte of *Capias* vpon the same originalle.*b* And then vpon his appearance, the pleyntiffe, doth declare agaynst hym in an accion of debt of a 1000£ or more or lesse, for which yf he sued by originall in*c* the Chauncerye he ought to paye a fine by the auncyient Course of the Chauncerye, and yf he sued by *Latitat* in the Kinges benche, he ought also to paye a fine, according to the ordr latelye taken*d* there.[1] But by this new practyze the kinge is deceyued of his fyne in both Courts. [3r]

iii. 8. Now of late also the Court of Comen plees, doeth houlde plee, of all penall statutes, and that by writte of *Subpena* awarded under the Iudiciall seale of that Court, and not by originall writte sued out of the Chauncerye.

iiii. 9. The lyke course is used by the Kinges benche and Commen place, and (as it is sayed) by the Iudges of *Nisi Prius*, to make writtes of *subpena ad testificandum*, for wytnesses.[2] All these writtes of *subpena*, they make without lawfull*f* warrant or authoritye, and thereby his maiestie is defrauded of the profette of his great seale.

f. 10. How so euer the questions touchinge Prohibicions shall be decided, yet it is convenient that the writtes of prohibicion be reduced to more breuitye, accordinge to the precedentes and examples of the Register, and not to be extended to such excessiue and unmeasurable length, as of late they haue bene.[3] Wherby the charge is so great that many, specially the poore clergye, are much impouerished,*g* and fynde yt better to lose theyr right, then to vndoe theym selues by suynge for it. [3v]

g. 11. And where prohibicions be grounded upon suggestions *de modo decimandi* and etc., according to the statute *anno* 2. Edward

a no *inserted before* finable.
b originalle *inserted after* same.
c out of] in.
d there *inserted after* taken.
e Which *deleted before* all.
f lawfull *inserted before* warrant.
g that the poore clergye is undone] that many, specially the poore clergye, are much impouerished.

[1] 'Liber Thomas Egerton', his commonplace book, Ellesm. MS 492, ff. 3–6.

[2] The problems posed by decentralisation, patronage, and corruption in *nisi prius* trials are explored by Cockburn, *Assizes*, 141–50.

[3] These rec's. were set out in greater detail in Ellesm. MS 766b, f. 1r. Exs. of Ellesmere's panacea for lengthy depositions are in Hawarde, *Reportes*, 55, 263.

6,[1] Order shoulde be taken that the proffe of the suggestion be more directe and pregnant, and by more sufficyent wytnesses, then of late haue bene allowed and suffred. And that for lacke of such directe and sufficyent proffe, Consultacions be graunted with all facilitye, and good Costes to be gyven in that Case*a* according to that statute.[2]

h. 12. Of late the Iudges of the Comen place, vpon suggestions made vnto them, haue used commenlye to make writtes*b* of *Habeas Corpus* to remoue persons Imprisoned, before theym in that Court, wherby Iustice is greatlye hyndred; and such writtes*c* ought not to be granted but out of the Chauncery of the Kinges benche, where the plees be houlden as before the king hym selfe – his Royall person.[3] And the Comen place ought not to awarde any such wryttes upon suggestions*d* but in Cases where sutes are Iudicially depending before theym by originall writte.

v. 13.*e* No process of outlary ought to be made *f* agaynst any deffendant in any personall accion, unlesse there be first four seuerall writtes awarded agaynst hym, *viz.*, the originall, a *Capias*, an *alias Capias*, and a *pluries capias*; and there ought to be 15 dayes betweane the awarding and making and the Returnyng of euery of the [4r] same wryttes, and yf the deffendant can not be arrested, or*g* doe not appere upon summon of the same writtes, then an *Exigent* is to be awarded agaynst hym, whervpon he is to be outlawed. Now all thos writtes*h* of *Capias, alias & pluries*, which by the true institucion*i* and auncient practyce of the Lawe were realle and essentiall, are by late practyze formed into matters of mere formalitye, and neuer sued out ordrlye and distinctely, nor deliuered vnto the shyreff and Returned by hym*j*

---

a in that Case *inserted after* given. *The handwriting becomes more hurried beginning with the following section.*

b Of late the Comen place, hath commonly made writtes] Of late the Iudges of the Comen place, vpon suggestions made vnto them, haue used commenlye to make writtes.

c and that Court] and such writtes.

d upon suggestions *inserted after* writtes.

e Before any subiecte can be outlawed in any personal action, if he make *crossed out after* v. 13.

f awarded] made   *g* can not be arrested, or *inserted after* deffendant.

h true *deleted before* writtes.   *i* institucion *inserted after* true.

j nor deliuered. . . by hym *inserted after* distinctely.

[1] The act referred to can not be found in the statute book.

[2] The two parags. above were abstracted from his book of 'Remembrances 4 Iune 1609', Ellesm. MS 452, f. 1r–v. The Chanc's analysis of this and other statutes on prohibitions is contained in 'Some Obseruations vpon ye Statutes', Barlow MS 9, ff. 13r–22v.

[3] Ellesmere soon changed his mind on the scope for the issuance of the writ by K.B. in 1615: *supra*, Chap. VII.

as they ought; But made all at once with antedates, and Retourned in the shyreffes name, by Clerkes and Attourneyes.¹ Wherby the sub-iectes are put to great charge, and yf any parte of this idle formalitye be omitted, the proceding is erroneous. None gayne by this but Clerkes and Attourneyes. Wherfore, synce this on ≪e≫ tyme wyll not suffr the first Institucion to be recountynued,ᵃ thes nedeles charges, for so vayne a formalitye, woulde be taken awaye for ease of the subiectes.

vi. 14. In all personall accions, and almost in all other sutes, one ≪of≫ the parties was to be fined orᵇ amercied in the ende of the pro-cesse, *viz.* either the plaintiff *per fals clamore*, yf he prevayled not in his sute,ᶜ or the defendant, if it passed agaynst hym. This forme is stylle contyned in the Recordes, but little or no proffette answerd to the King. Yt might be a matter of good value, yf it were loked vnto,² and the fynes and amercymentes to be proporcioned according to the value of the Coyne and money as it now runeth.ᵈ [4v]

vii. 15. Writtes of *dedimus potestate* for laking knowledg of fynes, haue of late yeares bene signed by some of th Iudges, to the ende that none Atturneys shoulde be trusted to be Comissioners in such Cases, but men of Integritye and sufficyencye, and so knowne by some of th Iudges, and allowed vnder theyr hande wrytinge. A course well de-uised by th great wysdome of Sir N. Bacon; but now abused and neglected by th Iudges, for comenlyeᵉ without regarde of the suf-ficyency of th persons named to be Comissioners, they indorse theyr name vpon the wrytte, and tak an excesse fee, *viz.* [————] or more for the same.³

viii. 16. The Iudges of th Kinges bench and Commen place haue of late yeares taken vpon theym as Chancellorsᶠ to mak orders in Equitye, according to theyr owneᵍ discrecions, not regarding nor

---

ᵃ synce this ... recountynued *added after* Wherfore.

ᵇ fined or *inserted after* to be.

ᶜ yf it passed against him] yf he prevayled not in his sute.

ᵈ and money at this time] and money as it now runeth. *The remaining sections of the manuscript are poorly abbreviated and sloppily written.*

ᵉ for comenlye *inserted before* without.   ᶠ as Chancellors *inserted after* theym.

ᵍ owne *inserted before* discrecions.

¹ An ex. of the Chanc. fining a sheriff heavily for making out a *capias* with a blank for the name is in Hawarde, *Reportes*, 113.

² The background for the coll. of such fines is in his tract on 'Govt.' 10–11. It should be noted, however, that it had become customary for the K.B. and C.P. to reserve such fines in meeting the costs of the courts; see Chief Justice Fleming's memo. to Sir Julius Caesar's complaint in Add. MS 10.038, f. 240 (30 Jan. 1607/8).

³ Ellesmere's orders for these commissioners are in *Chancery Orders*, 70–9; and Ellesm. MS 2960.

standing vpon, the stricte rules of Lawe, (whervnto they use to saye they are sworne);[1] and yf any such orders so made by theym, be[a] disobeyed, They awarde writtes of Attachement and Imprison the parties for disobeynge and contempt[b] of theyr orders. And so confounde the distincte Jurysdiccions of comen lawe and of equitye, challenging and taking[c] bothe to theym selues; and yet desire, to graunt prohibicions to staye sutes in Courtes of Equitye, where they thynke good.[2] [5r]

[a] such orders ... be *inserted before* disobeyed.
[b] They awarde processe of Attachement for contempte] They awarde writtes of Attachement and Imprison the parties for disobeynge and contempt.
[c] of lawe and equitye, taking] of comen lawe and of equitye, challenging and taking.
[1] Based on the Chanc's speech on judges interpreting statutes by equity against the intent of the makers and the rules and grounds of the law: *Rep. Chanc.* 7.
[2] This concl. is based on concepts which were expressed in the *Post-Nati*, 31–45, 54–8, and worked out in the common law–Chancery debate (*supra*, Chap. VII).

XIV

'SOME NOTES, AND REMEMBRANCES, CONCERNING PROHIBITIANS, FOR STAYING OF SUITES IN THE ECCLESIASTICALL COURTS, AND IN THE COURTS OF THE ADMIRALTIE'[1] (1611)

1. 《 Payment of Tithes 》

Tythes are payable *de Jure Communi*: And if there bee noe Prescription att all, eyther in *non[a] decimando*, or in *modo decimando*, it were good for ye Church and Common weale.[2] For when the tenth is truely payd to God, wee may trust in his Goodnesse, that hee will ye better prosper and increase the Nine parts to vs.

2. 《 Right of Tithes 》

The right of Tythes, is properly to bee tryed, and determined, in the [40] Ecclesiasticall Courts, And therefore when ye right of Tythes appeares to bee in Question, the Temporall Iudges ought to surcease, *ex officio*, although the partie doe not pleade against their Iurisdiction.

The[b] Right of Patronage, beeing a laye Inheritance, is properly to bee tried, and determined by the Common Lawe in ye Temporall Courts; and therefore, when ye right of Patronage appeares to bee in Question, the Ecclesiasticall Iudges ought likewyse to surcease. And this Difference is common in all the Bookes of ye Common Lawe.

3. 《 Trial of Tithes 》

When a suite touching the Right of Tythes is well commenced in the Ecclesiasticall Court euerie Circumstance or matter incident, which may barre or exclude ye Plainetiff from that benefitt which common Right giues him, may and ought to be tried in the same Court by the Iudges Ecclesiasticall, as a Custome or Composition for ye manner of

---

[a] modo *deleted after* non.   [b] *Item 3 crossed out in margin.*

[1] Barlow MS 9, pp. 49–8. A marginal note of the copier reads: 'Treatise of ye Lord Chancellor, Lord Elsemere'. At the conclusion is this: 'Tho. Egerton Ld Chauncellor of England, his Notes'.

[2] *Modus decimandi* is a composition for the payment of the tenth part of the property or goods for tithe.

payeing of Tythes; or a gift or sayle of the Corne, or Hay, etc. although the matter pleaded were otherwyse properly to bee tried by the Common Law.[1] For if it should not bee soe, then the Ecclesiasticall Iudges cannot determine the right itselfe, which appertaines to them only, and not to the Temporall Iudges.

And soe *via versa*, If a suite bee well commenced in the Temporall Court in many Cases, matters which are properly triable by the Ecclesiasticall Lawe shall bee tried by the Common Lawe; where the suite beganne: as in the *quare impedit* Habilitie, or Disabilitie alleadged in a dead Parson; soe whether the Church bee voide, or not voyde; soe Parson, and not Parson: soe wife, and not wife, etc.

4. « Prohibition »

And this Difference likewise is common in ye Bookes of ye Common Lawe. When a Prohibition is graunted vpon this suggestion, That hee yt sueth for the Prohibition, pleaded in the Ecclesiasticall Court, a Custom or a Composition etc, and that they refused to admitt and allowe his Plea. It is necessarily implyed therein, that if they had admitted his Plea, then hee had had noe cause to sue for a Prohibition; And, consequently it followeth, that if they had admitted itt they had power and Iurisdiction to trye and iudge it. And then in reason, this suggestion that hee pleaded such a matter in the Ecclesiasticall Court, and that the Iudges refused to admitt it is Trauerseable, and ought to bee putt in yssue, and tried; For if it bee a lye and false, it ought not to bee the ground of ye Prohibition; for it cannot bee warranted by lawe, nor Reason, that the Ecclesiasticall Court should loose their lawful Iurisdiction vpon an vntrue suggestion, and not bee admitted to haue any triall, whether the matter suggested bee true or false. And there is noe good authoritye extent in the printed Bookes of the Common Lawe, to prooue the contrarie.[2]

But if hee that sueth for ye prohibition, will suggest, That hee hath a deede or a Composition, or a Custome, or a statute to pleade which ought to bee determined by the Common Lawe, and that the Ecclesiasticall Court ought not to haue Iurisdiction thereof, then

---

[1] This was in fact legislated as the law of the land: 'An Acte for the true payment of Tithes', 2 & 3 Edward VI cap. 13, in *Stat. Realm* IV, 57; a statute which he discussed more fully at pp. 42–4.

[2] The Chanc's logic was impeccable. There were, however, few pr. law books concerning cases since the 1580s in circulation by 1611. The precedents in ms. law reports and treatises go both ways, and these are cited *supra* in Chap. VI.

there must bee deuised and framed a newe forme of Prohibition, and the forme nowe vsed (which is commonly grounded vpon vntruethes) must bee left. And soe it may That the Iurisdiction of the Ecclesiasticall Court may bee directly questioned and brought into Iudgement. But, then, how and by whome ye same is to bee iudged, will bee another question.

5. 《 Statutes Concerning the Jurisdiction of Tithes 》

The statutes Anno 32 Henry 8 cap. 7 and Anno 4 Edward 6 cap. 13 are full and plaine both in words and meaning, for ye true payment of Tythes, and for ye Iurisdiction of the Ecclesiasticall Courts in all Cases where Right of Tythes is in question. And it will bee heard to prooue by lawe or Reason, but, that the statutes concerning [41] Tythes or any other matter Ecclesiasticall, should bee construed and expounded by the Ecclesiasticall Iudges; As well as statutes concerning matters Temporall, are to bee construed and expounded by the Temporall Iudges;[1] specially, since the abrogating of the vsurped authoritie of the Pope, now that the King is (as in right hee was allwayes) supreame Gouernor of ye Church, and all Ecclesiasticall Iudges deriue and haue their Iurisdiction from him, and from none other. And yet in the Prohibitions, it is absurdly alleadged That the suites in the Ecclesiasticall Courts, bee in *Contemptum Domini Regis*.

The statute Anno 4 Edward 6 cap. 13 hath (amongst many others) twoe speciall Braunches.[2]

1. That noe Person[a] shall take away any thing, whereof prediall Tythes are to bee payd, before hee haue iustly diuided and sett forth ye Tythe, the Tenth part of the same, vpon peyne of forfeyture of treble value of the Tythe soe taken away. Soe, this braunch is only where ye Tythes are not sett forth att all.

2. That if any doe, willingly, withdrawe his Tythes, or doe stopp or lett the Parson or Vicar etc. to veiwe, take, and came away their Tythes, by Reason whereof ye Tythe is lost, impayred or hurt, then hee shall pay the double value of the Tythe soe taken, lost, with-

---

[a] *Read* Parson *for* person.

[1] Ellesmere was reacting here to Coke's charge that eccles. judges could not interpret statutes. The Chanc. defended their right to do so — while leaving himself in the chair of arbiter — in his speech to the P.C. of 23 May 1611: Tanner MS 120, ff. 10r–11v.

[2] The statute is mis-cited; it is 2 & 3 Edward VI cap. 13, and the branches are caps. 1–2 (*Stat. Realm* IV, 55–6). The analysis below follows the text of the statute very carefully.

drawen or carried away. Soe by this Clause, although the Tythe were once deuided, and sett out; yet if it bee after withdrawne, or if the Parson or Vicar etc, bee stopped or letted, to viewe and haue it, the partie offending is to pay the double value. And it is further expressely prouided, That it shall bee lawfull to ye Parson, Vicar, etc. or his seruants, to see their Tythes truely sett forth, and seuered from ye nine parts. And soe was the Common Lawe before this statute.

Now in these twoe Cases, where euer ye Treble value, or ye Double value is to bee payed, it is properly to bee tried and determined in the Ecclesiasticall Court. For first, before any Iudgement or sentence can bee giuen for the Treble or Double value, that Right of the Tythes must bee determined, and that appertaines meerely to the Ecclesiasticall Courts: [1] And if the Temporall Courts take vpon them to decide and Iudge of the right of Tythes, they doe that which is not warranted, eyther by the Common Lawe, or by any statute. And by the expresse wordes of this statute, the suite for the double value, is to bee before ye spirituall Iudges. And, after there followeth another Clause, That it shall not bee lawful for any person etc. to sue any with-holder of Tythes, before any other Iudges then Ecclesiasticall.

And the intent of this statute, and howe it ought to bee constructed in this point, may bee the better vnderstood by the words of the former statute: Anno 32 Henry 8, which are theis in the Negatiue: *viz.* That that Act shall not giue any remedye or Cause of Action or suite in ye Courts Temporall against any person which shall refuse to sett out his Tythes, or which shall with-hold or refuse to pay his Tythes, but the partie shall take his remedie in euerie such Case in the spirituall courts. [2] And the latter statute Anno 4 Edward 6 doth giue a greater penaltie in these Causes, but doth not restreyne or abridge the power or Iurisdiction to ye Temporall Courts, to decide or iudge of the right of Tythes, which before they could not doe; But, doth expresly ordeyne that the suites shall bee in the Ecclesiasticall Courts, and not before any other Iudges. And therefore, if in those Cases any suites bee in the Ecclesiasticall Courts, for the not deuiding or setting out of Tythes, or for stopping or [42] letting the Parson or

---

[1] A summary of his brief of statutes on tithes, Barlow MS 9, pp. 13–22 at 13–14.

[2] 32 Henry VIII cap. 12, in *Stat. Realm* III, 719–22. His recitation of the statute which follows is faithful to the statute roll. The part of the bishops and eccles. law in the enforcement of matters relating to the Church was made clear in a later statute of Henry VIII – 'An Acte for thadvauncement of true Religion', 34 & 35 Henry VIII cap. 1, in *Stat. Realm* III, 894–7.

Vicar to viewe and take his Tythes, noe Prohibition ought to bee graunted.

Besides this, the statute 32 Henry 8 doth not only authorize and inable the Iudge Ecclesiasticall to trie and determine the Right of Tythes; but doth alsoe direct their forme of proceeding in suits for Tythes, and addeth greater strength to their Iurisdiction, then before they had.

1. And, first it appeareth that they shall proceede ordinarily, or summarily, according to ye Course of Ecclesiasticall lawes.

2. If any doe appeale from ye sentence of ye Ecclesiasticall Iudge then the same Iudge shall forthwith adiudge, to ye other partie, his reasonable Costs of suits therein before expended, and shall compell the Appellant to pay ye same Costs by Compulsorie processe, according to ye Ecclesiasticall lawes.

3. If after Definitiue sentence giuen by ye Ecclesiasticall Iudge, any Person doe obstinately refuse to pay his Tythes, Then twoe Iustices of Peace (whereof one to bee of ye quorum) haue authoritie, vpon information to them by the Ecclesiasticall Iudge that gaue ye sentence, to cause ye Person soe refusing to bee attached, and committed to ye next Jeole,[a] there to remaine without Bayle or Maineprize, vntill hee finde sufficient suretyes to bee bound by Reconuzance to performe the sentence.

There is a like prouision in the statute 27 Henry 8 cap. 20 giueing like authoritie to any of the Kings Priuie Counsell, or to twoe Iustices of Peace.[1]

These prouisions will bee fruitlesse, and of none effect if in these Cases the Ecclesiasticall Iudges shall bee stayed by Prohibitions: or if the Treble value, or Double value shall in these Cases bee sued for and recouered in Temporall Courts, and soe the Right of Tythes bee decided there, and not by the Ecclesiasticall Iudges. And since the making of the statute Anno 4 Edward 6 there hath not any Action vpon that statute beene brought in any of ye Temporall Courts, for ye

---

[a] Ieoge[l] or [Ieege[l]] Ieole (Goal).

[1] 'An Acte conteynyng an Order for Tithes thorowe the Realm', 27 Henry VIII cap. 20, in Stat. Realm III, 551–2. There was, however, one most important exception – the City of London. The exception made it possible for common law courts to judge such matters through legal fictions and still remain within the purview of the statute. Thus the Chanc's allied attack on legal fictions below at pp. 45–7, and in his later tract on 'Iudicature', ff. 1v–4r, where he refers to the exs. here.

Treble or Double value of the Tythes, before《Alton》Woods Case in the Exchequer Anno 28 Elizabeth.[1]

And if such Actions shall bee continued, it will, in tyme, fall out, that all suites for Tythes, will bee drawne into ye Temporall Courts, and soe they will determine of ye right of Tythes in all Cases. For noe Parson or Vicar etc. can haue any cause of suite for Tythes, but eyther where the Tythes are not sett forth, and deuided from ye nine parts; or else, when after they bee soe deuided, and set forth, they bee taken away by the owner, or ye Parson or Vicar etc. is stopped and letted to take ye same.

6. [Costs and Damages vpon Consultations]

The statute Anno 4 Edward 6 cap. 13 giueth double Costs and Damadges to ye plaintyffe that sueth for Tythes in the Ecclesiasticall Court, and was stayed by Prohibition, and after hath a Consultation for that the suggestion was not prooued within sixe moneths, by twoe honest and sufficient wittnesses.

These Costs and Damages, are seldome graunted; for such witnesses and such proofes are commonly receyued, as fewe Consultations passed in this Case.

And in other Cases, where Consultations bee granted, yet the partie grieued, hath neyther Costs nor Damages, bee the Case neuer soe cleere, although the delay haue beene long, and the vexation and expences great and grieuous.[2]

If it bee obiected, there is noe lawe to giue Costs and Dammages in such Cases, It may bee answered that ye Iudges may doe it by discretion since there is noe direct lawe against it. For they doe many other things by discreation, as abridging and [43] increaseing of Damages in many Cases. And oftentymes, they extend their Discretion, if not *contra legem*, certainly *praeter legem*. As in taking vpon them to bee Iudges of Aequitie, and by colour thereof, sometymes

---

[1] *The Alton Woods Case*, 38 and not 28 Elizabeth, that was reported by Coke in 1 *Co. Rep.* 26r–53r, and criticised later by the Chanc. in 'Eg. on Coke', f. 48r. The disc. in this and the following section is directed to Coke's arguments, and this disc. formed the basis of one section of Ellesmere's observations on Coke's Reports at ff. 32v–6v.

[2] The statute should read as 2 & 3 Edward VI cap. 13, and is discussed above in pp. 283–4. There was a major discrepancy between the courts with ref. to costs, and the extremely low ones of the eccles. authorities proved harmful to their judicial development as the century progressed. The background is in Christopher Hill, *Economic problems of the Church* (Oxford 1963 ed.), pt. 2. A very different interp. of the statutes discussed by Ellesmere above is contained in Hill's study at pp. 77–92, 106–8, 125–8.

they staye Iudgement, as long as seemeth good vnto them in their owne Discretion. And which is more, sometymes they take vpon them the Office of Chauncellor, and make orders in Aequitie and awarde Attachements against such of the parties as disobey the same, and deteyne them in Prison, vntill they performe their orders.[1]

7. [For Probate of Testaments]

Of late in Cases of Probate of Testaments, new Prohibitions bee deuised newe both in matter and forme. As in this Common Case.[2] A man makes his last will and testament, and by the same deuiseth his landes, and giueth legacies of his goods, and nameth Executors, and soe dyeth possessed of leases for yeares and of moueable goods of great value, hauing alsoe many debts owing vnto him, amounting to a great summe. The Executors offer the Will to bee prooued in the Ecclesiasticall Court. A Prohibition is deuised and graunted.

1. The Pretence is first, that the right and title of the landes is to bee tried by the Common lawe.

2. That the Testator was not *sanae memoriae.*

Soe by this meanes the will is not proued, and before it bee proued, the Executors cannot haue any suite against ye Common lawe for recouery of the Debt or for any other thing in Action. Soe this Prohibition stayeth, not only the Ecclesiasticall lawe, but the Common lawe alsoe, as touching the Debts.

And for *non sanae memoriae,* if the principall suite bee well commenced in the Ecclesiasticall Court, they haue alsoe power to trie and iudge this point, falling incidently. And before Aueryes late Case, there was noe Lawe against it: And it is straunge to presume or suppose that a lay Iurie can haue more knowledge or vnderstanding to trie and iudge whether the Testator were *sanae memoriae* or not, then graue and learned Iudges in the Ecclesiasticall Court.

8. [Touching partiality of Ecclesiasticall Iudges]

To maintaine and conteyne this Current of Prohibitions, specially in Case of Tythes, there is a supposedd, or an imaginarie conceipt, that

---

[1] Emphasised later in his tract on 'Iudicature', f. 5r.

[2] Ellesmere's disc. here formed the basis of a longer commentary in 'Eg. on Coke', ff. 33v–4v. The problem, as that of tithes, was historic. The ramifications have been disc'd in the works of Michael Sheehan, particularly *The will in medieval England* (Toronto 1963).

the Iudges in Ecclesiasticall Courts, will not bee indifferent for triall of compositions, Prescriptions, and Customes, *de modo decimandi*, and such like.[1]

For answer to this.

1. It is to generall and preiudiciall to ye godly and Reuerend Fathers, the Arch-Bishopps and Bishopps, and to the graue and learned Iudges in the Ecclesiasticall Courts. And the lawe prouides Remedie by Appeale, if the sentence bee vniust.

2. The like may bee obiected against all Temporall Iudges, and with more reason and probabilitye, for they haue large possessions, for which they and their Tenants (which are many and wealthie) ought to pay Tithes.

3. And for the Ecclesiasticall Iudges, as it is well knowne, that many of the Reuerend Bishops, haue lay Possessions and Children to inheritt them. And all or most of the Bishops, Chauncellors, and Iudges in the Ecclesiasticall Courts, are laye men, and haue wiues and Children, and haue laye Possessions alsoe. And it is not likely that Bishops, or Chauncellors doe think or imagine that their Children shall succeed them in their places. And therefore it is not to bee doubted, but such Ecclesiasticall Iudges will respect fauourably enough their owne laye [44] Possessions, which their Children are to inherite and possesse after them.

9. [*Out of which Courts and how Prohibitions out to bee sued*]

Furthermore touching Prohibitions, a Principall point will bee out ⟨⟨of⟩⟩ which Court they ought to bee sued.

1. It is cleare an agreed by all men, that originally and properly Prohibitions are to bee sued out of ye Chauncerie, and to bee graunted vnder the great seale of England, which is [_____] *Regni*,[a] with the *teste* of the King Himselfe, *viz, Teste meipso*.[2] But of late yeares few or noe Prohibitions bee sued in Court, for all are ingrossed elsewhere.

---

[a] *word before* Regni *obliterated*.

[1] This was expanded in 'Eg. on Coke', ff. 35r–6v, after the pub. of parts 8–11 of Coke's Reports. The subject of this section had been a major concern of the Chanc's since approximately 1608: *supra*, Chap. VI.

[2] His concept of the seals, and of process sued out of the Chancery, was developed in 'Brief Chanc.', ff. 1v–2v, 4r–v, 11r–v.

2. Alsoe for many yeares past Prohibitions haue beene likewise sued out of the Kings Bench vpon suggestions made there, and haue passed vnder the subordinate seale of the Court, with the *Teste* of the Chiefe Iustice of that Court, *viz Teste* I⟨ohn⟩ Popham. But what sufficient ground or warrant in lawe there is for that Court to award Prohibitions vpon meere suggestions only, is to bee considered, for there appeares nothing in the Auntient printed Bookes of the lawe to warrant it. And it seemeth it hath growne there by Incroachment, by little and little, *tacite et sensim sine sensu,* as the abuse of *latitats* hath likewise done.[1]   And as ye Popes vsurpation did, not ouer all Bishopps onely, but att ye last, ouer all Emperours and Kings alsoe.[2]

And Plowden noteth the forme of proceeding in Prohibitions sued in that Court, [Plowden fol. 471. Sobeys Case.] and Taxeth it to bee straunge, and not consonant to the old Lawe or Order, and that it seemeth rather a Confederacy then a true suite, and grownded vpon lyes, and sheweth diuers Inconueniencies and Absurdityes in it, and setteth *de* [_____]*ᵃ* ye right and auntient forme vsed *ᵇ* in the Chauncerie. Yet it is not to bee denyed (for there are many bookes for it) that when Actions haue beene Commenced in the Kings Bench, and after a suite hath beene brought into ye Court Ecclesiasticall, for or concerning the same thing, which depended in Plea in the Kings Bench. In that Case the Iudges of the Court haue graunted Prohibitions grounded vpon the Record before them; but not vpon nude suggestions only.

And it appeareth alsoe in diuers Bookes, that the Iudges of the Court of ye Common Pleas, in suites depending of that Court, haue followed the Example of ye Kings Bench, and haue likewise graunted Prohibitions vpon the Record before them; but haue denyed to graunt any vpon suggestions only when noe such suite was depending there.

For the Iurisdiction of that Court of Common Pleas, is to hold Plea vpon writts originall sued out of ye Chauncerie and returned before ye Iudges of the same Court, and not otherwise (vnlesse it be in some few Cases of Priuiledge only); howsoeuer of late yeares, Prohibitions grewe common and current alsoe there: which belike is because they

---

ᵃ word after de *obliterated.*

ᵇ Note added later: Mr. Attourney Hubbart notes yt he speaketh against Prohibitions vpon bare surmise out of any Court, and quaere whether Ployden doth not require sight of ye libell euen in the Chauncery vpon Plea depending. In appendice to his discourse of Exposition of statutes.

[1] 'Iudicature', ff. 3r–4r.

[2] Part of the thesis of his 'Brief Chanc.', ff. 6v–11v.

would not bee behinde the Kings Bench, in a matter soe advan-
tagious.[1]

10.[a] [After adiournment of ye Tearme noe Prohibition ought to bee graunted in ye Court adiourned.]

But howsoeuer these Courts challenge vnto themselues this Iurisdiction, and authoritie to graunt Prohibitions vpon bare suggestions
only, yet it is euident (and cannot bee gaine sayed) that after ye Terme
ended, they haue noe such authoritie att all. For by the adiournment
of ye Terme their authoritie of Iudiciall proceeding ceaseth, or else,
to what end serueth the adiourning of ye Tearmes.

But to meete with this there hath beene of late a New and Straunge
practise deuised in ye Kings Bench contrary to ye Ordinarie Course of
Iustice and against all Lawe and Reason. That is, in the Vacation
tyme after the Terme adiourned, euerie one of ye Iudges (although
their authoritie for Iudiciall Proceedings ought by Lawe to cease),[b]
by vertue of ye Adiournment aforesaid, doe take vpon them to graunt
Prohibitions, Writts of *Habeas Corpus*, Writts of *supplicauit* for ye
Peace etc; Writts of *Supersedeas* and *Latitats*, giuing an Antedate, and
Teste to ye same the last day of ye last Terme before: to ye ende that it
may seeme to haue beene lawfully done in ye Terme tyme, when indeede they passed vnlawfully and indirectly after the Adiournment of
the Terme, as is aforesaid. [2] And sometymes vpon [45] new matter
growing in the vacation tyme after ye Terme was adiourned and not
before. And soe by this shift and practice the Lawe is defrauded and
Iustice greatly hindered. Specially by Prohibitions (by which Iustice
is stopped) and by Writts of *Habeas Corpus*, by which Prisonners that
are committed for great Contempts, or for Execution vpon lawfull
Iudgements, or sentences are enlarged, before ye Cause bee examined
or vnderstood. [3] And what law can be found to maintaine and iustifye
such vacation worke, for antidating of such writts, and vsing them
in this fashion *ipsi viderint*, for in the old printed Bookes of ye lawe,
there is noe such President to bee found. And what good cometh

---

[a] the figure does not appear in the text.   [b] parenthesis added here.

[1] The problems of the courts to which he was referring were those that have been sketched
by John Baker in 'New light on Slade's Case', *CLJ* XXIX (Nov. 1971), 215–25.

[2] He made the same charge, but not as complete, in his tract on 'Iudicature', ff. 1r, 2v, 3v,
among other indictments of a similar nature.

[3] This proved to be the background for his contest with Coke on the supremacy of the
Chanc's decree discussed in Chap. VII.

of it, or what aduancement of Iustice, appeared lately in Fullers Case.[1]

If it bee sayd, That[a] by this meanes, many bee relieued, which otherwise (if they should stay all ye vacation, vntill the next Tearme) should bee much hindered and preiudiced for want of Iustice. It may bee answered, that the Court of Chauncerie is neuer adiourned, but is allwayes open, as well in Vacation as in Tearme; and therefore whosoeuer haue any iust Cause, may there haue Prohibitions, Writts of *Habeas Corpus*, Writts of *supplicauit* and *supersedeas*, according to ye right and antient Course of lawe, and Iustice. And for the Incracher (Latitats) if hee did waite, and stay till the Terme, Iustice would speede ye better.

If this fashion of graunting Prohibitions etc. in ye vacation tyme with Antidates, bee alsoe comming into the Common Pleas, it is good to stay it in tyme.

11. [Noe Prohibition to bee graunted, but in open Court.]

And it is honourable and iust, and verie requisitt that noe Prohibition bee graunted att all, but in open Court, and that vpon sight and consideration of ye Libell and before ye suite in Ecclesiasticall Court bee readie for sentence. For it falleth out oftentymes, that Prohibitions bee sued eyther after sentence, or when sentence is readie to bee giuen.[2]

12. [The High Commission.]

For the High Commission in Causes Ecclesiasticall, if that Court doe proceede in Causes expressely mentioned in the Commission,[3] and according to the Tenour and effect thereof, there is noe Cause nor Reason they should bee stayed by Prohibitions.

And if anything bee inserted in the Commission, not warranted by the statute Anno 1 Elizabeth or else by the Common Lawe and the Kings supreame authoritie in Causes Ecclesiastical,[4] his Maiestie

---

[a] by this *deleted before* That.

[1] *Nicholas Fuller's Case* (KB, 1607), 12 *Co. Rep.* 41–4.

[2] Precisely what the Chanc. did in his own court with respect to the injunction against proceedings at common law.

[3] His later reforms for the Commission, 1613–16, which compromised his earlier position that is stated here, are disc'd in Chap. VI.

[4] 'An Acte restoring to the Crowne thauncyent Iurisdiction over the State Ecclesiastical and Spirituall', 1 Elizabeth cap. 1, in *Stat. Realm* IV, 350–5. The relevant sections are caps. 1, 7–8, 14; but there is nothing in this statute that precludes the common law.

hath been deceaued in graunting the Commission. And the Commissioners abused by colour of ye Kings Commission vnder his Great Seale. In that by these Prohibitions they are charged, as Contempers of the King and of his Crowne, whereas their endeauour is dutifully and diligently to execute his Maiesties Commission, and doe not presume to dispute, or doubt of His Highness Supreame Authoritie, and regall Prerogatiue, for graunting of the same: And this fault, (if any bee) must needes light specially vpon those learned men, that haue penned those Commissions, and presented the same to his Maiesties signature. And it cannot but touch alsoe, the Reputation of many graue and Reuerend Iudges of ye Common Lawe and other learned men of profession, that haue heeretofore executed the like Commission, whose examples the now Commissioners doe imitate and followe. Where if nowe after 50 yeares, the Iudges bee more quick of sight or of better Iudgement, then their Predecessors haue beene; they might doe well, rather to informe the Kings Maiestie what Errors or defect, they finde in ye Commission, and soe to cause it to bee reformed, then to trouble the Realme and interupt the quiet Course of Iustice, with such Prohibitions as they doe to ye discreditt of ye Commissioners, and to the dishonour of the King that graunted it, and to the great mislike and offence of many of His Highness faithfull and louing subiects.[1]

13. [The Admiraltie.]

For the Court of ye Admiraltie, the Prohibitions bee for the most part graunted vpon suggestion, that the suite in that Court, is for some matter done, or happening within the Body of the Sheires, and not [46] vpon ye sea or beyond the seas; wherefore it were requisite, that hee that sueth for a Prohibition vpon such a suggestion, should eyther make oath that his suggestion (or att least that part of it) is true; or else vtter[a] into Bond with suretyes to proue the same to bee true. And the Court may in discretion cause the partyes to take such an Oath, as in the Exchequer they doe sometymes cause ye Informers vpon some penall statutes to doe. [Plowden fol 1.]

And soe on the other side, it were meete, that hee that libelleth in the Admirall Court for any matter done vpon ye sea, or beyond the seas, or otherwyse, within ye Admirall Iurisdiction should make the

---

[a] read enter for vtter.

[1] Ellesmere himself was among the commissioners in 1605–13: Roland G. Usher, *The rise and fall of the High Commission* (Oxford 1968 ed.), 350.

like oath, that his libell is in that point true, or else enter into Bond with suretyes to prooue ye same true. But suites for matters properly determinable in the Admirall Court, are withdrawen from that Court, to the Courts of the Common Lawe (specially to ye Kings Bench) by an other late Deuise, more Common and worse then the Prohibitions; That is, by Actions vpon ye Case grounded vpon a false suggestion, and vaine fiction of a Trouer.[1]

Supposing in some Cases, that some Goods or Marchandizes, that indeed neuer were in England; and in some Cases, that a Shipp itselfe was lost in Cheapside in London, or in some other place in Middlesex, and there found by the Defeandant, and conuerted to his vse. And soe that matter, which naturally, and properly ought to bee decided in the Admirall Court, for that the grounds and Cause of the suite is matter happening on ye sea, or beyond ye seas, is indirectly, by an vntrue and vnlawfull fiction, drawne to bee tried by a lay Iurie of London or Middlesex and iudged by the Common Lawe. This practise, is, lately growne too common, and as it is now put in ure,[a] it doth not only wrong the lawfull Iurisdiction of the Court of Admiraltie; but doth alsoe make a great Breach in a Principall Maxime of ye Common Lawe itselfe, which is, that all things (specially the right and Title of Lands) ought to bee tried in their owne proper Country. But by this shift, vpon a fiction, That Tinne, Leade, Coles, Corne, Hay, Timber, and such like whatsoeuer, that did growe and come out of ye Landes in Cornewall, Yorkeshire, or Wales, were lost, and found in Cheapside or Middlesex;[2] the verie right and Titles of the Land itselfe is brought in triall there. A matter full of inconuenience and against the true Rules of ye Common Lawe, and therefore meete to bee reformed.

14. 《 Conclusion 》

And it would bee great quiettnesse to ye subiects, and a good meane to uoide much needeles trouble and expenses, if the Iurisdiction of all Courts, were conteyned within some knowne, certeyne, and Reasonable Bounds, and limitts; and that all Iudges would remember these words of ye Lawe: *Ne Iudices alienum iurgium putent suam quaedam.*[3] [1. 9 Tit. 27 *lege* 3.]

---

[a] jure *or* use implied.

[1] Milsom, *Historical Foundations*, 326–32.

[2] 'Iudicature', f. 2r–v. The importance, for Ellesmere, of preserving the jurisd. of local and provincial courts – both lay and eccles. – is discussed *supra*, Chap. VI.

[3] Based on Ellesmere's conception of the const: 'Parl. 1604–10', *passim* and f. 1r.

The*a* statute Anno 23 Henry 8 cap. 9. That noe person shall bee cited to appeare out of his Diocese, cannot extend to ye High Commission.[1]

1. It was made before any such Commission was graunted, and when ye vsurped Iurisdiction of the Pope had full Course in England, and before ye King had resumed his Regall Iurisdiction in Causes Ecclesiasticall. And therefore it is against Reason and absurd, to applye that statute to ye High Commissioners, whoe deriue their Iurisdiction from the King, by vertue of his Greate Seale of England, and not from any other forreigne or vsurped power.

2. The Preamble of the statute sheweth what High Courts are meant by the Parliament, *viz* the Arches, the Audience, and other High Courts of the Archbishopps of this Realme: But the Court of the High Commission is none of these.

3. The wordes of the Body, and purueiwe of that statute doe extend but to Ordinaryes, Archdeacons, Commissaries, Officialls or other spirituall Iudges; which generall words (or ther [47] Spirituall Iudges) are to bee intended of Iudges inferior to these that are before named; and not to the High Commissioners. And these High Commissioners are not properly to bee tearmed Spirituall Iudges, when they proceede by vertue of the Kings Commission vnder the Great Seale of England in Spirituall Causes committed vnto them by the King.

4. The Cases they deale in, are for ye most part none of the Cases mentioned in that statute; *viz.* for Defamation, with-holding of Tythes, or such like, but are some of the speciall Cases excepted in the statute. As;[2]

1. When the Inferiour Iudge hath committed, or done some thing hee ought not; or hath omitted or neglected something hee ought to haue done.

2. In Cases of Appeale.

---

a begins another section unnumbered and not titled.

[1] 'An Acte that no personne shalbe cited oute of the Diocese where he or she dwelleth excepte in certayne cases', 23 Henry VIII cap. 9, in *Stat. Realm* III, 377–8. The statute does, however, circumscribe closely the matters which can be brought to the courts of the Archb., and the tenor of this clause is perhaps closer to Ellesmere's conception of the eccles. courts and commissions than he alludes to in this brief.

[2] Some of the more interesting case studies that discuss these actions are those of R. Marchant, P. Tyler, and J. P. Anglin.

3. When ye Partie findeth him selfe grieued or wronged by the Ordinarie or Inferior Iudge after ye suite commenced there.

4. When ye Inferior Iudge dares not, or will not conuent[a] the Partie that is sued.

5. Wher the Bishopp or inferior Iudge is partie, directly, or indirectly, to the matter or Cause of suite.

6. Where ye Bishopp or Inferiour Iudge doth make request or instance to the Arch-Bishopp or superior Iudge, to examine, and determine ye matter, and where the Ciuill and Canon Lawe doth admitt such request, or instance.

7. Where Testaments are to bee prooued before the Arch-Bishop by his Prerogatiue.

8. The Arch-Bishopp may cite and call any Person in Case of Heresie, if the immediate Ordinarie consent thereunto, or doe not his dutie in punishing ye same.

9.[b] If any Archbishopp, or other superior Iudge offend in this kind, the statute inflicteth the punishment, *viz*, To ye Partie cited, double damages, and 10£ to bee forfeited to ye King: but taketh not away the Iurisdiction from ye Archbishop, nor giueth any Prohibition in such Cases. [48]

[a] Conuent (?).
[b] read 9 for 5.

XV

'THE LORD CHANCELLOR EGERTONS OBSERVACIONS VPON YE LORD COOKES REPORTES' (1615)

In the Reuiew of my Lord Cookes Reports.[1] Whereas in the debate of Causes brought to ye Iudgement seate they may all be reduced to one of theis 4 heads: either such as Concerne

1. The right of the Church
2. The power of the Kings Prerogatiue
3. The Iurisdiccion of Courtes: or
4. The Interest of the Subiect.

It is to be obserued throughout all his bookes, That he hath as it were purposely Laboured to derogate much from the Rights of the Church and dignitye of churchmen, [p. 1] and to disesteeme and weaken the power of ye King in the ancient vse of his Prorogatiue.

To traduce or els to cutt short the Iurisdiccion of all other Courts but of that Court wherein himselfe doth sitt,[2] and in the Cases of subiect.[a]

Sometimes to report them otherwise then they were adiudged. Sometymes to report them to be adiudged which were not. Sometimes by running before the Iudgement, as in publishing the case depending the writt of Errour whereby the first Iudgment should bee better examined; and oftentimes in setting [32r] downe that for Resolue which himselfe drawes in vpon the By and tendeth nothing to the point in Iudgement.[3]

In all which points, It is not easily to be discerned whether he hath erred more in setting downe the sudden opinions of Iudges for re-solucions, which is more then the Iudges themselues intended, or in scattering or sowing his owne conceits almost in every Case by takeing occasion though not offered to range and Exspaciate vpon

---

[a] *This paragraph was excluded from the printed edition.*

[1] Harg. MS 254, ff. 32r–50v. The page refs. are to the printed ed. (n.d.), the folio numbers to the ms.

[2] A theme of his speech to the P.C. on prohibitions and the eccles. courts, 2 May 1611 (Harg. MS 278, f. 259v), and of his tract on 'Iudicature'.

[3] The context of these charges stems from the Chanc's views on the common law that were expressed in the *Post-Nati*, 33–8, 50–66, 84–6.

by-matters. And albeit in the pervsall of all his workes it may be truely said of theym *sunt mala, sunt quaedam mediocria, sunt bona plura*; yett if the evill, that of it selfe possesseth much roome, may be drawen into a lesser, then the residue which are *bona* or *mediocria* will the better appeare and the more firmely be established.[1]

There shall therefore be given a tast how in every of the former points there is offence left, *et quia a Jove principium*. First shall be sett downe some such Cases wherein he doth too much disestimate the Church and Churchmen.[2]

In the Case of the Bishopp of Winchester (44. 45).[3] The plaintiff in the surmise of the prohibicion to remoue a suite [32v] for Tythes out of the Speritall Court alledged how he had pleaded before the Ecclesiasticall Iudge that he was farmer for yeares to the Bishopp of Winchester of the Mannour of Estmoure, and that the Bishopp his predecessours tyme out of mind had held the said Mannour for him and his Tennants for yeares discharged from payments of Tythes, and though he had pleaded this before the iudges Deligates and offered to prove it yett they refused to admitt his Allegacion and his proofes. To which the defendant said that the Iudges [p. 2] Delegates had allowed the Alligacion and admitted the plaintiffe to his proofes and Trauersed; *Absque hoc* that the Dellegates refused to admitt the Allegacions and proofes of the plaintiff, which Trauerse by the Report was resolued to be insufficient; for saith he the Allegacion of the Refusall of the Ecclesiasticall Iudge are words more of Course then of effect and substance. For in the Case of discharge of Tythes or *de modo Decimandi*[a] the Iudges of our Law know well that the Iudges Ecclesiasticall will not allow such Allegacion.[4]

---

[a] *Spelled* Decimondi *inaccurately by the transcriber.*

[1] These hot words were expanded on greatly by Sir Francis Bacon in *The Remaines* (London 1648), 20–7.

[2] Ellesmere's outline for this section of the draft is in Harg. MS 254, ff. 54r–5r. Some marginal notations on Coke's reports of cases concerning the eccles. jurisd. are contained in Ellesmere's copy of *The Fift Part of the Reports of Sir Edward Coke Knight* (London 1605), Hunt. RB 60778. This section of the Chanc's tract was reviewed by a contemp. lawyer in Add. MS 14.030, ff. 91r–2r.

[3] *The Bishop of Winchester's Case* (KB, 1596), 2 *Co. Rep.* (1602), ff. 38r–45v. See also Coke MS Rep. C, ff. 182v–4v. Since the cases are generally known by their English titles, the author has given the titles from the modern ed. (English) of 1826. As the calendar years of cases are not always precisely rendered by editors, the author has dated the cases in accordance with the contemp. calendar (Old Style). The refs. to the cases and their original date of pub. are cited from Coke's first edition (in Law French).

[4] Based on his position in the P.C. debate on the third question of the Archb. of Cant., 23 May 1611: Tanner MS 120, ff. 10r–11v; and also reported fully in L.I. Add. MS G.2, I.T. Misc. MS 20, Rawl. MS B.202, Petyt MS 518 and 511/16, and Harg. MS 278. For *de modo Decimandi*, see Barlow MS 9, ff. 23r–7r, and Petyt MS 538/55, ff. 30v–4v.

1. Now herein are the Ecclesiasticall Iudges much [33r] Taxed as if there Iustice were not Equall *Partibus Litigantibus.* But yet they will Condeme the defendant though he produce sufficient proofes to acquite him.

2. As if the Iudges of the Comon Law *ex officio* tooke notice of the partialitie of the Sperituall Iudge which they doe not nor can take notice of.

3. It appeared to the Court by the case it selfe that the sperituall Iudge had admitted the allegacion and proofes of the partye, and therefore is the imputacion laid vpon them the greater, as that they shalbe said to deny that vniustly which in the course of Iustice *et de vero* they had admitted.

In the case of the Marquesse of Winchester (*liber* 6: 23a).[1] It is reported to be *Concessum per ⟨Curiam⟩*[a]: That if a man by his will devise lands to a younger sonne or to any other and by the same will bequeath alsoe many Legacyes, the heire may haue a prohibicion vpon surmise his father was not *sanae memoriae* at the time of makeing his will of the Land, and by this stay the whole proceeding in the Ecclesiasticall Courte [33v] Aswell for Legacies and Bequest in the personaltie as for the land, ⟨shall be suspended⟩.[b] If this should be Law then in this Case and all other cases wherein the will of land may be suggested to be voyd (which are infinite) it will Close vp the hands of most of the Ecclesiasticall Iudges and also be mischeuious to many subiects.[2] [p. 3]

1. For that the probate of wills is proper for the Ecclesiasticall Court and the Common Law medleth not therewith; and by takeing the probate from them their Right is taken from them and yett given to no other.[3]

2. In the same will there being both Land deuised and goods bequeathed, the Law doth distribute the power according to the nature of the thinges conteined in the will. The will for soe much as concerneth the land to be tryed att the Common Law; for soe much as

---

[a] Chartum] Curiam *in the printed edition.*

[b] *Omitted in the MS ed.*

[f] *Pawlet Marquess of Winchester Case* (KB, 1599), 6 Co. Rep. (1607), f. 23r–v.

[2] The Chanc's opposition to the extensive use of prohibitions against the eccles. courts was well expressed in his tract on law reform: 'Iudicature', ff. 3v–4r.

[3] Among several items listed by the Chanc. wherein 'The Comen place to grant no prohibitions' – Ellesm. MS 766 (b), f. 1r–v.

Concerneth the goods to be Tryed att the^a Sperituall Court. And therefore since the Common Law hath onely power over the Land and noe power over the goods, it is noe reason that the Common Law should probibite the Ecclesiasticall Iudge generallie but to grant a [34r] Consultacion *quoad bona et Legata*; and soe the prohibicion to be for the land onely, and hereby to leaue to each Court his proper power; and this the rather because the probate of a will in the Ecclesiasticall Court Concludeth not the Courtes of the Common Law.

3. By staying the probate of the will as to the goods and Legacies the Executours of the parties are disabled to sue for any debts due to their Testatour, for they can mainteine noe such suite without shewing forth the Testament proued vnder the seale of the ordinarye, and this may bring in many Mischeifes: That the Executours cannot pay debts because they cannot Recover them; that Legates cannot haue the thinges given them because the hands of the sperituall Iudge are tyed; that they cannot proceed vpon any parte of the will vpon such bare suggestion of the demise of a Little land onely. [p. 4]

In the Case of Trollop (*liber* 8: 68b).[1] The Point in Iudgement was whether Excomunicacion pleaded in the Exchecquer against the plaintiff in *Quo Minus* under the Seale of the officiall, [34v] And with a speciall direccion of *omnibus Clericis & etc.* which could not comprehend ⟨the proper Direction to⟩[b] the Courte, bee good or noe.

Yett the cheife Iustice in his Report starts aside to other matters and setts it downe as Resolued: That the Iudges of the Common Law shall Iudge vpon ye matter and in some cases vpon the matter[c] in the Certificate of Excommunicacion, adding withall that the Certificate of the Bishopp must Comprehend in particuler the Cause of the Excommunicacion, to the end that the Iudges of the Law may Iudge whether the Ecclesiasticall Court hath Conusance of the Originall Cause.[2]

Now the matter in question could not drawe in this discourse, but rather the desire of the Reporter to intrude vpon other mens profession and to weaken the power of the Ecclesiasticall Court, as if

[a] in *deleted before* the.   [b] *Omitted in the MS ed.*   [c] *For* matter *read* Manner.
[1] *John Trollop's Case* (KB, 1609), 8 Co. Rep. (1611), ff. 68r–9r. Coke's original is in MS Rep. E, ff. 20v–1v.
[2] This formed a major theme of Ellesmere's 'Brief Chanc.', f. 5v. Coke had argued this point consistently; as for ex. in MS Rep. A, ff. 726v–7r, 739r, 741r–v.

they were not absolute in themselues in Iurisdiccions naturally belonging to them, but Subordinate ⟨to⟩ *a* the Iudges of the Common Law to be Controlled in thinges that fall not within ye Leuall of the Common Lawe.[1] [35r]

For if the Cause of Excommunicacion be warranted by the Common Law and the Common Law shall iudge the same insufficient, if now the Bishopp shalbe Compelled to absolue him he shall doe against the knowne Iustice of his owne Court which were most inconvenient.

The like fancy he sheds (*liber 5: 57*) ⟨in⟩ *b* Specote Case:[2] that the Bishopp refuseing a Clerke presented to him for Schisme shalbe forced to returne the speciall pointe wherein the partie is a Schysmatick; yett he deenies not but that the Iudges of Common Law can neither examine nor iudge the point of Schisme no more than of heresye. [p. 5]

In which points the Bishopps and Ecclesiasticall Iudges are much embased both in there honours and professions, as if in things meerely Concerneing the Church they had any other eyes over them saue the Kings onely.

In the Case of Magdalen Colledge (*liber 11: 7b*).[3] Though the point of the case be only whether Colledges be disabled by the statute of the 13 of Elizabeth to giue any Lands and etc. to the Queene [35v] and soe now to the Kings Maiestie;[4] As if he tooke delight a little to Lash the Clergie though nothinge pertenent to the matter in question he degresseth to vse these Words: A parson that hath the cure of souls and is non-resident *non est dispensator sed dissipator, non speculator sed spiculator*, which words being spooken soe generally and absolutely without respect of person or cause, strike att the Roote of all dispensacions And Pluralities tollerated by the statute of 21 H. 8, and which

---

a *Added to the pr. ed.*   *b* *Added to the pr. ed.*

[1] This was precisely the purpose of a number of common lawyers. According to one observer the jurisd. of the eccles. courts was growing inordinately, and constantly encroaching on the jurisd. of the common law. Thus prohibition, *significat*, *supersedeas*, and *praemunire* were legitimate writs to restrain the bishops and their courts: 'Law', F-H MS 75, esp. ff. 9r–34v. Coke made these views public in 1611, and they have been pubd. in *Const. Docs.* 156–63.

[2] *Specote's Case* (KB, 1589/90), 5 *Co. Rep.* (1605), ff. 57r–9r; and the reps. in Edmund Anderson, *Les Reports des mults principals Cases* (1664), I, 189–91; [William Leonard] *Reports and Cases of Law* (1658), III, 198–200; and John Goldesborough, *Reports of Courts at Westminster* (1653), 35–7.

[3] *The Case of the Master and Fellows of Magdalen College* (KB, 1615), 11 *Co. Rep.* (1615), ff. 66v–79r. See also Hale MS 83, ff. 161–6.

[4] 'An Acte agaynst fraudulent Deedes, Gyftes, Alienations, etc', 13 Eliz. cap. 5 (1571), *Stat. Realm* IV, 537–8.

necessitie of theis times still enforceth to be continued;[1] yett how bitterly doth he brand them, though in a bie discourse wherein he discovereth his small affection to ye Clergie of theis tymes.

In Godferies case (*Liber* 11: folio 43):[2] wherein the point in Iudgement was onely whether a Steward of a Leete vpon Contempt of a Iury in refuseing to present some articles in a Leete might impose a Ioynt Fine vpon all the Iurors, or that he ought to assesse particuler fines vpon every particular Iuror. Notwithstanding to discredite the Ecclesiasticall Courte and to make them lightly esteemed of though no [36r] fitt occasion be offered hee hath theis words: Some Courts cannot inprison, fine, nor amerce as Ecclesiasticall Courts held before the ordinary, Archdeacon, and etc. or their Comissaries, and such like Courts as proceed according to the Cannon or Civill law; wordes which extend not onely to the Bishopps Courts but the high Commission, the Prouiciall Councells, the admiraltie, the Court of Requests, and the authority of the Councell Table it selfe.[3] [p. 6]

CONCERNEING CASES YT CONCERNE HIS MAIESTIE.[4]

Whether they be in point of Estate or in point of power, in all his reports he hath stood so much in phrase vpon the King«s» honour, as in his Resolucions he hath had no respect to the Kings profitt. But in all his Cases sett forth by him since he was a Iudge every Pattent is made good whereby the King parteth with his Inheritance, and every Pattent is made void by which his Maiestie would expresse his Power in dispencing with thinges forbidden, or grant his power in doeing

---

[1] 21 Henry VIII cap. 13, on 'Pluralities' (1529), *Stat. Realm* III, 292–6, especially clauses 9–18.

[2] *Richard Godfrey's Case* (KB, 1615), 11 *Co. Rep.* (1615), ff. 42r–6r. See also Ellesmere's abridg. of Coke's rep. in Harg. MS 254, f. 29r–v.

[3] The Chanc. was easily perturbed by individuals who challenged the structure and auth. of the court system. Earlier he referred to such individuals as being subversive to the commonwealth: 'Parl. 1604–10', f. 5r. He had a list drawn up, for ex., of causes in eccles. courts which should not be disturbed: 'Some noates and remembrances', Tanner MS 176, ff. 1r–5v, and Barlow MS 9, ff. 40r–8v, which was sent to the Archb. of Cant. on Christmas Day 1608. For Coke's attack on the Court of Arches see his opinion in the *Rochester Case* (CP, 1608), Cleo. MS f. II, ff. 467r–78v.

[4] His outline of this section is in Harg. MS 254, f. 54r. Neither the *Prince's* nor *Wiseman's Case* was discd. in the earlier draft. Elsewhere, Yelverton's critique of Coke's reports was devoted to the subjects of 'the power and jurisdiction of courts and commissioners', and 'the Kings prerogative': Stowe MS 153, ff. 39r–40v. Reversing these two subjects in their order of appearance, the outline of cases in this section of Ellesmere's tract is similar to that in Yelverton's.

such thinges as formerly had beene done by the like Pattent; to instance but in a few for all.[1] [36v]

1. In Darcies case (*liber* 11: 88),[2] or the Cheife Iustice doth report it to be resolued: That the dispencacion or Licance of Queene Elizabeth to Darcy to haue the sole importacion of Cardes notwithstanding the statute of 3. Edward 4 was against the Law.[3] But those that obserued well the passage of that case and attended the Iudgment of the Court in that case, Doe know that the Iudges never gaue any such Resolucion in that Point, but passed it by in silence because they insisted vpon the body of the pattent; whereby the Trade of makeing Cards which was Common to all was by the patent appropriate to Darcy and his Assignes, which the Iudges held against the Law because it sounded in distrucion of a Trade whereby many subiects gott their Liueing.[4] But in point of Dispensacion it hath ever been allowed in all ages, and the defference taken Betweene *Malum in se et Malum prohibitum*, the Kings cannot dispence with the first with the other he may. But that new difference invented by the reporter, that the King may dispence with *Malum prohibitum* but cannot dispence with a Statute made *pro bono publico*. [37r] But the troth is the onely reason of the Iudgment was that which is mencioned by the Reporter but *obiter*, which was because Darcyes patent might excuse him vpon an informacion brought vpon the Statute but could not giue him an accion of the case against another. [p. 7]

2. In the Princes case (*Liber* 8: 29:30),[5] he restrayneth the Dukedome of Cornwell Litterally to the First begotten sonne of the King and not the eldest sonne *pro tempore*, which is a great Diminucion to the Kings honor, and in a manner a disherison to our noble prince Charles who by the Death of his brother without issue is now *filius primogintus Regis existens*.

[1] Ellesmere's criticism refers to his earlier tract, where he writes of the duties of judges and ministers to preserve the rights and revenues of the Crown: 'Govt. 1615', 7–8.

[2] *The Case of Monopolies* (Ex. Ch., 1602), 11 *Co. Rep.* (1615), ff. 84v–8v: Moore, *Cases*, 671–5; William Noy, *Reports of Cases* (London 1656), 173–85; and Yelverton in Stowe MS 153, f. 40r. See also the lengthy rep. in Add. MS 25.203, ff. 543r–8r, 558r–9r, 576v–88r, 678v, discovered by Dr Baker. Coke's original is in Coke MS Rep. C, ff. 571v–4r. A coll. of the pr. reps. was pubd. with notes by M.B. Donald, *Elizabethan monopolies* (Edinburgh 1961), 208–49.

[3] 3 Edward IV caps. 1–4, especially cap. 4 on the evils of importing manufactured goods, or products made domestically by aliens. *Stat. Realm* II, 392–8 and 396–8, respectively.

[4] The parag. above is a close copy of Yelverton's critique in Stowe MS 153, f. 40r.

[5] *The Prince's Case* (Chanc., 1606/7), 8 *Co. Rep.* (1611), ff. 14r–36r. See also *The Declaration of ovr Soveraigne Lord the King* (1613), of which Ellesmere's copy was Hunt. RB 17713.

And vppon this Rocke did he voluntily Fall without being accompanied with the Opinion of any one Iudge, and without any occasion being in the life of prince Henry.

3. In Baskeruiles case (*Liber* 7: 28):[1] Cited to be adiudged it sounded much in preiudice of the King. As that a Title of presentacion devolute to his Maiestie by Laps may by the presentment of the true [37v] Patron and death of his incumbent be taken from the King.

1. For yt is against the receiued Maxime, *quod nullum tempus occurrit regi.*

2. It is cast vpon the King by Act in Ley in default of the patron and the meanes Ordinaries, which Defalt the Law hath appointed shalbee repaired by the King and therefore cannot be taken from him.

3. The King cometh to this Title by Lapps not onely as supreame ordinary but also as supreame Patron; and so is the presentacion setled in him in point of Interest, which by the Act of no other can be drawen from him for the Law preserueth the possession of the Crowne.[2]

4. In Wisemans Case (*Liber* 2: 15).[3] The point was Tenants in Taile the Remainder in Fee. Hee in ye remainder in Consideracion and to the intent aswell, that all the Lands should contine in his family name and blood, as for other Consideracions doth Covenant. That he will stand seised of all his lands to the vse of [p. 8] himselfe and the heires Males of his body, and for defalt of such issue to the [38r] vse of Queene Elizabeth, her heires and successors, Kings and Queenes of this Realme.

The Cheife Iustice doth report that as it is said. It was resolued to be no Consideracion to rayse the vse to the Queene for their wanteth *quid pro quo.* And admitting that the Covenantor has said in his Indenture: In consideracion yt the queene is the head of the Com-

---

[1] *Baskerville's Case* (CP, 1585), 7 *Co. Rep.* (1608), f. 28r; and Leonard, *Reports and Cases*, I, 280–1; II, 50–1.

[2] The Chanc. maintained in an earlier draft of his tract that Coke 'doth misalledge the text which I recited in my speech and frameth others of his owne' (Harg. MS 254, f. 56v), and 'whereof it may be doubted whether the law be as he hath reported it' (*ibid.* f. 57r). Ellesmere was Att.-Gen. at that time.

[3] *Wiseman's Case* (CP, 1585), 2 *Co. Rep.* (1602), ff. 10r–6r; and Anderson, *Les Reports*, II, 140–3; Moore, *Cases*, 195; and Sir John Savile, *Les Reports de divers Special Cases* (London 1675), 80–1. Compare Coke's pr. rep. of the case with his MS Rep. C, ff. 303r–4r, where the version is highly abridged.

mon wealth and hath the charge and care aswell to preserue the peace of the Realme as to repell forraine hostilitie, which is imployd in this word Queene; yett this is no Consideracion to rayse the vse, for Kings *ex officio* ought to governe and preserue their subiects in peace and Tranquilitye.

1. This reason doth relish ill for it soundeth as if the subiect might challenge proteccion and defence of his soueraigne merely of duty, and that he were nothinge bound to the King for the same nor could any way recompence the King for it; whereas proteccion and defence is the most reall and most benificiall Consideracion to the subiect that can be, and therefore will vndoubtedly change the vse and settle it [38v] in the King ells wee shall make the King, who is *pater patriae*, inferior in desert to our naturall parents, which may not bee.[1]

2. He might haue been better advised then to haue filled the subiect with such a Conceite as that the King in all his cares and paines should be but an vnproffitable servant to his people, haueing done but that «which» he is tyed to theym in duty to doe. The rather, because by ye reporters owne words it was but a Tale told him from some other that it was Resolued. Soe as this report resteth not vpon his owne Creditt but vpon the Creditt of the Tale bearer, which may well be suspected. [p. 9]

TOUCHING THE POWER AND IURISDICCION OF COURTES AND COMMISSIONERS,[2]

Which are established by the Common Law by continuall vse and practice within the Realme, or by Act of parliament. It is a point of great danger and breedeth occasion of much Contempt in the inferior subiects when they see the same either questioned, impeached, or weakened. And therefore as it is fitt that each streame should [39r] keepe his owne Current, yett is it as vnfitt in a settled state that the Current should be stopped or made strayter then by Continuall vse it hath been. Yett the Cheife Iustice in his reports hath scattered many

---

[1] The basis of this reason was discd. fully in the 'Prerog.', f. 7r–v; and in the *Post-Nati*, 67–76, 98–104.

[2] The outline of this section is in Harg. MS 254, ff. 55r–6r. It omits disc. of the *Clark, Ely, Godfrey*, and *Ipswich* cases, and contains the *Rowland Heyward Case* that was not included in the final version. Yelverton's brief on Coke's reps was devoted primarily to a critique of this subject, and Yelverton's analysis of it is similar to that of Ellesmere: Stowe MS 153, ff. 39r–40v.

suddaine opionions in Diminucion of the lawfull power of many Courtes, not onely in Abridgeing but in a manner wholy suppressing the Iurisdiccion of some of them: To giue instance in some few.[1]

1. In Godfries Case (*Liber* 11: 44),[2] hee taketh occasion without any dependance vppon the case in question, out of his owne Fullnes, to say some Courtes cannot imprison, fine, nor amerce, as Ecclesiasticall Courtes before the ordinary, Archdeacon and etc., or their Comissaries and such like which proceed according to the Cannon and Civill Law.[3] Wherein he secrettly striketh att the Iurisdiccion of the high Comission, the prouinciall Counsells of Wales and Yorke, the Court of Requestes, and the admiralty, all which haue by Constant vse ever used to fine and imprison for Comtempts and such like offences, and trencheth (as was said further) to the very authority and ⌈39v⌉ practise of the Councell Table; ⟨which⟩ *a* passage of his might well haue been omitted, the same being accompained with the opinion of no other Iudge, but that he purposed vnder hand to shoote att the power of those Courtes.[4]

2. In Docter Bonhames Case (*Liber* 8: 118).[5] The Case in question being what power the Colledge of phisicions had by their Charter and by the Act of parliament of 14 H. 8 to imprison any other phisicion that practised here in London without the licence of the Colledge; he letteth fall not ⌈p. 10⌉ att vnwares but *de industria* this paradox, that in many cases the Common Law shall Controll Acts of parliament and sometimes shall adiudge them to be vtterly void.[6] For sayth he, when an Act of parliament is against Common right and reason the Common Law shall Controll it and adiudge it to be void; which dero-

---

a with] which *in the pr. ed.*

[1] The theoretical background of this theme was set out in the 'Prerog.', ff. 1–2v, 4r–v, 9r–v; and in the 'Brief Chanc.', ff. 1v–2v.

[2] *Supra*, p. 302, n.2.

[3] The general controversy between the eccles. and common law courts usually prompted parties and their lawyers to bring forward cases such as these. For ex. a contemp. coll. of cases, precedents, and proceedings gathered by a common lawyer (Petyt MS 518, ff. 1–99), and by a canonist (Petyt MS 538/38, ff. 256–309).

[4] The above parag. is a close copy of Yelverton's critique in Stowe MS 153, f. 39r. Some of the consequences of this interference with the local courts were spelled out in Ellesmere's tract on 'Iudicature', ff. 2r–3r.

[5] *Dr Bonham's Case* (CP, 1610/11), 8 *Co. Rep.* (1611), ff. 114r–21r, and Coke MS Rep. E, ff. 90v–5r. Other refs. to the case are cited above in Chap. VI, p. 149, nn. 2–3.

[6] The phraseology that has been rendered famous by the debates of historians. Cf. S. E. Thorne, 'The constitution and the courts', *LQR* 54 (1938), 543–52; and J. W. Gough, *Fundamental law in English constitutional history* (Oxford 1955), 31–8. The letters patent were recited in the statute for the college of 14 Henry VIII cap. 5 (1522), *Stat. Realm* III, 213–4.

gateth much from the wisdome and power of the parliament, that
when the three estates – the King, the Lords and the Commons – haue
spent their Labours in makeing a Law, then shall 3 Iudges on the
bench distroy and frustrate all their points because the Act [40r]
agreeth not in their particular sence with Common right and reason,
whereby he advanceth the reason of a particular Court aboue the
Iudgement of all the Realme. Besides, more temporately did that
Reverend Cheife Iustice Herle in the time of Edward 3 deliver his
opinion, 8 Edward 3: 30 (cited by my Lord Cooke), when he said:
some Acts of parliament are made against Law and right which they
that made them, perceiueing would not putt them in execucion. For
it is *Magis Congruum* that Acts of parliament should be corrected by
the same penn that drew theym, thayn to be dasht in peeces by the
opinion of a few Iudges.[1]

3. In Baggs case (*liber* 11: 98)[2] in the Kings bench, wherein the point
in question only was what cause was sufficient for a Corporacion to
remoue a Burgesse from his place, He digresseth from his matter and
sayth it was *Resolve*: That to the Court of Kings Bench belongeth
authority not onely to Correct Errours in Iudiciall proceedings, but
other Errours and misdeameanors extra iudiciall tending to ye [40v]
Breach of peace or oppression of the subiects, or to the rayseing of
faction, Controversie, debate, or to any manner of misgovernement;
soe that no wrong and iniury either publike or private can be done,
but that this shall be reformed or punished by the due course of Law.
Werein in giueinge excesse of authorye to the Kings Bench he doth
as much as insinuate that this Court is all sufficient in it selfe to
manage the state. For if the Kings Bench may reforme any manner of
Misgovernement (as the Words are), it seemeth that their is little or
noe vse either of the Kings Royall Care and authorye exercised in
his person and by his proclamacions, ordinances and imediate direc-
cions, [p 11] nor of the Councell Table, which vnder the King is ye
cheife watchtower for all points of misgovernement, nor of the Star
chamber, which hath ever been esteemed the highest Court for ex-
tinguishment ⟨of⟩[a] all riotts and publike disorders and enormities.
And besides, the words do import as if the Kings bench had a super-

---

[a] *Added to the pr. ed.*

[1] The parag. is nearly identical to that in Yelverton's critique, Stowe MS 153, f. 39r–v.
Ellesmere's criticism stemmed from his conception of the const. 'Parl. 1604–10', f. 1r; and the
Post-Nati, 50–4, 104–10.

[2] *James Bagg's Case* (KB, 1615), 11 *Co. Rep.* (1615), ff. 93v–100r. See also the Chanc's
abridgement in Harg. MS 254, ff. 30v–1r.

interdependency over the governement it selfe, and to iudge wherein
any of theym doe misgoverne.[1] [41r]

4. In the Case of the Taylors of Ipswich (*Liber* 11: 54),[2] he sayeth it
was Resolved that the statute 19 H. 7 Cap. 7 doth not Corroborate
any of the ordinances made by any Corporacion, though they be
allowed and approued by the Lord Chancellour, Lord Treasuror,
Cheife Iustice of either Bench or 3 of them, or by the Iustices of
assizes in there Cercuits as the statute speaketh,[3] but leaueth them[a]
to be affirmed as good or disaffermed as vnlawfull by the Law; and
that the sole benefitt the Corporacion gaineth by such allowances
⟨is⟩[b] that they shall not incurre the penaltie of 40 £ mencioned in
the Act if they putt more such ordinances. This detracteth much from
the power of Corporacions and will be an occasion to make the
younger and inferior sorte among them to insult vpon there governors.
It taketh much also from the honour of the Lord Chancellour and the
other great persons whome the statute trusteth with the allowance or
disalowance of such ordinances; that what in their Iudgment they
shall approue [41v] to be good and holsome for the Corporacion
shall yett be subiect to the Censure of every perticular Iudge to be
overthrowen, whereby ye great Lords shall bestow their paines in
vaine and the Corporacions be putt to vaine expences in sueing for
such allowances. Whereas the true meaneing of the statute of 19 H. 7
was that such ordinances made by Corporacions and allowed by the
great Iudges of the Realme should stand Confirmed by Act of parliament.

5. In the Case of the Marshalsey (*Liber* 10: 57b).[4] Hee suffereth to
fall from him this noveltie as a principall (vizt): And it is to be observed
that where a statute probibiteth any thing, a man may haue a *supersedeas* in nature of a prohibicion to any Iudge that holdeth plea
against any statute. This rule is known not to be law, For then in the

---

^a *Read* them *for* then.   ^b *Added to the pr. ed.*

[1] Ellesmere considered the exercise of auth. such as this as collective: the statement in
the *Post-Nati*, 50–2; and his introd. to the 'Brief Chanc.', f. 1r. His arg. in this case is
similar to – but much more detailed than – that of Yelverton's in Stowe MS 153, f. 39v.

[2] *The Case of the Tailors...of Ipswich* (KB, 1615), 11 *Co. Rep.* (1615), ff. 53r–4v; and
Godbolt, *Reports*, 252–4. See also the Chancellor's abridgement in Harg. MS 254, f. 29v.

[3] 19 Henry VII cap. 7 (1503/4), *Stat. Realm* II, 652–3. Ellesmere's interp. follows clearly
the intent of the statute, which was to confirm all municipal ordinances but 'unlawful and un-
reasonable' ones.

[4] *The Case of the Marshalsea* (KB, 1613), 10 *Co. Rep.* (1614), ff. 68v–77v. The ms. version
of Ellesmere's critique of this case is considerably better than the printed one.

first Case may a prohibicion*a* goe out of the Kings Bench with *teste*
[p. 12] *Edwardo Cooke* to ye Lord Chancellor into the Chancery,
where the style is *Teste Meipso*. Besides the Rule is put soe indefinitely
as it Comprehends noe Certaintie, neither out [42r] of what Court
such *supersedeas* should goe, nor to what Iudge Speritualll or Temporall.[1]
And in saying to any Iudge, the Lord Chancellour is not Excluded,
nor Lords of the Star chamber, nor the Lord Treasuror and the
Court of Exchecquor Chamber, nor the Court of wards, nor the
Court of Dutchy; so as the Chiefe Iustice doth imploy Tacite yt all
theis may be prohibeted, vnto the putting in practise whereof it
seemeth this Case should bee aleading.

6. The Case of Clarke (*Liber* 5: 64)[2] reported thus: that Queene
Elizabeth by reason of the plague in London apointed the Terme to
be kept att St. Albans. The Maiour and Burgesses, by generall assent
among themselues and by force of their Chartre, assiss a somme vpon
every inhabitant toward the charges in erecting the Court of Iustice
there, and ordained that if any refused to pay the summe assessed
vpon him the Maiour*b* inprison him, for which Clarke «was» imprisoned. The Cheife Iustice reporteth it was adiudged yt ye imprisonment was against Law because the ordinace made by ye Maiour and
Burgesses was against the Statute of *Magna Charta, Nullus Liber Homo
imprisonetur.*[3] [42v] If there were such a Iudgement it were fitter to
haue lyen silent then to haue seene light; for ye assessement being in
advancement of the generall Iustice of the Realme, and the ordinace
being in furtherance thereof, the Statute of *Magna Charta* never ment
to protect such obstinate persons as should refuse to sett forward
erection of the Court of Iustice.

Soe as by Casting this report abroad he hath much weakened the
Iurisdiccion of all Corporacions and dishartined them to further his
Maiesties service, Ther being no such bridle to curbe froward Com-
painions as Restrainte of their libertie.

In the Case of the Isle of Ely (*Liber* 10: 143),[4] which by his owne
reporte came not Iudicially into the Court but was by the Lords of

---

a their *deleted before* a prohibicion.
b for which *transposed from the line below and inserted before* Maiour.
[1] The Chanc. has distinctly in mind the precedence of his court, discd. *supra*, Chap. VII.
[2] *Clark's Case* (CP, 1596), 5 *Co. Rep.* (1605), f. 64r.
[3] Magna Carta was frequently misused in this period, but usually with reference to
eccles. courts and not corporations: Faith Thompson, *Magna Carta* (Minneapolis Minn.
1948), for ex., 209–19.
[4] *The Case of the Isle of Ely* (CP, 1610), 10 *Co. Rep.* (1614), ff. 141r–3r.

the Councells referred to him and other Iudges, he sayth it was by them Resolued: That a [p. 13] generall Taxacion vpon a Towne to pay so much towards the repaire of the Sea Bankes is not warranted to be done by the Comissioners of Sewers, but yt the same must be vpon every particular person according to the quantitie of his Land [43r] and by number of acres and perches, and according to the porcion of the profitts which every one hath there.

If this should be Law it giveth a great blowe to the power of that Comission and may bring much mischeife with it. For if a Sudden Inundacion of the sea happen, and the walles and bancks against the sea be caried away by the sudden violence of the streame, if the Comissioners of sewers shall stay their Taxacion for the repaire of the walls and Bancks till every mans Lands be knowne and till every acre or pearch ⟨be⟩ [a] by Survay devided and numbred, which cannot be the worke of one day but of many monthes, The whole Countrey hapely may be drowned.[1]

And therefore in Cases of necessity the Law allowes those wayes that are of most expedition and of quicknest dispatch, which is by setting a generall Tax, and then the Landholders among themselues to rate themselues in particular that the Worke may goe with speed. [43v]

CASES THAT CONCERNE YE SUBIECT.[2]

As for cases of the Subiects the Conceite of the Reporter besides or beyound the Iudgment are too many to enumerate of them; therefore those onely shalbe inserted which fall within theis Excepcions. [p. 14]

Cases where the Report of the Iudgement is not warranted by the Record or by the authority alledged.

1. Gages Case (*Liber* 5: 45b).[3] The writt of Covenant to levy a fine did beare *teste* 24th Aprill Returnable 15 *pasche*, which in truth was

---

[a] *Omitted in the MS ed.*

[1] The Chanc's defence of the powers of commissioners, and their role in encouraging the draining of the Fens, was elaborated in a brief he composed with John Popham: Lans. MS 110, f. 21r–v. He also took part in the P.C. discs. and the resulting corresp. in this case (*supra*, Chap. VI).

[2] The outline for this section is in Harg. MS 254, ff. 56r–7r. The section underwent considerable revision. The earlier draft did not contain discs. of the *Boswell, Legate, Lynn, Michelborne*, and *Poulter* cases; and the *Styles, Digby, Pythington*, and *Philens* cases were deleted from the finished copy.

[3] *Gage's Case* (KB, 1599), 5 Co. *Rep.* (1605), f. 45v; and Moore, *Cases*, 571.

the 15th of Aprill, and so the Returne of the writt was before *teste*. It is reported to be resolued *per Curiam* that this should be amended. But the Record it selfe being viewed waranteth noe such report.

2. Michelbornes case (*Liber* 6: folio 18).[1] A writt of Error was brought vpon a Iudgement given in the Court of Marshalsey in an accion vpon the Case vppon a Trover and Convercion within the Verge, where neither of the partyes were of the Kings household; and for this cause it is reported that the Iudgement was reversed. But the Record being seene it appeareth yt to this day ye Iudgement was never reversed. [44r]

3. Boswells case (*Liber* 6: folio 48b).[2] A writt of Error was brought in the King Bench vpon a Iudgement given in a *quare impeditt* in the Common pleas, wherein the matter in Law questioned was onely whether the Iudges of the Common pleas had not erred in the very point of their Iudgement, because they had awarded a writt to the Bishopp for the plaintiffe notwithstandinge *Reclamacione* of the Defendant and of Lawrence Boswell a stranger to the writt, or of either of them. In which the Court gave no Resolucion att all, but *pendet huiusque indiscussum*, and was ended by Arbitrement. [p. 15]

Yett doth the cheife Iustice say that it was *Resolve* that the plaintiff should haue his writt to the Bishopp generally. And for all the rest reported in that Case it is merely his owne discourse, for neither did the matter beare Any such argument ⟨and⟩.[a] neither was there ever any such point argued either att the Barr or att the Bench.

4. In Alexander poulters case (*Liber* 11: folio 34ab),[3] the point being but whether Poulter for maliciously burneing a House att New markett should haue his Clergie. To draw in his owne [44v] Conceipt of another matter (nothing pertinent to the point in question) he falls vpon the Exposition of the statute of 27 E. 3. car. 1 of *premunire*, against them which sue in any other Court to defeate or impeach the Iudgement given in ye Courte of the Kinge: That they shall haue day

---

[a] *Added to the pr. ed.*

[1] *Michelborne's Case* (KB, 1596), 6 *Co. Rep.* (1607), ff. 20v–1r. Ellesmere's ms. cites folio 18 incorrectly. The case is on the plea roll at KB 27/1337/263–4, where there is no indication of a reversal in judgment.

[2] *Boswell's Case* (KB, 1606), 6 *Co. Rep.* (1607), ff. 48v–52r. Compare the pr. rep. of this case with the ms. one in Coke MS Rep. C, ff. 652r–7r, where there are several insertions.

[3] *Alexander Powlter's Case* (KB, 1615), 11 *Co. Rep.* (1615), ff. 29r–37v. See also the Chancellor's abridgement in Harg. MS 254, f. 29r.

conteyneing the space of 2 monthes and etc. And if they come not att the same day in proper person they shalbe out of proteccion.[1]

A question (sayth the reporter) was moued 30 E. 3:11, which was within 3 yeares after the makeing of the Act: if the offender doth not make default but appeare and plead, and be Condemned, whether he shall haue the high and penall Iudgment of *premunire* given by the said Act. But after (sayth the Reporter) in the 39 E. 3: folio 7, Iudgement was given against the Bishop of Chicester, who appeared, yt he should be put out of Proteccion.[2] But if theis two bookes be examined they proue not the matter for which they be wrested in, for neither of them say that if the partie appeare within two monthes given by the statute of 27 Edward 3 and be after Condemned, That the Iudgement shall be [45r] to be out of Proteccion; for in 30 E. 3: 11 no such Iudgement att all could be because the partie was not Condemned in any writt brought vpon the Statute of *Premunire*, but onely vpon an attachment of Probibicion att the Common Law. And in 39 E. 3: 7 the Iudgement was that he should be out of proteccion because he appeared not att all in person but by Atturney, which in this suite is no appearance. And where the cheife Iustice in the same place sitteth, Ferebies Case 44 E. 3: 36ab to be adiudged:[3] that when the defendant in case of *premunire* appeares within the two [p. 16] monthes and pleads and is found guiltie, that he shall haue Iudgment vpon the said statute of 27 Edward 3 to be out of proteccion.

The Booke case it selfe proueth no such matter, For it is this. In a writt sued for the King vpon the Statute of Provisors In the Kings Bench – att the suite of William Fereby against T – processe was sued till the defendant offered to averr that he hath sued noe plea and etc. And therevpon att *Nisi Prius* att St. Martaines before Ingleby it was found against the defendant, wherevpon he had Iudgement in the Kings bench to be out of the Kings Proteccion [45v] and his Body to be taken. But that he came within the 2 monthes after warneing, which is the point the cheife Iustice insisteth vpon, appeareth not att all by the Booke. And by the bookes of 43 E. 3: 6 and 8 H. 4: 7a where Gascoigne giueth ye rule, It appeareth that the forfeiture of his Landes

---

[1] The statute and the background to this subject were discd. fully in the 'Brief Chanc.', ff. 8r–9v.

[2] Coke's position here is similar to the wealth of args. that were presented in 'A discourse vpon the statutes of Praemunire and Prohibition, how farre foorth they may be extended agaynst ecclesiasticall Iurisdiction': Cleo. MS F. II, ff. 450r–8r, and the precedents at ff. 458v–64r.

[3] No comments helpful to the disc. could be located in notes from the printed Year Books.

and goods growes onely vpon his Contempt in not appeareing within
2 monthes after warneing giuen him by the sheriffe, which is the
Cause why the Sheriffe in his Returne must sett downe the very day
when he warned the person, that the Courte may see whether he be
warned according to the statute, and soe is the booke expresley 42 E.
3: 7a.[1]

CASES REPORTED THAT HAUE BEENE ADIUDGED CONTRARY TO YE REPORTES

1.   Barwickes case (*Liber* 5: folio 93).[2] Queen Elizabeth granteth
ye Mannour of Sutton to Humfrey, *Habendum a die Confeccionis
capdum Patent* for 3 liues. It is said to be resolued that the lease was
voyd because a Freehold cannot by the Common Law Comence *in
futuro*, but must take his effect presently. The reason alledged is true
but the Law shall Construe the Patent to take noe effect att all [46r]
Till that the estate by rule of Law may commence, and therefore *a
Die confeccionis* shalbe taken to be *a Tempore confeccionis*. For the
cheife Iustice in Cleatons Case (*ibm* 1b) sayth that from the date and
from the daye of the date is all one, and nothinge is more vsuall in all
the Courts of Law att Westminster, both in the [p. 17] Case of the
King and in the Cases of Common Persons, for the Iudges doe make
such Construccion. And that the grants and Leases made to poore
farmers may not by such nice Construccion be made void and il-
lusory; and so did my Lord himselfe, being Cheife Iustice of the
Common pleas, over rule the same against the Bishopp of Oxford,
who vpon the like point wood haue overthrowne a lease for liues
made by his Predecessors *per 9 Jacobi Regis*.[3]

2.   Blumfeilds Case (*Liber* 5: 86b).[4] It is reported by ye Cheife Iustice
to be resolued *per Curiam*, That if a man Condemned in debt be taken
and inprisoned and dye in Execucion, that the plaintiff may haue a
new Execucion by *Elegit* or *fieri facias*. But the Contrary to this was
adiudged Hillary 4 *Jacobi* in the Kings Bench by the Lord Popham and
[46v] the other fower Iudges in Lamb and Cutleres his case: that the
death of the partie in Execucion discharged the debt forever. For

---

[1]   *Barwick's Case* (Exch., 1597), 5 *Co. Rep.* (1605), ff. 93v–5r; and Moore, *Cases*, 393–4.
[2]   The background was sketched in 'Brief Chanc.', ff. 7r–8v, 10v–11r.
[3]   *Clayton's Case* (CP, 1595), 5 *Co. Rep.* (1605), f. 70r–v. The ref. in the text is not
understood.
[4]   *Blumfield's Case* (KB, 1596), 5 *Co. Rep.* (1605), ff. 86v–7v.

Mors soluit omnia, and accordingly hath been lately adiudged in the Common Pleas in Doctors Fosters Case.[1] Soe as both the Courts haue Concured against the Resolucion Reported by the Cheife Iustice.

3. Sir Henry Neviles Case (*Liber* 11: folio 17),[2] Reported by ye Cheife Iustice to be Resolued That a Customary Mannour may be held by Coppie, and that such Customary Lord may keepe Court and grante Coppies. The Contrary to which *Terminis terminantibus,* and Betweene the same parties was adiudged by the whole Courte of Kings Bench (*Michaelmas 8 Jacobi*) in a *quo warranto,* and by Iudgement was ousted to keepe any Courte as belonging to any such pretended Customary Mannour.

CASES PUBLISHED WHILE WRITTS OF ERROR WERE DEPENDINGE.

Legates Case (*Liber* 10: 109),[3] adiudged before the Cheife Iustice and his Companions in the Common Pleas, and printed while the writt of Error was depending in the Kings bench to haue the first Iudgement better Examined. [47r] [p. 18]

The Case of the Mayour and Burgesses of Lynn (*Liber 10: 122*),[4] about the Misnomer[a] of the Corporacion adiudged in the Comon pleas while he was the Cheife Iustice there, and presently published before it could be determined vpon the writt of Error in the Kings Bench. Wherein my Lord may seeme to haue overrunne the Law. For ye Law is in a manner stopt by the printed Case and the partie[b] is dishartened to prosecute his writt of Error.

Magdalen Colledge case (*Liber* 11: 66)[5] adiudged in the Kings bench, and that vpon a new point contrary to the long receiued opinion: That the statute of 18 Elizabeth did enable Colledges, Deanes, Chapters and etc. to passe their Lands to the King, yett

[a] Misnomer *inserted for* Mannour *to correct the error of the transcriber.*

[b] stopt whereby the printed Case the partie] *changed to read like the pr. ed.*

[1] See in add. Ellesmere's abridgement in Harg. MS 254, ff. 29v–30r.

[2] *Sir Henry Neville's Case* (CP, 1613), 11 *Co. Rep.* (1615), ff. 17r–8r. The Chanc's abridgement of the case is also important: Harg. MS 254, ff. 28v–9r.

[3] *Arthur Legates Case* (CP, 1613), 10 *Co. Rep.* (1614), ff. 109r–15v; and Godbolt, *Reports,* 257–8. See Ellesmere's abridgement in Harg. MS 254, f. 27v.

[4] *The Case of the Mayor and Burgesses of Lynn* (CP, 1613), 10 *Co. Rep.* (1614), ff. 120r–6r.

[5] *Supra,* p. 301, n.3.

being now Ruled that such Colledges and etc. remaine still disabled.[1]
While the Argumentes were even warme in the Iudges mouthes the
Case was likewise warme in the presse and published, though their
was a writt of Error presently brought vpon the said Iudgement In
the Exchecquer Chamber which yett dependeth, ⟨and⟩ though by
the Confidence vsed by the reporter in setting downe the Case the
partie is much discouraged in his prosecucion.[2] [47v]

Now allthough by the former instances it apeareth that many
Cases, which haue fixed their feet in this Impression of the Cheife
Iustice, might with more safty and honour both to his Maiestie and the
Law haue taken their wings and fled away; yett in the exact peruall
of his 11 volume⟨⟨s⟩⟩ their arise infinite more cases that can endure
neither the Hammer nor the Furnace, but will either fly in peeces as
dissonant from the true and antient reason of the Comon Law, or else
turne to drosse and proue Reprobate Silver. Neither is it to be forgotten how in every one of his bookes he transgresseth his owne Rules
propounded to himselfe as a Reporter.[3]

1. For when in Alton Woods case (the *reports* 50):[4] He sayth Reporters
doe wisely to omitt opinions spoken accidently and which tend not to
ye point in question; yett he himselfe in many Cases, haueing slighted
over the present point in Iudgement – as *Liber* 2: 36 Sir Rowland
Howard case, *Liber* 11: 29 Alexander Poulters case, *Liber* 6: 63 Sir
Mile Finches Case,[5] and diueres others – Hee exspaciates into new
feilds, and stuffeth his [48r] volumes [p. 19] with graines of another
kind as if they were rather Common Places for store of different[a]
matters then true observacions of the Reasons of the Cases then in
Iudgement.

2. Wherein his Epistle to his third booke hee profereth theis bookes
of his ⟨to⟩[b] haue in them the true vnderstanding of every case, and

---

[a] Read different *for* disserent.   [b] *Added to the pr. ed.*

[1] The Chanc. also stated in his earlier draft that 'for my part I never heard it of the judges
with whom I often conferred': Harg. MS 254, f. 56v.

[2] Discd fully in *supra*, Chap. VII: *The Magdalen College Case, The Earl of Oxford's Case*
(the case pending here that was eventually judged for the plaintiff in the Chancery), and
Dr Googe's Case (the def. who attempted to have the original decision of the K.B. restored).

[3] Namely, in his preface to the *First Report*, sig. 11r–v.

[4] *The Case of Alton Woods* (Exch., 1595), 1 *Co. Rep.* (1600), ff. 26r–53v.

[5] *Sir Rowland Heyward's Case* (Wards, 1595), 2 *Co. Rep.* (1602), ff. 35r–7v; *Alexander
Powlter's Case* (Ex. Ch., 1614), 11 *Co. Rep.* (1615), ff. 29r–37v; and *Sir Moyle Finch's Case*
(CP, 1606), 6 *Co. Rep.* (1614), ff. 63r–70v.

that by resting or inference of witt he hath not drawn them from their proper and naturall sense.[1] A Man with smal labour shall obserue thorough all his Labours how oftentimes a Cleare Case is Clouded and obscured by the Subtilty of a difference he adioyneth of his owne. Vpon which haueing discoursed in his large maner, he drawes is this Conclusion more vsuall then true (vizt): And thus bee all your bookes reconceiled; which being perused warrant not att all the inference or difference propounded by himselfe.

3. Wherein his Epistle to his fourth bookes he vseth theis words after *Suetonius*:[a] '*que praeter consuetudinem et morem maiorûm fuit, neque placent, neque recta videntur*'; adding further, that old Lawes and new meates are fittest for vse.[2] Yett as [48v] forgetting his owne prescript, he hath strawed more novelties then old Corne in theis feilds of his; and theis sometymes so nice as hardly to be discerned, sometymes so Contrary to vse as not easily to be beliued, nay as himselfe is forced to haue recalled. One instance whereof is seene in Herlakendens Case (*Liber* 4: 62),[3] where he Traduceth 2 Reverend Iudges of our times, Wray cheife Iustice and Manwood cheife Baron,[b] as that they Resolued that notwithstanding the Clause of 'without impeachment of wast' Conteined in a Lease or assurance, yett the Tenant for Life or yeares might not take the Trees, but they belonged to him in Revercion. Against which Conceipt (soe fathered one them) the practise of former tymes had been for many yeares. Yett did this opinion (scattered by him) draw att first many to doubt, and more Lessors and sonnes to attempt suttes against their farmers and fathers for such Trees, which Troubled (of late times) the Realmes much: Though now att last when hee saw the Reverend Iudges hold fast to the antient Law and to desert this new opinion, Hee hath sounded the Retreate himselfe, and (*Liber* 11: 80) [49r] [p. 20] In Bowles case, renounceth this Child of his as illegitimat, and is Content to Resorte to the old Fountaine, and to lay aside this fresh and Rawe opinion first printed by himselfe.[4]

---

[a] of *deleted before* Suetonius.   [b] *Read* Manwood *for* Manhood.

[1] The accusation is not substantiated by a reading of the preface to the *Third Report*, sigs. Cij-Ej.

[2] The preface to the *Fourth Report*, sig. B3.

[3] *Herlakenden's Case* (KB, 1589), 4 *Co. Rep.* (1604), ff. 62r–4r, and noted in Coke MS Rep. C, f. 22v.

[4] *Lewis Bowles Case* (KB, 1615), 11 *Co. Rep.* (1615), ff. 79v–84r. See also Ellesmere's abridgement in Harg. MS 254, f. 30r.

Wherein his Epistle to his 7 booke he would make men beleiue that in all his Reports he had avoyded obscurity and Noveltie; for that (to vse his owne words) he ever held all new or private interpretacions or Opinions, which haue no ground or warrant out of the reason or rule of our bookes or former presedents, to be dangerous and not worthy any observacion.[1] Yett who soe doth read Adams and Lamberts Case (*Liber* 4: 105),[2] shall runne into a wood or thickett out of which he shall not easily wind himselfe. He hath so darkened the Case by many intricate differences, whereof the Court that Argued the same did never dreame.

And for Noveltie, in Docter Bonham Case (*Liber* 8: 114)[3] the cheife Iustice haueing no president for him, but many Iudgements against him,[a] yett doth he strike in sunder the Barrs of Governement of the Colledge of phisicons; and without any pawsing on the [49v] matter frustrates the patent of King H. 8 whereby the Colledge was erected, and Tramples vpon the Act of Parliament 14 H. 8 whereby that Patent was Confirmed, blowing them both away as vaine and of no value. And this in Triumph of himselfe, being accompanied but with the opinion of one Iudge onely for the Matter in Law when three other Iudges were against him, which case possessed a better roome in the presse then it deserued.

1. It giueing such a blow to the governement of so graue a Companie as the Colledge of phisicians,

2. Leaueing such Liberty to emperiokes within the Cittie of London, as that they may all practise Pell Mell without restraint or feare of Imprisonment, which both the pattent of Henry 8. and the parliament ment to suppresse.

3. Leaueing such a slur[b] and taint vpon his Maiesties power and prerogatiue as is vnfitt to be digested (vizt): that the King hath not power by his patent ioyned [p. 21] with the parliament, to exclude strangers from practising Phisick within the Cittie till they be approued by the Colledge vpon paine of Imprisonment. [50r]

---

[a] but many Iudgements against him *repeated twice in the manuscript.*

[b] assar *corrected to* slur *from the pr. ed.*

[1] Preface to the *Seventh Report*, sig. A4.

[2] *Adams and Lambert's Case* (KB, 1602), 4 Co. Rep. (1604), ff. 104v–16v; and Moore, *Cases*, 648–54. The Coke MS Rep. C, ff. 506r–8v, is identical to the pr. rep.

[3] *Supra*, p. 306, n. 5. The criticisms of the Chanc. which follow were rejected by a later lawyer in his annotations to a L.I.'s copy of the tract: L.I. Add. MSL, p. 21.

4. By this opinion of his he peruerteth the intent both of the patent and parliament, which hath by approued practise ever since the makeing thereof been allowed by most of the Iudges in seuerall ages; and lately also vpon an assembly of the Lord Popham and other Iudges att the house of the now Lord Chancellour, by his Maiestie expresse Comandement.[1]

Soe as men had need be wary what fayth they build vpon theis Reports, they being in many places like hollow grounded green-swardes: one The Top seemeing faire to the eye, yett such as they can take little sure footing, they walke so incertainely among so many Noveltyes, which cann never settle their Iudgementes but rather draw them from the old way in which is best abideinge.[2] [50v] [p. 22]

---

[1] In particular, Ellesmere's 'Brief Chanc.', f. 5r–v.

[2] The pursuit of the 'old way' was his response to the legal problems of the period: 'Iudicature', f. 1r.

XVI

'A BREVIATE OR DIRECCION FOR THE KINGES LEARNED COUNCELL COLLECTED BY THE LORD CHAUNCELLOR ELLESMERE, *MENSE SEPTEMBRIS* 1615.ᵃ *ANNO JACOBI REGIS*'¹

PRAEFATIO.

The gravitie and discrecion of the Iudges in auncient tyme hath bine such as in doubtfull cases and espetially in construccion of statutes, they desyred to conferr with the Kinges privie councell, whereof there bee many examples some of which are Cited in the case of *Post nati*,² and this ought to bee spetially regarded where the aucthoritie and Iurisdiccion of the Kinges Courtes is to bee brought into dispute and question: For *Grauius priuatorum damno peccatur cum intra summos magistratus Curia sue maiores de imperio certatur* [Bodin lib. 3 ca. 6 pag. 435]. And in those Cases the Iudges should haue private and loveing conference together before publicke disputes,³ according to the emperours Commaund, *Alloquor illum ne rem iniustam faciat.* [Bodin lib. 3 cap. 6 pag. 504].

SOME NOTES AND OBSERUATIONS VPON THE STATUTE OF *MAGNA CHARTA* ca. 29, AND OTHER STATUTES CONCERNING THE PROCEEDINGS IN THE CHAUNCERIE IN CAUSES OF EQUITIE AND CONSCIENCE.ᵇ

The statutes which bee now vrged and stood vpon against the Chauncery⁴ are first *Magna Carta* [*Magna Carta* ca. 29],ᶜ where

---

ᵃ 'A Breviate for the Kings Learned Councell collected by the Lord Ellesmere', *the title of Copy E*; 'An Apologie for the Chancerye by the Lord Elesmor', *the title of Copy F*; 'The Privileges and Prerogatives of the High Court of Chancery', *the title of Copy G. The titles of Copies B, C, and D begin with the first sub-title after the* 'Prefatio'.

ᵇ *The text of B, C, D, and G begins here.*

ᶜ Cap. 90 *in F, cap. 9 in G. The paragraph is shortened considerably in G.*

¹ Folger MS v.b. 190.   ² *Post-Nati, passim.*

³ As he stated earlier in asking the judges for their opinions on a few causes in the Chancery, 'good discretion to follow the example of wise men': Add. MS 48.056, p. 34.

⁴ Most of the texts quoted were from his own coll. Ellesm. MS 34/A/9.

the words bee *nisi per legale Iudicium parium suorum vel per legem terrae.*
It is *Lex terra.* That as the Iudges of the Common law shall determine
questions [1r] in lawe, *et pares et Iuratores* to trye matters in fact,*a*
Soe the Chancery is to order and decree matters of Conscience and
equity, which can not be remedied by the stricte rules of the Common
Law. And the same rule serveth for vnderstandinge of the statute of
Anno 25 E. 3 cap. 4 vpon these words, s'ilne foit dorment mesne en
response et foreiudge dicelles per voye *b* del ley.[1] And it appeareth
that the cause *c* of makeing that statute was to restraine privat suggestions made to the Kinge or to the Counsell: But not meant to take
away the ordinary Iudiciall proceedinge and heareing of the causes of
Conscience and equitie in the Chancery. The statute 28 E. 3 cap. 3.
hath the same words in effect as Magna Charta cap. 29,*d* vzt: Without
being brought in to answeare by due processe of Lawe.[2] For understanding whereof it is to bee remembered, That those that are sued in
the Chauncery ⟨⟨are⟩⟩*e* brought to answere by due processe of lawe
for Cases of equity and Conscience and that is *per legem terrae.*

Anno 2 E. 3 cap. 8, that it shall not bee comanded by the great
Seale ⟨⟨nor⟩⟩ *f* the little seale to disturbe or delay common right. And
tho⟨ugh⟩ such Commaundmentes doe come, the Iustices should not
therefore*g* leave to doe right in any point.[3]

For the understanding of this statute, the ordinary judiciall
proceedinge by the Chancery according to conscience and [1v]
equitie, is not any disturbance or delay of common right. But is the
doeing of Right and Iustice in Cases which the Common law cannot
help: For Common right standeth not only in the strict right and

---

a *Several sections of this paragraph are blotted out in A, and confused in E–G. It is supplemented*
with B.

b voye] roye *in B.*

c Course *inserted above the crossed out* cause.

d answere by due proces *cancelled after* cap. 29.

e are *inserted for* and.

f Nor *inserted for* me. *The statute above is incorrectly cited as* cap. 4 *in A.*

g Therefore *often omitted in other copies.* Cap. 4 reads cap. 8 *in F and G. The paragraph, torn
in A, is supplemented by B.*

[1] Neither this direct quote, nor the arg. that the purpose of the statute was to restrain
private suggestions made to the K. or the P.C. can be found in this statute: 'The Statute of
Provisors of Benefices', 25 Ed. III stat. 4 (1350–1), *Stat. Realm* 1, 316–18.

[2] 'The Statute of the Twenty-Eighth Year of King Edward III', 28 Ed. III cap. 3 (1354),
Stat. Realm 1, 345, a direct quote.

[3] The parag. 'That ... point' is a direct quote from the 'Statute made at Northampton',
2 Ed. III cap. 8 (1328), *Stat. Realm* 1, 259. The citation in Copy A is wrongly ascribed to cap. 4.
The justices referred to in the Statute are the JPs, and the topic is the method of local law
enforcement.

extremity of law*a* (for often *summum Ius est summa iniuria*), but rather is doeing right according to conscience. And the Iudges of the Common law themselves doe almost every day, extend theire discretion to stay and mitigate the right *b* and strictnes of the common law; And in soe doinge they doe well notwithstandinge the strict wordes of theire Oathes.[1]

14 E. 3 cap. 24,*c* declareth the law concerninge writes of search, and in the end of the same statute there are these wordes vzt; that by the commaundment of the great seale*d* «or» privie seale noe point of this statute (vzt concerning search) shall bee put in delay, nor that the Iustices of whatsoever place it bee shall let to doe the Common law by Commaundment which shall come to them under the great Seale or privie seale.[2]

The Common law hath alwayes allowed the proceeding in the Chauncery in Cases of Conscience and equitie: And therefore the wordes (to doe the Common Law) must not bee construed too precisely and therby to stopp all Courses of Equity. For it standeth with the Common law as well that equity and Conscience bee ministred where the common law cannott help, as that strict Iustice be ministred [2r] according to the Common Law, when the Common Law may serve.[3]

The Chancerie doth not commonly send any writt or commaund to the Iudges under the great seale, Commanding them to stay to doe Iustice. But awardeth Iniunccions to the parties that seeke to haue the advantage of the strictnes of the Common law against Equity and Conscience.

Nevertheles there bee plentifull examples that writes of *Supersedeas* vnder the great seale haue bine directed to the Iudges in divers speciall Cases, and haue in all tymes, vntill of late bine dutifully obeyed,

---

a and equity *added after* law *in F and G.*   *b* rigor *used for* right *in B, F, and G.*

c cap. 14 *in F. The paragraph is omitted in G.*

d Kinges *cancelled before* great seale; no *inserted after a plausible* or.

[1] The Chanc. did not allow this discretion to the judges of the common law in his private memo. on law reform that was composed shortly before this tract: 'Iudicature', f. 5r.

[2] The parag. 'That ... seale' is a direct quote of the 'Statute the First', 14 Ed. III, cap. 14 (1340), *Stat. Realm* I, 286. The citation in Copy A is wrongly ascribed to cap. 24, but correct in Copy B. Since the statute concerns the export of wool, the writs of search are for wool, and the 'commandment' is by Parl. Ellesmere's interp. is partially distorted.

[3] Ellesmere's approach to the law and equity problem was completely different from the pro-equity args. advocated by ardent royalists: Anthony Ben, 'Discourse touching the Praemunire', the copy in the Caesar coll., Lans. MS 174, ff. 205r–15r; and the later Caroline copy in Stowe MS 177, ff. 190r–8v. Close to Ellesmere's opinion was a later, and carefully researched, common law tract on the K.B. and Chanc. that was addressed to Coke: C.R.O. DDX Misc. Doc. 15, pp. 9–32.

As in Cases of priviledg[a] and to stay the proceedinges *Rege Inconsulto* and divers others.

Also it is to bee[b] remembred that many Iudges of the Common law have complyned and sued for remedie in the Chauncery and haue beene sued, and haue answered there, and haue obayed the Orders of that Court in Cases of Equitie and Conscience which would not bee releived by the Common Law.

42 E. 3 cap. 3. This statute is pursuing[c] two former statutes: One 37 E. cap. 8, which giveth *paenam Talionis* [2v] against those who make false suggestions to the King,[1] The other 38 E. 3 ca. 9, which confirmeth the former statute in all thinges saveing *pro paena Talionis*.[2] And this 42 E. 3 explaneth the two former, and provideth that the people bee not greived by false accusers that doe oftentymes make theire accusacions more for vengeance and singular profitt then for the profit[d] of the Kinge or his people. And therefore ordayneth that none bee put to answere (which is to be intended vpon such accusations[e] and false suggestions) without (first) presentment before Iustices, or (secondly) matters of record, or (thirdly) by due processe,[f] or, (fourthlie) by writt originall according to the old law of the land.[3]

In this statute the intent is to bee considered. First to explaine the two former statutes 37 E. 3 and 38 E. 3 as is before noted. Secondly that the auncient law of the land bee observed, that is: That for matters determinable by the Common Law, none bee put to answere but by presentment, of matters of record, or by due processe, or by writt originall But herein is not meant, that the ordinary Iudiciall proceedinge in the Chauncery in matters of Equity and conscience (not being remediable by the strictnes of the Common law) should bee taken away or restrayned;[4] But that in such Cases they may proceed against the parties called in by due process, for that it is according

---

[a] privitie *for* priviledg *in B. This paragraph is omitted in G.*

[b] *Crossed out word before* to bee *is indecipherable.*

[c] pursuing] prosecuting *in B. Some copiers cite the following statute incorrectly as* cap. 28.

[d] then for the profit *added before* of the Kinge.

[e] accusations *inserted above the crossed out word* occasyons.

[f] processe] proof *in B.*

[1] 'A Statute Concerning Diet and Apparel', 37 Ed. III cap. 18 (1363), *Stat. Realm* 1, 382.

[2] This statute confirms the former indirectly, providing a procedure for proceeding against false complaints: 'Statute the First', 38 Ed. III stat. 1 cap. 9 (1363–4), *Stat. Realm* 1, 384.

[3] A concise summary of 'A Statute Made at Westminster', 42 Ed. III cap. 3 (1368), *Stat. Realm* 1, 388.

[4] The statute of 37 Ed. III gives recourse expressly against such false suggestions to the Chanc., Treas. and K's Co: *ibid.* 382.

to the auncient law of the land: And soe the practise and experience hath in ever since, which is the [3r] true and certayne interpretacion of this statute and of all other statutes.[1]

Statute 4 H cap. 23, the wordes bee these: Where aswell in Plea Reall as in plea personall after Iudgment given in the Courtes of our Soveraigne lord the kinge the parties bee made to come upon greivous payne sometyme beefore the Kinge himself, sometyme before the Kinges Councell and sometyme in the parliament to answere thereof anew[a] to the great impoverishing of the parties aforesaid and in the subversion of the common law of the land; it is ordayned and established that after Iudgment given in the Courtes of our soveraigne lord the kinge, that partie and theire heires shall bee thereof in peace till the Iudgment bee vndone by Attaynt or by Error if ther bee Error as hath bine vsed by the lawes in the tyme of the Kinges progenitors.[2]

For the [b] understanding of this statute the question is,[3] Whether there bee any thing in the wordes or intent of this statute to take away or restraine or impeach the Iurisdiccion of the Chancery to give remedy and releife according to conscience and Equity in Cases which cannot bee remedied by the strict Rules of the Common Lawes by Attaint or by writt of Error.

For resolveing of this question it is to bee [3v] Considered what hath bine vsed by the law before the makeinge of this statute. And to this point I must say That I haue not seene any record or presidentes that the Court of Chancery hath bine restrayned to heare and determine cases of Conscienc and Equity and to give releiffe accordingly aswell after[c] as before Iudgment given by the Iudges of the Common Law: But before the makeing of this statute there be many presidentes

---

[a] whether *crossed out after* anew.   [b] *Added from B.*   [c] after] against *in B.*

[1] Coke had disagreed, and Ellesmere did not meet his precise objections to the Church's use of the injunction: see Coke's 'Dangerous and absurd opinions', items 8–10.

[2] The parag. is a direct quote of the 'Statutes of the Fourth Year', 4 Hen. IV cap. 23 (1402), *Stat. Realm* II, 142 (This is the second cap. 23, as a new series beginning cap. 21 appears after the first 34 chapters). Ellesmere's discussion in the following four parags. is a very precise analysis of this statute.

[3] The question had been put earlier by the Doctor to the Student, and the latter replied that the purpose of the statute was to eschew the delays and vexations of men who sued in courts other than those of the common law for actions which could be remedied there by orig. writ. The statute did not prohibit the equitable jurisd. of the Chan. but did prohibit the re-exam. of judgments concluded before the royal courts: Christopher Saint German, *The fyrste dyaloge in Englysshe* (1532 ed.), ff. 40v-1r. Ellesmere's reply formed the basis of a Restoration attack on Coke (through his interp. of the statute in his *Third Institute*) in 'A Vindication of the Judgment given by King James', *Collect. Jurid.*, I, at 35–41, 54–78.

and recordes*a* to prove that the King and his counsell and the Kinges Commissioners appointed to bee *Auditores Quaerelarum*, and*b* the Court of Rome and some pretending to haue power and authoritie from the pope, did take vpon them to examine such Iudgmentes, and to reverse and vndoe the same, which seemeth to bee the point meant to be remedied by this statute. And this is with the direct and precise wordes of this statute where vpon it may bee inferred and concluded, That if the wordes shalbe taken preciselie in the strict sence, Then the king himself and his counsell and the parliamentes (who in the tyme of the Kinges progenitors*c* vsed to examine and reverse Iudgmentes) shall bee bound and restrained by this statute.

But the Chauncery medleth not with the reversinge of the Iudgmentes given by the Iudges of the Common Law, but (alloweing the same to bee good and iust according to the strict rules of the Common Law, wherevnto the Iudges are sworne) [4r] doth examine only the equity of the case according to the rules of Equity and Conscience and take order with the party to see that which in equitie and conscience ought to bee done which the Iudges of the Comon Law haue noe power to doe.[1] And that seemeth to bee the true reason that the statute doth not once mention the Chauncery.*d*

And it cannot reasonablie bee conceived that the parliament meant either to binde the Chauncery (which is not named) or the King and his counsell and the parliament it self (which are expressly named), that they should not releive parties that are greived by the rigor of the Common Law against equity and Conscience in Cases wherein*e* the Iudges of the common law cannot releive them, by attaint or Error or other wise.[2] For *sententia Iudiciis non praeiudicat veritati*:

a F and G *cite* 29 E. 3 c. 1, *for which there was no Parliament.*

b and *added after the crossed out words* or his.

c progenitors *added after the crossed out word* prerogative.

d G *omits the following four paragraphs, and the fifth through* whom they serve.

e wherein *inserted above the crossed out* which.

[1] The view that the judges of the common law could do little more than this was based on the Chanc's conception of the devolution of the powers of the royal prerog: 'Prerog.', ff. 4r–5r, 7v–8r. The maximum use of discretion allowed to the judges was set out above at ff. 1v–2r.

[2] There is an important note on this problem in the margin of Harl. MS 4265, f. 39r. 'It is plaine by this statute yt ye Chancerye is not named therein becase ye English way of proceedinges in Equity was not then broached, for which need ye King to assigne auditores querelarum if ye Englishe way of proceedinge in Chancery had then been vrged, & it is vnreasonable to conceive yt ye Parliament would bind ye Kinges hands & his Counsell & their owne too, & leave ye Chancery free in their English way of proceedinges in Equity, ye proceedinges whereof are altogether excentricall to ye common law.'

And *Iudicatura naturalem obligationem non tollit: Ita conspurcatam laesam que conscientiam non purgat.*[a] And some doe truly and aptlie defyne equity thus: *Equitas est publici Iuris moderatio a pectore regis velut ab oraculo pretenda.* And an other saith thus: *Equitas in potestate moderatoris esse debet multa contra scriptam facere et dicere.* An other saith *Equitas Justitiam aciem refundit*; And St. Augustine sayth: *Lex quia seip sum moliri non potest mitiganda est, et contemptus, fraus et dolus in curia regis minime subvenire debeant.*

《1.》 And furthermore for the true vnderstanding of this statute and all other statutes this [4v] rule should bee observed: First to vnderstand and consider what was the mischeefe at the Comon law which the parliament meant to remedie, which in this statute appeareth to haue been the reverseinge and undoeing of Iudgments by the king or his counsell or commission or parliament, which might and ought to bee examined by attaint and error as is aforesaid. But not the ordinary iudiciall proceedinges in Chancery according to equity and Conscience to give releiffe to the partie greived by the strict rigor of the Comon law in Cases which could not bee remedied by Attaint or Error, or by ony other ordinary meanes by Course of the Common law; And where they in that equitable proceeding did not attempt to reverse and impeach the Iudgment given by the Common Law, But to admitt and allow the same to bee good and iust as is before declayred.

2. The next is how this statute was understood and expounded att and soone after the tyme of the makeing of it. For in all such cases *Contemporanea expositio* is spetially to bee regarded. And for that (as I said before) I haue not seene any record or president that this statute hath bine expounded to restrayne the Chancery from proceeding in theire ordinary Course of giving releiffe in Cases of Equity according to good conscience neere the tyme of the makeing of it, or many yeares after. And I suppose noe such materiall record or president can bee shewed.

And for the later tymes, as in the tyme of King H. 7 and since, the presidentes and examples [5r] bee soe frequent, soe plaine and direct[b] as noe thinge is more common. And it is a certayne and true rule, *Intellectus currit cum proxi.*

---

[a] *The most accurate Latin forms are given from B.*
[b] soe *crossed out before* direct.

And if any ambiguity or doubt should bee conceived vppon the wordes and intent of this statute, Sithe it concernes the Iurisdiccions of the Kinges Courtes which haue noe power nor authority but from the King whom they serve, One Court ought not to take vpon them to iudg and decide theire own Iurisdiccion and*a* of an other of the Kinges Courtes: But then Bracton's rule is to bee holden, that is that the Kinges interpretacion is to bee expected who is to declare and expound all doubtful and obscure wordes in *Chartis Regiis et factis regum.* For all statutes are *facta regis* made at the request and by the Consent of the Lordes Spirituall and Temporall and by the Commons.*b*

And where some new conceptes haue bine latelie imagined that the partie greived should haue complained before Iudgment, or els it is not to bee heard or releived after Iudgment by reason of the Statute: This is but a cavill and sophisticall distinction not worthe the answeringe. For before hee bee hurt he hath noe cause to complaine, and that which hurtes him is the Iudgment grounded vpon the strictnes and rigor*c* of the Common Law against Equity and Conscience.

And when hee feels the wound it is tyme for him to complaine, and to seeke the remedie by Complayning of the wronge which is done vnto him by the rigor of the Comon Law contrary to equity and good conscience. [5v]

And of this sorte bee the presidentes and examples before mencioned. And the wordes of the statutes before Anno 4 H. 4 make noe such distinctions. And therefore *Ubi lex non distinguit, nos non distinguimus.* And for the statute Anno 4 H. 4 the Cause, reason, and true vnderstandinge*d* of it, according to the experience and practise is, as is before declared.

Lastly it is to bee lamented that auncient common lawes are soe much neglected, contemned, and almost growne obsolete and out of use that for the most part we haue not the substance but the shadow of the auncient Common lawes, *Manet magna nominis vmbra.e* And therefore his majestie at the beginning of his gratious raigne of England did most princly, prudently, and iudiciously shewe his mislyke of the vncertanty of the Iudicature in the*f* Courtes of Justice

a the jurisdiction *added after* and *in G.*
b Bk. 2 f. 34 cap. 16 *cited in F and G.*
c and rigor *deleted in F. The following two paragraphs are omitted in G.*
d vnderstandinge *added after the crossed out word* meaning.
e *Taken from the best version in B.*
f *Read* his *for* the *in F.*

in England, and required and commanded his Iudges to take mature
consideracion*a* of it. But what hath followed I will say noething of.[1]

Therefore lett the Iudges now consider how they observe in theire
Courses and proceedinges the wordes and intent of this statute,
whether after the Iudgment the parties bee in peace vntil the Iudgment bee vndone by attaint and Error, whether after Iudgmentes
in writtes of *Eiectione firmae*[b] they suffer not new accions and verdict
against verdict, and Iudgment against Iudgment without Attaint or
Error to the manifest deludinge of the true and antient Maximes of
the common law. And without regarding the wordes of the statute.

And thus suites for one and the self same cause are carried from
Court to Court as power and might [6r] of the parties or favor and
affeccion of the Iudge, or Corruption of the Sheriffes, or sub-
ordinacion and periury of wittnesses, or such lyke shiftes and trickes
as can best accomodate the busines.

*De Chartis Regiis et factis Regum non debent nec possunt Iustitiarii,
nec priuatae personae disputare: Nec etiam sive illa Dubitatio oriator
possunt etiam interpretari et in dubiis et obscuris vel si aliqua dictio duos
continet intellectus Dominum Reges erit expectanda interpreta et
voluntas cum eius sit interpretari cuius est concedere.*[c] [Bracton lib. 2.
f. 34 ca. 16.][2]

*Maneant termini patrum et inter fines proprios se quisque contineat,
sufficiant limitos quos sanctorum patrum providentissima Decreta
posuerunt.* [Leo: epist. 17. et. 94.][d]

SOME NOTES AND OBSERVACIONS VPON THE STATUTES
OF PROVISORS AND *PRAEMUNIRE* ESPECIALLY
CONCERNINGE THE PROCEEDINGES IN THE COURT OF
CHAUNCERY AND OTHER COURTES OF EQUITY;

The wordes bee [Stat. 25 E. 3, Cap. 22][e] because some doe purchase
in the court of Rome Prouisions to haue Abbies and Priories in

---

a consideracion *added after the crossed out* delib. *b Read* Errour *for* Eiectione firmae *in* F.

c ejus ... condere *in* B, ejus sit interpretari cujus sit condere *in* A. *Word endings in these
two paragraphs are more confusing in A than in B, which is used in such places instead of A.*

d et 29 *in* B. *The two paragraphs above were omitted in F and G.*

e Given incorrectly as 23 E. 3 *in* A. *Other copiers revise often to* 23 E. 3 *incorrectly. This is
actually* 25 E. 3 *statute five.*

[1] This was a theme of his tract on 'Iudicature'.

[2] With the exception of a few confused endings, this is an accurate quotation from his
printed copy of *Henrici de Bracton de Legibus & Consuetudinibus Angliae Libri Quinque* (1569),
Hunt. RB 97059.

England in distruccion of the Realme and holy religion. It is accorded That every man that purchaseth such prouisions of Abbies or Priories, that hee and his Executors and procurators which doe fine and make execucion of such provisions shalbee out of the Kinges proteccion. And that a man may doe with them as of enemyes of our soveraigne Lord the Kinge and his realme.[1] [6v] *Nota*: The vsurpacion of the Church of Rome in this Case iudged at that tyme to bee the destruccion of the Realme and Religion:[2] And the partie himself and his executors and procurators putting in execucion such provisions, iudged to bee enemyes of the King and realme and out of the kinges proteccion (and soe in worse degree then Traytors). And that therefore every man might iustify the takeing of their goodes from them by force and killing of them, and not bee questioned or impeached for doeing the same.[3]

There is an other statute intituled, *Statutum de provisioribus* [Anno 25 E. 3],[4] declaring the great mischeefe that the King and the Realme sustayned by the vsurpacion of the Pope in Cases of Provisions and Reservations of Benefices, recyteing the lawes ordeined by King Edward 1,[5] and adding further revenge[a] and severe punishment against the offendors that noe processe or suite should bee in those Cases in the Court of Rome nor in any other Court.[6]

Both these statutes were spetially provided to restraine the vsurpation of the Pope and Church of Rome in those Cases of provisions and reservacions.[b]

By the statute of 27 of Ed. 3 [Stat. 27 Ed. 3 《cap. 1》], that notwithstanding the two former statutes Anno 25 E. 3, yet the vsurpation

---

[a] revenge] remedy *in B*.

[b] *This and the following four paragraphs are omitted in F and G.*

[1] 'The Statute of Provisors of Benefices', actually 25 Ed. III stat. 4 (1350–1), *Stat. Realm* I, 316–8. The Court of Rome, however, is not mentioned specifically; the statute is directed against abbots, priors, and governors of religious houses both native and alien, who subject such houses to heavy taxes and impositions without the consent of the K. and his nobility.

[2] The problem of the jurisd. of the Bishop of Rome was a contentious one throughout the Middle Ages for lay and eccles. society. Some Coll'd contemp. papers on this subject are in Yale Law MS G. R. 24, ff. 55r–70v.

[3] Some of Ellesmere's notes on these matters are in his copy of Rastell's *Statutes*. The notes are made later than his orig. notations, probably just prior to his draft of this tract. Cf. William Rastell, *A Collection of all the Statutes* (8th ed. 1572), Hunt. RB 59499, ff. 414r–20v, 464r, 469r, 561r.

[4] See p. 320, n.1.

[5] 'The Statute of Carlisle', 35 Ed. I (1306–7), *Stat. Realm* I, 150. It is cited inaccurately as 23 Ed. I in the statute of 25 Edward III itself (*Stat. Realm* I, 316).

[6] It was noted by Ellesmere in one of his ms. eds. of the statutes: Ellesm. MS 34/A/9, fol. 59.

of the pope and Church of Rome was soe exhorbitant That the Nobles and Commons complayned in this parliament and prayed further remedy for the same. Alleadging that divers of the people haue bine drawne out of the realme, to answere of thinges whereof the Cognizaunce pertayneth to the Kings Court ⌈7r⌉ or of thinges whereof Iudgmentes bee given in the Kinges Courtes, or with fine in an other Court, or defeat or impeache the Iudgmentes given in the Kinges Court in preiudice and derision*a* of the Kinge and his Crowne and of all the people of this realme. And the vndoeing and distruccion of the Common Lawes of the same realme at all tymes vsed.

This was *b* the mischeefe which was complained of and was desired to bee remedied. The offendors against who remedie is sought, are those which drawe any out of the Realme in Plea, where as the conusance that appertayneth to the Kinges Court are of thinge whereof iudgmentes bee given in the Kinges Court,*c* or which doe sue in any other court to defeat or impeach the Iudgmentes given in the Kinges Court.

The remedy provided is That such offenders shall haue garnishment *d* by two monethes to bee before the Kinge and his counsaile or in his Chauncery, or before the Kinges Justices of the one Bench or the other, or before the ⟨⟨other⟩⟩ Justices of the Kinge, which to the same shall bee deputed to answere in proper person to the Kinge for theire contempt done in this behalf. And if they come not, then to bee out of the Kinges proteccion and etc. Provided where they come before they bee outlawed they shall bee received to answer and etc.[1]

Now it will appeare manifestlyie that the intent of the parliament was not to restraine or punish any that complayned or sued in Chancery to bee relieved according to equity and conscience in Cases wherein by the strict Rules and rigor of the Comon Law they could not ⌈7v⌉ bee relieved: Nether are there any wordes in the statute which can without violence be strayned or racked to serve any such vnreasonable construction.

---

a disherison] derision.

b was *inserted above crossed out* is.

c are of things ... Kinges Court *inserted later in A*; *original in B*.

d garnishment] punishment *in B*.

[1] The lengthy analysis of this statute is similar to the anon. tract entitled, 'That the Courte of Chauncery Cannott be intended within the Statute of XXVII Edward 3. ca. 1'. Of the many copies, see John Selden's in Hale MS 83, ff. 272–94; and William Hakewill's in Lans. 174, ff. 226r–35v. The general arg. of the tract, however, is concerned with clerical patronage, the misuse of wealth, and interference with lay govt.

For the better vnderstanding hereof the partes of the statute are to bee divided and severally considered: [1]

1. As first the mischeefe complayned of.
2. The offendors, against whom, and the forme of proceeding therein. [a]
3. The remedy provided, against whom, and the forme of proceeding therin.

1. For the mischeefe the parliament finding that the Pope and Court of Rome did not only continue their vsurpacion in Cases mencioned in the former statute Anno 25 E. 3, but did also extend it further, in draweing the people out of the Realme to answere thinges whereof the Cognizance pertayneth to the Kinges Court, or of thinges whereof Iudgmentes bee given in the Kinges Court in preiudice, and etc.

In this preamble, wherin the mischeeffe is declared, it appeareth that the draweing of the people out of the Realme to answere in these Cases specially remembred was the greiffe of the people for which they prayed remedie.

But by suites in Chancerie to bee relieved according to equity and Conscience in Cases to which the Iudges of the Common Law could not give remedie, the people were not drawne out of the Realme, nor Iudgmentes given in the Kinges Courtes [8r] sought to bee defeated or impeached, but conscience and Equity to bee observed. Nor such suites in the Chauncery cannot bee accounted to bee in any other Court then the Kinges Court: For the Chancery is one of the Kinges supreame Courtes of Justice, and as much or more greived by the inordinate vsurpacions of the pope and his courtes, as any other of the Kinges Courtes. [3]

Neither[b] could such suites in the Chauncery (being the Kinges

---

[a] and the ... therein *omitted in B. The paragraph was omitted in G.*

[b] Neivertheles *cancelled before* Neither.

[1] This procedure was drawn from the one he used as a practising lawyer in the 1570s: for example, Ellesm. MS 482, ff. 42r–52r, 77v–9r, 90r–8v. A more elaborate form of this contemp. method is found in the treatise of Sir George Carew, a Chanc. Master, on 'Directions for ye ordily Reading of the lawe of England', Rawl. MS C. 207, ff. 238–42. The procedural developments were analysed by Samuel E. Thorne, 'The equity of a statute and Heydon's Case', *Illinois Law Rev.* 31 (1936), 302–17.

[2] Ellesmere's view of the role of the preamble in the understanding of statutes was set out in the *Discourse*, 114–17.

[3] His interp. of the phrase 'out of the realm' was seized on by later writers as the correct one, and as the fundamental error of Coke's attack. See Francis North, Lord Guilford's tract on 'Praemunire', Add. MS 40.160, esp. ff. 17v–8r.

owne supreme Court) be in preiudice or disherison of the Kinge and
his Crowne, and of his people, or the vndoeing or destruction of the
Common Law at all tymes vsed. And I suppose that there can noe
Record or warrantable president bee shewed that such proceedinges
in the Chancery will haue in tymes before bine vsed, that is before
the 27 E. 3 haue bine construed to bee the vndoeing and ^{a} destruccion
of the Common Law.

2. And herevpon it may bee inferred and concluded, That those
which complaine and sue in the Chauncery for relieffe and remedy
according to Equity and Conscience in such Cases as the Iudges of
the Common Law cannot remedie, are not any offenders within
the wordes or meaning of this statute.

3. And this will appeare more playnlie by the remedie which is
provided, that is that the offenders shall haue warning by two
monethes to appeare before such Iudges as are assigned to give
remedy in the cases before mentioned in the ⌈8v⌉ statute, which are
these: the king and his Counsell, The Chauncery, The Kinges Iustices
of the one Bench or the other, or other Iustices of the Kinge which to
the same shall bee deputed.

Wherein it is to bee noted, that the Chancery is the second Court
which is appointed to give Iustice against such offenders as the parliament meant, and is placed next after the kinge and his Counsell, and
before the Iudges of the one bench or the other: Betweene whom in
this Case the parliament giveth noe priority nor preiudice and addeth
such other Iustices as the king shall depute. By which power the king
may by this statute exclude both those Courtes, and appoint other
Iustices if it shall seeme soe good vnto him.

Now it is too absurd to say, or imagine ^{b} that the ordinary and
Iudiciall proceeding in the Chancery, by the kinges owne authority in
the Case before remembred, can bee in preiudice or dishersion of the
kinge or his Crowne, or distruccion of the Common Law, or that the
parliament did soe meane or vnderstand it, sith they haue designed the
Chancery to bee a speciall and ^{c} prime Court to punish offenders
against the statute, and to resort to the rule, *Contemporanea expositio*.
For *intellectus currit cum proxi*: I haue not seene nor heard that any
person hath bine Charged or impeached by suit in the nature of a

---

^{a} and⌉or *in F and G.*
^{b} or imagine *added before* that.
^{c} and⌉or *in F and G*; prime *inserted above crossed out* privie.

Premunire vpon this statute for suing in the Chancery in Cases before remembred or in any other lyke Cases.

The statute 27 E. 3 was grounded vpon the exhorbitant vsurpacion of the Pope and Church of Rome, which were in some sort provided for by the former statute anno 25 E. 3.[1] But the parliament of 27 E. 3, finding the same to《o》weake, and that the Church of Rome did not only continue their former vsurpacion: bud did dayly increase the same more and more, did therefore devise further remedy against theire insolent and outragious excesse.[a]

Wherein it appeareth that the speciall marke wherevnto [9r] both those parliamentes aymed and directed theire accions was to provide and give remedy against the wicked proceedinges of the pope and the Court of Rome, and not to restraine the Iurisdiccion and authority of any of the kinges owne Courtes in theire ordinary and Iudiciall proceedinges ether in law or equity as by that which is before remembred is sufficiently declared. Yet the same if made more manifest by the statutes Anno 38 E. 3 stat. 2 chap. 1.2.3.4, by which it appeares that in 9 yeares space after the parliament Anno 27 E. 3, the pope and Church of Rome ceaseth not to goe on still in their wicked and enormous vsurpacion vpon the king and Crowne. And therefore that parliament Anno 38 E. 3 declareth plainely and directly that it was the court of Rome that dealt in Cases whereof the cognizance and finall discussion pertayneth to the kinge and his Royall Court, and for remedy thereof ordayneth that the former statutes made Anno 25 E. 3 and Anno 27 E. 3 shall bee in all thinges affirmed and executed. Adding alsoe some further provisions and punishmentes against the offendors directing the proceeding therein to bee before the kinge and his counsell, only without mencioning any other Court as 27 E. 3 did.[2]

Soe as vpon conferring together these 3 statutes (vizt) 25 E. 3, 27 E. 3, et 38 E. 3, it appeareth that the intent of all these parliamentes was onely to punishe offendors that maintayned the vsurped and pretended Authority of the pope and Church of Rome, and prosecuted any accion or sute by vertue of the same in any case whereof the Conusance and finall discussion perteined to the king and his Courtes.

---

[a] *This paragraph is omitted in G. The following sentence is omitted in F and G.*

[1] See p. 320, n. 1, and p. 328, n. 1.

[2] The statute was the fullest on the subject to date, and was composed with far more contempt of the papacy than previous statutes, or this brief summary suggests: 'Statute the Second', 38 Ed. III caps. 1–4 (1363–4), *Stat. Realm* I, 385–7.

And therefore if any doubt bee conceived vpon any wordes in the statute 27 E. 3 it is to bee explayned by the statut 38 E. 3 comming soone after.

After all these statutes,[1] yet the ambitious vsurpacion and greedy coveteous extorcion of the pope and Court of Rome ceased not, but still continued and increased more and more, wherevpon the parliament anno 16 R. 2 c. 5, reciting some particuler Causes vzt: That Iudgment being given in any of the Kinges Courtes for recovery of presentmentes to Churches and Benefices, And the same Iudgmentes dayly executed by the Archbishops and Bishops as they ought to bee, that[a] there vpon the Archbishops and Bishops haue bine excommunicated by the popes Censures for executing the same Iudgmentes. [9v]

And also that the pope did ordaine and purpose to translate some prelates out of the Realme, and some from one Bishoprick to another here in the Realme, without the assent or knowledg of the kinge, by which the kinge should bee destitute of his Counsell, and the Treasure of the realme[b] bee essoyned out of the realme. And so the regality and Crowne should bee made subiect to the pope in perpetuall destruccion to the King and his Crowne, and all his Realme.

In which cases and all other cases attempted against the kinge, his Crowne, and Regalitie, the lordes temporall and Commons did promise to stand with the kinge and Crowne, and to live and die.[2] And the lordes spirituall did promise to stand with the king in the lyke cases before remembred, and in all other cases touching the Crowne and regalitie, as they bee bound by theire Alledgeance, yet with a speciall protestacion and saveing of the popes authority in excommunicating of Bishops and translateing of prelates according to the law of holy[c] Church.

And herevpon it is ordayned and inacted that if any purchase or pursue in the Court[d] of Rome or elswhere any such translation, processes and sentences of excommunicacion, Bulles, instrumentes, or other thinges touching the kinge against him, his Crowne and regal-

---

[a] that *inserted above the crossed out word* and.

[b] and soe the regalitie *crossed out after* realme.

[c] holy *inserted above crossed out* the.

[d] Church of the *crossed out before* Court.

[1] The background and context of these re-enactments is explained by Bertie Wilkinson, *Constitutional history of medieval England, 1216–1399*, (1958), III, 380–7.

[2] Ellesmere's rather nationalistic interp. of English medieval history was sketched in more detail in his *Post-Nati*.

itie, or his realme, as is aforesaid; And they who bringe or receive the same within the realme or make therof notificacion or any other execucion within the realme or without, that they shall forfeit and etc, and bee put out of the kinges proteccion and bee *a* attached and etc, and processe of premunire and etc, as against others which sue *b* in other Courtes in derogacion of the Kinges regality.[1]

By this it appeareth plainely that as the pope and Court of Rome contrived still, and proceeded *c* further and further in theire exorbitant vsurpacion *d* vpon the Crowne, and the Kinges Regality, and the Common Lawes of the Kingdome: Soe this parliament endeavored to meet with and withstand the same, namely in the particuler Cases which are spetially mencioned. Vzt, concerning Iudgmentes given in the Kinges Courtes in these pleas and Cases, and in translateing of places and etc, and in other pleas attempted against the Kinges Crowne and regalitie.

But it is manifest that the intent, scope, and drift *e* of the parliament was onely against the Pope and Court of Rome, and against those persons that pursued any translacions, processes, and etc, or other thinges which touched the king *f* or was against his Crowne and regalitie, or his [1or] realme as is aforesaid, or which beinge received, notefyed, or executed the same *g* in the realme or without. These bee the offendors which the parliament had cause and meant to punish. And it is strang and improbable that any learned Iudges of the Common lawes of England should strecht or extend the wordes of this statute further then only against the vsurped authority of the pope and Church of Rome.[2]

But *h* it seemeth that some that take pleasure *ludere in verbis in*

a shall *crossed out before* bee.

b sue *added above the crossed out word* fine.

c proceeded *inserted above the crossed out word* exceeded.

d vsurpacion *added after the crossed out word* courses.

e and the *before* scope *and* drift *are omitted in A.*

f Items *in A are in the singular number.*

g which *is deleted after* same.

h *New paragraph as in E–G. The best construction for this sentence is taken from B.*

[1] A complete summary of the statute of 16 Rich. II cap. 5 (1392–3), *Stat. Realm* II, 84–6.

[2] This statement, objecting to the extension of the words of the statute, and the argument that follows in the next parag., comprised the core of a later tract on the interp. of these statutes: the anon. 'Preemunire', Harg. MS 146, ff. 1–2r. A contemp. coll. of precedents outlining the limitations is contained in the anony. tract, 'Certaine Extravagant Reasons', discussed *supra*, Chap. VIII, pp. 191–2.

sentebus dormitare, And soe dispute *de apicibus Iuris equi^a et boni ratione pertermissa*, And professe learninge *peritia literali non intelligentia spirituali*, And soe are contented *verba legis tenere, et vim legis ignorare*, haue gone about to presse and straine the wordes of the statut, not only against the pope and Church of Rome, But also against the Kinges owne high court of Chancery and other his majestyes Courtes of Equity in England, grounding that theire opinion and conceipt on^b these wordes of the statute: If any purchase in the Court of Rome, or elswhere any such translacions, processes, or other thinges which touch the kinge and etc.¹ And for the better vnderstandinge hereof it is to bee remembred that the Pope and Court of Rome kept theire sees and Courts not at Rome onely, but some tymes at Avignion, sometymes at other places: And divers Anti-Popes being at one and the self same tyme, kept their severall Sees and Courtes at severall places, and yet each of them pretended^c to haue supreme Iurisdiccion, power, and authority aboue the kinge and his Crowne and regality in the Cases before remembred. And therefore it was requisite and necessary for the King and the parliament to withstand and provid remedy for the same: And that is the true and right vnderstanding of [10v] the wordes ou ayllors.²

For^d it is too absurd to say or imagion that the kinge or the parliament meant to extend the same against the kinges owne Courtes of equitie in England:³ which derived theire authority and Iurisdiccion from him onely; and heard and determined as his substitutes according to equitie and conscience, such Cases as the Iudges of the Common Laws could not by the strict Rules of the Common Laws iudge and determine.⁴ These Courtes, and the Iudges and ministers therof, the kinge had power to suppresse, alter and punish at his pleasure. And therefore against those the Lordes Temporall and Commons needed not to ingage themselves to stand with the king and the Crowne and to live and die, Nor the Lords Spirituall and Clergie

---

^a aqui *in A*; equi *from B.*   ^b on *inserted above the crossed out word* of.

^c pretended] challenged and pretended *in F.*   ^d *New paragraph as in F and G.*

¹ His interp. of the words of these statutes follows the first rule of his former strictures on the subject: the *Discourse*, esp. 123–9, and more generally 154–61.

² The interp. was later misunderstood in the 'Vindication', *Harg. Law Tracts*, I, 41–53.

³ His earlier discussion of where the words could, and could not, be extended was contained in the *Discourse*, 171–2 and 143–53, respectively.

⁴ However, the Chanc. had noted earlier that a statute of 23 Hen. VIII that referred to damages and costs in the K's courts did not extend to the Chan. and the S.C. – William Rastell, *A Collection of All the Statutes* (8th ed. 1572), Hunt. RB 59499, f. 125v.

to promise to stand with the kinge, as they were bound by theire alleadgianc with theire Cautious protestacions for the popes authority. For by the ordinary legall and iudiciall proceedinges in the Cancery and Courtes of equity according to conscience the Kinge, nor his Crowne nor Regality, nor the Common Law were not in any danger: But the danger was by the Ambitious vsurpacion of the pope and the Church of Rome, and by the proceedinges in the Courtes holden by the vsurped authority. And therefore against them the parliament provided this statute: followinge the example to the former parliamentes 25 E. 3, 27 E. 3, 38 E. 3. And those bee the Courtes which this parliament Anno 37 E. 3 cap. 1 noted to bee in*a* derogation of the kinges regality and distruccion of the Common Law, but not the Kinges owne Court of Conscience and equity.

And for the further Clearing of this doubt (yf it bee worthie to bee made a doubt) how *ou ayllors*[b] shall be vnderstood in 5 E. 4 there is this note: *Nota que le statute de praemunire est in Curia Romana vel alibi le quel alibi est intendre[c] en les Courtes des huesques ipsum que si home soit excommenge[d] en Court del huesque per chose que appeirt al royall maiestie sur chose ad comen ley il eur praemunire et issint[e] adiudgei.*[1] And Fitzharbert abridging that [11r] Case saith (11 H. 7),[f] the opinion of the Court was soe which hee himself heard.[2]

By which it appeareth that the Iudges did then vnderstand by[g] the proceedinges by the Bishop in the spirituall Courtes (which were by authority deryved from the pope and Church of Rome), was onely meant by the wordes *vel alibi*, But not the proceedinges in the kinges owne Court of Chancery by authority derived from him onely in Case of Equity and Conscience not remediable other wyse; For that were to sett the kinge against himself which is too inconvenient and absurd.

1615 T. Ellesmere Canc. [11v]

---

a in] the *in A.*
b ayllors *added above* autres *in A, but in the original in B.*
c intendre] interdue *in B.*
d *Perhaps this is a contemporary form of excommunico. B has* commenque.
e issint] essuit *in B. Other readings in this sentence differ in B.*
f 11 H. 7] 11 Ft. 7 *in A. This sentence and the following paragraph are omitted in F and G.*
g by *deleted in A, added from B.*

[1] There was no Parl. in 5 Ed. IV, and the statute cannot be found in those of 4 or 7 Ed. IV.
[2] Anthony Fitzherbert, *La Graunde Abridgement* (1577), Pt. II, f. 105.

INDEX OF PERSONS AND PLACES

149, 189–90, 203n, 297–318; monopolies, 150–2, 303, 306–7; *praemunire*,
141–2, 311–13; privy council and
politics, 93, 97–8, 102–3, 127, 130–1,
176–8; prohibitions, 136–40, 298–9,
308–9; royal prerogative, 66, 131–4,
302–6, 311; sewers, and commissioners
of, 150–2, 309–10; tithes, 140, 142,
144, 284n, 287–9, 297–300. *See also*
Thomas Egerton *and* James I
Coleman, Mr 58n
Coleshill, Manor of (Flintshire) 23
Colet, John 7n
Cope, John 25n
Cornwall, Duchy of 132, 252, 275, 294
Cotton, Robert 69, 171, 178n, 192, 230n
Courtney, Mr 171
Coventry, Sir Thomas (later Baron
Coventry) 179, 180n
Cowell, Dr John 71, 74–5, 161
Craig, Thomas 70
Cranfield, Sir Lionel (later Earl of
Middlesex) 59, 86, 94, 101–2, 185, 265n,
271n
Cranmer, Thomas (Archbishop of
Canterbury) 52, 107
Croke, Sir John (Serjeant) 80, 126, 223
Crompton, Richard 80n
Cujas, Jacques 69–70

Dackambe, James 168
Dalton, Richard 5n
Daneau, Lambert 49, 60
Daniel, Samuel 41n, 58n, 62n, 128, 152,
230
Darcy, Edward 151, 303
Davies, Sir John (Judge) 62n, 71n, 106,
217n, 274n
Davies, John of Hereford 41n
Davies, Katherine (née Ravenscroft), *see*
Elizabeth Mainwaring
Davies, Robert 171
Davies, Robert (of Gwysaney) 10, 12, 25n
Dee River and Estuary 1n, 2–3
Dee Vale Royal 2–4, 6
Defoe, Daniel 3n
Demosthenes 40, 273
Denbigh, Borough of 25
Denbighshire 1, 4–5, 10–11, 22–5, 57
Derby, Alice, Countess of, *see* Alice
Spencer
Derby, 3rd Earl of, *see* Edward Stanley
Derby, 4th Earl of, *see* Henry Stanley

Derby, 5th Earl of, *see* Ferdinando
Stanley
Derby, 6th Earl of, *see* William Stanley
Derby, family of, *see* Stanleys
Devereux, Robert, Lord (3rd Earl of Essex)
18, 30, 56, 59
D'Ewes, Sir Simonds 185
Doctors' Commons 137
Dodderidge, Sir John (Judge): Anglo-Scots
Union, 184, 232n; common law actions,
107; judicial opinions, 132n, 172; legal
thought and writing, 69, 71, 162n, 184,
232n; royal prerogative, 71
Dodleston, Manor of (Cheshire) 23, 52n, 56
Doneau, Hugues 69
Donne, John 25n, 53n, 54
Dove, Dr John 54
Downall, Gregory 83n
Downame, George 42
Downame, John 42, 53n, 55n
Drayton, Michael 58
Duaren, François 69
Dudley, Robert, Lord (Earl of Leicester)
3n, 8, 10, 23, 145
Dumoulin, Charles 70, 74
Dunchurch, Manor of (Warwickshire) 24
Durham, County Palatine of 147
Dutton, John (of Dutton) 11n
Duttons (of Dutton) 10, 11n
Dyer, Sir John (Chief Justice) 50–1, 126,
241, 276
Dymocke, Thomas 10

East Anglia 146, 153
Eastmore [Eastnor], Manor of (Hereford-
shire) 298
Eaton Hall (Cheshire) 4, 23
Edge, Manor of (Cheshire) 23
Edinburgh (Scotland) 235
Edward I 209, 231
Edward II 231
Edward III 231, 243
Edward VI 22, 234
Egbert (King of the West Saxons) 219n
Egerton, Alice (née Spencer), *see* Alice
Spencer
Egerton, Dorothy (of Ridley) 30–1
Egerton, Elizabeth (née More), *see*
Elizabeth More
Egerton, Elizabeth (née Ravenscroft),
see Elizabeth Ravenscroft (of Bretton)
Egerton, Elizabeth (née Stanley), *see*
Francis Stanley

INDEX OF SUBJECTS AND TERMS